AMERICA
AND THE
FRENCH NATION,
1939–1945

AMERICA
AND THE
FRENCH NATION,
1939–1945

JULIAN G. HURSTFIELD

The University of North Carolina Press

Chapel Hill and London

©1986 The University of North Carolina Press
Manufactured in the United States of America

Library of Congress Cataloging-in-Publication Data

Hurstfield, Julian G., 1949–
America and the French nation, 1939–1945.

Bibliography: p.
Includes index.
1. World War, 1939–1945—Diplomatic history.
2. United States—Relations—France.   3. France—
Relations—United States.   4. France—Foreign opinion,
American.   5. Public opinion—United States.
6. Roosevelt, Franklin D. (Franklin Delano), 1882–
1945—Views on France.   I. Title.
D753.H83   1986   940.53'22   85-20899
ISBN 0-8078-1685-X

To my mother,

Betty Hurstfield,

and in memory of my father,

Joel Hurstfield

CONTENTS

PREFACE

This study is conceived as an essay in American history, an exploration of American behavior toward France during the Second World War. After 1940, the French nation, defeated and divided, offered to an apparently sturdier republic a remarkably complex spectacle of divided loyalties and fratricidal conflict. Some splinters from this fracture, the French émigrés, presented themselves in the United States, for closer scrutiny. The American investigation of France during this period thus took a number of forms.

Of these, diplomacy was the most public, and remains the most straightforward to chronicle. Very simply, it consisted of a steady reliance upon representatives of the French nation who were in no way associated with the French resistance or the movement around General de Gaulle. The successive appeal of these men, Marshal Pétain, Admiral Darlan, General Giraud, to American policymakers, from President Roosevelt downward, is thus one central topic to be examined in this book.

But alongside these political and military developments, other, less formal exchanges were occurring. These cannot be so precisely described. Some of them, in addition, ran athwart the actual course of diplomacy. For while the American administration was conducting its policy, a vocal element within the American public campaigned for a reversal of that policy, and for whole-hearted recognition of de Gaulle. The result was an unusual situation, in which the administration was criticized by its usual admirers and supported by its usual enemies. This historical anomaly commands attention quite irrespective of any influence that public opinion may have exercised on events.

The book is so organized as to attempt to do justice to these themes. It is broadly chronological, and can be read as a consecutive narrative. At the same time each chapter examines a distinct area, which may be the experience of one particular person or group, or the course of a particular episode. Always the aim has been to consider a point of intersection between the two countries. The frequent direct quotations are intended to convey something of the polemical flavor of what proved to be, on all sides, a deeply controversial encounter.

The author of a work such as this has the very pleasant experience of acquiring debts that both parties know can never be adequately repaid. My earliest teacher of American history, Professor H. G. Nicholas, was a generous, tactful, shrewd, witty, endlessly knowledgeable supervisor. Professors

Max Beloff and Alec Campbell offered genuinely helpful and constructive advice at an early stage. My colleagues Professor Christine Bolt and Dr. R. J. Crampton read drafts of several chapters with great insight, as did, in Indiana, Professor George Juergens. For incidental, particular acts of kindness and assistance I am deeply grateful to Professors Henry Blumenthal, Wayne Cole, Francis Haber, John McVickar Haight, Jr., and Douglas Johnson. Janet Rabinowitch provided some indispensable counsel. Only the very great authority of these friends, colleagues, and teachers tempts me toward the otherwise rash admission that any residual errors can only be my own. Dr. Graham Clarke, working in an adjacent discipline and thus exempted from reading drafts, was, nonetheless, an unfailing source of wisdom.

I am also grateful, for their patience and toleration, to the librarians and archivists of the following institutions: in England, the British Library and the Public Record Office, London, and Rhodes House, Oxford; in France, the Bibliothèque Nationale and what was once the Comité d'histoire de la deuxième guerre mondiale; in the United States, the George Arendts Research Library at Syracuse University, the Chicago Historical Society, the Houghton Library at Harvard University, the University of Illinois at Chicago Circle, the Library of Congress and, within it, the Manuscripts Division, the Lilly Library at Indiana University, the National Archives in Washington, D.C., Princeton University Library, the Franklin D. Roosevelt Library, and the Sterling Library at Yale University. Wherever I went I met only the warmest generosity. Neither my broken French nor my British accent proved an obstacle to a form of collaboration so much happier than that recounted in this book.

Essential financial assistance was provided, at different times, by the Department of Education and Science, the British Academy, and the Faculty of Humanities at the University of Kent, to all of whom I am most obliged.

The manuscript was prepared, in several stages and drafts, by a number of gifted typists, including Susan Davies, Pam Duesbury, and Sheila Hawkins. Eve Hurste was, by a pleasing coincidence, chiefly responsible for both the first and final drafts, and I thank her for her lavish care. The index was prepared with the expert technical assistance of Dotty Esher. The entire manuscript benefited appreciably from the editorial scrutiny of Gwen Duffey at the University of North Carolina Press.

All the time the work was moving toward completion, Geraldine Mary Hurstfield supported, encouraged, inspired.

J. G. H.
Whitstable, Kent, England
St. David's Day, 1985

AMERICA
AND THE
FRENCH NATION,
1939–1945

CHAPTER I
WILLIAM C. BULLITT,
THE AMERICAN ADMINISTRATION,
AND THE END OF
THE THIRD REPUBLIC

othing so well illustrates the American distance from Europe in the 1930s as the contrasting strategies for avoiding war. Whilst the diplomacy of the European democracies was conducted, however obscurely, with some regard for the realities at hand, in the United States long-range planning and idealistic, often abstract goals were substituted. Europeans struggled to avoid the outbreak of war; Americans debated tactics to ensure their own neutrality.

The American public was thus presented with a bewildering variety of proposals to ensure peace. The League of Nations and the World Court, disarmament and arbitration, collective security and international law: each had its advocates; and there were in addition other, more precise plans advanced: the Neutrality Acts of 1935, 1936, and 1937, ingeniously framed to avoid a repetition of America's entry into the First World War, and the Ludlow Constitutional Amendment that, if passed in 1938, would have required a national referendum before a declaration of war.[1] Meanwhile, the secretary of state, Cordell Hull, led his department to advocate free trade—the progressive reduction of economic rivalry—as the only effective international healer.[2] And the president, Franklin D. Roosevelt, descended from high rhetoric only to offer American mediation to ensure, in effect, that Hitler's proposed revisions of the Treaty of Versailles were performed peaceably.[3]

This welter of conflicting voices drowned out any possibility of a settled diplomatic approach. Always, when crises arose, the initiative apparently lay elsewhere. The result was that the United States came to seem a copartner in the Anglo-French appeasement of Germany, all the more so as Hitler's demands on behalf of the German people grimly mocked the American faith in national self-determination. A further effect was that when diplomatic crises did arise, the opinions and activities of American ambassadors abroad acquired a fresh importance. These men could, in their far-flung outposts, lay claim to a greater expertise than their superiors in Washington; and so many of them, in their different, sometimes opposed ways, did attempt to influence policy: in Britain Joseph P. Kennedy, in Russia Joseph E. Davies, in Germany

Professor William E. Dodd, in Spain Claude G. Bowers, and in France, perhaps the most remarkable of them all, William C. Bullitt.[4] As a preamble to examining the response of the American administration to the events of 1940, the career of one of its more flamboyant agents may first be considered.

Bullitt was a man of intense, but brittle loyalties, making his one of the more intriguing careers in American diplomatic history. For it possessed a distinct rhythm, in which an early enthusiasm was invariably superseded by vindictive animosity. So it proved with Woodrow Wilson, whose protégé he once was; with the Russian Revolution, which he once urged Americans to favor; and with Franklin Roosevelt, in whom he once placed great trust. All of them came in time to disappoint him; and Bullitt's wrath, once aroused, was boundless.

He attacked Wilson in the conventional manner—speeches, articles, congressional testimony—but also, more originally, in a psychobiographical caricature, written in collaboration with Sigmund Freud and fortunately unpublished till 1967.[5] Bullitt was likewise transformed from the well-disposed first American ambassador to Soviet Russia into a doctrinaire anti-Communist and geopolitical strategist, outlining during the Second World War the contours of the next, imminent global conflict.[6] And Roosevelt, once (like Wilson) conveniently dead, was remorselessly abused by Bullitt for not following the adviser's advice.[7] His most relentless vendetta was conducted against another man with whom he might be imagined to have much in common, Sumner Welles, Roosevelt's under secretary of state. Victory came, in 1943, with the removal of that talented man from public office.[8]

This may suggest that Bullitt had an unstable or wayward personality. Yet, while that may be so, he also had the knack of foreseeing, even when not influencing, the future course of American diplomacy. The irony—and perhaps, to him, the tragedy—of his career was that all his recommendations, those vigorously argued, densely documented position papers, arrived not early but prematurely. He earned little credit and great distrust. Though ominous, it is scarcely surprising that in 1947 he can be caught sight of on an investigative foray in Indochina.[9]

One key to Bullitt's career is that he belonged to the generation of disillusioned Wilsonian idealists;[10] and his disillusionment had come at the hands of the master himself, when Wilson declined to consider the draft treaty that Bullitt had negotiated with Lenin in 1919. A member of the Philadelphia aristocracy, a Yale graduate, Bullitt had at the age of twenty-eight the intoxicating experience of being admitted to the innermost circles of government, just when a new world was being fashioned. Not to see the start of that new era, to have it instead indefinitely postponed by diplomatic intrigues and partisan maneuvering, chastened all its advocates. Franklin Roosevelt, for example, then Wilson's assistant secretary of the navy, resolved never to repeat Wilsonian errors, and developed a more flexible rhetoric in foreign affairs as well as a more astute sense of tactical politics. He shrank from that precision of thought which his mentor had so ardently promoted.[11] Walter Lippmann, then a friend of Bullitt, turned toward a cooler, harder appraisal of politics generally.[12] Bullitt, by contrast, withdrew from public life and joined, in effect, the intellectual exile of the 1920s. He married the widow of John Reed, the apostle of American Communism; he wrote a novel; he roamed the world.[13]

There was in all this an ummistakable element of self-dramatization, ambitious, idealistic, touched with frustration. To his friend Upton Sinclair he wrote feelingly in 1920 of his hopes for his "generation." It might accomplish "nothing less than the integration of the whole planet in some sort of an international system that will really mean a unified humanity."[14] For his part Bullitt had already announced his determination "to employ the next few years in learning a great deal more about this country and the Far East than I do at present."[15]

How natural it was then that in 1932 Bullitt should attach himself to the rising star of Roosevelt; and, once the president had overturned his predecessor's policy of nonrecognition of the Soviet Union, what more natural place was there for Bullitt's talents than the new American embassy in Moscow? In fact those were unhappy years for Bullitt. Recognition did not bring the two countries closer together: it only enabled Bullitt and his staff to gain firsthand impressions of the new Communist regime. Bullitt's were the most critical. He was affronted by all aspects of Soviet life, of which the personal harassments were only the least annoying. "The physical discomforts," he wrote early on, "would make life hellish if all the men were not such good pioneers."[16] More serious were the prolonged wrangles over matters that were supposed to have been settled, like the question of war debts. Discussions of such issues were never easy with the Russian Foreign Office because, Bullitt wrote, "in that institution the lie is normal and the truth abnormal and one's intelligence is insulted by the happy assumption that one believes the lie."[17]

One flagrant breach of faith occurred in 1935 when the Third International, meeting in Moscow, resolved to continue to spread the Communist gospel, although the Russian-American agreement of 1933 had specifically required that Moscow refrain from propaganda in the United States.[18] Bullitt was growing restless, and the next year, when the Stalinist purges resumed in all their savage enormity, he left for the Paris embassy as an implacable enemy of Communism. "It must be recognized," he wrote to Cordell Hull, "that Communists are agents of a foreign power whose aim is not only to destroy the institutions and liberties of our country, but also to kill millions of Americans."[19] For Bullitt, personal vexations, philosophical differences, and a lack of trust had been interwoven, as they so often were in him, to produce the most profound hostility.

In Paris Bullitt was back at the center of things. Moving from a dull proletarian state to a lively cultural center made him very happy. He quickly succeeded in gaining the confidence and affection of numerous members of the French political elite, left and right, from Léon Blum to Paul Reynaud. He enjoyed the sophistication, the cabinet intrigues, the honorary degree from the University of Nancy. Perhaps he relished the metropolitan life rather too much, for his dispatches to Washington tended to dwell on political gossip at the expense of political analysis. But on the major diplomatic issues of the day he did hold pronounced views, and while these owed a great deal to his own, rather personal understanding of the dangers of Communism, they also harmonized well with the wishes of the French cabinet.

In 1937 the dream was of Franco-German rapprochement, the soothing, by direct negotiation between Paris and Berlin, of all outstanding differences. Here an American ambassador had an important, lubricating task to perform, and thus Bullitt greatly welcomed the appointment as American ambassador in Berlin of the career diplomat Hugh Wilson to replace the intellectual anti-Nazi William Dodd ("I have felt like singing a *Te Deum Laudamus*," he wrote to President Roosevelt).[20] In 1938, once that dream had faded, the new objective was the avoidance of European war, by acceding to revisions in the Treaty of Versailles. Again, American influence might prove helpful, and long before the Munich settlement in September Bullitt was active in prompting his government to bless the peaceful dismemberment of Czechoslovakia. "I think," he wrote to Roosevelt in May, "we should attempt to find some way which will let the French out of their moral commitment."[21] And when finally, in 1939, war did come, Bullitt was no less resourceful in backing French pleas for American aid, endorsing the various proposals of Jean Monnet to purchase American airplanes.[22]

Thus following the French government through all its reverses, from appeasement to war, Bullitt might have seemed a mere spokesman for it, a rare point of stability amidst all the cabinet shuffles and conflicting signals. Yet there was for him, if not the Quai d'Orsay, an ulterior consistency of purpose, coming from his sorry experiences in Russia. Henceforth the stemming of Russian influence—what a later generation would term "containment"— would be a primary goal for Bullitt. And both the appeasement of Germany before the Nazi-Soviet Pact, and the declaration of war following it, satisfied, however indirectly and inadequately, that need.

In short Bullitt was never just a propagandist for a doomed French regime. Moreover, much of his strength as ambassador came precisely from his flaunted intimacy with President Roosevelt. He would enjoy phoning the president in order to abuse the British and French foreign offices, after announcing that they were bound to be listening on the line; and Roosevelt equally would enjoy telling the story to his poker-playing friends.[23] In Paris, as before in Moscow, Bullitt was Roosevelt's most trusted servant in foreign affairs, albeit at a time when the president's main interest lay elsewhere. The two men shared a distrust of the State Department bureaucracy, and from the time of his arrival in Paris Bullitt acted unofficially as Roosevelt's personal emissary, an ambassador at large, keeping in close touch with other diplomatic missions and advising Roosevelt on foreign-service matters generally. On more than one occasion, a list of proposed State Department appointments was forwarded to Bullitt from the White House for his comments.[24] But the best illustration of the convergence of his American stature and French loyalties can be seen in his reaction to an early, but significant event in the Second World War: the mission of Sumner Welles to Europe.

War had been declared on 3 September 1939. There followed eight months of what was called "phony war," but was in fact a period of intense fighting in Poland, Finland, Norway, and Denmark, and, for Britain and France, a time to define war aims and formulate strategy. Bullitt, playing his customary dual role, spent his time requesting American aid for France while warning the French that such aid would not be very great.[25] Then, in February 1940, came the announcement that Roosevelt was sending Welles on a mission for talks in London, Paris, Rome, and Berlin. Whatever the supposed purpose of such a visit—to gather information, or simply to reassure American isolationists that the president was indeed aiming at peace, not intervention—in practice this turned out to be a last-ditch attempt at appeasement.

So it appeared to the British, who resented Welles's assumption that peace could be secured via disarmament.[26] So it appeared to the French, many (though not all) of whom equally resented his assumption that peace could be secured via Italian mediation.[27] And so it appeared to Bullitt, who now had personal and professional reasons to hate Welles, a man whose intimacy with the president rivaled his own, while his intrusion into European politics challenged Bullitt's supremacy there too. Of course the mission itself was a failure, doomed by the sealing, even as Welles was in Europe, of the Rome-Berlin axis at the Brenner Pass on 17 March.[28] But the event is not without significance, revealing as it did the prolonged life of American appeasement.[29] It also highlights Bullitt's own position. He profited from Welles's failure. He felt strong enough with Roosevelt even to administer a mild rebuke, reporting back to him how Welles's praise of Mussolini had (according to Bullitt) dismayed prominent French politicians like Reynaud, Blum, Edouard Daladier, and Camille Chautemps.[30] Elsewhere he expressed himself more violently, and referred to Welles as a "fascist."[31]

So it was that when the "phony war" ended, and a more authentic one began, Bullitt recovered his old prominence. As the German blitzkrieg opened on 10 May with an invasion of the Low Countries, he conducted his own telegraphic blitzkrieg, bombarding Roosevelt with messages, often several in one day, crammed with intelligence, advice, and pleas for further assistance to the French.[32] At the same time he maintained the closest possible contacts with the French leaders. On 14 May he interrupted a meeting of the French War Cabinet to provide the prime minister, Reynaud, with news of the latest Italian moves.[33] On 15 May he learned of the collapse of the Belgian Army directly from the minister of war, Daladier, the only other civilian who knew.[34] On 31 May he actually attended the same meeting of the Supreme War Council for which the new British prime minister, Winston Churchill, and his deputy, Clement Attlee, had flown over from England.[35]

What is more revealing, Bullitt also came to share many of the French leaders' most distinctive attitudes during the months of crisis. Like them, he was greatly impressed by the German military machine, so much so that when he later passed through Madrid on his way back to the United States his feelings bordered on "defeatism," according to the British ambassador, Sir Samuel Hoare.[36] Like them, though for a shorter period of time, he half expected Britain to arrive at a compromise peace with Germany; and on 16 May he sent a telegram to Roosevelt advising him, in such an event, to secure the removal of the British fleet to Canada.[37] Finally, like the French leaders, he subscribed to the rumors then current about the imminence of a Nazi-inspired Communist revolt in Paris. From this, in part, came his decision to remain in the capital, after the French government had fled, so as to provide the inhabitants with such protection as he could.[38]

This was Bullitt's finest hour. It had moreover been well prepared. As long ago as October 1939, he had written to his friend, the secretary of the interior, Harold Ickes, "I simply will not pull down the American flag here."[39] As a symbolic gesture, Bullitt's action achieved two things. It gratified his own anti-Communist ardor, while also elevating him into the ranks of earlier American ambassadors in Paris, Elihu Washburne and Myron Herrick, who had also risked their lives to comfort the inhabitants. So, in order to supervise the peaceful occupation of Paris, Bullitt willingly neglected his more obvious diplomatic responsibility, to accompany the fugitive French government to Tours, to Bordeaux, and thence to Vichy.

His decision, naturally, was rather unpopular in the State Department; but, equally naturally, Bullitt escaped reprimand by invoking his intimacy with the president. Bullitt had announced to Roosevelt that in the event of a German occupation he would remain in Paris; and he had further gained an assurance that, if this happened, he would be appointed a cabinet member, secretary of the navy no less, to ensure his safety.[40] In fact nothing came of that, but nor did anything come of Cordell Hull's attempts to have Bullitt stay with the French government. Roosevelt later confessed that if he had ordered Bullitt to leave Paris he knew he would not have been obeyed.[41] Even Hull, while deploring his ambassador's indiscipline, admitted that not much would have been accomplished with the French. Had Bullitt been in Tours, Hull bluntly remarked to Adolf Berle, an assistant secretary of state, he would have been "spinning around like a goose that had been hit on the head with a corn cob."[42]

Bullitt was in Paris for the last three weeks of June, and by the time he caught up with the French government at Vichy it had greatly changed complexion. Gone were the strong men, the resisters. General Charles de Gaulle, lately under secretary of war, was in London. The most determined parliamentarians, Daladier, Georges Mandel, César Campinchi, Yvon Delbos, had sailed for North Africa in a last forlorn attempt to prolong the fight, doomed to futility as soon as the forthcoming armistice was signed. In their place was a cabinet whose first act had been to ask the Germans for information about armistice terms, and a National Assembly soon to vote itself out of existence. Thus the first impression Bullitt had on his arrival was that the French leaders wanted "to cut loose from all that France has represented during the last two generations." The new premier, Marshal Philippe Pétain, explained to him that all the parliamentarians responsible both for the war and for French unpreparedness "should be eliminated from the French government"; he intended "to dismiss every politician who had been connected with the Blum government"; indeed, "the system in France must be changed." In the same spirit Admiral François Darlan, minister of marine, blamed the defeat less on the armed forces than on "the entire system of parliamentary government in France which had been rotten"; once again, "a complete change in French ways of life was needed." Moreover, such a change might yield immediate, tangible benefits. "If a dictatorship . . should be introduced in France before the peace," Bullitt was told, "France would obtain much better terms than . . . under a . . . parliamentary system."[43]

But what kind of dictatorship? To Camille Chautemps, who had contrived the request for armistice terms, "the model would probably be the German constitution when Hindenburg had been president and Hitler chancellor. Pétain would be Hindenburg and Laval would be Hitler."[44] No greater gesture of contempt for the Third Republic can be imagined than the rising, out of its ashes, of Pierre Laval, the political fixer, opportunist, appeaser, the symbol of all its worst features. Rejected at the Popular Front elections of 1936, he was now back for revenge. "This Chamber threw me up," he declared to the new foreign minister, Paul Baudouin, "now I shall throw it up."[45] The repudiation of that French political regime whose members Bullitt had known so well for four years was neatly exposed by the reemergence of the most dangerous parliamentary exile of those same years.

The rejection of the past, then, was total and unanimous; but what of the future? Two questions in particular arose in Bullitt's mind: how would France behave toward her former ally, Britain, and her current master, Germany? It was to be expected that Anglophobia, already visible as Britain withdrew from the fighting in France, would be sharpened by the British attack on the French fleet on 3 July, with the ensuing loss of over a thousand French lives, that "hateful aggression," as Pétain called it in a letter to Roosevelt.[46] Darlan for his part only smiled when Bullitt inquired whether he relished the prospect of a British defeat.[47] By contrast, as Britain declined, Germany rose in French eyes; the Germans could even exploit the prevalent hatred of Britain by relaxing some of the armistice provisions. Pétain thought that the Germans would "do everything to obtain the goodwill of the people of France," while Darlan believed that they "desired to make France a willing vessel of Germany."[48]

Such were the common, general assumptions. But with regard to the future shape of French policy there appeared little accord in the new government. Bullitt did, however, regard Pétain as holding a commanding position. On those two crucial, related questions—hostility against England and collaboration with Germany—Pétain could seem to be taking a resolute stand against the opportunists in his cabinet. For there were those, Baudouin in the first instance, Laval in the second, who were, it seemed, prepared to sacrifice long-range French interests for the sake of immediate gain. But, according to Bullitt, Pétain at least recognized that only the defeat of Hitler could "restore independence to France"; he was, therefore, "secretly desirous of a British victory."[49] Moreover, he appeared to exercise real authority. In the immediate aftermath of the attack on the French fleet the question had been raised in the cabinet of going to war against England. Yet Pétain, almost alone, had, it seemed, been "resolutely opposed to anything more than a break in diplomatic relations."[50] Nor did he weaken. Bullitt's last impression was that "little stands between French acts of war against the British except the good sense of Marshal Pétain."[51] It was therefore a testimony to that "good sense" that, with the exception of some minor reprisals against Gibraltar, no such acts of war occurred.

If there was a consensus at Vichy, it was a very uneasy one. All the new French leaders assured Bullitt that the fleet would never be surrendered, to Britain or Germany, that Vichy's foreign policy would be one of inflexible neutrality. But, even in the short while that he was at Vichy, Bullitt could discern the growing divisions. Having withdrawn from the war, Vichy politicians could justify their continued power only by their success in two undertakings: alleviating the plight of their subjects and appeasing the conqueror. Their power would thus depend not on the bare fact of neutrality, but on what that neutrality would provide. And each leader spoke with a different priority. Pétain seemed bent on a moral renaissance in France. Darlan was preoccupied with the integrity of his fleet, and Laval wanted to secure a cozy niche for France in Hitler's new Europe.[52] The future of Vichy, and thus the American policy toward it, would be determined by the blending of these different tendencies, the outcome of the power struggle. Bullitt saw Pétain, who nicely combined a fatherly devotion to the forty million souls entrusted to his care with an acute grasp of strategic realities, to be the likeliest winner.

Such were the impressions Bullitt carried home from Vichy. He left on 10 July, the day the Third Republic expired; and practically his first words on American soil were in defense of Pétain and Vichy France. "I don't know if it is right to call it a fascist state," he told reporters; Pétain had "a tremendous reputation," was "thoroughly honest and straightforward," "universally respected," "doing his best to bring order out of a desperate situation." In short, Pétain was "absolutely the boss."[53] Nor was this statement mere diplomatic tact. Bullitt's respect for Pétain was perfectly genuine, as his colleagues in Washington soon discovered. The new secretary of war, Henry Stimson, was treated to an enthusiastic review of Pétain's accomplishments, while Harold Ickes began to wonder if Bullitt had succumbed to a European disease, that of calling upon Nazism and Hitler "to ward off the dangers of Communism."[54] Increasingly in his public speeches Bullitt would concentrate on the "lessons" taught by the failures of the French war effort, not the actual punishment visited upon the delinquents. In his "Report to the American People," a major policy address delivered at Independence Hall in Philadelphia on 18 August, a speech frankly designed to aid Roosevelt's presidential campaign, there were no references to the Vichy regime, only to the mistakes of its predecessor. There were horrifying descriptions of Nazi strategy, the devious propaganda, the Fifth Column, the military machine, against all of which Americans were duly instructed to commence preparations. But the outcome of defeat, the government of Marshal Pétain, was not included in Bullitt's catalog of the horrors of war.[55]

Bullitt's central beliefs—that the sovereignty of Vichy was real, that Pétain was in control and sympathetic to the Allied cause (if not to the former ally), that such collaboration with Germany as ensued would have to be forced upon him—these were to be the underlying assumptions of a new American policy. Yet if Bullitt inspired that policy he played little part in its formulation; he even came to abandon its original premise. His return from France marks the beginning of his involuntary retirement from governmental service, though not public affairs. He was denied his coveted secretaryship of the navy, which went to Frank Knox, the Republican publisher of the *Chicago News*; he was offended at the manner in which William D. Leahy was appointed to succeed him at Vichy;[56] and he was refused, again and again, a commission in the army.[57] For as Roosevelt was required to interest himself more in foreign policy, with at least the possibility of a war in sight, he turned increasingly to new (though often old) men; loyal, unobtrusive subordinates, like Colonel Knox, Admiral Leahy, and, at the War Department, Colonel Stimson, men who, conscious of the imperatives of military discipline, would not hamper presidential activities. By contrast, Bullitt, in 1940, must have seemed excitable, independent, unruly; and, thus excluded, he began to lead a strange, twilight existence.

At first it appeared that there was work for him in the Roosevelt administration as ambassador-at-large, or personal aide to the president, making fact-finding tours of the Near East, and reporting on the American army's training camp for future military governors in Charlottesville, Virginia.[58] But these were marginal activities, and Bullitt's reports, like his later, more substantial offerings, however cogent, received little attention. "I am doing nothing in this war," he wrote pathetically to Roosevelt in June 1942. "If there is anything I can do with you or for you, I want to do it."[59] Roosevelt's attitude towards him, however, was shifting from indifference to hostility. Bullitt's intrigues in Washington, culminating in the whispering campaign against Roosevelt's friend, Sumner Welles, effectively closed the White House doors to him as well as to Welles.[60]

There now seemed little for him to do. He tended his Pennsylvania farm; he delivered ceremonial speeches on behalf of French resistance and Franco-American friendship;[61] and he tried to defend himself against criticisms of his diplomatic record: he had not, he correctly insisted, encouraged the French to go to war or guaranteed American aid.[62] Then, in 1943, he made a most unwise, and unsuccessful, intrusion into Philadelphia politics.[63] The following year, realizing that he would not be allowed any influence on the settlement at the end of the war, he enlisted, in a superbly ironic masterstroke, in the French army of General de Gaulle, the leading opponent of that American policy toward France of which Bullitt had been, not the author, but the prophet;[64] and from Algiers, as special correspondent for the Henry Luce papers, he wrote for *Life* an article, "The Future of France," which asked Americans to adopt a kindlier, less suspicious attitude to the new France of de Gaulle.[65]

Bullitt's skills lay in foresight, not action; they were, that is, intellectual rather than practical ones. He never had any direct effect on American foreign policy, however close he liked to feel to the center of power. At times, indeed, he seems more a European than an American figure, far more comfortable in the intrigues and ideologies of Europe than in the democratic politics and governmental machinery of the United States. Yet his career is instructive for precisely that reason; the Roosevelt administration worked under different pressures, with different priorities, yet arrived at the same destination. While Bullitt was impulsive in his loyalties and his feuds, the government moved, for the first fifteen months of the European war, with deliberate caution.

It can still be debated at which point Roosevelt decided that the United States would not escape war with Hitler; but it was certainly not in 1940, when every step was accompanied by doubts and hesitations. Not until March 1940, for example, was the Anglo-French contract for American-built planes finally signed (and deliveries would not begin until September). There the Allies were themselves partially to blame for the delay.[66] But nearly four months elapsed between Churchill's request for some American overage destroyers and the completion of the Destroyers-Bases deal in September 1940, that disingenuous piece of constitutional evasion: four months, critical to Britain's survival, during which every potential source of opposition, like the United States Congress, was effectively neutralized.[67] Then too it is symptomatic that a plainly unneutral measure, which brought the United States closer to war, was proposed to the American public as one to keep war at bay. "This is not inconsistent in any way with our status of peace," Roosevelt assured Congress.[68] Even when Roosevelt's rhetoric was vigorously pro-Ally, as in the Charlottesville address of 10 June, it did not imply any change of policy. In that speech Roosevelt castigated Mussolini, who had just declared war on France, in language of a vehemence itself appropriate to a declaration of war, employing a term, "stab in the back," first used in that context in a telegram from Bullitt.[69] Yet, four days later, he declined to give Mussolini's victim, Reynaud, any substantive aid.[70]

Thus 1940 did not see any novel departures in American foreign policy. The most, it seemed, to be expected from the American administration was a renewed commitment to the status quo. On the day, therefore, when the French asked the Germans for details of prospective armistice terms, Cordell Hull summoned a conference of Latin American representatives to reaffirm the Monroe Doctrine;[71] and in August negotiations were opened with the new French high commissioner for the Western Hemisphere, Admiral Georges Robert, with the same objective: to insulate the entire continent against the shocks emanating from a European conflict now threatening European colonies.[72] This American stance may be termed, not unfairly, *attentisme*: waiting to see if Britain would last the summer, waiting to test American opinion in the November elections (and thus consolidate domestic support), waiting for the outlines of the new France to appear. The fruits of Britain's survival, and of Roosevelt's victory at the polls, came in March 1941, with the passage of the Lend-Lease Act. But in the meantime Washington had already embarked on the first stage of its Vichy policy.

The prelude to any analysis of Washington's policy must be the recognition that, in American eyes, a period of French history had, with the Armistice, drawn to a close. The claims that the Third Republic had made on American loyalties, however tardily acknowledged, were now finally extinct. That had been, of course, Bullitt's impression at Vichy. The speedy replacement of democratic politicians by soldiers, sailors, and former political outcasts presaged a more profound shift. It was tempting, therefore, to reach beyond German armed might for an explanation of the defeat, and to locate it, as Bullitt did in his Philadelphia speech, in various manifestations of democratic inertia: susceptibility to foreign propaganda, the Fifth Column, Communist pacifism.[73] However, to accept those explanations was also to go far toward accepting the legitimacy of the Vichy regime, which would in due course, taking that logic to extremes, actually bring to trial leading politicians of the Third Republic. Bullitt had been one of the earliest to allow a measure of French responsibility for the French defeat, and to adopt the paradoxical view that French politicians having failed in war, French soldiers might succeed at peace; but he was not alone, as the case of Anthony Drexel Biddle demonstrates.

The former ambassador in Warsaw, Biddle had moved in to stay with Bullitt in Paris when Poland was overrun in September 1939; and the following June he was the senior American official with the fleeing French government, while Bullitt stayed in Paris. For a second time Biddle witnessed governmental morale dissolve in the face of a Nazi attack; and on 1 July he sent his impressions of the defeat to Roosevelt in a memorandum that stressed "moral" factors. To Biddle the event was an illustration of a nation "gone soft"; between the wars there had been revealed "a bankruptcy of leadership in France."[74] Robert Murphy, counselor of the French embassy, likewise viewed prewar French political life with a certain skepticism, and titled the relevant chapter of his memoirs, "Frenchmen Expect the Worst and Get It."[75]

Thus informed on the causes of the French defeat, the American administration tried to analyze the new regime. But in the early stages all that was known with complete certainty were the terms of the armistice of 22 June; and this was, precisely, an armistice, not a peace treaty, nicely balancing current German needs and prospective French anxieties.[76] Its terms were, therefore, by no means free from ambiguity, though they may have seemed, at first glance, straightforward enough. They provided for the ending of all hostilities, the demobilization of all troops, the immobilization of all war matériel, and, the most humiliating measure, the occupation by Germany of about three-fifths of the country, including the whole of the northern and western coasts.

But over the remainder of French territory, including the empire, the French government would continue to exercise sovereignty. Indeed article 8, regarding the French fleet, was explicit on this point: the German government "solemnly and expressly" undertook not to interfere with the neutralized French war fleet, nor would it make demands on the fleet when peace was concluded. The carrot—continued French sovereignty over unoccupied France, the fleet, and the empire—was however accompanied by the stick. Article 3 provided that the Germans would, in occupied France, exercise "all the rights of an occupying power," and article 18 that the French government would, in turn, uphold and finance them. But what were those "rights"? That question was left tactfully unanswered, though the costs of their exercise were eventually calculated at four hundred million francs a day. French compliance was further encouraged by the retention in Germany of two million French prisoners of war, not to be released until the final peace (article 20), and by the threat (article 24), to "terminate the agreement at any time" if the French proved recalcitrant. Sterner measures would then be imposed.

The armistice terms, therefore, could not serve as a guide for American diplomatic action. On the contrary, they contained, in embryo, all the problems that were to plague American policymakers in their dealings with the French regime over the next thirteen months, fostering skepticism about the reality of Vichy's sovereignty, concern over the continuing immobilization of the fleet, doubts as to the strict neutrality of the empire. Given that, by 1940, German guarantees were to be treated with some caution, the crucial question for Americans was always how far France would go in the direction of placating, or resisting, her overlord. The French fleet, on either side, could tip the balance in a naval conflict, as could, in a global conflict, the French empire.

But Vichy's behavior, like her spokesmen, bordered on the inscrutable. At home, collaboration with Germany was initially so ardently desired that in September 1940, a potential opponent of it, General Maxime Weygand, was forced out of his post as minister of national defense; yet three months later the chief exponent of collaboration, Laval, was himself removed from office by Pétain. Abroad, French sovereignty was maintained in North Africa, bartered in the West Indies, surrendered in Indochina. Nor did Vichy officials display much consistency in their statements. Sometimes a German victory was proclaimed inevitable, sometimes unlikely. A British defeat was first desired, then feared. In the end, only two principles emerged with any clarity from the welter of confused and confusing declarations by the new rulers of France: hostility to the Free French movement of General de Gaulle, and friendship toward the United States.

How did all this seem in Washington? In the grim days of June and July, when there seemed a possibility of war between Britain and France, and more than a possibility of a British defeat by Germany, official opinion was vehemently hostile to Vichy. Cordell Hull saw the armistice terms as "complete capitulation," and complained that the French government "had gone entirely to pieces under Herr Hitler's intimidation." He told the French ambassador, in a discussion of the British attack on the French fleet, that "the whole of American opinion supported Great Britain's action." He was, he said, "utterly disgusted with the present French government which certainly did not represent the real France and seemed solely concerned to play up to Hitler." In the same way Sumner Welles called the armistice terms, which ensured, in his opinion, German control of the French fleet, "the most degrading surrender in history."[77]

But these harsh views, formed during an especially tense period in the war, soon yielded to a subtler, more cautious interpretation. As British and French tempers started to cool, as Britain failed to go down to defeat, Vichy came to be viewed not as a prelude to disaster, but as a rather more complex phenomenon. Once again, one of Bullitt's insights proved compelling: the notion that Vichy was not a solid, uniform structure, but an arena, in which competing policies, and politicians, struggled for preeminence. The American chargé d'affaires in Vichy, H. Freeman Matthews, saw various "schools of thought" at work there. One, led by Laval, worked for "an active pro-German policy"; another, "weak and uninfluential," but with the "real but inarticulate support of the overwhelming majority of French opinion," was pro-British; in between were Pétain and his entourage, willing to bargain and maneuver with the Germans. As for the French people as a whole, according to Matthews, they regarded the whole political situation as "entirely ephemeral."[78]

If that were so, then an opportunity was presented to American diplomacy. Rather than merely respond to Vichy's actions, it might itself, through skillful intervention, influence them, tip the scales this way or that. Two contrasting examples will show how the American administration came to sustain the belief that it could influence events at Vichy. The first is the Montoire meetings. As part of a coherent Mediterranean strategy, Hitler paid in October personal calls on all the relevant dictators, Mussolini at the Brenner Pass on the fourth, Franco at Hendaye on the twenty-third, Laval at Montoire on the twenty-second, and Pétain in the same place two days later. Whatever the Montoire encounters meant in practice, they were at the time a frightening portent, a symbol of German control and French obeissance, coming as they did only a few weeks after a speech by Pétain which anticipated France's liberation from "traditional friendships."[79]

The American response was swift and pointed: a vigorously worded personal message from Roosevelt to Pétain, warning that any "assistance to Germany and her allies" carried dire penalties. It would "wreck the traditional friendship between the French and American peoples"; it would discourage American relief activities; and it would deter the United States from helping France, "when the appropriate time came," to retain her overseas possessions.[80] Thus French imperialism, American humanitarianism, and Franco-American friendship were all invoked to restrain French collaboration. And the message seemed to have some effect. Pétain's answer was, compared to his reply to a similar note from King George VI, soothing and restrained. He too emphasized "the friendship which since the founding of the United States has bound the French people to the American people," and suggested that the tone of Roosevelt's note could only be due to "misunderstandings," since France had solemnly promised never to surrender the fleet. Britain, on the other hand, had adopted a stance toward her "to which the French people cannot consent," and France would "know how to enforce respect, with honour, for her essential interest."[81]

But Montoire did more than provoke immediate American diplomatic pressure. It further encouraged the interpretation of the relative positions of Pétain and Laval that Bullitt had earlier suggested. The meeting convinced Matthews at Vichy, for example, that the French government, "which means Laval behind the glorious name of the aging Marshal," had just made a strong bid for collaboration with Germany.[82] All that could slow Laval "in his march towards Hitler's new Europe" would be the assurance of a British victory, and of American aid to Britain.[83] It followed that American policy could exert a telling influence on events at Vichy. In Paris, likewise, Maynard Barnes, the first secretary of the American embassy, found Laval increasingly aware of the

American attitude, and conscious of his own isolation within the governing circle. Laval had, it seemed, come back from Montoire expecting to stimulate American interest in a compromise peace. Meeting with an outright refusal, he had begun, thought Barnes, to realize that he had not given enough attention to the American role, and that, moreover, "the mass of the French people" did not support him.[84] On one occasion Laval disarmingly suggested that French and American policies differed only with respect to the "small question" of a British victory.[85]

As Laval emerged a devout collaborationist, Pétain, by contrast, came to seem comparatively innocuous. To Matthews he stressed that French collaboration would "be only economic . . . and in no sense military aid to Germany." He even claimed that "a British victory is what France must hope for," although he expected a drawn peace. Above all Pétain insisted that he would never consent "to any step which by his lights and standards and in his words is contrary 'to the honour of France'." "He sold me completely on that," was Matthews's revealing conclusion.[86]

The aftermath of Montoire seemed to validate certain American assumptions: that the United States possessed a measure of influence at Vichy, and that the differences between Pétain and Laval were real and profound, ripe for American exploitation. This second belief was strengthened still further by the events of 13 December, when Laval was dismissed. As with Montoire, what actually took place was unclear, but, like Montoire, it was the impression that mattered. Just as the simple knowledge that Pétain had met Hitler had earlier fostered the belief that France was treading the road to collaboration, so now the simple knowledge that Laval had been expelled from the cabinet, and placed under house arrest, fostered the view that she might be abandoning it. Whatever the actual motives behind Pétain's dismissal of Laval, whether personal differences, as Pétain explained to Hitler, or a complex intrigue within the French cabinet, as Baudouin explained to Murphy,[87] the incident soon acquired the significance of a complete repudiation of all that Laval stood for. In particular, Matthews reported to Washington, it reflected "the unpopularity of his enthusiastic and determined march down the path of collaboration with the Nazis and of the bad name which that policy is giving France abroad (especially in the United States)." In view of the vast power that Laval had wielded, as string-puller behind the scenes at Bordeaux, as vice-president of the council and minister of foreign affairs at Vichy, his elimination could only strengthen Pétain's power and prestige and, by extension, French self-respect. So, according to Matthews, did the French people ("including ordinarily timid and discreet government circles") view the event.[88] So did the American administration. Hull told the British ambassador, Lord Lothian, on 21 December, that he was expediting the departure to Vichy of the new American ambassador, Admiral Leahy;[89] and Leahy's instructions, dated 20 December, indicated the extent to which the administration put its faith in Pétain. The first "principle" of American policy, they noted, was that "Marshal Pétain occupies a unique position both in the hearts of the French people and in the government."[90]

What in practice did this mean? As far as metropolitan France was concerned, continued American recognition of the Vichy regime presented no immediate problems. Rather it fulfilled the requirements of that fundamentally conservative policy to which, in 1940, the United States was committed. But French sovereignty stretched beyond metropolitan France into areas where it was, after the armistice, increasingly threatened by a varied assortment of rival groups and powers.

These overseas threats included the traditional Spanish claims on Morocco, and Italian claims on Tunisia, which always surfaced at times of French weakness. There was also the new threat from de Gaulle's Free French movement, which, with British support, was winning over such parts of the empire as Chad and Equatorial Africa, and aimed to spread the infection elsewhere. Indochina lay in the path of Japan's southward expansion. As for France's possessions in the Western Hemisphere, while these came under the protection of the Monroe Doctrine, that mantle, as reaffirmed and invigorated by all the American powers in the Act of Havana on 30 July, was alarmingly overprotective: it foresaw, if any danger arose of a non-American possession getting embroiled in the European conflict, the establishment, by the American nations, of "a regime of provisional administration."[91] In general, therefore, the further a French possession was from metropolitan France, the more severe were the threats it faced. It remains to be examined to what extent the American commitment to the status quo within France influenced its attitude to France overseas, in these scattered outposts of the French nation.

The French West Indies presented an especially tortuous problem. The islands themselves were of little strategic value, though there was always the lingering possibility, as Churchill feared, of their being used as bases for German U-boats.[92] But some recent acquisitions provided an immediate cause for both British and American concern. Several French warships were stationed there, along with 106 American airplanes (purchased by France, to which they were on their way at the time of the armistice); and there were also on the islands three tons of French gold (on their way from France to Canada for safekeeping). The armistice, which froze this situation, could scarcely have come at a more inopportune moment. Understandably covetous of the airplanes, and concerned about the future disposition of the French vessels, the British, having failed to dislodge the governor general's allegiance to Pétain, instituted a blockade on 5 July. Clearly some American initiative would have to be made if war were to be kept from the Western Hemisphere; and negotiations were soon opened in Washington to secure the more effective neutralization of the islands and the repatriation of their purchases.[93]

The Washington discussions, while abortive, did serve to clarify the two countries' positions. On 20 July the French ambassador in Washington, Count René de Saint-Quentin, delivered a series of proposals to Sumner Welles. One was that Vichy would ask the Germans for permission to give the United States an official guarantee that the French war vessels then in Martinique would not leave French territorial waters. However, if the vessels were perchance removed, the American government would, paradoxically, be notified in advance. In addition, the ambassador suggested that an American naval officer could be stationed in Martinique to see whether the agreement was kept. Welles found the proposals "totally unsatisfactory." They made no reference to the American airplanes, and would confer no authority on the American naval officer. Above all Welles stressed the German role in the proceedings. He found the notion that the Germans could determine events in the West Indies "exceedingly distasteful"; and in any case, "what assurance was there that such an agreement would be given[?]" Yet, four days later, after some discussion with Roosevelt, Welles presented alternative proposals that only differed in requiring the immediate return to the United States of the airplanes. They did not demand any authority for the American naval officer; and they retained that earlier obnoxious principle that German permission be sought.[94]

As direct negotiations between Washington and Vichy thus drifted into deadlock, the State Department began to apply what came to be called the "Greenland technique." The idea was to premise negotiations with a local representative upon his presumed independence of the central government: to accept, in the case of Greenland, the actions of local officials as the actions of the Danish government, on the theory that Greenland was the "surviving remnant," as Assistant Secretary of State Adolf Berle put it, of an autonomous Denmark. This enabled Britain, the United States, Canada, and the governor of Greenland happily to conclude negotiations to ensure the effective neutrality of the islands, guarantee supplies of food, and fulfill, in spirit at least, the Monroe Doctrine. In the same fashion, since Vichy had refused to release the American airplanes from Martinique (impossible, it was alleged, under the armistice terms), the United States sent Admiral John W. Greenslade on two missions to Martinique, in August and November, to deal directly with Admiral Robert. Washington was therefore acting on the theory that, in Berle's words, "the French government is not in full exercise of its sovereignty."[95]

But the analogy with Greenland was inexact. The French high commissioner was not, as Berle thought, sitting on the fence; he was scrupulously loyal to the home government and hostile to Britain; and since his sentiments were not shared by the native population, he moved swiftly to crush all dissidence, suppress the General Council, and institute a strict military regime.[96] Throughout the negotiations he stressed his devotion to Pétain, and, by extension, his fidelity to the armistice terms. The difference between Greenland and Martinique, between Governor Aksel Svane and Admiral Robert, was the difference between a defunct central government and a regime whose very existence depended on a jealous regard for its prerogatives. The upshot was that, while Robert freely gave assurances about the vessels and the gold (no more than had been offered in Washington), the airplanes were left to rust on the islands, to the chagrin of the British Foreign Office, whose officials saw in French tactics "a transparent attempt to get the United States to promote Vichy's legitimacy."[97] Washington's position was indeed ironic: having failed to mount the merest challenge to Vichy's policy, it had been required to collude in a diplomatic fiction, even while acknowledging, as Hull said, "that when the French naval commander at Martinique gets a message from Vichy it might well be a message from Berlin in disguise."[98]

In Indochina, by contrast, the United States remained passive before a surrender, not an assertion, of Vichy's sovereignty. There, in 1940, the French made two strategic concessions to Japan: in late June, at their weakest, they yielded to a Japanese demand for the closure of the railway from Haiphong to Kunming, by which about ten thousand tons of war matériel, chiefly of American origin, had been sent to China each week; then on 22 September they signed comprehensive military and political accords with Japan, under which the Japanese secured within Indochina three airfields, bases for six thousand troops, and transit rights, in return for recognizing "the sovereign rights of France over all parts of the Indochinese union."[99]

These measures, by tipping the scales heavily against China in her war with Japan, also altered somewhat the balance within the Roosevelt administration. By demonstrating Japanese intransigence, they fueled the arguments of those —the secretary of the treasury, Henry Morgenthau, Stimson, Ickes, and the chief of the State Department's Far Eastern division, Stanley Hornbeck—who had been pressing for stricter economic measures against Japan, such as an embargo on oil and scrap-iron exports; and they correspondingly weakened the arguments of those, Hull, Welles, and others in the State Department, who feared that such measures would bring the United States closer to war. The result was a splendid Rooseveltian compromise, a partial embargo loosely administered through the State Department; but it was nonetheless a marked shift—"a victory in substance," Stimson called it.[100]

However controversial these incremental measures of economic warfare were within the Roosevelt administration and within the State Department, there was one area of more general agreement: that such measures should always fall well short of force or the threat of force; and it is within the context of that American policy that the French surrenders can be most charitably viewed. For American advice to the French in their dealings with the Japanese had always been the same: delay, temporize, negotiate—the same policy, in fact, as the Americans were following, although they could supplement it with an embargo.[101] The policy was adopted with skill and resourcefulness by the French governors-general in Indochina, first General Georges Catroux, then after 20 July, Admiral Jean Decoux; and it is quite possible that they succeeded to some extent in postponing the final surrender. But while the French kept Washington fully informed about the progress of their talks,[102] they in turn were never deceived about American intentions. The ambassador, Saint-Quentin, for example, well understood that when Americans spoke of providing every possible assistance "within the framework of our established policies," that phrase excluded "military or naval force in support of any position which might be taken to resist the attempted Japanese aggression on Indo-China."[103] In Vichy the foreign minister, Baudouin, was told by Murphy that it would be vain to expect more than "a verbal condemnation of Japanese initiatives."[104] And Welles admitted that in the circumstance the United States could hardly "reproach the French Government for according military facilities to Japan."[105]

The United States could not, in 1940, behave otherwise. While it is true that the official announcement of the Franco-Japanese accords received some rather sharp rebukes from the State Department,[106] that outburst of ill-feeling was only a brief departure from the normally sympathetic American approach. This can be explained perhaps by Vichy's statement that Washington had actually approved the accords (Hull and Welles had always tried to make the most of the distinction between acquiescence and assent);[107] perhaps by a previous French failure to keep Washington informed about some earlier military accords;[108] or, not improbably, by the demonstration of the hollowness of the State Department's, as distinct from Stimson's or Morgenthau's, approach to Far Eastern issues. In any event, after the immediate crisis had died down, relations became more cordial; and there even arose a possibility that the United States might supply Indochina with material aid, though the only actual proposal made—to transfer the American planes on Martinique—was blocked by the Germans.[109] The central point remains: the hard bargaining of Catroux and Decoux, and the determined negotiations by Vichy in Tokyo and Washington, both plainly demonstrated the French reluctance to relinquish any part of the national patrimony. The irony of the Indochinese crisis, which was not lost on the American administration, was that Vichy's sovereignty, even when she was forced to surrender it, remained a fact of diplomatic life.

That left France's possessions on the African continent. Here the situation was indeed confused, and remained fluid for some months. It was not immediately obvious what were the governing principles, if any, of the resulting American policy. There was undisguised American approval of the successful British bombing of the French fleet at Oran in July, and of the markedly less successful Anglo–Free French raid on Dakar, the strategic port on the tip of French West Africa, in September.[110] But there was also the American support of French sovereignty in North Africa against all aggressors (and the Americans tacitly accepted the French inclusion of Great Britain among potential aggressors) by, among other means, a program of economic assistance.[111] With regard to the only areas that the Gaullists did manage to detach from Vichy, the State Department took a resolutely noncommittal stand; in September the American consul in Leopoldville was informed that the department wanted to avoid "any question of principle" in its dealings with the Free French, and he was reminded in November to do nothing "which might in any way commit this Government."[112]

Yet there was in all this an underlying consistency, which emerges once the African colonies are viewed not as separate issues but, as the American administration itself came to see them, in the light of an overall Vichy strategy. In the closing stages of the Battle of France, American representatives in Vichy and Africa were instructed to report fully on the prospects of France continuing the war from the colonies; but if there was one clear message that came out of all the confusion at Vichy, it was the determination of the new government to hold on to whatever was French, and to enforce its neutrality. The spasm of anger that swept through Vichy after the British bombing of the fleet is one illustration; the successful repulse, with the aid of hastily dispatched reinforcements, of the Anglo-Gaullist assault on Dakar is another.

The most impressive example of Vichy's resolve was in North Africa. There it made the most strenuous efforts to bring into line the French colonial officials of Morocco, Algeria, and Tunisia, along with their restless native populations. Already by the end of July those efforts, by General Auguste Noguès, the commander of the French North African forces, his commander in chief, General Maxime Weygand, and Marcel Peyrouton, the resident general of Tunisia, had brought some success; and the tide of dissidence, whether from more junior civil and military officials or from hopeful émigré politicians like Daladier and Mandel, had been stemmed. From Casablanca, Algiers, and Tunis, American consuls now reported on the willingness of colonial officials to obey orders from Vichy. There might be some dissident groups, but they either left North Africa to join the Gaullist cause or, lacking any leadership, submitted to the pressing need to maintain colonial order. "In short," concluded the American consul general in Casablanca, "the spectacle is of human nature at its worst, acting just as Hitler would have it act."[113]

The Gaullist successes on the African continent, which appear to contradict this general pattern, in reality confirm it. The Gaullist campaign in Equatorial Africa, begun in August, was complete with the winning of Gabon in October. But Vichy officials did not disguise from the Americans their intention to reverse the situation. Robert Murphy heard from both Pétain and Baudouin of a proposal to secure German permission for a French expeditionary force to expel British or Gaullist forces from Chad. Similarly Pierre Boisson, governor general of French West Africa, strongly hinted that his forces would not merely defend their territory but, in the event of further Gaullist moves, take countermeasures against British colonies.[114] Thus the effect of Gaullist successes had been actually to strengthen Vichy's colonial ardor; and it was on that basis, rather than in the hope of Allied successes in the future, that American diplomats chose to act. Convinced of Vichy's resolve to cling to her colonies, the State Department adopted a noncommittal attitude toward the Gaullist colonies, whose future was uncertain, and cultivated more amicable relations with the Vichy authorities at Dakar, whose future, with the Gaullists repulsed, seemed clear.

In North Africa, however, and especially Morocco, there did seem scope for more direct, though cautious, American intervention. As a result of the British Mediterranean blockade, Morocco was cut off from France, its principal supplier and market; and on 26 August, Emmanuel Monick, the secretary general, discussed with Matthews the possibility of establishing closer economic relations with the United States. He spoke of the "strong independent spirit in Morocco, its chagrin at the armistice . . . and the excellent morale of the colonial forces stationed there." On 6 September the American consul in Tangier sent a long memorandum to the State Department arguing that the British blockade was "superfluous as a war measure," creating hardships for the potentially friendly native population, aiding German propaganda, and setting France against Britain. A neutral power could, he concluded, perform "a real service" by getting the belligerents to see "the futility, from all points of view, of the hardships imposed upon this country by the throttling of its trade." Three days later he reported a request from the Moroccan representative of the Socony–Vacuum Oil Company of New York, A. G. Reed, to use American influence with the British to secure a relaxation of the blockade sufficient to procure supplies of gasoline, the greatest shortage in Morocco. But while the State Department's Near Eastern division was beginning to take an interest, official policy remained fixed, and the American consul was instructed to tell Reed that "in view of the well known attitude of the British Government in this matter the Department considers that it would be useless to transmit his request."[115]

What changed matters was the arrival in Algiers in early October of General Weygand. He had resigned the previous month as minister of national defense, and then been appointed, by Pétain, delegate general in French Africa. It was an intriguing appointment, prompting much speculation about the purpose behind it. Ostensibly he was to ensure the defense of the entire French African bloc, and to promote its economic fortunes, by coordinating the work of all the French residents and governors general. Beyond that, Pétain explained to Murphy that Weygand had been sent to quell the dissident (that is, Gaullist) movement, which seemed, in the wake of Dakar, to be gaining strength.[116]

But there were other, more hopeful signs. Weygand's known animosity to Laval, and his presumed hostility to Laval's policy of collaboration (the apparent cause of his resignation), suggested him as a strong candidate for Allied aspirations.[117] By 18 October, Felix Cole, the American consul in

Algiers, was concluding that there were grounds for optimism. He felt that
Weygand's policy, though initially anti-Gaullist and anti-British, would soon
be changed to one "based on opportunity."[118] According to the consul in
Casablanca, Weygand was advising his officers to "grit their teeth, prepare
very quietly and await the opportunity that might come."[119] And from Vichy
Matthews reported a certain unease among French officials at an apparent
change of heart by Weygand who, so they feared, had been "much impressed
upon breathing the free air of North Africa." He now thought a British victory
more probable, and "the spirit of resistance" seemed to have revived in him.[120]

Thus tempted, the Americans revived the idea of an economic aid program
for North Africa and sought an understanding with Weygand. One of their
earliest confidential messages to him included, to Vichy's annoyance, information about the peace proposals allegedly made by Hitler at Montoire, over
which the French cabinet was said to be divided.[121] But the Americans did not
try to weaken that allegiance to Pétain which Weygand so often and so vehemently affirmed, and which one of his associates called "a matter of hon-
or."[122] Once the excitement over Montoire had died down, American policy
was limited to seeking French goodwill, and thus assuring French neutrality,
by economic favors. Murphy, who was sent to North Africa in mid-December
to begin negotiations on the spot with Weygand, was expressly instructed to
convince him that the United States did not propose to create any discord
between him and Pétain.[123] Seen in this light, the program for American aid to
North Africa, while aimed at future benefits, served in the meantime to
stabilize the colonial situation; and to the extent that it succeeded it enhanced,
rather than impaired, Vichy's control over her empire.

Wherever possible, it seems, the United States sanctioned and reinforced
Vichy's colonial rule. Only in the Far East, where there were obvious constraints on American action, were the efforts made on France's behalf mini-
mal. Elsewhere the Americans, in pursuing their own conservative strategy,
also advanced Vichy's goals. They vetoed a proposed Anglo-Gaullist assault
on French Guiana;[124] they acquiesced in Admiral Robert's repressive rule in
Martinique lest, as the French put it, the natives receive "an invitation to
licence through the removal of all the symbols of authority";[125] and they
supported Weygand's attempts to quell dissidence in North Africa.

This is a long way from the pronounced anticolonial stance of later years. In
1940 the United States could neither reproach Vichy for the concessions in
Indochina, nor seek to detach dissident colonies from the mother country. Nor
could the administration, at least, engage in the gratifying practice of anti-
imperial rhetoric. This was how Roosevelt replied to a question on the French
colonies at his press conference on 5 June: "Martinique is a French colony and
they have a very interesting form of government for nearly all Negroes. They
get on extremely well with the small number of white people who are down
there. They never have any trouble. They have a low standard of living but that

is so all through the West Indies. They are a happy, cheerful people and, surprisingly, they have a much better education among the Negroes of Martinique than we have in most of the states in the South. Now, that is an interesting fact and that is a French colony."[126] Roosevelt did occasionally hold over Pétain's head the warning that the United States would not, if provoked, exert herself on behalf of French overseas possessions, as for example when the Montoire meetings threatened increased French collaboration with Germany.[127] But American practice in 1940 never went beyond that threat; and in December Roosevelt instructed his new ambassador to France, Admiral Leahy, to inform Pétain of the president's "sympathetic interest" in Vichy's efforts to maintain its authority in North Africa.[128]

So ended the first phase of America's Vichy policy. The sending of Leahy as United States ambassador to Vichy was the logical outcome of the events of the summer and autumn, as viewed in the United States and as initially interpreted by Bullitt: the collapse of French resistance, the pivotal role of Pétain, the threats of collaboration with Germany, the dangers as well as the opportunities presented by the fleet and the colonies, all suggested the wisdom of a forceful American presence at Vichy, one neutral power sustaining another, American intervention without American belligerence, the characteristic pose of 1940. These diplomatic and strategic realities, not Vichy's unseemly domestic practices, were the determinants of American policy. That policy had, moreover, the additional merit, in American eyes, of alleviating two other difficulties that had run through Franco-American relations since the fall of France: the relatively straightforward, though crucial, matter of the inadequacy of communications between the two countries, and the rather more complex issue of British policy toward France. It would be part of Leahy's mission to ease both these strains.

Certainly the rulers at Vichy desired closer relations with the United States. As a source of material supply, as a prop to Vichy's legitimacy, as an arbiter in the desired compromise peace, the United States could exert an altogether welcome influence. Vichy's spokesmen therefore endlessly stressed their affection for America and American institutions. Pétain spoke warmly of his old comrade-in-arms, General John Pershing, of the American Constitution, "which fortifies the executive power and separates it from the legislature," and of the common ideals of French and American democracy, "founded on respect for the human individual and love of justice and humanity."[129] Laval assured Murphy that France was hoping "to adapt its political forms to the best it could derive from the American Constitution" (as well as the German and Italian forms of government).[130] Newspapers in the unoccupied zone advertised all signs of American appeasement, especially the election speeches of Roosevelt, which naturally stressed his desire for peace.[131] Georges Bonnet, himself a fairly consistent appeaser, called on Matthews to encourage the

American administration to follow his example. He wanted the Americans to bring their influence to bear in favor of an early peace, "the sooner the better for France." The British, he felt, were ready for a "reasonable" peace, unless the United States "push them too far and encourage them too much."[132]

One theme above all dominated these conversations: the French belief that the United States did not "understand" the true position of Vichy, which sought merely relief from German oppression, not partnership in the Nazi enterprise.[133] The most peculiar complaints came from Laval, who blamed American incomprehension on "those miserable people who fled France—most of them Jews—who are now conducting such abominable and traitorous propaganda in the United States." To combat their activities a new ambassador, Gaston Henry-Haye, was sent to the United States in August. He would explain to Americans the "factual situation resulting from Germany's victory and the unintelligent attitude of Great Britain," and how the work of "national reconstruction [a word that might echo in American minds] is necessitated by the political decomposition of the previous regime." His chief task, however, was to stress that French "intentions and sentiments towards the United States are above all suspicion."[134]

Henry-Haye arrived in Washington with handsome endorsements from Bullitt and Murphy, and with a long record of pro-American behavior behind him.[135] Yet his mission cannot be counted a success. This was partly because his association with some of the least attractive features of Vichy was rather too intimate. He had worked ardently before the war for Franco-German rapprochement through the *Comité France-Allemagne*; he was a longtime admirer of Pétain and associate of Laval; and soon he was alleged to be operating a form of espionage system in the United States to keep watch on those same French emigrés whom Laval had mentioned.[136] None of his initial meetings with Roosevelt, Hull, or Welles was marked by any cordiality.[137] More seriously, it quickly became apparent that, even with a Vichy ambassador in Washington, and possibly because of him, communications between the two countries were still far from perfect.

By the end of 1940 complaints had been voiced on all sides. Welles expressed his concern to Henry-Haye that Vichy had taken a full week to issue, through the ambassador, a denial that peace proposals had been discussed with Hitler at Montoire, at a time when the world's press had been filled with rumors of the negotiations, and when Vichy "was well aware of the tremendous importance which American public opinion attributed to this matter."[138] Hull for his part objected that in the absence of such direct communication he was obliged to turn to press rumors, and reports from other countries, to keep abreast of French developments affecting the United States.[139] Henry-Haye himself felt aggrieved at a general lack of confidence in him; on one occasion he "burst into a state bordering on frenzy" when informed at the State Department that Laval, having ignored all his similar suggestions, now welcomed an

American proposal to use the planes on Martinique for the defense of Indo-china.[140] Laval, equally, and one of his subordinates, Jean Chauvel, voiced their dissatisfaction with the paucity of information they received from Henry-Haye and the garbled form in which it sometimes arrived.[141] And Matthews was no doubt surprised to learn that in transmitting Roosevelt's message to Pétain after Montoire Henry-Haye had neglected to stress its personal nature, and softened the language.[142]

Would an American ambassador at Vichy be of more use than a Vichy ambassador at Washington, the information more reliable, the communication more direct? So the British Foreign Office had come to feel by late October, when Lord Lothian was instructed to urge the State Department to establish "some closer link with Vichy than is afforded by the maintenance of a Chargé d'Affaires there or by the notorious M. Henri-Haye [sic] at Washington."[143] This may seem strange, especially in the light of later wartime developments when Britain and the United States seemed to diverge in their policies toward France. It is tempting to read back those later disputes into 1940 and to assume that even then the two countries were moving in opposite directions: Britain from the highpoint of wartime alliance with the Third Republic—at the climax, proposing to unify the two nations—to then, with the French defeat, ending relations with Vichy and supporting the alternative, rival movement of General de Gaulle; the United States by contrast swinging from the provision of moral and some material aid to the Third Republic to recognition of the Vichy regime, while displaying little interest in de Gaulle.

Yet this is to ignore the full complexity of Anglo-French relations in 1940. From the different timings of their declarations of war on Germany to the hastily improvised and soon abandoned project for Anglo-French Union, the two countries had never shown any real success at coordinating their policies. Rather, they had paved the way for the mutual recriminations and actual bloodshed, at Oran and Gibraltar, that followed the French defeat. But even then, with formal relations broken, the British never wholeheartedly endorsed de Gaulle's movement, certainly not after the Dakar episode, and always refrained from conferring any governmental status on him. Indeed they strove to keep in contact with Vichy through various intermediaries like Professor Louis Rougier and Pierre Dupuy, Canadian chargé d'affaires at Vichy.[144]

Initially, to be sure, Britain favored the ostracism of Vichy and welcomed any signs that Washington might recognize an alternative government.[145] When in fact Vichy did assert her sovereignty, and American policy did not challenge it, Britain still approved of the withholding of an American ambassador as a standing rebuke to Vichy. As late as 1 October, W. H. B. Mack, a senior Foreign Office official, commented that it was "just as well that Vichy should realise to the full the bad effects for them of their conduct and attitudes since the third week of June."[146] And, according to Matthews, there was no doubt that the absence of an American ambassador was "causing the Vichy

Government both embarrassment and a certain amount of misgiving."[147] But if Vichy was courting Washington while also flirting with Berlin, then an insistent American presence at Vichy might aid British interests. There was always the matter of miscellaneous intelligence to be gathered at Vichy, from which Britain was then cut off; and there was the attractive possibility of embroiling the United States still further in European affairs. But the greatest advantage was the moral weight that an American ambassador might lend the British cause. Twice Churchill asked Roosevelt to advise the French of the dangers, in loss of American goodwill, of surrending any part of the French fleet to Germany. Moreover, he added, "they will pay great heed in Vichy to such a warning."[148] Not surprisingly, then, when Leahy's mission was announced, Mack commented, "I should think that the appointment can only be helpful to us."[149]

The American policy that crystallized with Leahy's appointment was not, however, a mere prop to a complementary British policy. Before the year was out clear differences had emerged between the two countries. While accepting the primacy of British interests in maintaining the blockade of metropolitan France, the Americans were concerned that the Mediterranean blockade might be used "to curb arbitrarily American exports to Morocco."[150] Adolf Berle threatened that if the British policy with regard to trade with Syria continued to remain obscure, it might be necessary for the United States to consider taking an independent line.[151]

Beyond such economic issues, more fundamental differences over diplomatic strategy came to light. These were summarized in a telegram from Nevile Butler in the British embassy in Washington on 22 November: the Americans did not want to see the French West Indies brought to such economic straits that "internal troubles" would break out and a Gaullist movement take power; they regarded de Gaulle's movement as "rather an unfortunate if necessary improvisation on our part"; and they simply thought that the best way to deal with France was "to bring pressure on the French North and West African territories and on General Weygand to resist German and Italian infiltration."[152] If all that were so, concluded Lord Lothian, then how far could Britain ever achieve her goals by adopting a different line from the United States?[153] In short, far from the United States following the British policy, it was Britain that would have to stay in step with the United States.

America's Vichy policy was thus America's own. The events of the outside world were being interpreted and handled from a fixed national position, which outsiders were powerless to influence; and if that applied to foreign governments, how much more so did it weaken their official and unofficial emissaries. From Vichy there came in 1940 Camille Chautemps and René de Chambrun, both of whom were, in a sense, counterproductive. Chautemps, the author of the original French proposal in June to ask Hitler about possible armistice terms, was more of an opportunist than an apologist for Vichy.

Although after his arrival in December he cultivated Sumner Welles, and was granted one audience with Roosevelt, he was viewed with suspicion by the French embassy itself. Within a year he had broken completely with Pétain.[154] De Chambrun, who came on two missions, in June and October, to plead for food supplies, was entirely unsuccessful. The son-in-law of Laval, he already bore a considerable stigma, and so unpopular did he become that Roosevelt even contemplated depriving him of that honorary American citizenship to which, as a descendant of Lafayette, he was entitled.[155] Nor, it should be added, were critics of Vichy any more effective. Jean Monnet, who had the ear of Stimson and of Roosevelt's adviser Felix Frankfurter, did not win the administration round to his view that the "Stimson Doctrine"—that diplomatic recognition should be withheld from governments established by military conquest, as with Manchukuo in 1932—be applied to Vichy.[156]

Just as American policy reflected distinctive national concerns, so it also reflected certain developments within the administration, especially the increasing control that Roosevelt was exercising in foreign policy. Both the candidates for the post of ambassador to Vichy, General Pershing, who declined on grounds of ill health,[157] and Leahy, were personal friends. Leahy, Roosevelt's former chief of naval operations, famous for his tireless advocacy of a two-ocean navy, willingly left his post as governor of Puerto Rico to undertake a mission for the president to whom he was unquestionably devoted.[158] Roosevelt further determined the policy his ambassador would carry out.

On his arrival in Washington on 2 December, Leahy spent nearly three weeks studying French affairs in the State Department. But it was only too clear to a seasoned naval officer that there was a definite lack of direction there. He noted privately that while Roosevelt's oral instructions had been clear, he was now "unable, after discussion with the officials of the Department of State, to find unanimity as to what actually was the policy of the United States towards the French government in Vichy."[159] So there took place a remarkable exchange. Leahy asked Hull to get from Roosevelt written instructions on basic United States policy. He was then asked what Roosevelt had said to him in their conversations. He replied that the president had made three fundamental points: that Leahy should try to get as close as possible to Pétain, that he should urge the French not to join in any war against England, and that he should use his naval prestige to convince French officers not to permit Germany to use French naval bases or the French fleet. On the basis of Leahy's recollections, draft instructions were drawn up in the State Department, sent to Roosevelt for his signature, and thence back to Leahy who had thus, by a circuitous route, instructed himself.[160]

The precise outlines of America's Vichy policy were vague, and its course lay ultimately in the hands of the president. Yet it still displayed the prevailing assumptions of the entire American administration. It was in no sense a "gamble." Rather it grew almost inexorably out of the distinctive American experience of Vichy—grounded upon the conservative dictates of American foreign policy, premised upon a particular interpretation of the French defeat, fortified by the successes of Pétain and the failures of de Gaulle. "In America nothing fails like failure," commented a British Foreign Office official after the French defeat,[161] but the comment applied more aptly to de Gaulle after Dakar than to Pétain after the armistice. The transition that Bullitt had made in the space of a few July days, from contempt to respect for the Pétain regime, had taken the American administration five months.

CHAPTER 2

AMERICAN ATTITUDES
TOWARD FRANCE
IN 1940

The historian who examines the American newspapers for the month of May 1940 may wonder how much of ourselves we saw in that mirror.
—*Saturday Evening Post*, 6 July 1940

Foreign affairs are not the same to the diplomats who observe them and the public that attends to them. That is not only because diplomats are more directly involved, and should be better informed. They also work within a distinct frame of reference. William Bullitt, and after him the American administration, responded to the French defeat in the light of a presumed national interest. He analyzed the causes of the defeat, and his superiors, looking at political and strategic matters, arrived at a policy, the recognition of Vichy France. There was, in 1940 at least, a consensus in American governing circles that this was the correct policy. Nor was there, in 1940 at least, any demurral from public opinion at large. It was not only a sensible but a prudent policy. After the fall of France Americans were, with some notable exceptions, agreed upon the desirability of staying out of the war, while providing aid to Great Britain, declining to appease Hitler, and implementing, with all dispatch, a comprehensive national defense program. That much is evident from the raw data of public opinion polls;[1] and it is equally evident that the policy toward Vichy harmonized well with those anonymous preferences.

Behind the agreement on policy there also lay a general assent in the premise of that policy: that the causes of the French defeat lay in French internal weaknesses. This was, in a sense, a cultural rebuke, from the United States to France, and it was delivered in a number of striking ways. In October 1940 the *New York Herald Tribune* held its Tenth Annual Forum on Current Problems. The speakers' rostrum was graced by celebrities and opinion-makers of various political persuasions, who differed among themselves on matters great and small. They included Eleanor Roosevelt and Walter Lippmann, Dorothy Thompson and Clare Boothe Luce, Robert Sherwood and Wendell Willkie. Yet when they discussed Europe, in particular when they reflected on the French defeat, they spoke with one voice. To Lippmann, the event showed that "no people can settle down in complacency and self-indulgence to enjoy the blessings which they inherit from their forefathers." To Clare Boothe Luce, the men of Vichy were merely the "opportunist liquidators of a democratic bankruptcy." To Archibald MacLeish, "the collapse of France was a collapse from within, a collapse of will and conviction and belief."[2]

Another illustration is afforded by the art critic Harold Rosenberg in an essay for *Partisan Review* in 1940 titled "The Fall of Paris." To be sure, Rosenberg sharply distinguishes himself from those "former friends and present enemies" of France who saw its defeat as the product of some internal weakness, like "softness" or "sensuality." Nevertheless the argument of the essay did suggest a cultural fault, though the analysis was conducted in intellectual, not political, terms. To Rosenberg, "twentieth-century Paris was to the intellectual pioneer what nineteenth-century America had been to the economic one." But "for more than a decade there had been a steady deflation of that intellectual exuberance which had sent out over the earth the waves of cubism, futurism, vorticism—and later, dadaism, the Russian ballet, Surrealism." That deflation, that "general ebb," was a dissipation of the energies of Modernism, of that cultural internationalism whose capital had been Paris, steadily adulterated by that political internationalism whose capital was Moscow. It was in the name of this bastard internationalism that the artistic innovators, the "defenders of culture," in Paris had enrolled in the Popular Front. As a result, the loudest intellectual criticism of the "criminal burlesque" of the Moscow trials had come not from some present-day Emile Zola crying "J'accuse," but from American thinkers like John Dewey. The Parisian culture thus evaporated, German tanks found in their path nothing but "a pile of decomposed scrapings."[3]

The views of a cultural critic and of political commentators intersected neatly. Yet, for all this, American opinion in 1940 was also marked by divisiveness, rancor, and suspicion. It was no ordinary presidential election year, for it was widely assumed that the American people would issue judgment on the past eight years of New Deal reform, on the candidacy of President Roosevelt for an unprecedented third successive term, and on the appropriate American posture toward a darkening European scene. Between liberals and conservatives, Democrats and Republicans, interventionists and isolationists, the debates were heated and bitter; and in these feuds events in France were both mourned and also welcomed as a vindication of partisan views. They had become debating points, exploitable by all factions. To see how this came about, it is necessary to start with the outbreak of the war itself.

Americans reacted to the opening of hostilities in September 1939 with a mixture of complacency and concern. According to public opinion polls the overwhelming majority expected and wanted the Allies to win (only about 10 percent foresaw a German victory). At the same time the overwhelming majority also made it their first priority that the United States should stay out of the conflict. Thus while majorities could always be found to support the general proposition of aiding the Allies, there was never a majority in favor of any such specific measure. On the question of Allied war aims, opinion divided almost equally between those who felt that the war was "a struggle of democracy against the spread of dictatorship," and those who saw in it "just another struggle between the European nations for power and wealth."[4] The tone was set for these varied reactions by President Roosevelt in his "fireside chat" on 3 September. Making a deliberate contrast with Woodrow Wilson who in 1914 had urged Americans to remain resolutely neutral in word and deed, Roosevelt stated, "I cannot ask that every American remain neutral in thought as well."[5]

It is an interesting exercise to delve into the ethnic, regional, religious, and economic sources of Americans' views on the outside world. It can be shown, for example, that isolationism was particularly strong in the northern middle western zone, from Ohio to Idaho, with its tradition of radical hostility to Europe; in the provincial, traditional, northern New England states; and among German and Scandinavian immigrant communities as well as urban, Anglophobic Irish Catholics. By contrast, interventionism was strongest in the states along the eastern seaboard, parts of New England, and especially the South, which was historically oriented toward England, free trade, and a world market. Similarly, it can be shown that women, the poor, the young, and the old were more inclined toward pacifism than men, the middle-aged, and the wealthy.[6] The distinction, in 1939–40, was primarily between those who feared a war and those who feared a Nazi victory.

But, however suggestive, this process of sociological categorization can only chart tendencies; it plainly does not expose uniform blocs of opinion. Isolationism and interventionism may be found throughout the United States, scattered among all ages and income groups. More is revealed by going beyond the surface manifestations of public opinion and investigating their origins. Though these views were indeed in conflict, they will be found to have arisen from the same attitudes: in the first place, a fear of war, to which Roosevelt eloquently appealed in his speech in Chautauqua, New York, in August 1936 ("I hate war");[7] and, second, a suspicion of European power politics, as expressed, for example, by Ernest Hemingway when he called Europe a "hell broth."[8] Those were the continuous traditions of American opinion, subsequently refined through a whole series of regional, political, and emotional ties.

The First World War strengthened both traditions. It was the memory of that crusade, and its shabby aftermath, that lay behind the neutrality legislation of the 1930s. Those laws, restricting foreign trade and travel, were designed specifically to prevent the United States from being embroiled in another war in the same way that she had been involved in that earlier conflict.[9] But they were not the only method proposed to keep America at peace. There was in fact a fundamental conflict within the peace movement, which became steadily more acute as the decade wore on. It was between those, the "isolationists," who saw the only safeguard for peace to lie in a vigorous maintenance of American aloofness from European affairs, and those, the "internationalists," who felt it to lie in American support for collective security in Europe. That the two wings of the movement, represented by the Keep America Out of War Campaign and the American Union for Concerted Peace Efforts, were diametrically opposed over the means to be used does not alter the fact they had in common a paramount desire to keep the United States out of war.[10]

If a militant desire for peace was to be found equally among isolationists and internationalists, so too was a suspicion of European politics. France was viewed with particular disquiet. Though she might be the junior partner in the British alliance in 1939, her prewar conduct seemed at least as heinous as that of Britain. Much of the revisionist historical writing dealing with the origins of the First World War was concerned with France's role in the prewar crisis.[11] Thereafter, the Treaty of Versailles, the occupation of the Ruhr, the bombing of Damascus, French rule in Morocco and Indochina, and the Munich settlement all added up, in many eyes, to a most unsavory record. Challenging the idea of a community of interests between the Old World and the New, the liberal Oswald Garrison Villard wrote to the leading isolationist Senator Burton K. Wheeler, ". . . would it not help in your next speech to point out that France is no longer a democracy?"[12]

Once war had broken out, Americans were even further distanced from a sympathetic appraisal of what was happening in Europe. For war brought in its train all the apparatus of censorship, which constricts the flow of information, and propaganda, which inflates and distorts it. The basic principle of wartime censorship is, naturally, to prevent the dissemination of any news that might help the enemy. In the case of France this definition covered an uncomfortably large area, and American correspondents were required to compose their reports from extremely scanty military bulletins; the official French war communiqués were always shorter than the British or German ones. Not until the blitzkrieg was well under way was any reference permitted to the weaknesses of the French war effort—the civil unrest, for example, or the political disputes—news of which, in the hands of such Francophile correspondents as Edgar Ansel Mowrer, might actually have helped arouse public opinion to the seriousness of France's plight. However the correspondent for the *Chicago Tribune*, Edmond Taylor, did admit subsequently that he had not reported fully on what he saw of French morale and attitudes toward the war because he found it "too disturbing."[13]

By contrast, French spokesmen in the United States reflected with confidence and enthusiasm on the French war effort. Addressing the Chicago Council on Foreign Relations, André Philip of the Anglo-French Purchasing Commission explained that France "had come to the point when Hitler had to be stopped"; his listeners could be sure that "we are unanimous in France on this point."[14] At the same forum, in April 1940, the French ambassador, Count René de Saint-Quentin, reiterated the message: ". . . there is no one among the five million men in our army that is ready to lay down his arms."[15] It is therefore not too surprising that when Reynaud replaced Daladier at the head of the French government, a move that might have suggested severe internal dislocations, the *New Republic* only commented, "France is not dependent on any one individual for ability to fight. That is her democratic strength."[16] As late as 7 June an editorial in the *New York Times* bore the title "France Undaunted."

The French had never considered propaganda as an integral part of the war effort. The Ministère de l'Information was originally the Commissariat de l'Information under the brilliant but hardly warlike Jean Giraudoux, author of *La guerre de Troie n'aura pas lieu*. It was organized only after war had broken out, and its head acquired cabinet status only after the fall of the Daladier government in March. Even then it retained, under men like Paul Hazard, the distinguished historian of ideas, and André Morize, the former head of the French department at Harvard, a scholarly and literary aura that made it rather less effective for wartime propaganda than its Nazi counterpart. Moreover, it had to reckon with the well-known American suspicion of propaganda, as shown, for example, by the reluctance of American correspondents to repeat rumors of German atrocities, such as the use of poison gas. In February 1940, on his return to the United States, Mowrer told the *Editor and Publisher* that "France sees no need for propagandizing in this country, mainly because French governmental leaders have been tipped off that the less they try to influence neutral America, the better for them."[17]

Nevertheless, when Pierre de Lanux undertook a mission to the United States in the same month—February 1940—he blithely announced on his arrival that he was making a "propaganda tour." Of course, he encountered heavy sales resistance. Adopting a didactic approach, he brought with him a fifteen-page mimeographed handout titled "Anti-French Opinion in the United States." This listed the "twelve chief attacks" made on France by American critics, which were then optimistically countered with "twelve answers concerning France." As *Time* pointed out, these answers suffered under the distinct handicap of being rather less convincing than the original questions. Thus to "Attack One—France is imperialistic," de Lanux's reply was hardly reassuring or even tactful: "France," he wrote, "like England and the United States for that matter wishes to preserve what she possesses. Unlike some of them [sic] she does not wish to acquire any new territory."[18] From March to May an average of one-third of respondents to opinion polls affirmed that England and France were fighting mainly to preserve their power and wealth.[19]

Some propaganda was less overtly political. This stressed the sentimental features of a France at war, the theme of Eve Curie's three-month lecture tour. The daughter of the discoverer of radium spoke at literary luncheons and social gatherings on the life of French soldiers, the grace of Paris, chestnut trees in spring, women in wartime, and democracy. Some of this propaganda simply proclaimed the delights of French life in general, through anonymous advertisements in leading American newspapers for "French gloves," "French champagne," and "French liberty." This drove Raoul de Roussy de Sales, then head of the Havas news agency in New York, almost to despair. "The French government," he noted in his diary, "has begun to spend hundreds of thousands of dollars on publicity in the papers here. Beautiful France—her cheeses, her wines, her fashions, are vaunted. It is the stupidest kind of propaganda imaginable."[20]

Within limits, however, this sentimental propaganda was successful. It was, for some quarters, accurately gauged. While Americans might have some grave reservations about the current French political leadership or the motives for French participation in the war, the older, affectionate bonds between the two nations were only strengthened by the outbreak of war. It had been assumed from the beginning that, as in the First World War, of the two Allies France would bear the heavier burden. In a matter of days after the outbreak of war, a host of charitable and humanitarian organizations had been founded or, since some dated back to the earlier war, reanimated; and, as was customary, they were sponsored and directed by members of that polite society where, in any case, Franco-American links were particularly strong. The American Friends of France was directed by Anne Morgan of the J. P. Morgan family, and Le Paquet au Front by Mrs. Seton Porter, once married to the head of the Morgan concerns in Paris; the treasurer of L'Aide Lafayette was H. Leigh Hunt of the National City Bank in Paris. Much was accomplished: clothes, ambulances, and Christmas presents for French children were all provided through the generosity of Miss Morgan and those who supported her cause.[21]

It is not, therefore, to belittle that generosity to suggest that these activities represented an emphasis on the sentimental and humanitarian issues presented by the war to the exclusion of all else; or to point out that these were the same impulses—and in some cases, like Anne Morgan, the same people—that had promoted similar activities on behalf of General Franco in the American Union for Nationalist Spain. In the eyes of the sentimental supporters of France, the war was free of ideological complexities. There was an easy assurance of a French victory (as Anne Morgan said, "France will win; the French feel so, I feel it must be so"), and everything French was idealized. Exploiting the nostalgia of Americans for a French life could be most rewarding. Thus at a gala held on the roof of the St. Regis Hotel in New York, the guests arrived appropriately dressed for "A Night in Cannes," which was rivaled only by "A Day in Cannes" at the George Washington Hotel. As if to underline the nostalgia, the resulting ambulance brigades were named after figures from a glorious and distant past in Franco-American relations: Benjamin Franklin, Myron T. Herrick, General Pershing.[22]

Propaganda and censorship from France, nostalgia and sentimentality in America—each made its contribution toward muddying still further the already opaque waters of Franco-American understanding. Partly as a result of all this, the keenest interest that Americans displayed did not concern the war, but rather the nature of the forthcoming peace. The earliest demand made of the Allies when war broke out was for a statement of "war aims" consonant with the idealism that Woodrow Wilson had taught Americans to expect from the waging of war. Even someone as sympathetic to the Allied cause as Herbert Agar could write in November 1939 that the absence of a declaration of precise war aims was the Allies' single greatest failure.[23] It remains one of the ironies of the American suspicion of foreign "war" propaganda that the German brand was designed to encourage American pacifism, and the British and French brands to portray the blessings of the coming peace.

But the Allies' attempts to satisfy American cravings met little success. For one thing, there was what seemed in the United States to be a division of opinion between Britain and France. While some British spokesmen—Lord Lothian, Clement Attlee, Lord Halifax—were prepared to entertain the idea of a federally united Europe—a satisfying goal to all shades of American opinion—and while a joint Anglo-French Purchasing Commission made sense to Americans, French declarations were rather more muted.[24] It was not long before many Americans felt that France was intending to impose a punitive, Carthaginian peace on Germany; that, as many believed had happened in 1919, France would dominate the peace conference to secure a settlement containing only the germs of yet another conflict. Specifically, the editor of the *New Republic*, Bruce Bliven, expressed his alarm that French war aims might include the dismemberment of Germany and the occupation of the left bank of the Rhine;[25] and the cry was heard in other papers including some, like the *New York Herald Tribune*, actually sympathetic to the Allied cause.[26] Beyond that, there was the familiar American suspicion of European politicians, which tended to make even their most idealistic proclamations sound vaguely disreputable. Writing in the *New York Post*, Ernest Meyer foresaw that "once pushed all the way in it may be our historic role once more not to dictate justice but to underwrite a redivision of the spoils of gangsters."[27] In short, the failure of Allied propaganda was a failure to adjust the war to American expectations.

The net result was that in the absence of a clear Allied lead, the more sympathetic American commentators, the internationalists, filled the void. They began themselves to draft the outlines of a satisfactory postwar world. "Fighting against Hitlerism is not enough," declared the *Chicago Sunday Times*.[28] Walter Lippmann concurred, as did Dorothy Thompson.[29] In these circles the topics up for discussion included the economic foundation for peace, a United States of Europe, even world government. Here indeed was an unintentional reminder of the earlier conflict. Once again, Raoul de Roussy de Sales perceived the truth behind the illusion:

In 1917 it was the Americans who drafted war aims: "Make the world safe for democracy." Left to themselves the Allies had found nothing more inspiring than the struggle against Kaiserism. They did not dare say that they were simply fighting against an attempt at German hegemony, and in this war the same thing is true. Long before this war began —from the birth of Nazism—it was the Americans who said that western civilisation and democracy were at stake. Dorothy Thompson, Lippmann and Roosevelt in particular have tried to formulate war aims for the Allies. England and France, through opportunism and to please the United States, adopted this idea of conflict between two forms of life and two concepts of civilisation.[30]

But only the very exceptional writer went beyond a declaration of American concern with the shape of the postwar world to propose actual American involvement in the war to bring that world about. Archibald MacLeish, the poet and Librarian of Congress, caused an outcry when in May 1940 he published in the *Nation* his article "The Irresponsibles," castigating his fellow intellectuals for their indifference toward the totalitarian assault on the common Western cultural heritage: "Nothing is more characteristic of the intellectuals of our generation than their failure to understand what it is that is happening to their world."[31] Waldo Frank, the novelist and social critic, went further than MacLeish in maintaining American responsibility for the European crisis. In his article "Our Guilt in Fascism," published the same month in the *New Republic*, he attacked what he identified as "empirical rationalism," the scientific, mechanical, materialist conceptions of social life that lay behind the current collectivist manias that were assaulting all civilized existence. Taking as his text the lines from Hosea, "For they sow the wind, and they shall reap the whirlwind," he argued that the chief responsibility lay with the intellectuals, who had promoted abstract, collectivist experiments divorced from an organic conception of social reality; and even when that scientific collectivism had taken a brutal and sanguinary form, the intellectuals, though they might be critical, were not to be numbered among its fiercest opponents. This intellectual guilt, Frank argued, underlay the disastrous foreign policy of Roosevelt, "the President who uttered one deep truth, 'our frontier is the Rhine,' and let his actions toward Japan, China, above all toward Spain, betray us." Frank concluded with a Lincolnian antithesis: "This world cannot permanently survive, half fascist and half free."[32]

On their lofty intellectual plateau MacLeish and Frank could not escape attack. MacLeish earned the robust criticism of Edmund Wilson, Rexford G. Tugwell, and Dwight MacDonald; Frank was shortly to resign from the *New Republic*. To generalize about the popular mood in the United States in 1940 may be rash, but it does appear to have been marked by a desire to remain at peace, sympathy for the Allied cause tempered by suspicion of its leaders and fear of its propaganda, and such confidence in an Allied victory that the only issues worth discussing concerned the postwar settlement. As the *Washington Post* claimed, "the eventual peace is our concern, even though we may argue that the war is not."[33]

It was against this backdrop of American opinion that on Friday, 10 May 1940, the Nazi war machine lurched forward, quickly overcoming Holland, Belgium, and Luxembourg, soon to strike into the heart of French territory. The prospects of an early peace, of an Allied victory, of American isolation were all rapidly brought into question.

To employ the language of 1940, the French armistice was not so much a defeat as a "fall," a "collapse" of all that France symbolized. In order to measure the shock delivered to the United States, it is necessary to record more than the obvious political and strategic repercussions—the prolongation of the war, the renewed demands for aid to Britain, the Atlantic threat posed by Germany's capture of France's western coast and possible seizure of her fleet. The psychological blow dealt by the surrender of such a seemingly undaunted nation must also be examined.

One by one, the easy certitudes of 1939 had crumbled—the Maginot Line, the defense of Paris, "no separate peace." "The Allies," said the *Cleveland Plain Dealer*, "will stand or fall together."[34] As the blitzkrieg got under way, the *New Republic* commented, "No matter who wins this war, it means the end of 'la douce France'—sweet, mild, agreeable France, where living was easier than anywhere else in the world."[35] The fall of Paris in particular was the occasion for much lugubrious reflection. "Paris," said the *Atlanta Constitution* on 15 June, "for more than ten centuries has held aloft the torch of civilization." The same day, the *New York World Telegram* lamented that "This incomparable capital of the West is dead." It is perhaps symbolic of the American involvement in the war, with the emphasis on the sentimental bonds between the United States and France, that it was the American ambassador, Bullitt, who had ensured that, in order to preserve the capital in all its splendor, Paris should be declared an open city.[36]

But the melancholy is not to be explained in purely sentimental terms. It stemmed also from a sense of powerlessness. As the German armies swept through northwestern France, they created a situation of chaos, with thousands of refugees lining the roads, military morale dissolving, and the government in a state of panic. Out of this turmoil came plaintive pleas for help from, among others, Hamilton Fish Armstrong, the editor of *Foreign Affairs*, for planes, food, and medical assistance.[37] Premier Reynaud made three appeals to the United States for aid, to which Roosevelt could give only the vaguest of replies.[38] It was not simply that the American public was reluctant to give aid; the United States was, in the words of the *Atlanta Constitution*, ". . . empty-handed."[39] That a newspaper as sympathetic to the Allies as the *Atlanta*

Constitution should endorse Roosevelt's withholding of aid testifies to the popularity of that stand.

How tempting it was then to conclude that France had been defeated not for external reasons, the absence of aid, but for internal reasons, domestic failings. This temptation was strengthened by the seeming deception, perhaps self-deception, in which French spokesmen had engaged. All the assurances that France would never yield, would never make a compromise peace, seemed to have evaporated, and along with them American confidence in France. Even so shrewd a firsthand observer as Armstrong had been taken in: cabling that appeal for American assistance, he had noted that "French policy can be stated in one sentence: the army, the government and the people intend to win this great battle in the north at any and every cost." Soon a tone of reproach entered the analysis, once the initial period of mourning for a fallen bastion of civilization had passed. By 24 June an editorial in the *New York Herald Tribune* could recall that "France was pledged to a joint war together with Great Britain and no separate peace."

For it was not only the fact of France's defeat, but the very completeness of her "fall" that so shocked Americans; and in 1940 that "fall" seemed cause for despair. As one academic observer, the historian Hans Kohn, noted, Poland also had been defeated and invaded, yet no Pole had been found to head a submissive government; Norway and the Low Countries had been invaded and captured, but their governments were continuing the fight in exile, leaving behind a people hostile to the occupying power. The French government, on the other hand, having declared that Paris would fight to the last man, had surrendered the capital with scarcely a shot. It seemed like a betrayal of trust, damaging to the hopes of isolationists and internationalists alike.[40]

The earliest adjustment to the shock was naturally to find an explanation for so unexpected a defeat. The search displayed considerable partisan bias, since this was an election year, since internal causes had to be stressed, since the event was harmful to all points of view. The "fall of France" nicely combined the elements of a mystery story with those of a morality play; and in finding culprits and drawing lessons, American writers exposed their domestic preoccupations rather more than their love of France. Isolationists and interventionists, Republicans and Democrats, supporters and opponents of the New Deal, all pointed to France as a tragic warning of what would befall the United States unless she heeded those lessons—lessons about appeasement, about the Fifth Column, about preparedness, about the New Deal. A presidential election is habitually an opportunity to debate four years of American history. In 1940 it also gave a chance to debate twenty years of French history.

To one group of writers the explanation for France's defeat was beguilingly simple: it lay in the Popular Front government of Léon Blum. So the word went out: If the United States were to avoid a like fate, she must abandon the New Deal, dismiss its directors, repudiate its doctrines, whether of creeping socialism or creeping internationalism. That theme was developed, with various embellishments, throughout the whole range of the American press: mass-circulation dailies, provincial newspapers, trade papers, popular magazines, and journals of opinion. Always the analogy between the United States and France was considered exact. Always the purpose in making it was ruthlessly didactic, to the extent that some of the comparisons were rather vulgar, as in a photographic section in *Scribner's Commentator*, a leading organ of rightwing isolationism. Under the banner, "These Wrecked France," Geneviève Tabouis, the journalist, became "the Dorothy Thompson of France"; Henri Bernstein, the playwright, emerged as "the Robert E. Sherwood of France [who] showed little feeling for the past of France with the usual communist technique [sic]: he ridiculed in his plays Catholicism and the country's long record of success"; and Maurice Thorez, head of the French Communist party, was none other than "France's Happy Warrior, but unlike Al Smith he took his orders direct from Josef Stalin in Moscow." In short, concluded the writer, if Americans listened, they would realize that "those who betrayed democracy in France are precisely those who out-Ickied Ickes in praise of its benefits."[41] In a similar vein, a leading Republican isolationist, Senator Arthur H. Vandenberg, had printed in the *Congressional Record* a lengthy and more scholarly indictment of the Popular Front and, by extension, the New Deal. Written by an economist, Hartley W. Barclay, for the journal *Mill and Factory*, in July 1940, it documented, with an array of tables and statistics, the "planned sabotage of national defense by social reformists" in France, who had "opened the door to Hitler's triumph in a way which can be paralleled by a Fifth Column in any democratic country."[42]

Not all newspapers made the cruder analogies. An editorial in the *New York Herald Tribune* suggested that "for the sake of clear thinking it should be borne in mind that the weakness of the French system finds no precise parallel in this country." Actually, it continued, that weakness, the development of narrow factions or personal cliques, was precisely what George Washington had warned his countrymen against in his *Farewell Address* at the very start of American history. Nevertheless, in the last paragraph, the editorial returned to the important theme. There were, sadly, some slight resemblances between the two countries. In the United States, as in France, the democratic process was sometimes "cumbersome and, in many respects, inefficient." Fortunately it was not too late to learn; perhaps "under wise leadership—leadership such as Wendell Willkie offers—there is the chance to clean house."[43]

The fall of France was the *locus classicus* for opposition to the Roosevelt administration, to liberal social reform, to interventionism. But there arose, dialectically, a contrary interpretation. In the liberal and internationalist press can be found an explanation every bit as simple and appealing, but with the ideological coordinates reversed. It was not the Popular Front and the Left that had made France vulnerable, but the sabotage of the Popular Front from the

Right, which had then in addition provoked a more extreme left-wing reaction. This argument was particularly seductive once it was realized that the defeat had brought into prominence old enemies of the Popular Front. The Vichy regime could be made to appear the culmination of an ancient plot. As early as 24 June the *Cleveland Plain Dealer* was sure that "the truth is that the Pétain Government is a front for those who have for years admired and worked for the totalitarian system." Similarly, the French journalist "Pertinax" (André Géraud) wrote on his arrival in the United States a number of articles that anticipated the argument of his later book, *Les fossoyeurs*, laying the blame for the defeat at the door of the moneyed classes and political reactionaries who feared democracy and the social consequences of even a victorious war.[44]

The chief task, however, was to defend the Popular Front. Here the argument was made that, far from being a cause of disunity, it was a worthy attempt to solve the problems of an already perilously divided France. This was how Russell I. Hare of the New York and Paris law firm Coudert Brothers explained the situation on his return to the United States after twenty-three years in France: "Léon Blum and the Popular Front government, the forty-hour week, paid vacations, and the collective contract were not the causes of disunion and sabotage in France. Low wages, long hours of work, deplorable living conditions, little leisure and no place to spend it, except in saloons, brought on the Blum social revolution."[45] Similarly, Melvin M. Fagen, on his return from six months as a relief administrator in France, wrote at length on the "lesson" of France, which was as much a defense of the Popular Front as an endorsement of the New Deal: ". . . French industry produced more goods more quickly during the Popular Front regime than it did at least six months before or twenty months after."[46] Similar conclusions were reached by a writer in *Foreign Affairs*.[47] And Pierre Cot, formerly Blum's minister of aviation, then in exile in the United States, defended the Popular Front's record, and his own, at length in the American press, cautioning that "the legend of the incompetence of the Popular Front is one which democratic Americans should be wary of accepting."[48]

To some liberals this line of argument might have presented certain difficulties. It was necessary, for example, for the *Nation* to forget the editorials it had delivered in the thirties on the "merchants of death" theme, denouncing the British and French armament programs, or exposing the alleged Anglo-French interlocking munitions empire, or attacking the western allies' belligerency. Instead, a new charge was placed that France had been defeated because French private enterprise had failed in the crucial area of national defense. Ironically, part of the defense made of the Popular Front was to the effect that it had by 1938 to a large extent abandoned social reform and embarked on a program of rearmament. Some liberals were, however, aware of the confusion in their position. Writing in the *Nation* in September 1940, Albert Guérard, professor of comparative and general literature at Stanford University, admitted that "one of the causes of France's fatal hesitancies was that we, American liberals, unwittingly acted as a Fifth Column. For twenty years we kept denouncing the iniquities of Versailles. Our attacks sapped France's self-confidence."[49]

The essential point, however, remained. When all the allowances were made for liberal pacifism in France, or liberal isolationism in the United States, the real guilt lay with the opposition. Thus Heinz Pol, a German émigré journalist, included in his series of articles for the *Nation* titled "Who Betrayed France?" one essay on "The Guilt of the Left," in which he attacked the pacifism of Paul Faure, Léon Jouhaux, and the Radical Socialist party; but he safely concluded that ultimately it was the French Right that had sold out, since it aimed at "a victory over the socialist masses."[50] In the same fashion, Colonel William J. Donovan and Edgar Ansel Mowrer, in their series of articles for *PM* on "Occupied Europe," put the greatest emphasis on right-wing hostility to the Third Republic, particularly among "a hesitant officer class . . . and a majority of cynical and cowardly politicians."[51] For the liberal Edmond Taylor of the CBS news service, the weaknesses in French democracy, which had caused the French defeat, stretched back beyond the Popular Front to 1934, the year of the riots inspired by the demonstrations of right-wing groups like the Croix de Feu. In that year, Taylor wrote, "democratic leadership, through timidity or necessity, abdicated in the face of an insurgent minority and turned over power to a compromise formation which proceeded to nullify the majority will—as expressed in the last elections—in both home and foreign policy . . . In short, French democracy collapsed because democratic morale between 1934 and 1940 dropped steadily lower, while antidemocratic morale rose steadily higher."[52]

With the comments of Edmond Taylor a consensus seems to emerge. At first there appears to be little common ground between the two rival interpretations, each postulating different villains in the tragedy of France's downfall—Nazi sympathizers and Communist agents, social reformers and political reactionaries, selfish workers and greedy businessmen, appeasing politicians and bellicose publicists, treacherous generals and pacifist soldiers. But the common ground is plainly the belief that France was defeated not by external blows, but by those identifiable "enemies within" whose counterparts already lurked in the United States. These internal foes had so damaged the whole fabric of French society that it had collapsed; France had been defeated through a failure of will.

This thesis can be observed in the writings even of those who eschewed the cruder partisan analogies. Dorothy Thompson, for example, who had once stood on the Maginot Line, used the occasion of the French defeat for an orgy of self-criticism on behalf of democratic institutions and democratic values everywhere. "They know now, in France," she wrote on 7 June, "that frivolous waste of time, inconsequential playing of politics, weighing of personal interests and downright corruption have contributed to the French military weakness and lack of coordination."[53]

The only remedy for democratic inertia was, Dorothy Thompson predicted, a democratic renaissance. In this context the phrase that repeatedly occurs is "militant democracy," which neatly combined toughness and idealism. Only a society as honeycombed with antidemocratic influence as France could have gone down to such an easy defeat; only a militant posture in the face of such influence could prevent the United States following the same road to disaster. "Militant democracy," had in fact two complementary features: first, a maintenance of open hostility against internal foes, the Fifth Column, lest, in the words of the *Greenville* (S.C.) *News*, American citizens be "lured into looking with some approval upon the delusive pictures of Utopian conditions under Marxist or Nazi programs."[54] But this hostility could only be maintained if there were a renewal of the fighting spirit, the other side to "militant democracy." In a well-informed article in the *Washington Star*, Jay Franklin revealed that the Roosevelt administration had taken considerable alarm at the revelations of treachery and appeasement among senior French government officials, the discovery that in a country traditionally hostile to Germany (unlike, for example, Norway), leaders had been found to head a submissive government. That, it was felt, marked "the spiritual conquest of France by the forces of greed, the lust for power, and the spirit of class hatred at the top, rather than the bottom of the social pyramid."[55] The shock of the French defeat had, on all fronts, served to promote a demand for militant democratic renewal, which, had the phrase not been preempted, might also be called moral rearmament.

The French defeat may have sharpened certain issues for Americans at home; but the problem, the mystery of France, remained. Moreover, there were now two successors to the stricken Third Republic, Vichy and Free France, and in formulating their responses to each of them, Americans were confronted with the same obstacles as before: censorship (only now it was censorship imposed by Germany on France) and propaganda (only now there were two rival sources of propaganda). The emphasis of any news item depended upon its dateline. From Spain and Portugal, American correspondents recently in France, like Edgar Ansel Mowrer, sent reports describing the chaotic situation they had just left; from neutral Switzerland came uncensored discussions of the new French regime leaving no doubt of its presumed fascist tendencies. But from France itself the dispatches came delayed, censored, and "wired via Berlin." According to an Associated Press correspondent, news from Paris was not instantly transmitted to Berlin by telegraph; it was sent more gradually by train, car, or plane.[56]

Those dispatches routed through Berlin attempted to portray a picture of contentment, order, and a return to normal. Thus P. J. Philip cabled the *New York Times* on 1 August a story from Lyon where, he claimed, he had encountered among "persons of all classes . . . the perfectly frank and honest disposition to revise their opinion of Germany under Nazi Control." Earlier he had found only blind opposition; now he detected a "tendency even toward admiration, especially for the work of economic reconstruction that has been done under Hitlerian rule."[57] One correspondent, G. H. Archambault, even seemed at first to be enthusiastic about the regime. In July he wrote that the French people realized that the first necessity was discipline, and were looking with confidence to the new regime to maintain it. But, he added, "there is no question of France not remaining democratic."[58] In August he sent in a laudatory report on Marshal Pétain and the "new French state." He described sympathetically Pétain's concern for "truth" and "liberty," his affection for "the common people, farmers, workers and the like," and the widespread feeling "that the situation must remain delicate for some time."[59] But in November, on the occasion of a French complaint about American lack of understanding, he explained to his readers how he and his colleagues had in fact been prevented from displaying "that frankness toward American public opinion which has ever proved the best policy."[60]

What effect had the earlier dispatches had upon American readers? Evidently the intention had been to create the impression that the Vichy regime was based on consent, not compulsion, that it was not an imposition by an alien elite but a response to pressure from below. This would be particularly difficult for Americans, supposedly so affectionate toward the French people, to accept, and newspaper editors sometimes inserted their own parenthetical comments into the published version of their correspondents' stories. For example, an Associated Press dispatch reporting Vichy's admission of Gaullist defections in French Africa was headlined variously, "Three French colonies to aid Britain," "Three French colonies to take protection of Britain," "Churchill blamed for Chad revolt," and "French East African rebellion admitted." Only one newspaper echoed the AP writer's prescribed phrase, "France strikes back," in connection with Vichy's formal dismissal of the rebellious governors.[61] Sometimes editors devoted entire editorials to the correction of what they saw as false impressions. Thus in answer to Archambault's stress on the widespread French desire for "discipline," an editorial in the *New York Times* argued that if discipline were the supreme need, this could have been achieved under temporary military rule, "exercising trusteeship for the Republic."[62] From the beginning of July editors and columnists were warning their readers not to believe any story emanating from France. To the *New York Herald Tribune* the news stories from France bore "the unmistakable marks of Nazi censorship."[63] The *Christian Science Monitor* likewise argued that "this isn't France—this imitation of totalitarianism that is being set up at Vichy."[64]

But despite this determination to resist foreign propaganda, Vichy news management did score one remarkable success. This was over the Dakar incident. The strategic importance of Dakar had long been recognized. The announcement, on 17 August, that the United States was to open a new consulate there was described by the *New York Herald Tribune* as "a belated recognition by the United States that the French West African possessions may serve as the point of departure for German attacks against both South Africa and the British African colonies."[65] Correspondingly, alarm was expressed a month later when it was rumored that the French ships that had slipped past Gibraltar were going to Dakar to suppress an incipient revolt. Thus when the news of the Anglo-Gaullist attack did break it was greeted with enthusiasm, particularly by the military experts. But the news was coming exclusively from Vichy. On 25 September an AP dispatch conveyed "unconfirmed and conflicting reports that Dakar had surrendered to the 'Free French' and British expeditions." By the afternoon, sympathetic American newspapers were developing this news with headlines like "Dakar surrenders to British." Meanwhile, no news was coming from Dakar itself (except for a report that the radio had been damaged), and the British, according to the London correspondent of the *New York Times*, were "reticent, the Admiralty said it knew nothing, and the Foreign Office was snappish."[66]

Thus, relying on sources in Vichy, American newspapers repeatedly ran stories favorable to the Allies. An initial London story that de Gaulle was withdrawing was swept off the front pages by Vichy-inspired rumors that Dakar was surrendering, only to be replaced late on 25 September by the definitive announcement from London of complete withdrawal; Major George Fielding Eliot had to rewrite his entire military analysis just before the *New York Herald Tribune*'s deadline. The net effect was to make the expedition seem even more muddled than it had been, and for both Britain and the Free French a propaganda defeat was added to a military repulse. One newspaper survey concluded that it had been the hardest blow given to British prestige since the beginning of the war, detracting even from the glory of the Battle of Britain.[67] The *Nation*, later to become one of de Gaulle's great champions in the United States, referred to the expedition as a "blunder."[68] The *New York Times* concluded that de Gaulle's leadership had been severely questioned: "The authority of General de Gaulle as the spokesman of 'Free France' has been discredited. The effort to detach the French colonies has suffered a setback, and may have to be resumed in other ways, perhaps with other leaders."[69]

The Dakar incident was a fine illustration of the success that subtle management of news could achieve. Here it paralleled the achievement of the Vichy government in convincing Washington that Vichy's sovereignty was real and effective; and it thus appeared to justify the Roosevelt administration's noncommittal posture toward de Gaulle. But the more blatant efforts to influence opinion tended to go awry. For example, official news items stressed those features of the new French order that were expected to strike a responsive chord in American hearts—the task of "reconstruction," the "back to the land" movement, the gospel of work, the introduction of religious teaching in schools, even the prohibition of alcoholic consumption; that last attempt at a renewal of moral vigor must surely have been hard for most Americans to take seriously.

The new French order thus won few converts, save those already predisposed to one or another aspect of it. The admittedly remote *Lancaster* (Pa.) *Intelligencer Journal*, for example, could happily announce that the disaster of war might be France's "remaking," through a recovery of her rural traditions; all Americans too, it suggested, should "buy a farm."[70] But there was overall a stridency and stern moralism about Vichy's propaganda that scarcely encouraged goodwill. What, for instance, were Americans expected to make of a blast from Adrien Marquet, Vichy's minister of the interior, concerning the danger confronting the United States? Of his first visit, in 1932, he recalled that it had seemed a healthy and buoyant country; a young man with average intelligence, average brawn, and an average will to work could have hoped, and did hope, to amass enough to live comfortably. But when Marquet returned in 1939 he had been astonished to find American youth no longer willing to work and no longer ambitious, preferring the relative security of a civil service job to running in the race for a fortune. "It is probably this attitude," he somberly reflected, "which has allowed the spread of the infection manifest by three critical signs—women filling the jobs of men in industry and commerce, wearing too much makeup, and refusing to bear children. I warn you, when a nation generally exhibits these three manifestations of decadence it is time for that nation to look to its future and awake."[71]

Frenchmen, of whatever persuasion, had one formidable obstacle to overcome before reaching American opinion: the popular revulsion against propaganda, "that special breed of cultivated untruth," as Herbert Hoover called it.[72] The most dangerous aspect of propaganda, in American eyes, was that by appealing to the emotions it fostered irrational forms of behavior. It diverted the individual from the rational pursuit of his self-interest; it undermined the rational foundation of democracy. That certainly was a frequently drawn lesson from the First World War. Both the American entry into it and some murderous outbreaks of xenophobia that followed were laid at the door of foreign propaganda.[73] The result was that when war broke out again in Europe there arose in the United States a strange and paradoxical phenomenon: propaganda *against* propaganda. For example, the newly formed Institute for Propaganda Analysis—scholarly, respectable, its membership largely academic—periodically issued exposures of foreign intrusions into the American opinion-forming process.[74] There was also the familiar isolationist plaint that every statement that favored the Allies over Hitler was by definition foreign propaganda, even, or perhaps especially, when issued by the American administration.[75] Such an atmosphere scarcely encouraged clear, or objective, thought. Americans, observed de Roussy de Sales, "have all become so obsessed by the word 'propaganda,' and so alert at detecting it everywhere, that no one can be sure that his innermost and most personal convictions are not the result of it."[76]

France was unique in being, after June 1940, at once a purveyor and a victim of propaganda. That placed a special burden upon the numerous French arrivals in the United States in the second half of the year. The suggestion by the columnist Westbrook Pegler that they should all be herded into camps can be dismissed as eccentric; but even Dorothy Thompson cautioned her readers to distrust all Frenchmen lest they turn out to be secret agents. In fact the newcomers defy easy classification. There were authentic exiles like the journalists Geneviève Tabouis and "Pertinax," hostile to Vichy without entering the Gaullist orbit; literary men, of as yet undefined political loyalties, like Antoine de Saint-Exupéry and Jacques Maritain; discreet, retired civil servants like Alexis Leger, formerly secretary general of the French Foreign Office, who now elected to devote himself mainly to poetry, under his pseudonym Saint-John Perse; unofficial emissaries from Vichy like René de Chambrun; and the new French ambassador, Gaston Henry-Haye, whose arrival precipitated a rift within the French diplomatic corps.[77] This period saw a number of departures from the French embassy and consulate staff, in protest, as it seemed, against the direction taken by the mother country: among others, Maurice Garreau-Dombasle, commercial attaché to the embassy, who was dismissed, Paul Pazery, vice consul in Philadelphia, and Comte de Fontnouvelle, consul in New York, who resigned.[78] All of these people sought, according to their lights, to influence American opinion—by gathering support for either de Gaulle or Pétain, by raising funds either for ambulances and medical supplies for the Free French or for food and clothing for a metropolitan France threatened with famine. In so doing they, perhaps unwittingly, imported into the United States precisely that spirit of antagonism and divisiveness which, to so many Americans, had characterized French prewar society and brought about its defeat.

The leading target for hostility came to be the new ambassador, Henry-Haye. Despite a record of pro-American activities stretching back to the First World War, the publication of some friendly articles about him by American correspondents in France, and a public endorsement, in the warmest terms, from Robert Murphy, who was "proud to call him my friend," he remained subject to deep suspicion in the United States.[79] Rumors about his alleged pro-Nazi sympathies had preceded his arrival, and he was greeted at New York by a handful of pickets carrying placards that read "Heil Henry-Haye."[80] In less than a month his critics had what seemed more substantial grounds for attack, for many newspapers reported that in the wake of the new ambassador there had also arrived a four-man French "Gestapo," among whom were some of Henry-Haye's former associates when he was mayor of Versailles. They had, it was alleged, orders to investigate the activities of those Frenchmen in the

United States who were following an anti-Vichy line and, presumably, to threaten them with reprisals against their families and property in France.[81]

Nothing could have touched more acutely American sensitivity about foreign activities on American soil. When Henry-Haye claimed in his defense that all Frenchmen in the United States still had to obey the laws of France, he was roundly rebuked in the *New York Times*: "Surely he understands that Frenchmen and other foreign nationals are subject to American law while here. They are also protected by American laws from molestation by their governments at home or by its agents in this country."[82] Perhaps most indicative of Henry-Haye's growing unpopularity was his loss of favor even in fashionable Washington circles, where fund-raising drives for stricken France had succeeded those for France at war. The society leader Mrs. Harrison Williams was described by the gossip columnist Walter Winchell as "a very dead pigeon indeed" by virtue of her association with Henry-Haye.[83]

Equally illustrative of the temper of American opinion was the animosity aroused by Count René de Chambrun on his visits to the United States. Normally, he would have been an ideal representative of his country to plead the case for sending American relief to ravaged France. He was a direct descendant of Lafayette (thereby possessing honorary American citizenship) and the nephew of Nicholas Longworth, a former Speaker of the House of Representatives. But he was also the son-in-law of Laval and therefore a highly suspicious figure.[84] Moreover, he did not confine himself to personal talk with Roosevelt, but chose also to launch himself as a celebrity in the United States with the publication in October of his book *I Saw France Fall— Will She Rise Again?* This work repeated the familiar condemnation of the Popular Front; it bemoaned France's lack of moral and physical strength that had made the defeat "logical and desperately necessary"; and it concluded with an enthusiastic commentary on the great spiritual reformation that, under Vichy, France was undergoing. Even the forthcoming trials of various prewar politicians were to be seen as the result not of "unhealthy political or class hatred but merely an intense desire for justice."[85]

The book's thesis harmonized well with certain tendencies in American political commentary; it received favorable notices in, for example, the *Chicago Tribune* and *Scribner's Commentator*.[86] But it also attracted widespread dissent. While acknowledging that it was ably written and that the descriptions of actual fighting showed considerable skill (Henry Stimson, who read it in bed, found it "a good read"),[87] most reviewers considered it to be primarily a fascist apologia for Vichy. They noted the author's silence on such vexing questions as the degree of influence that Hitler was exerting upon the Vichy government, and often made bitter comments about the author's personality, political affiliations, and activities in the United States. "I do not care," wrote Samuel Grafton in the *Washington Post*, "for the idea of titled pro-Vichyites giving our people wrong information on what killed a sister republic."[88] The most savage commentary was made by Ulric Bell in the *Louisville Courier Journal* on 16 October. Bell was a high official in the Fight for Freedom Committee, a militant interventionist group, formed shortly after the French defeat, which engaged in the most energetic lobbying and propaganda efforts on Britain's behalf, and which had released Bell's statement for nationwide distribution the previous day. His lengthy diatribe is a useful illustration of the extent to which a belligerent hostility to foreigners of certain persuasions, and a phobia about foreign propaganda, could be found as much among internationalists as isolationists.

"Now come the men of Vichy," Bell announced, ". . . Publication of *I Saw France Fall* is the latest in a long series of episodes dovetailing into a pattern of suspicious import." He then explained that the plot was to soften American opinion so as to permit relief to be sent to metropolitan France, thus simultaneously hampering the British war effort by breaking the blockade of the continent, and easing the economic strain on Germany. Involved in the plot, in addition to Henry-Haye, de Chambrun and the four French police officials, were their American friends, Herbert Hoover, who (as in the First World War) was in the vanguard of all relief efforts to Europe, and socialites like Mrs. Harrison Williams. For, "the swank Riviera set, superimposed now upon New York café society, offers one of the easy avenues of access to the American scene. . . ." But, Bell cautioned, it was not just a matter of "palaver over the caviar and champagne. . . . A new kind of Gestapo has made its debut in our midst."

A climate of opinion unfavorable to Vichy propaganda might be presumed to be more charitable towards anti-Vichy efforts. But the anti-Vichy exiles, lacking diplomatic recognition and official status, did not have a particularly easy time. Some of them, like "Pertinax," only managed to enter the United States through the energetic intervention of sympathizers like Walter Lippmann.[89] The earliest public efforts to ventilate criticism of Vichy were in fact undertaken by Frenchmen already on American soil.

On 26 June a statement was issued in New York by a group of distinguished and influential Frenchmen, including Gilbert Chinard, professor of philosophy at Princeton, Richard de Roussy de Sales (Raoul's brother), formerly a French consular agent in Dallas and now New York correspondent of *Paris Soir*, Albert Grand, Washington correspondent of the Havas news agency, and Robert La Valeur, former director of the French news service and professor of economics at Columbia University. Their statement began cautiously. "At a distance we cannot pass judgment on the motives which determined the French government to accept the terms of the German and Italian armistices." Nevertheless, "we consider that the present French government . . . is no longer in a position to represent and safeguard the permanent interests of France."[90]

Other steps soon followed. The France Forever organization came into being late in August under the enthusiastic leadership of Eugene Houdry, a

French industrial chemist who had settled in Philadelphia and amassed a considerable fortune through the invention of a cracking process for distilling gasoline with a high octane content. The organization began an intensive campaign to counter Vichy propaganda, publicize the activities of de Gaulle, and win the adherence of Frenchmen and supporters of a Free France in the United States.[91] There were also the official Gaullist representatives, who were not yet the exiles from France—men such as Jacques de Sieyès, the perfume manufacturer who was de Gaulle's former classmate at St. Cyr, the French military academy.[92] So long as Vichy, not Free France, was recognized by the American government, these men could never acquire any independent status. But they did receive assistance and advice from British propaganda agencies. In early July a small party, under Lord Strathallan, arrived in New York to work with them.[93] A British initiative also lay behind the publication and distribution to the United States of James Marlow's pamphlet, *De Gaulle and the Coming Invasion of Germany*, described on its cover as "a powerful brief for carrying the present war, once technical superiority is achieved, into the heart of Nazidom." This was "a fighting book for all Americans who want no false Maginot line of defence between democracy and dictatorship."[94]

An atmosphere of intrigue swirled around all these propaganda forays. For example, there was formed the Groupement des Français d'Amérique, under Paul Séguin, a French veteran of the First World War, now an American citizen, known to the British as "a most unmanageable creature."[95] This organization had the laudable objective, so it claimed, of exposing "the activities of those few Frenchmen in the United States who, under pretext of obedience to the Vichy Government, endeavor to bring this country to the ideas and precepts of the Nazi doctrine."[96] Leaflets were distributed, and President Roosevelt was invited to contribute to a new journal, *Freedom* (he declined).[97] But the movement was not what it seemed. In reality it was a covert operation to gain American support for the proposal to send relief to metropolitan France and thus break the British blockade. While the preview issue of *Freedom*, in December 1940, included a tribute to Roosevelt, an explicit disavowal of the armistice, and the recognition of Great Britain as an ally, the first proper issue, in April 1941, was larded with Vichy propaganda and contained an attack on American foreign policy.[98] Séguin was also anxious to combat the rumor that there were Vichy spies in the United States.[99]

The autumn of 1940 was, in short, a dangerous time to launch an anti-Vichy propaganda offensive. Even apart from the presence of impostors, there was the domestic distraction of a presidential campaign together with widespread anxiety over propaganda, especially strong among native isolationists where refugee interventionists were concerned. Above all, de Gaulle was simply not well enough known, or known only for the Dakar bungle, and thus by no means immediately popular among Frenchmen abroad. The "France Forever" group certainly benefited in its membership drive from not being formally associated with him. As Strathallan pointed out, "some good Frenchmen are still not willing to be tied to de Gaulle and yet want to help Free France. The solution here of an independent Houdry committee makes their adherence possible."[100] Moreover, if Vichy propagandists were tainted with Nazi backing, Free French propagandists could hardly afford an obvious identification with a British government known to desire American involvement in the war. So Strathallan explained to Houdry that the British "did not wish to appear too openly associated with them lest it do harm to their work." Indeed, the exuberant Houdry, whose first act had been to give an ambulance to the Free French directly, rather than through the Red Cross, thus violating the Neutrality Act, had to be warned not to press for American recognition of the Free French—a step not even the British had taken.[101]

Hence a kind of voluntary restraint emerged among anti-Vichy sympathizers. "Pertinax" had mentioned to the Ministry of Information before leaving Britain that, while he intended to do everything to assist the British cause, he was "very anxious not to have it suspected" that he had any "special contacts" with the British and therefore would be "rather guarded in action and words to begin with."[102] Similarly, Mme Tabouis's public utterances, in her lecture tour of the United States in October and November, and in her magazine articles, were confined at first to straightforward denunciations of the Vichy government and assertions of her faith in her country's democratic spirit—"I affirm," she wrote, "that it *will* not perish. To doubt this would be the only treason."[103] Only in these modest, cautious, fragmented ways was the anti-Vichy cause advanced.

In this context the case of William C. Bullitt is once again worth mention. He was not, of course, a Frenchman, but it was precisely his affection for France and his close association with the French government that made him suspect. And what is most revealing is that suspicion was vented on all fronts. Bullitt was at the same time—though to different groups—responsible for the French declaration of war and subsequent defeat and an apologist for the successor, Vichy regime. In a particularly savage attack, entitled "Teacher's Pet," the *New York Daily Mirror*, a member of the Hearst chain, accused him of misinforming Roosevelt about France's ability to resist invasion, while encouraging French hopes for American intervention: "Thus again has our playboy Ambassador messed up the foreign relations of this nation, whose viewpoint he had long since lost 'somewhere in Europe.' "[104]

By contrast the interview he gave on his return to the United States, in which he denied that the Vichy regime was fascist and praised Pétain as a sincere patriot who was trying to bring order out of chaos, earned him rebukes from the opposite side; thus editorials were published with titles like "Is Mr. Bullitt dumb?" and "Mr. Bullitt likes French fascism."[105] His claim in his Philadelphia speech that refugee Communists in France had performed sabotage and espionage for the German army made the *Nation* very uneasy. At a time when the Smith (Alien Registration) Act was the law of the land, the journal argued, Bullitt's charges deserved "careful and public substantiation," as "the continued toleration of the Communist Party as a legal organization in the United States may hang on the accuracy of Mr. Bullitt's report"—a significant stand from those who were rather less skeptical about rumors of sabotage and treason credited to more conservative elements.[106]

These limitations, external and internal, upon the American perception of France did not mean that Americans necessarily lost interest. On the contrary, Vichy was and remained a fascinating enigma; and unlike the fall of France it was not a mystery to which there were any clear-cut, ideologically imposed solutions. On certain grounds, to be sure, there did develop a kind of consensus. For example, there was the belief, the faith, that France would rise again. This was first expounded, appropriately enough, by the Reverend Dr. John Maynard, speaking at the French Church of the Holy Spirit in New York on 16 June. "One thing is certain," he proclaimed, "there is going to be another miracle in France . . . the miracle of a country old and new, realistic and human, peace-loving and courageous."[107] Thereafter this theme became part of the stock-in-trade of most commentary on French affairs. For it reinforced the prevalent view that the French defeat had demonstrated deep-seated structural weaknesses in French society, from which any recovery would have to be in the nature of a rebirth.

Beyond this there were specific events that prompted a uniform response. The British bombing of the French fleet at Mers el-Kébir won widespread American approval; it was as comforting to isolationists as it was gratifying to interventionists.[108] On the other hand, there was equally widespread disapproval after the announcement by Vichy that many leading politicians of the Third Republic would shortly be tried by a special court for crimes relating to the preparations for war—a particularly extreme form of judicial retribution that few American democrats were prepared to countenance.[109] As the *New York Times* put it, if those men were guilty, "the people who elected them are guilty, democracy is guilty."[110] Nor did Americans have any kind words for Vichy's attacks on Jews, Spanish Republicans, and German refugees. Only very rarely was there any note of disquiet at the mounting American criticism of Vichy, such as Felix Morley's comment in the *Washington Post* that a cynical and hostile attitude on the part of the United States would only serve to make France's position more difficult and drive her further into the arms of Hitler.[111]

These attitudes sprang largely from humanitarian sentiments, addressed to specific incidents. They were not the fruit of an attempt to grapple with the substantive issues raised by the existence of Vichy France: what was the nature of the regime, how much domestic support did it have, where did power ultimately reside, in Berlin or Vichy? Of greater interest for the American public, as it was of greater importance to the American State Department, was the clash of personalities, as indicated by the comings and goings at Pétain's court, whose very opacity invited speculation. The effect was, as de Roussy de Sales bitterly noted in his diary, that commentary on French affairs was reduced to a guessing game: "I had dinner last night at C. D. Jackson's [a *New York Times* correspondent], together with Valeur and a man from *Time*, their correspondent in France, who had just come from there. We tried to settle the question of 'what should be thought of France.' It appears that Harry Luce absolutely insists on thinking something. The result of our deliberations was not conclusive."[112]

But by the end of the year *Time* had made some headway. After Pétain's dismissal of Laval, the magazine observed, in a characteristic plethora of adjectives that nonetheless captured the contrasting impressions Americans were receiving of Pétain, that he was "old, crotchety, painstaking, slow. He is also honorable, patriotic and, when he takes the advice of a few trusted friends, often a clever tactician."[113] But this judgment too, it has to be remembered, was a direct response to a particular event, Laval's departure; and it was the same as the response of Roosevelt and the State Department, and the great majority of the press. In the view of the *Christian Science Monitor*, the event seemed "reflective of a public opinion that does not sleep easily under oppression"; and the *New York Herald Tribune* contended that "to the extent that Pétain's moves have been influenced by a rebirth of national spirit in France . . . Americans must welcome them." Only the *New York Times* sounded a note of caution, suggesting that possibly the British were right in considering the changes not necessarily to be for the better, since whatever the patriotism of Weygand and Pétain, they remained unfree.[114]

More candid was the judgment of Ralph Ingersoll, the editor of *PM*, who confessed that ". . . so great is our curiosity about what's what and who's who in Vichy that it leads us, the press, into a kind of foolishness. We will print practically any rumor that comes out of free Fascist France [sic]—in the hopes, I suppose, that one of them may be right and we can spend the rest of our journalistic lives pointing back to it." He then listed the theories: "Premier Pétain is a dribbling old man. He is so strong he aspires to set up his own fascist state. M. Laval is the boss. He is only a stooge. He is the pro-French fascist stooge for M. Pétain. He is the pro-German stooge for M. Pétain. It's three other fellows and neither M. Pétain nor M. Laval means anything."[115]

In short, when one realizes the limitations under which American foreign correspondents operated, the nature of the propaganda engaged in by Frenchmen of all persuasions, and the ideological quality of so much American commentary on French affairs, then one begins to appreciate the truth of Walter Lippmann's observation that public opinion is "primarily a moralized and codified version of the facts."[116]

What then may be concluded about the American response to the French defeat: that it alerted the American public to the seriousness of the European situation and the possible danger to the Western hemisphere; that it accelerated the American drift toward intervention in the European war, while also broadening the base of public support for that policy; that it ensured the renomination of Roosevelt, the nomination of Willkie, and the victory of the Democrats in 1940? Such grand assertions, seductive in their obedience to the logic of events, deserve close examination. For there is much evidence to sustain an opposing thesis, that very little did change in the American perception of the outside world: ignorance of the French war effort, the product of wartime censorship, was succeeded only by ignorance of developments at Vichy, the result of German censorship; deep suspicion of the French politicians who had been waging the war was superseded only by an equally deep suspicion of those who had brought it to a close; and the intuition that France would win was replaced only by the intuition that France would "rise again." Had that combination of skepticism and sentimentality with which Americans historically regarded France simply been adapted to new conditions?

The public opinion polls do not permit any easy generalizations. For example, it is clear that there was a movement in public opinion in the second half of 1940 with regard to aiding Britain. In July, 37 percent were prepared to help Britain even at the risk of war, while 59 percent were not; in October the figures were almost exactly reversed, 59 percent to 36 percent.[117] But fear of a Nazi attack on the United States seems actually to have declined over the summer. In April, 65 percent felt that if Germany defeated Britain and France she would sooner or later make war upon the United States; in August the figure dropped to 42 percent.[118] There are other, more striking inconsistencies. Though clear majorities could now be found to support the general proposition of aiding Britain, no majority could be found in 1940 to support any specific measure, except on two occasions. The first exception was in a poll published on 30 June, in which 80 percent approved, retrospectively, the sale of American airplanes; the second, published on 5 September, showed 60 percent in favor of selling American destroyers.[119] However, within two months the same proportion, 60 percent, was opposed to any change in the Neutrality Act that would permit American ships to carry supplies to Britain.[120] Finally, there is the contrast between the rising expectation that America would go to war in Europe—51 percent in May, 59 percent in October—and an overall decline in the desire to do so—14 percent in July, 12 percent in December.[121]

These inconsistencies—optimism combined with fatalism, a broad willingness to aid the Allies, together with a reluctance to enter into any specific commitment—may be more apparent than real. Differences of 1 or 2 percent are not statistically significant. Moreover, it is the understanding of such professional students of public opinion polls as Hadley Cantril, who was highly regarded at the Roosevelt White House, that these reverses and contrasts only emerge if public opinion is calculated on a simple mathematical scale, in terms of percentages and majorities.[122] If, instead, an analysis is made on the basis of blocs of opinion—isolationist, interventionist, and a middle group of non-interventionist, Allied sympathizers—then a more consistent pattern appears. Then the fall of France can be seen to have created an emergency, producing both short-term and long-run effects on public opinion, with an impact varying from group to group. Indeed, once one recognizes that Americans viewed the French defeat as an emergency, a crisis, a profound shock, then it is not even necessary to break up public opinion into its constituent parts in order to reach certain preliminary general conclusions. The year 1940 presented to an overseas audience a succession of such emergencies—the Russo-Finnish war, the invasion of the Low Countries, Dunkirk, the Battle of Britain—involving a variety of combatants and raising a number of complicated issues—appeasement, national and hemispheric defense, propaganda, the Fifth Column. This complexity hindered, as Allied propagandists bemoaned, the formation of a clear-cut attitude to the war on the part of American public opinion; and it is in this light that the various fluctuations in the polls, with regard to overseas aid, national defense, and the expectation that the United States would go to war, must be considered.

One conclusion, however, is clear: public opinion does not anticipate such emergencies; it only reacts to them. Thus it was only after the French defeat, in a poll published on 20 July, that a clear majority, 69 percent, felt that it would be personally affected by a German victory.[123] It is also in the nature of emergencies that their greatest impact on opinion is felt immediately. Just as blitzkrieg warfare, like Hitler's diplomacy before it, tended to promote short, sharp military and political crises, so too those crises produced short-lived responses in American public opinion: an expression of concern over the particular emergency, then a relaxation of tension, followed by a shift to the next, different crisis. And finally, there is the perennial problem of public opinion in a democracy at a time of international crisis. In critical situations, the public seems willing to assign more responsibility to politicians than hitherto, but at the same time it finds the government more remote, and participation in its affairs less real. This irony lies behind the 10 percent rise in Roosevelt's popularity during the critical month of May, even while his chosen policies never commanded the same approval.[124] It also lies behind the seeming contrast in the polls between an expressed desire to stay out of the war and the fatalistic acceptance that war would come. And it also explains why some opposition to particular governmental policies may coexist with a willingness to concede to that government vast powers over, for example, conscription and the organization of industry and labor. As the government's actions toward an unruly and dangerous world drift further away from the individual's control, so correspondingly his desire for its protection, and for leadership that guarantees that protection, seems to be magnified.

One more fundamental conclusion may be drawn from the polls, though it may seem self-evident—that opinion is colored by desire. This is where the different component groups of American public opinion are significant. Once the distinct frames of reference are acknowledged, it is apparent that there was a general consistency to the expressed opinions, and that this consistency survived the events of the summer. It survived, that is to say, not merely the shock of the fall of France, as one might expect, but also the announcement on 27 September of the Rome-Berlin-Tokyo pact: a move expressly aimed at American public opinion and intended to deflect it from aiding Britain by threatening trouble with Japan.[125] By the end of the year it remained true that those who felt themselves most personally threatened by a German victory were those who thought Britain would win and who sought to increase American aid; those, on the other hand, who doubted that they would be personally affected by a German victory also doubted that Germany would start a war against the United States and opposed any increase in overseas aid. What had occurred in the course of the second half of 1940 was that the former group, the "interventionists," had swollen from slightly more than a third of the sample to well over a half. But the primary determinants remained constant. The South continued to be the most interventionist section, the Midwest the least; upper-income people under thirty continued to be the most isolationist group, middle- and upper-income people over thirty the most interventionist.[126]

Public opinion polls intimate more than they affirm. In this case they suggest that the opinions they measured derived from deep-seated personal convictions. Insofar as those opinions changed, they did not do so in response to Allied propaganda, or to Axis intimidation, neither of which penetrated deeply, but rather to specific events, crises, emergencies. Having measured the opinions, therefore, it is still necessary to explore the attitudes; and there the professed spokesmen are the most reliable guides—editors, publicists, congressmen. Such people are not, of course, ideally "representative." In varying proportions they both reflect and mold public opinion. But even when perverse or idiosyncratic, they were responding to the same issues, and their views are as much a part of the historical record as the most formal, scientific calculation of public opinion. Sometimes, indeed, a kind of eccentricity is more pertinent to an inquiry into public attitudes than mere conformity. The journalist John T. Flynn, for example, was no more representative of the American public than William C. Bullitt was of the American administration. Both were, by the end of 1940, bitter, disillusioned individualists, Bullitt excluded from government service, Flynn in exile from the growing interventionism of the *New Republic*, the one an impatient internationalist, the other a passionate isolationist. Yet both were articulating views of enormous future import—Bullitt a keen anti-Communism, Flynn the basic identity of totalitarian forms of government. And just as Bullitt's career is most revealing about the developing views of the American administration, so is Flynn's about the drift of American liberalism. The publicist is very rarely a neutral commentator. He may be a spokesman for a widely held point of view or he may be a lonely voice. Either way, his views merit attention.

There was, it is clear, on all sides, a decisive shift toward interventionism in the weeks after the French defeat. This was the period of Roosevelt's appointment of two renegade Republicans, Henry L. Stimson and Frank Knox, to the War and Navy departments, a unilateral step toward a bipartisan foreign policy, or, as it seemed to hostile Republicans like Thomas Dewey, "a direct step towards war."[127] It was a period when, as is customary in presidential elections, the critical decision about the choice to be offered the electorate was made at the convention of the opposition party. The Republicans met in Philadelphia when the French armistice was two days old, and the event hovered over all their deliberations. The choice of Wendell Willkie was ultimately a preference for internationalism over the competing forms of non-interventionism represented by District Attorney Dewey, Senator Arthur Vandenberg, and Senator Robert Taft. This was also the period when the socialist journal *Common Sense* and the liberal journal *New Republic* both adopted a clear-cut stand in favor of aid to Britain, in their editors' beliefs that the achievement of socialism and the fulfillment of liberalism were now each dependent on the defeat of Hitler.[128] It was the period when an independent, non-partisan movement for a peacetime conscription law began in Congress. And it was the period that saw the formation of the shrewdly named Committee to Defend America by Aiding the Allies, with a Kansas Republican, William Allen White, at its head, and of the more advanced, interventionist body, the Century Group based in New York. From their activities issued most of the pressure, and much of the public support, for the Destroyers-Bases deal of September.[129]

But there was another side to 1940. That year saw not only the quickening of interventionist, but also the hardening of isolationist sentiment. The defection of the bulk of American liberals from its ranks left American isolationism with a conservative, at times reactionary, aura that it retained until Pearl Harbor. It might still command the allegiance of individual reformers, such as the liberal Oswald Garrison Villard, the socialist Norman Thomas, the trade unionist John L. Lewis, the radical Charles Beard; but after June 1940 the characteristic isolationists, the speakers most in demand, were simon-pure conservatives like Taft and Hoover, disillusioned, second generation progressives like Senators Gerald P. Nye and Burton K. Wheeler, and the popular hero Charles A. Lindbergh.

This shift was reflected in the composition and location of two rival pressure groups. Though each could boast a nationwide organization and the support of national celebrities and folk heroes, the interventionist Century Group, whose membership was drawn from the liberal, Anglo-Saxon, Protestant establishment, was based in New York; while America First, the isolationist organization founded in September, the creation of western businessmen like R. Douglas Stuart of Quaker Oats and General Robert E. Wood of Sears, Roebuck, was based in Chicago. Moreover, it was in this period that American isolationism began to acquire its most illiberal features. Increasing publicity given to Henry Ford's anti-Semitism, Joseph Kennedy's defeatism, and Lindbergh's apparent admiration for fascism served greatly to discredit the isolationist cause, and America First was never able to cut itself free of association with pro-Nazi elements like the Coughlinites and the German-American Bund.[130]

It would appear that the effect of the French defeat was not merely to tilt the balance of opinion toward interventionism, but also to simplify somewhat the composition of the two opposing movements. Henceforth, interventionism would appear liberal and progressive, faced only with a purged, conservative, rump isolationism. But these terms are in fact deceptive, as can be seen from the bitter controversy that arose over the question of sending relief to the occupied countries of Europe, particularly France. Here was an immensely complicated moral issue, in which matters of public policy collided with instincts of private philanthropy. There was no question that the inhabitants of the occupied countries, and unoccupied France, were faced, as a result of German plunder and the British continental blockade, with a chronic shortage of food in the coming winter; and while prisoners of war were able to receive supplies through the Red Cross, no such relief was possible for the civilian populations, who were the inevitable victims of the last, critical weapon at Britain's disposal.

In the second week in August, Herbert Hoover, who had fed starving European populations before, proposed that the British be persuaded to relax their blockade sufficiently to permit only the passage of food, while requiring the Germans not to interfere with its distribution. The strategic damage would be slight, Hoover and his supporters argued, as there was no way in which, for example, condensed milk could be used as an offensive weapon.[131] The proposal naturally met considerable opposition from those pro-Allied groups who saw any reduction in the effectiveness of British economic warfare as a minor victory for Hitler. Churchill rejected the suggestion outright, and within the United States the ensuing controversy plainly reflected the new balance of forces. The *Chicago Tribune* seized upon the proposal as "evidence that American sympathies have been aroused by the sufferings of the non-combatants in the European war . . ."[132] And a group of writers associated with the Century Group stated that "there is more at stake than temporary physical relief and we urge our countrymen who share our love and respect for the true France to give no heed to the spokesmen of appeasement and betrayal."[133]

On strategic grounds the opponents of the scheme were probably correct; a loosened blockade could assist Germany. Yet that hardly made its advocates "spokesmen of appeasement and betrayal."

There were other instances of the new interventionist drive for conformity. One of the more notorious was the full-page newspaper advertisement of 10 and 11 June, titled "Stop Hitler Now," drafted by the playwright Robert E. Sherwood, which contained the crucial sentences, shocking Oswald Garrison Villard, "Will the Nazis considerately wait until we are ready to fight them? Anyone who argues that they will wait is either a fool [in some versions "an imbecile"] or a traitor."[134] A more general illustration is afforded by the ongoing discussion of national morale. The absence of a sense of national purpose had seemed, for many writers, the critical weakness of the French war effort. Here the writings of Edmond Taylor are of particular interest. A journalist of Missouri French descent, Taylor had spent some years locked in controversy with the publisher of the isolationist *Chicago Tribune*, for which he was the Paris correspondent. From the French defeat, which he had observed at first hand, Taylor drew a number of specific conclusions, relating to the peculiar weaknesses of democracies at a time of total war. In the first place, democrats had become "suspicious of the very idea of leadership and had to a considerable degree abandoned it to the enemy." Second, they were reluctant to acknowledge that "crisis in our age was endemic." Finally, they were clinging to democratic forms in a conflict with antidemocratic forces: "Merely seeking to perfect democracy . . . would not suffice to protect it against . . . attacks, and might in some cases even contribute to weakening it. Ideological enemies who did not depend on their ideas alone to destroy us could not be defeated solely by better ideas."[135]

Thirty years later, Taylor admitted that "everything seemed a great deal simpler in 1940."[136] This is certainly what emerges from the flurry of books and articles that he produced in the aftermath of the French defeat. In the first edition of *The Strategy of Terror*, published in 1940, he assumed that Hitler and Stalin were plotting together to destroy democracy; in the second edition, two years later, after the German invasion of Russia, he wisely concluded that "there was no plot." Nevertheless, the diagnosis of democratic stagnation remained intact: "The military defeat of France produced a political and moral collapse because the democratic leaders of France—and the democratic masses—had developed, like the generals, a kind of political Maginot complex." The problem was not treachery, but defeatism, and in 1940, "under cover of peace, the Axis powers were attacking us with the same techniques of psychological and political warfare which had proved so effective in the case of France." Given the diagnosis, the remedy was clear. Although democracy did suggest diversity of opinion, debate, and dissent, these were now to be understood as luxuries, to be discarded in the interests of a larger cause: "The important thing is to shut up the propagandists before they have a chance to do any undermining."[137] True to his principles, once the United States was in the war, Taylor joined the propaganda wing, headed by Robert E. Sherwood, of the Office of the Coordinator of Information, where he became, in his own words, a "well-poisoner."[138] The paradox, which he acutely foresaw in 1940, was that a war for democracy might need to employ some rather undemocratic means.

This phenomenon—an emerging internationalist consensus that increasingly sought to silence opposing views—did not escape the attention of the folksy, eccentric editor of *PM*. Ralph Ingersoll characteristically observed political affairs with considerable perception, only to bring forth bizarre prescriptions for their improvement. In an editorial on 1 August titled "Silent Enemies," he began by noting that every major political party seemed agreed that "our enemy is the expansive force of fascism." But far from being a healthy state of affairs, this was rather perilous, since "there are not only good arguments in favor of Fascism, but there are an enormous number of people in this country . . . to whom these arguments are real and compelling." To deny such people an effective voice would only drive them "underground," where they would become dangerous. "What I lament," Ingersoll confessed, "is that there is no recognized political party in this country, frankly standing for appeasement of the dictator Hitler, the realistic dealing in trade with him, the revamping of our political institutions to use the more effective of his political creations." The absence of such a party was almost as much a threat to democracy as its presence would be: "What's going on is that in a democracy which needs an opposition to survive as a democracy, we the majority have no open and aboveboard, outspoken and articulate opposition to fight—and are forced into the position of assuming we are at war with a foreign power before war is declared, just to have an enemy we can identify."

"Just to have an enemy . . ." An overstatement, perhaps, but a suggestive one. The French defeat had made internationalism seem progressive and isolationism reactionary. Moreover, dogmatic internationalism and intolerant isolationism were feeding off one another. The conformist tendencies of interventionists, the shrill rhetoric of isolationists, and the bitter polemics between the two, all stemmed from the recognition that, since the French defeat, one viewpoint was in the ascendant, acquiring the status of a democratic creed, while the other was held only by a beleaguered, unpopular minority, tainted with treason. Even Ingersoll did not see fit to distinguish among isolationists, appeasers, and fascists.

If then a consensus of sorts was emerging, what part did foreign affairs play in the presidential election? From the election returns it would seem that domestic affairs were paramount. Roosevelt maintained intact the New Deal coalition of urban workers, the South, blacks, and some poorer farmers; Willkie gained in six western states where there was evident agrarian discontent. In the cities, which Roosevelt easily won, it was economic status that divided Democratic from Republican voters. Moreover, the result was in many ways a personal victory for Roosevelt. The party that won was not a labor party, or one pledged to internationalism, or the congressional Southern party, but the New Deal party, Roosevelt's own creation, a presidential Democratic party, as further underlined by his choice of running mate, Henry Wallace, a cabinet member devoted to the New Deal. As against this, Willkie's shortcomings, like Roosevelt's achievements, were largely personal: an ineptly handled campaign and the failure clearly to define any major issues. Ironically, inasmuch as foreign affairs affected the result they may actually have aided Willkie, who gained German, Italian, and Irish votes; in New York he even gained the larger portion of Democratic votes. Indeed, he only began to climb in the polls once he belatedly stressed the peace issue in October.[139]

It is equally true that the basic outlines of American foreign policy—to aid Great Britain, to stay out of war, to implement a defense program, to shun appeasement—were not at issue, as shown by Willkie's implied willingness to retain Hull as his secretary of state.[140] When debate was joined it usually concerned the domestic record of the New Deal. The past was thus used to illuminate the future; the administration's domestic record was held to prefigure its performance in the outside world; and in this context European events were easily harnessed to partisan causes. From the very start of the campaign, the lessons of the French defeat were most prominent in the debaters' armory—Hoover's speech to the Republican Convention on 25 June attacking the "totalitarian 'liberals' . . . the spiritual fathers of the New Deal,"[141] Willkie's acceptance speech in Elmwood, Indiana, on 17 August drawing parallels between the New Deal and the Popular Front, Wallace's acceptance speech in Des Moines on 29 August identifying Republicans as the party of "appeasement."[142]

But the election did produce some novel arguments. For the differences between Republicans and Democrats were never, like those between isolationists and internationalists, or conservatives and liberals, purely matters of principle. They were electoral issues, with a strong pragmatic content, and the effort to tailor ideological interpretations of recent European events to these new requirements produced some odd reversals, most conspicuously in regard to the twin issues of "appeasement" and "preparedness." After June 1940 appeasement was to be avoided and preparedness to be endorsed. But what was the historical record of the two parties on those matters? The argument over appeasement was particularly involuted. Harold Ickes began on 19 August with a statement that "the Republican party in 1940 contains the equivalent of England and France's pro-Nazi Munich appeasers of 1938—the men with the black umbrellas." Wallace followed with his accusation that Republicans belonged to the party of appeasement. Then Willkie issued a nicely judged counteraccusation that in fact, at the time of Munich, Roosevelt, "the great appeaser," had "telephoned Hitler and Mussolini and urged them to sell

Czechoslovakia down the river" (a charge subsequently modified to read that Roosevelt had urged England and France to attend the Munich conference, "where they sacrificed Czechoslovakia").[143] Cordell Hull retorted, in a reply based on the official record, that Willkie "was grossly ignorant of the history of the last few years"; but Alf Landon, the Republican presidential candidate of 1936, then replied that, whatever Roosevelt's actual conduct had been, he "and his official family, immediately following Munich, proudly boasted of the part which Mr. Roosevelt had played in bringing about the Munich settlement for appeasement."[144]

The confusion over the appeasement charges and countercharges was, however, overshadowed by the more pressing issue of national defense. This required, if anything, even greater rhetorical flexibility. The two candidates faced virtually the same problem: how to mold a vigorous program of national defense onto an isolationist party record without appearing an irresponsible convert to interventionism; and the solution involved cursing the opposing party for the very existence of the problem. Thus, while advocating a policy of preparedness, the Republican party platform also blamed the New Deal for "our unpreparedness and for the consequent danger of involvement in war." In his keynote address to the convention, Governor Harold Stassen went even further, blaming the Roosevelt administration for being "too neutral": "We have . . . aided the manufacture of implements of destruction that Russia used upon Finland, that Germany uses against the Allies, that Japan uses against China, that Italy uses against France. How belated is our now exclusive assistance to the Allies."[145]

Willkie's main chance came with the announcement of the Tripartite Pact of Germany, Italy, and Japan in late September. This he claimed demonstrated the failure of Roosevelt's foreign policy, now faced with a formal alliance binding together all the potential enemies of the United States. Willkie accused the New Dealers of failing to prepare the country for the new danger, while also bringing the United States closer to war by bringing "the wars of Europe and Asia into American politics." Given the present situation, there was little electoral danger for Willkie in advocating preparedness. Roosevelt attacked the problem from a different perspective, but came up with an equally workable conclusion. Addressing an audience at Madison Square Garden on 28 October, he first accused the Republicans of "playing politics with defense . . . and the national security of America today." They had consistently voted against defense appropriations in the last decade, he argued, and he singled out the "perfectly beautiful rhythm" of "Martin, Barton, and Fish" for heavy emphasis. Then Roosevelt proceeded to take credit himself for the neutrality legislation of the 1930s—laws he had in fact vainly tried to oppose at the time—and blessed them as "measures to keep us at peace." Now, however, it was time to embark on a more vigorous defense program, unhindered by opposition from Hamilton Fish, Hoover, Vandenberg, and Taft.[146]

These partisan bickerings and revisions of history effectively blurred the fact that the candidates themselves desired much the same policy and were competing only for the opportunity to implement it. The basic political discourse of the campaign was thus a dispute within an internationalist circle, as would be clear in 1941, when Willkie endorsed every foreign policy move of the Roosevelt administration, in 1942, when he acted as Roosevelt's emissary abroad, in 1943, when he published *One World*, and in 1944, when he proposed running on a coalition ticket with Roosevelt.[147] But the political campaign of 1940, like the discussions within the press and among the American public at large, is significant not solely for the emergence of a consensus, but also for the idiom in which that consensus was expressed, an idiom permeated with allusions to recent European events. A year before the United States entered the war, her political language had absorbed the whole European wartime vocabulary of "appeasement," "Fifth Columnism," and "totalitarianism."

Not all of this can be accounted for by the French defeat, which was but one item in a catalog extending from the Nazi-Soviet Pact to the Tripartite Pact. But the French defeat did remain the basic American referent for the issues involved in the war, the stereotype of a nation misled by appeasers, betrayed by a Fifth Column, powerless before the forces of totalitarianism; and for this stereotype to retain its power, the future must remain obscure. Nor was it only Americans who wrote articles with titles like "France in the Shadows" ("An able foreign correspondent says that country will live as a great culture though perhaps not as a great power").[148] One Frenchman, the journalist Robert de Saint-Jean, wrote an article for *Harper's* on the "Failure of France" that concluded, "there is no living Frenchman who should not today declare his *mea culpa.*"[149] Another, the scholar Charles A. Micaud, posed the question, "Do the French Want Democracy?" and drew pessimistic conclusions.[150] And Heinz Pol, the German émigré journalist, wrote a book on the French defeat called *Suicide of a Democracy*, which he thoughtfully dedicated "to the preservation of democracy in America."[151]

This vision of a transference of the democratic mantle from France to the United States remains the most striking consequence of the French defeat. There were of course those who considered the postmortems premature, émigrés like Geneviève Tabouis and André Maurois, and the braintruster, turned political commentator, Raymond Moley. But their writings only reveal how they had to struggle against the prevailing views. "American public opinion," said Maurois ". . . should . . . be founded on facts and not on prejudices, on permanent values, and not on the fortunes and downfalls of individual statesmen."[152] "Let us be sure," cautioned Moley, "that our sources of information are trustworthy—that they are not the same sources that would have sacrificed what was democratic in France to communist ideology."[153] But to be hesitant in passing judgments on French affairs was to sound highly conservative in 1940, when an American near-monopoly on democratic values and liberal practice was being asserted with increasing vigor.

There is some irony in this. Previously it had been conservative isolationism, the isolationism of Herbert Hoover, that had stressed the incompatibility of Old and New World values. "When shall we learn again," asked the *Saturday Evening Post* in March 1940, "that Europe is Europe, America is America, and these are two worlds? When shall we believe again that our destiny is unique, parallel to nothing?"[154] In some conservative quarters this apparent contrast was only strengthened by the French defeat. Representative Martin Dies, chairman of the Special Committee on Un-American Activities, was on the floor of the House the day of the French armistice, drawing lessons about aliens and subversive organizations.[155] Within a week the Alien Registration Act had passed through Congress. By the end of the year Dies's committee was at the height of its influence, in no danger of having its funds terminated. As Dies claimed, "not a single one of the countries of Europe which have been overrun by Stalin and Hitler had the protection of a committee like ours." Beyond that, Dies emphasized that the totalitarian states in command of the European continent did not adhere to American principles: "I can see no distinction between brands of totalitarianism . . . any ideology that is predicated upon the atheistic philosophy that the State must be everything and the individual nothing, whether it masquerades under the name of communism, naziism, or fascism, is un-American, and is diametrically opposed to all our country stands for."[156]

The views that Dies here outlined, an updating of traditional conservative isolationism, were really only a vulgarized and simplified version of what had, under the shock of the French defeat, become an accepted version of events, expressed by government spokesmen and discussed in the popular press. Actually a reversal had taken place. With the spread of totalitarianism, the existence of a division between Old and New World values became rather more appropriate as an interventionist than an isolationist tenet. Henceforth it was the lot of unreconstructed isolationists, like John T. Flynn, to argue that under Roosevelt, the New Deal, and a policy of interventionism, that distinction had broken down as the United States acquired more and more "fascist," "totalitarian," and "corporative" aspects.[157] It became on the other hand the internationalist refrain that as the continent of Europe fell under the control of Fascist, Nazi, and Soviet powers, the contrast with American democracy was laid bare.

Every idealistic utterance was built upon that antithesis. When William C. Bullitt testified before the House Committee on the Judiciary, drawing upon his French experience to assist an investigation of possible legislation to prevent labor unrest, he was invited to contribute what one member called his "most enlightening" definition of civil rights, which was that they are "what no-one has any of under the dictator."[158] When on 6 January 1941 Roosevelt outlined in his message to Congress the Four Freedoms upon which the future world must be founded, he was explicitly countering the principles upon which totalitarian societies relied. He spoke not simply of freedom of speech and religion, but also of freedom *from* fear, freedom *from* want; and he had first explored the subject at his press conference within days of the French defeat.[159]

The growing frequency of these idealistic pronouncements was a direct consequence of the French defeat. That event had brought about a greater American involvement in the war, though in 1940, at least, American diplomacy was still marked by extreme wariness. What was more important was that the nature of the French collapse appeared to justify the beliefs of observers as diverse as Clare Boothe Luce, Walter Lippmann, Dorothy Thompson, and Edmond Taylor that the Allies' chief weakness had lain in the moral realm, as proved by their neglect of war aims. These publicists were always anxious to fill the void of idealism left by a diplomacy of caution, and they moved swiftly to supplement administration efforts with their own. "The time is past," Lippmann had written to the American Friends of France, Inc., "when it is a question of helping the Allies in some sort of condescending and charitable way. We are on the verge of a catastrophe which, if it occurs, will be irreparable for generations."[160] So, to counteract Vichy propaganda, the interventionist Fight for Freedom group sent circulars to leading churchmen throughout the United States on the need to combat any offensive; and it began to compile dossiers on Vichy's spokesmen.[161] Other interventionists also became more active. "I think," Hamilton Fish Armstrong wrote to Felix Frankfurter, "one of the secrets of totalitarian efficiency is synchronization of propaganda even more than volume of propaganda." He therefore proposed that Roosevelt be advised to employ "unofficial disinterested persons" like Robert Sherwood and Dorothy Thompson to outline in public the nation's foreign policy goals. "What I am hoping for," he later wrote, "is that the President will begin to exercise the moral leadership in the world which Wilson acquired in 1917 and 1918."[162]

This was, in a sense, private enterprise: countersubversion to aid the FBI, propaganda to aid the president and State Department. With the Four Freedoms address these publicists scored a notable triumph. Before she was in the war, America had defined her war aims. Nevertheless, a latent tension already existed. The view of the French defeat as a total, moral collapse had promoted, alongside this idealistic, democratic crusade for the Four Freedoms, that policy of diplomatic realpolitik with the Vichy regime which opened with the mission of Admiral Leahy. Over the next four years these two approaches were to collide with increasing confusion.

CHAPTER 3
AN AMERICAN AT VICHY:
THE MISSION OF ADMIRAL
WILLIAM D. LEAHY

Brilliant work in the field of diplomacy . . . displaying unusual tact in the handling of both men and situations, at a period that may well prove to have been a decisive turning point of the war.
   —Citation for honorary degree as Doctor of Law,
    University of Wisconsin, 1943[1]

William Leahy came to diplomacy as a raw recruit. His talents lay elsewhere. He had graduated fifteenth in his class in the United States Naval Academy in 1897, and seen action almost immediately in the Spanish-American War, then during the Philippine insurrection, and later in the Boxer uprising. Thereafter he rose steadily if undramatically up the naval hierarchy until his appointment as Roosevelt's chief of naval operations in 1937, two years before retirement. He was, however, one of the very few of Roosevelt's associates who knew him before his polio attack.

In 1913 Roosevelt, an inexperienced assistant secretary of the navy, had found Leahy, the seasoned professional, a wise and dependable adviser. In due course all kinds of apochryphal stories circulated about the degree of rapport between the two men. One had Roosevelt summoning Leahy to the White House after the Japanese sank the *Panay* in 1937 and inquiring, "Bill, what will it take to lick Japan?" "Fifty billion dollars a year—and I'd like the job," replied the admiral. "It's too much," said Roosevelt, "send for Cordell Hull." Another story was that when in 1939 Leahy retired from the Navy, to become governor of Puerto Rico, Roosevelt, presenting him with the Distinguished Service Cross, told him: "Bill, if we ever have a war, you're going to be right back here, helping me to run it."[2]

A bond, not exactly of friendship, more of mutual trust, existed between the sailor soon to be thrust into politics and the politician who loved sailing. Roosevelt's letters to Leahy in Vichy, with their nautical metaphors and their swashbuckling diction, suggest a cordiality reserved for his closest associates.[3] Sumner Welles may have taken the credit for first proposing Leahy's name to Roosevelt as ambassador to Vichy ("The President's face immediately lit up as it always did when a new idea appealed to him").[4] But he could hardly have suggested a man closer to Roosevelt in spirit and further from the State

Department in style. Already, as governor of Puerto Rico, he had impressed his superior, Harold Ickes, the secretary of the interior and a fierce critic of the State Department, with his firm resolution. Ickes, who could be the most combative man in the administration, found Leahy "thoroughly sane," "a good man," and certainly "the best Governor that we had ever sent down there."[5] Ickes's only reservations concerned Leahy's apparent disdain for the civil rights of the native population. He would, it seemed, instruct the police force, in the event of any "trouble," "to shoot first and investigate later."[6] He also viewed with equanimity the prospect that, should war break out, the several hundred Germans on the island, though only suspected of being fifth columnists, "simply would disappear; no one would ever hear of them again."[7] It may be, mused Ickes, that Leahy was not "as jealous as he ought to be for the civil rights of people generally": a peculiar streak, he thought, "in an American naval officer who had come out of the soil of Iowa."[8] But such misgivings were outweighed by Ickes's respect for a man who had, he claimed, advised going to war against Japan in 1937, and who shared Ickes's dismay at the State Department's caution. If the State Department had agreed to cut down on shipments of oil to Japan, the two men agreed, there would never have been a Pacific war.[9]

Such was Leahy's experience of politics and diplomacy when he went to Vichy, a posting in the European, not the Pacific, theater. Nor did he arrive encumbered by any deep understanding of French affairs. Given his background it would be unjust to expect that in him. He may have spent nearly three weeks in Washington studying the French situation with the available experts: Bullitt, Welles, Ray Atherton, head of the European desk at the State Department, and such French figures as the Vichy ambassador, Henry-Haye, the unofficial emissary from Pétain, Camille Chautemps, and Alexis Leger, the poet, formerly permanent secretary to the French Foreign Office.[10] But those discussions most probably revolved around personalities, not the broad political divisions of French society. Roosevelt's instructions to Leahy had already stressed the prevailing American view of the primacy of Pétain and his resolve to maintain a fixed neutrality. They had also fastened on Laval as the individual most set on active collaboration with Germany, with the remaining senior officials drifting from one course to another, while owing primary allegiance to Pétain.[11] Shortly after Leahy accepted the mission to Vichy, Pétain dismissed Laval. It would follow that Leahy would now need to know about those newly risen to prominence: the new foreign minister, Pierre-Etienne Flandin, and the minister of marine, Admiral Darlan. Those two, with General Charles Huntziger, secretary of state for war, composed Pétain's "inner cabinet."

Neither politics nor diplomacy nor France herself had ever been a consuming interest of Leahy. His presence in Vichy is best viewed as a mission from one court to another, a reversal to an earlier mode of diplomacy. When offering Leahy the post Roosevelt had described Pétain as "the one powerful element who is standing firm against selling out to Germany."[12] Now, in a personal message to Pétain, Roosevelt described Leahy as "a close personal friend of mine from the days of my first official connection with the United States Navy, nearly twenty-eight years ago, and in this administration he has filled, as you know, positions of the highest trust. He possesses my entire confidence."[13] Pétain in turn sent back word that he was delighted with the choice, "for two reasons, first because the new ambassador is a close and intimate friend of [the] President, second, because he is an admiral."[14]

These personal touches promised more than the customary diplomatic exchanges. Certainly the French Foreign Office, as reconstituted at Vichy, offered few enticements. A memorandum drawn up for Leahy by the embassy's counsellor, H. Freeman Matthews, mordantly recounted the failings of most of the officials: the head of the American section, Jean de Séguin, was "a stupid, dull little man . . . [who] spreads a gospel of pessimism concerning our war effort"; the head of the European section, Pierre Bressy, was "a Bonnet man, very close to collaboration"; the remainder, when they were not pro-German, struck Matthews as timid and of little influence, though there were some isolated exceptions like Charles Rochat, the secretary general, and Jean Chauvel, head of the Far Eastern section, who might promote a franker exchange.[15]

Leahy accordingly cultivated Pétain and his immediate entourage. For comparable reasons he also supplemented his formal, diplomatic dispatches to the State Department with private, more revealing letters to Roosevelt and to Sumner Welles, then rather more intimate with the president than was his superior Cordell Hull, to whom Leahy wrote less frequently. "I hope," Welles wrote to Leahy in February 1941, "you will continue to send me personal letters of this kind since they are extraordinarily helpful to me in this complicated situation."[16] They were, he added later, "useful in obtaining the background of your official reports."[17] The presumed advantage of personal, court diplomacy lies in its discretion, its flexibility, its independence of the bureaucratic machinery of a state department or a foreign office. Such at least is the expectation; and it was certainly a requirement during the ensuing sixteen months, during which Russia and the United States entered the war, and Allied military planners began to consider the most far-reaching strategic goals, the time of GYMNAST and BOLERO and SLEDGEHAMMER. But what emerges from Leahy's telegrams and letters is quite the reverse: uninvolved in the larger tactical discussions, he came to have profound misgivings about the value of his stay in Vichy, and to dislike and distrust almost all the senior Vichy officials. Yet he also found himself unable to exert any real influence on American policy toward France, still premised largely on the assumptions of 1940.

It is instructive to trace the course of Leahy's progressive disenchantment. His initial impressions were not all bad. Pétain, at eighty-six, displayed "vigor, and strength of character," though, to be sure, more noticeably in the morning than in the afternoon, and more openly when he was not flanked by subordinates.[18] Huntziger showed "patriotism, loyalty to his people, and a high determination to do the best for France that is possible under existing circumstances."[19] Flandin admittedly seemed "a compromiser . . . [who] leans pretty far over to the German side."[20] But within a month of Leahy's arrival Flandin resigned, leaving Darlan stronger than ever; and Darlan behaved in a most friendly fashion toward Leahy, assuring him that he would rather scuttle his beloved French fleet than hand it over to any other authority.[21] The first major blow to Leahy's optimism appears to have come with Darlan's visit to Hitler in Berchtesgaden in early May 1941 for what threatened to be a repeat of Montoire.

Leahy's suspicions of Darlan had been building up for some time. After 25 February 1941, Darlan was, in addition to minister of marine, vice-president of the Council, minister of foreign affairs, and minister of the interior—a concentration of power that might materially reduce Pétain's effective authority. At a meeting on 3 March, Leahy had found Pétain completely unaware of Darlan's new concessions to the Germans—the presence in Casablanca of a large German military mission and the order to General Weygand to deliver five thousand tons of gasoline to Italy. On this occasion it was Darlan who provided the excuses and denials.[22] On 18 March Pétain confided to Leahy, "Admiral Darlan seems to be getting closer to the Germans and to be playing more with them. I must watch him and I will restrain him as much as possible."[23] A month later, Pétain chose to receive Leahy at a time when Darlan would be busy with a cabinet meeting.[24] On 3 May Pétain admitted that he did not know the scope or purposes of Darlan's current talks with the Germans in Paris.[25] And on 13 May, after another interview with a nervous and perplexed Pétain still awaiting news from Darlan about German demands, Leahy concluded that "there are few demands except 'voluntary active military aid' that the Vichy government is likely to refuse."[26]

Leahy outlined his misgivings in two long dispatches to Washington. In the first, a letter to Roosevelt on 21 April, he rehearsed all the evidence of German pressure on Vichy, and then struck at the basis of the American position. Pétain, it now turned out, was in "a powerless position," and it was important for the American government not to "indulge in expectations that cannot be accomplished." The marshal would be unlikely to "move his government to North Africa or . . . direct General Weygand to join cause with the democracies." He may have promised not to turn over the French fleet and naval bases to Germany, but that provided no guarantee that the Germans would not seize them. In short, "any demands whatever that may be made by the Germans will either be granted by the Vichy government or permitted without active opposition." The only effective opposition that could be made to Germany would not come from within official circles at Vichy, but would have to take the form of "armed resistance and the use of sabotage methods." However, the French people "have no arms, no organization, and very little fighting spirit at the present time."[27]

It is scarcely surprising that such radical, albeit implicit, criticism of the policy should have caused some concern in Washington. Roosevelt forwarded the letter to the State Department for comment, and received a reply, dated 13 May, that sought to rescue some justification for the policy. In fact there was very little that could be said. Hull simply based his argument on the hope that American encouragement would be a force for stability (rather than opposition to Hitler). There was no question, nor had Leahy raised one, of halting the American supply of wheat to unoccupied France or of provisions to North Africa. "I see," concluded Hull, "no better course to pursue than to go on with these matters, subject, of course, to termination or reversal immediately upon Vichy taking any action detrimental to the British cause."[28] Beyond that, there were other grounds for optimism to which Hull alluded in a second memorandum to Roosevelt on the same day. Between 6 and 8 April Leahy had visited Marseilles to welcome a Red Cross supply ship, the S.S. *Exmouth*; there had followed demonstrations of pro-American sympathies in the unoccupied zone, and simultaneous denunciations of Leahy by the German-controlled Paris press, in which, for example, the Iowa-born admiral had been charged with "combining Anglo-Saxon hypocrisy with Jewish rapacity."[29] Hull now gratefully seized on these attacks as

> . . . a clear indication that the Germans are intensely annoyed at the success we have had in convincing the French people that this country is doing everything that it can to support them against the oppression and degradation the Germans are attempting to fasten upon them. This matter of the French public attitude is of tremendous importance in the backing of Pétain and even in the limiting of the Marshal's government in the extent to which "collaboration" might be accepted. As I see it our only course is to continue our present policy toward Unoccupied France, and the more attacks, such as the Admiral sends us, appear in the German-controlled press, the more will we know we are getting our policy across with the French people.[30]

But the May crisis at Vichy was by no means over yet. After a meeting with Pétain and the once resolute Huntziger on 13 May, Leahy came away with "the definite impression that following the British defeats in Libya, Yugoslavia, and Greece, the Marshal and his Government are moving rapidly towards 'collaboration' with Germany."[31] Darlan came back from Berchtesgaden to assure the French people that Hitler had not *asked* for the French fleet, a French declaration of war on England, or any French colonies.[32] But he maintained a studied silence with regard to what Hitler had actually asked for and received, merely stressing that it was the duty of the French people to follow the Marshal wheresoever he might lead them; later he was to tell Leahy that he could not say that the Germans had not asked for French bases.[33] Pétain himself developed that theme in a broadcast to the French people on 15 May, in which he stated that "it is no longer a question today for public opinion, so often anxious because badly informed, to measure our risks, to judge our gestures. It is a question for you Frenchmen to follow me without question on the paths of honor and national interest."[34] Toward the end of the month the press within Vichy began to refuse publication of anything that bore on American friendship toward France, an attempt, as Leahy saw it, at "building prestige for the Marshal's government by discrediting Americans and the assistance heretofore provided by America."[35] Finally, on 28 May, Darlan signed the Paris Protocols, the terms of which were never properly known until after the end of the war, but which, given the precedents and the circumstances, seemed ominous.[36]

These developments only deepened Leahy's concern. His telegram of 13 May to the State Department, in which he foresaw the trend of French policy, provided, as had his letter of 21 April, telling criticisms of the basis of American policy. Thus far, he argued, American influence in France had not been a determinant of French policy; nor had French public opinion. The government's calculations were being made with regard solely to the relative position of Britain and Germany, and the possibility, in that conflict, of tangible American aid: "Last winter," he noted, "when the British were advancing to Benghazi and beyond and when the progress of our Lease and Lend Bill led to exaggerated hopes in France of the implications of its passage in terms of immediate action, the Marshal's attitude was noticeably 'stronger' and his declarations as to the limits of collaboration beyond which he would not go were more promising than is the case today." Now, Pétain would either concede or not oppose any German demand, whether on the continent or in the empire; and he would not do anything to help the Allied cause: "The only deterring factor, with British prestige at its present low ebb, is the amount of pressure the Germans wish to exert and the importance to them of their objective."[37]

By this time Washington was sufficiently alarmed to take some action. The United States Coast Guard was ordered to place armed guards on French merchant ships lying in American ports.[38] Roosevelt issued a stern public statement, in which he called it "inconceivable" that the French people would let themselves be a party to a policy of collaboration with Germany, or any kind of voluntary alliance "which would deliver up France and its colonial Empire."[39] Cordell Hull concluded after a conference with Roosevelt that the best American course would still be to see what could be salvaged first from Vichy and then from Weygand in North Africa.[40] To that end he had a long talk with the French ambassador on 20 May, in which he spoke angrily about the new direction of French policy and concluded with a demand for "a clear statement and pledge by the French government to the effect that it will do no more than observe the terms of the armistice so far as extending any military favoritism to Germany is concerned, etc."[41] Sumner Welles sponsored the sending of a personal message from Chautemps informing Pétain of "the psychological mechanism which has brought about the present state of mind in the United States," and warning him that "it would be a mistake to think that it would be possible to push on to the limit collaboration on a military plane without being exposed to a conflict with England, and perhaps, with the United States."[42] That was, in sum, the American action taken.

What is immediately striking is the moderation, the reliance on moral suasion rather than action. There was only temporary suspension of the discussions about supplying North Africa, and no halt in the aid to unoccupied France. And Hull blocked a proposal made by Welles that the president should declare all the Atlantic islands and West Africa to be covered by the Monroe Doctrine.[43] Later, this moderation would be credited with causing French abandonment of the Paris Protocols, inasmuch as they were indeed opposed by Weygand in cabinet; and Weygand was expecting, in North Africa, to benefit from American aid.[44] But the proof is lacking. It was certainly true that the opposition to the protocols came from the empire, from men such as Weygand and Pierre Boisson; but, for them, American aid had always been a supplement to, not a prerequisite of, their resolve to keep the colonies free of German control. Given Leahy's low opinion of the French ability to oppose German pressure, a mere cabinet decision to propose renegotiation of the protocols is a less convincing explanation for their abandonment than other, later events in June—the Anglo-Gaullist assault on Syria (which rendered nugatory any French concessions to Germany there) and Hitler's attack on Russia (which temporarily distracted him from Mediterranean ambitions).[45]

The crisis of April and May 1941 prefigured the nature of Leahy's mission in Vichy for his remaining year. There is no reason to believe that he was ill-informed, at least not about the activities of the Vichy government. He was, for example, shrewder than his Washington superiors in recognizing that a personal message from Chautemps of all people—the Freemason, the wily democrat, the émigré—did not carry undue weight with Pétain.[46] Nor did he harbor any illusions about Vichy's ability to resist German pressure. He faithfully advised his government on both counts. But just as he was prevented, by his terms of reference, from stepping outside French government circles, so also the mechanics of American policy prevented him from effectively challenging the assumptions on which that policy rested. Though providing the information, he was not expected to draw the analysis that would govern future American action. It was because the range of his activities was thus circumscribed that he was drawn, almost in spite of himself, into a real loyalty toward Pétain. As the personal, diplomatic instrument of a government that relied on moral argument and humanitarian gestures to secure its goals, Leahy had little choice.

There is no mistaking that it was, for Leahy, a frustrating experience, whose full extent emerges most graphically from his own words. In July 1941 he heard of yet another French surrender of sovereignty to the Japanese in Indochina, the cession of bases, and noted, "Here endeth the French colonies in Asia."[47] In October, shortly after Pétain announced the end of parliamentary democracy in France, suggesting the attractiveness of the fascist system, Leahy wrote: "The present government of France is not essentially different from that of Nazi Germany."[48] Later in the month Leahy concluded that: "We have no reason to believe that the present Government of France accepts or even understands that . . . it [can] be maintained only with the assistance of German arms, a conclusion that appears obvious to most of us who have knowledge of the present political situation and alignment in unhappy France."[49] On 21 November, after the dismissal of Weygand from North Africa, at German insistence, Leahy suggested: "America may now very correctly base its relations with France on an assumption that it is a captive nation no longer free to make decisions and therefore no longer capable of maintaining political relations with the free peoples of the world."[50] On 12 December, with the United States now a formal belligerent, Leahy simply commented on receipt of a French note promising continued neutrality, "I have however no reason to believe that under German pressure the Marshal will be able to carry out the policies stated in these Foreign Office notes."[51] Finally, on 27 January 1942, after discussing with Pétain the mounting evidence of German pressure on North Africa, he concluded that "there is no indication at the present time that Vichy will give any assistance to the Allied Governments in an attempt to keep the Germans out of North Africa."[52]

The thrust of Leahy's analysis is perfectly clear. According to him, the German influence at Vichy was decisive and American influence was negligible; whatever the theoretical basis of Vichy's claim to sovereignty, that meant in practical terms little save assenting to German demands. The question therefore immediately arises, why did he not urge that American policy be brought into line with his perceptions? To doubt Vichy's sovereignty was, logically, to question America's policy. Yet on one notable occasion he actually pulled back from an earlier, vigorous recommendation. On 19 November 1941, after reporting a conversation he had had with Pétain warning him of the probable consequences of the removal of Weygand, Leahy listed a number of actions that he thought the American government should take, including the recall of the ambassador "for consultation" (the conventional diplomatic expression of disapproval).[53] When Hull invited him to reflect more on his advice, Leahy immediately reversed himself, and replied: ". . . it is my opinion that by remaining here for the present I may possibly be able to exercise on the Marshal a restraining influence, counter to additional demands for collaboration in Africa which are generally expected in the near future."[54]

Like an old trooper, Leahy remained at his post. More than a code of discipline was involved. He displayed a genuine humanitarianism, an authentic desire to do what he could to improve conditions for the suffering people of France. Both he and his wife were active in securing and distributing relief supplies;[55] and he often argued that such relief would be a means of reaching the French people over the heads of Vichy officials.[56] He therefore reacted angrily to a vituperative press attack on the United States for thus meddling in Vichy's internal affairs: "It may be difficult [he noted in his diary] for the professional officeholders of the Vichy Government to understand that there is little pleasure and no profit whatsoever to the people of America, to the President or to the Ambassador in their efforts to help the distressed people of France. They may be unable to appreciate that I personally am making a considerable sacrifice to remain here in the service of the President as ambassador, and that an early return home is the one bright hope."[57]

Occasionally a flicker of anger led him to propose that such relief be made conditional: renewed collaboration with Germany should end all humanitarian gestures towards Vichy.[58] But he usually advocated relief on compassionate, not strategic, grounds; and when, by February 1942, the prospect of a return to the United States seemed imminent, he wrote feelingly about the miserable country he was leaving, adding that "after more than a year in this defeated country where not only the material necessities of life but the spiritual values have been destroyed by an invasion of barbarians, the thought of returning to a free, undefeatable country is pleasing beyond the power of words to express."[59]

As long as he had to remain in Vichy, Leahy retained his concern for the physical welfare of the French population. But for that concern to have any practical effect, any chance of easing the plight of ordinary French men and women, he had, almost against his will, to accept the questionable claims to independence of Vichy officialdom. For one point had clearly emerged from the protracted Anglo-American negotiations over the breaking of the continental blockade entailed by any delivery of relief supplies: the British insisted that the reality of the demarcation line between occupied and unoccupied France be emphasized. If, that is, relief supplies were to go in, then Vichy must be accorded the status of a neutral country, with its rights intact, rather than be deemed a Nazi-occupied country, subject to British economic warfare. Even this allowance was grudgingly given. As Churchill noted in a telegram to Roosevelt, "The anxiety which we have always felt about this project is that it would lead to similar demands on behalf of our German occupied allies."[60] On that principle the limited relief that the United States did send was permitted into Vichy, thus showing how even the exercise of simple humanitarian feelings served to strengthen the position of the Pétain regime. Leahy was in the position of advocating a measure whose sole justification was the alleged independence of Vichy, even while, in telegram after telegram, he was reporting on actions taken, in France, North Africa, Indochina, that vitiated that very independence.

In still another way Leahy was drawn toward Pétain. Following Roosevelt's instructions, he confined his main contacts to the ruling clique at Vichy—Pétain, his cabinet, and his officials. But an American ambassador, in a nest of political and diplomatic intrigue, was not immune to the visits of persons less well situated. He might even be expected to take at least a passing interest in non-governmental sources of opinion; and, conscientiously, Leahy did so. Broadly, these were of three types: those in outright opposition, that is the resistance and the Gaullists; political outcasts of the old regime, like Edouard Herriot; and possible dissenters from the current one, like General Weygand. Leahy's dealings with these varied people drove him in fact further toward Pétain.

His first notice of de Gaulle did not augur well. Pétain mentioned to him that he had been told, confidentially, by Churchill that de Gaulle had been of no service to the British cause; and Pétain wondered why the British did not accordingly unburden themselves of him, since he also obstructed Pétain's maintenance of French neutrality. That frank bid for American understanding took place on 18 March 1941 and was duly reported to Roosevelt and the State Department.[61] But during the same period, as it happens, Leahy possessed an alternative source of information on the internal strength of the resistance movement. Three days before, Roosevelt had delivered an address to a dinner of White House correspondents, spelling out the American commitment to Britain in a characteristically lingering phrase, "the arsenal of democracy."[62] During the next week the American embassy in Vichy was deluged with letters that, taken together, gave some idea, albeit an impressionistic one, of French public opinion. "This more or less anonymous source of information," wrote Leahy, who read it thoroughly, ". . . indicates that the de Gaulle movement has a much larger following than one would think from official sources of information. It would appear that there are a large number of people in unoccupied France who have no confidence in officials of the Vichy government, particularly Admiral Darlan, and who would rather be placed on starvation rations for themselves and their children than make any concessions whatever to Germany."[63]

The tenor of these letters seems clear: resistance, Gaullism, was making inroads on a public not yet disenchanted with Pétain, but bristling nonetheless at his regime and German impositions, and willing to sacrifice present comforts for the prospective defeat of Germany. Yet Leahy chose to adopt the Pétainist interpretation of de Gaulle's movement, even as, on relief supplies, he had chosen to subordinate political to humanitarian considerations. That view was, first, that de Gaulle's removal would strengthen Pétain's hand with the Germans, and, second, that within France de Gaulle's movement represented a species of political radicalism. To Pétain as to Darlan, "Gaullist and communist" efforts were of a piece.[64] Leahy's fullest survey of Gaullism was in a letter to Roosevelt on 28 July, in which he asserted that "the de Gaulle movement does not have the following or the strength that is indicated in British radio news and in the American press." Even those Frenchmen who were noted for their British sympathies had little regard for de Gaulle, he went on; and while there was, in the occupied zone, a Gaullist organization engaged in propaganda and sabotage it did not command widespread support elsewhere: "The radical de Gaullists whom I have met do not seem to have the stability, intelligence and popular standing in their communities that should be necessary to success in their announced purpose. One of them recently told me that all the Ministers of the Vichy Government are under sentence of death which can be carried out at any time and which will be carried out when it suits the purpose of their organization."[65]

Thus de Gaulle's activities, insofar as they constituted a threat to Vichy, also imperiled American policy. What then of the liberal, democratic opposition? Here the obstacles to an American entente were just as formidable. For members of the old regime were as much a target of Vichy persecution as the resistance, perhaps rather more so since the legitimacy of Pétain's rule depended to a great extent on discrediting that of his predecessors. Thus four of them, Daladier, Blum, Guy La Chambre, and Robert Jacomet (together with General Maurice Gamelin, commander of the French Army in 1940) were, for most of Leahy's stay, awaiting trial by a special Vichy tribunal, which opened proceedings in February 1942.[66] Others, like Reynaud and Georges Mandel, languished in Vichy prisons without benefit of trial. Nevertheless, Leahy did make some contact with one or two of the others, parliamentarians rather than cabinet officials, to the evident displeasure of Pétain and Darlan. On 28 May 1941, he received an oral message from the marshal, delivered by Charles Rochat, acting secretary general of the French Ministry of Foreign Affairs, which ran, "The Marshal and his government find it regrettable that an ambassador accredited to the chief of the French State should constantly receive people like Louis Marin [a conservative deputy] and Edouard Herriot [president of the French Chamber of Deputies and the leader of the Radical-Socialist Party] whose hostility to the Marshal and his government is well known."[67] And at the first opportunity, on 4 June, Leahy went to explain himself to Pétain and Darlan.

He began by saying that the message appeared to be a direct reflection on his "loyalty," that he had seen Herriot only once (on Leahy's arrival he had come to pay his respects at the Embassy) and Marin not at all, and that he had not discussed political questions with anyone but the marshal and the minister for foreign affairs. That emphasis, on his loyalty to Pétain, was the central thread running through the conversation. He told the marshal, "I have consistently made every endeavor to obtain from my Government every possible support for the Vichy Government." When Darlan talked of secret police reports and telephone intercepts indicating that the American embassy had frequent contacts with individual members of the opposition who claimed to have American backing, Leahy replied that "the only information of any value received by the Embassy comes from officials of the Marshal's government who are not or have not heretofore been satisfied with the prospect of collaboration with the Germans."[68] This was certainly true, since Leahy tended to discount any political intelligence received from other sources. But in practice it meant that even though Sumner Welles later told the British ambassador in Washington that, in preference to de Gaulle, "if some man like Herriot could get out of France and lead the movement the situation would undoubtedly be very different,"[69] the American embassy at Vichy was finding its range of contacts severely limited.

This was but one episode in a consistent Vichy effort to undermine the American embassy and discredit its sources of information, even when those sources were American correspondents. Defending American journalists against French accusations, the embassy's counselor, Matthews, argued that they had an exceedingly difficult task, possessing as many of them did anti-Nazi and anti-collaborationist sentiments and being thwarted by censorship or ensnared by propaganda "plants": "In the field of journalism Franco-German collaboration is very nearly complete."[70] Leahy also reported on Darlan's complaints about American press coverage, and his threat that unless American correspondents repaid French hospitality in kind they would no longer be welcome in French territory.[71] Only those like Ralph Heinzen, of United Press, a friend of Laval, actually prospered.[72] It was equally necessary to warn members of the embassy against Vichy attempts to discredit them by the use of agents provocateurs, "travellers," for example, calling to inquire about contact with resistance forces.[73]

Thus insulated, the embassy needed to proceed with the utmost caution in dealing with anyone outside the official Vichy orbit, potential dissidents as well as outright opponents. Here the case of General Weygand is particularly illuminating. For American interest in him did not end with his dismissal from North Africa in November 1941. The following month saw the first conference with the United States a full belligerent, the Washington conference between Roosevelt, Churchill, and MacKenzie King, the Canadian prime minister, at which the critical decision was taken to launch the initial Allied move in North Africa, the project then known as GYMNAST; and Weygand's name came up again.[74] Would he support an Allied bid to pre-empt a German move into North Africa by helping to rally to the cause the French military and the inhabitants there? Matthews, then on leave in New York before taking up a new post as counselor to the London embassy, was summoned to the White

House on 23 December. There he was told of a proposal to induce Weygand to return secretly to North Africa and prepare for an Anglo-American expeditionary move. "I told them frankly," Matthews later recalled, "that I was convinced that Weygand would not act independently of Pétain and further that he would immediately inform the Marshal of our approach to him. I added that in view of the German contacts in the Marshal's entourage, they would almost immediately learn of our plans."[75] According to Matthews, his objections were overruled because Churchill was determined to bring the French back into the war, either by persuasion or by invasion; and the message to Weygand was duly sent. But neither Matthews nor Leahy was involved in its transmittal. Matthews, en route to London, could scarcely have stopped off in Vichy without arousing suspicion, any more than the ambassador could have left Vichy for the Riviera, where Weygand was living in retirement. So the message went from Washington to Vichy with Henry P. Leverich, second secretary in the American legation in Lisbon, and from Vichy to Nice with Douglas MacArthur II, third secretary in the American embassy in Vichy.[76] In short, precisely because there was an American ambassador at Vichy, he could not be employed on the most important and delicate mission of his tenure.

The message to Weygand was in two parts. The first, a written letter from Roosevelt, was simply an expression of hope, couched in vague terms, that Weygand's efforts to do everything possible for the French people had not ended with his departure from North Africa.[77] The second, more specific message, delivered orally by MacArthur, was based on coded notes that he subsequently burned. According to his, and Weygand's, later recollection, he first outlined a series of conceivable changes in the status quo—the elimination of Pétain, German use of the French fleet or bases, German penetration of North Africa. In such cases, he went on, the United States would be compelled to take action; and that action might well involve North Africa, where Weygand's assistance would be of great worth.[78]

Weygand's response was not just negative, but actually harmful. As Leahy reported, Weygand, though "courteous and agreeable," flatly refused to consider even the possibility of playing an active role in any future campaign. He refused even to suggest a substitute who might be interested. Moreover, though "specifically requested to keep message secret, [he] stated his duty requires that he inform the Marshal and that he will do so," trying, however, to avoid letting any others know.[79] Weygand was in fact only obeying the logic of his own understanding of the proper relations between the military and the civil arm, for he was not yet convinced of "the unworthiness or the illegality" of Pétain's regime.[80] So when, on 27 January 1942, Leahy had a conference with Pétain, Darlan, and Rochat, he could discern from Pétain's thorough preparation that a communication from Weygand had been received.[81] A more futile diplomatic venture seems hard to imagine.

Those last few months at Vichy must have been extremely dispiriting for an admiral whose country had been plunged into war by the bombing of its fleet. Already, with the entry of Russia into the war in June 1941, the European scene had, for Leahy at least, lost whatever charm it had once possessed. Then he had been reluctant for the American embassy to take over Russian interests at Vichy, which would have meant "looking after a large number of alleged 'Reds' who are being taken into custody."[82] Later, when Weygand was dismissed, it was Murphy in North Africa, rather than Leahy in Vichy, who successfully pressed for the maintenance of relations.[83] Now, after Pearl Harbor, the Pacific, not the European theater beckoned, and Leahy grew even more restless, wanting to serve "in the military-naval effort." He reacted angrily to the assurances of Lucien Romier, acting minister of foreign affairs, that France would stay neutral. "Of course," he wrote to Welles, "this spineless Government can do nothing to oppose Japan in the Orient or to help or injure either side in the Pacific War."[84]

As American battle plans began to be formulated, the Vichy embassy was no longer pivotal; and it was with an understandable lack of patience that Leahy continued his mission. On 12 December he proposed that if the embassy's code privileges were withdrawn, following the German declaration of war on the United States, the State Department should, for once, actually take the initiative and recall the embassy staff.[85] He at once received a curt reply from Hull to the effect that the United States would not squander the forceful gesture of a rupture of relations on a minor issue like code privileges.[86] It doubtless occurred to Leahy as time went by—as German penetration into North Africa seemed more likely, German influence at Vichy more evident, French reassurances less convincing—that he was living a paradox: remaining at Vichy for the sole purpose of quitting at an appropriate moment. On 20 February he wrote to Roosevelt about Pétain's failure to respond adequately to the president's demand for a French guarantee that no military aid of any kind would be given to the Axis.[87] That demand had been backed up by a firmly worded threat to recall Leahy if no satisfactory reply were given. As Leahy noted, that was "the first positive action taken by America in the matter of French-American political relations since my arrival in France. It very closely approaches an ultimatum."[88] Now, he wrote, was the time for him to be recalled, at least "for consultation," lest American threats seem mere bluff; and Roosevelt replied that military considerations elsewhere precluded any abrupt change in American policy toward France.[89]

Finally, on 27 March, the critical decision was taken. Already twice that month Leahy had written to Welles questioning the wisdom, in the long-term interests of American strategy, of the United States binding itself too closely to Vichy.[90] Now Welles informed him that when Laval's long-expected return to power took place—the final, public acknowledgment by Vichy of submission to Germany, as it seemed—"it would be impossible for this government to maintain diplomatic relations with the French government at Vichy."[91] But, once again, American action involved a distinct retreat. On 15 April, after Laval's return was announced, Leahy heard from Ray Atherton, of the State Department's European desk, that new instructions were being cabled to him.[92] In fact those instructions only provided for Leahy's recall "for consultation." No rupture of relations was planned.[93] After a short delay caused by the illness and death of Mrs. Leahy, he took his leave of Pétain (who assured him that Laval would furnish no military aid to Germany),[94] of Laval (who indicated that he would if he could),[95] and of Darlan (who hoped to retain American friendship).[96] Within two months Leahy had taken up a new post in Washington as chief of staff to the commander in chief, Roosevelt's closest military adviser.

Leahy's mission to Vichy was only a very limited success. It may, symbolically, have demonstrated the continued American attachment to France; and the resulting charitable efforts were, however circumscribed, not negligible. But in practical, diplomatic terms, performance scarcely fulfilled expectations. It exposed rather the dangerous illusion that the United States could influence the course of events at Vichy, could divert the trend toward collaborationism. Hence Leahy's disgust, for he was not personally to blame. With whatever acuteness he observed the moral deterioration of Pétain's regime, his conclusions had no observable effect on the formulation of American policy. On the contrary, particular circumstances, allied to his own innate conservatism, induced him to accept Pétain's self-image as the leader of Frenchmen, just as Roosevelt, in his original letter of instructions, had described him. The reduction of diplomacy to a kind of court intrigue left the monarch, whether Pétain in Vichy or Roosevelt in Washington, in a commanding position.

For Leahy himself, however, the experience proved most instructive. When he moved from Vichy to Washington, he brought with him an entire range of convictions that, through his new intimacy with Roosevelt, he could readily communicate: continued trust in Pétain, hostility toward de Gaulle, if for no other reason than that he was Pétain's foe, fear of the disruptive potential of Communism, and a certain disquiet at the activities of British diplomats. These views were unaffected by events over the next three years, and, being detached from any domestic political views, they possibly contributed to his appeal, to political strategists like Herbert Hoover, as secretary of war in a prospective Republican administration, in the brief period in 1943 when General Douglas MacArthur seemed a likely presidential candidate.[97]

Underlying all Leahy's principles was a deeply felt suspicion of European politics and politicians. Because de Gaulle appeared to have political ambitions, Leahy always preferred that the American administration have dealings with those whom he saw as the simple, straightforward, apolitical soldiers of France, Pétain, Weygand, even, in time, Darlan. When in fact Darlan was installed in North Africa following the Allied invasion in November 1942,

Leahy simply could not understand the ensuing outcry, given "our full adoption of Stalin."[98] Pétain he continued to respect, and was most upset at the marshal's ultimate imprisonment by the Gaullists "for purely political reasons."[99] De Gaulle he continued to despise, and even resented, at war's end, having to meet that "dirty frog."[100] The British he suspected for their financing of de Gaulle's movement, the Russians for their support of it.[101] Yet, as it happened, these were all—the Gaullists, the British, the Russians—America's European allies. No wonder the admiral was happier in Washington.

CHAPTER 4
GASTON HENRY-HAYE
AND THE ECLIPSE OF
FRANCO-AMERICAN DIPLOMACY,
1940–1942

Washington, however welcome to Leahy, was never a congenial place for his opposite number, Gaston Henry-Haye, ambassador from Vichy. Henry-Haye often remarked that Leahy in Vichy had a much easier time than did he in Washington.[1] For the burdens imposed on him were really quite unusual for an accredited ambassador from a recognized government.

Those burdens included more than the abuse heaped on him by the French émigré colony based in New York,[2] or the "investigatory" journalism of *PM* in 1940 and the *New York Herald Tribune* in 1941, which portrayed him as being at the center of a Nazi spy ring.[3] More troubling than the public attacks were the private intrusions, about which he knew less than was strictly proper. The embassy over which he presided did contain double agents, as he suspected;[4] and each official who resigned from it, as the contours of the Vichy regime became clearer, deposited with the American government a confidential account of the workings of the embassy.[5] The telephones were tapped, the cable ciphers broken, and in 1942 President Roosevelt was receiving from Colonel William Donovan of the OSS copies of telegrams between the embassy and Vichy within hours of their receipt or transmittal.[6] Donovan did show some awareness of the need to keep this domestic espionage secret and told Roosevelt that "it must be handled with great care and discretion and I dislike to let anyone know."[7] But the OSS made its services available to all branches of the government. When the secretary of the treasury, Henry Morgenthau, sought some information to aid him in the negotiations over the frozen French funds, he received a detailed, private memorandum about the relationship between Henry-Haye and Camille Chautemps.[8] Henry-Haye also had his personal mail, to and from his family in Occupied France, intercepted and read by the FBI. As a result, he only heard of his mother's death by radio,[9] and on one occasion he had the humiliating experience of having to request Welles to secure the return of his mail.[10] Finally, he had periodically to endure the quick temper of Cordell Hull as well as the cold anger of Welles.

These experiences he reviewed in a book of memoirs that he chose not to write until three decades had elapsed. He thus claimed a historical perspective that was not, for all their sense of history, at the disposal of other French memoir writers, de Gaulle, Admiral Emile Henri Muselier, Jacques Soustelle, or other servants of Vichy, Yves Bouthillier, Marcel Peyrouton, Pierre Pucheu.[11] More than them, Henry-Haye was a lasting victim of the historical processes he attempts, in the book, to explain, encountering at the end of the war the ordeal of flight and exile. Accordingly, he neither writes in the disciplined, austere prose of de Gaulle, nor does he provide a personal, detailed reconstruction of events, like that of General Giraud.[12] Conscious by now of all the ironies and failures, he adopts a sardonic style, ever noting the betrayals, broken promises, and deceits of his contemporaries. He supplies commentary rather than evidence, and the entire book reeks of irony, a memoir in the strict sense, not an autobiography or a historical essay. Thus instead of trying to defend Vichy's anti-Semitic measures, he simply notes the existence of segregated bathing facilities in Atlantic City;[13] instead of mounting any sustained criticism of the wartime de Gaulle, he is content to observe the developments in that remarkable man's career and to comment wryly that in the 1950s and 1960s de Gaulle achieved, with regard to the French empire, precisely what he had falsely accused Pétain of plotting in the 1940s.[14]

Leaving aside the grander historical generalizations, Henry-Haye's account of the war years, the actual period of "la grande éclipse franco-américaine," is perfectly straightforward; it is as would be expected from someone whose role in those years was ambassadorial. The souring of relations, the misunderstandings, the broken pledges occurred, he argues, primarily because France lacked critically situated friends in the United States, people who would combine a faith in Pétain's integrity with a purely humanitarian concern for his subjects. There were, to be sure, individual, though sadly powerless, Francophiles, for whom Henry-Haye does have kind words, General Pershing, Mrs. Harrison Williams and Sara Delano Roosevelt, the president's mother.[15] There were also the quiescent French-speaking communities of New England, which, he claimed, gave him a warm reception. Even there, however, the passage of time wrought certain changes. Immediately on his return from New England Henry-Haye exultantly told Sumner Welles that "he had won to the support of the Vichy government a group of influential French professors."[16] But thirty years later he came to regret that they were in fact rather reserved, reluctant to oppose an already converted American public opinion.[17]

Especially among American officials, Henry-Haye detected a certain duplicity coming from professed friends of France. There was William Bullitt, for example, who announced in 1937 that the United States would participate solely as an arbitrator in a future European conflict, only himself to push France into one two years later;[18] and there was Robert Murphy, who in 1944, during the liberation of France, refused to accommodate a desperate Henry-Haye in his flat in Paris when the latter was in fear for his life.[19] Those men (one of the frequent ironies of the book) originally recommended Henry-Haye to Washington.[20] Yet with men like that in high position, Henry-Haye believed, the American administration was able to afford the dual luxury of moralistic recriminations and opportunistic diplomacy, supervised by the conceited Roosevelt, the naive Hull, the austere Welles, and the uncharitable Morgenthau.[21] In all this Henry-Haye resembles no one so much as de Gaulle, who declared in a famous passage in his memoirs that "the United States brings to great affairs elementary feelings and a complicated policy."[22]

Henry-Haye and de Gaulle, civilian and soldier, rivals for American attention, shared nonetheless a suspicion of American diplomacy. They delivered what was in essence a cultural rebuke to the United States for disparaging certain features of the Old World. But their lofty judgments may serve to dwarf the particular details of their separate encounters with the American administration. Henry-Haye was, as will be seen, rather more than a diplomat, but even as a diplomat he had an uncommonly intricate assignment. Ambassador in Washington, titular chief of Vichy's representatives in the United States, he presided over a mission whose composition and objectives shifted with the ebbs and flows of Vichy's own policy. In September 1940 he arrived with his personal retinue at the embassy to replace the popular Count René de Saint-Quentin,[23] and was almost immediately engulfed in a feud with Camille Chautemps, who claimed a comparable, though unofficial, status with the American administration.[24] There also soon followed a number of resignations and dismissals from the staffs of the embassy and consulates in Boston, New York, and San Francisco;[25] still more left when Pierre Laval returned to power in Vichy in April 1942;[26] and the entire mission was of course convulsed when relations were severed between France and the United States after the Allied landings in North Africa seven months later.[27] In short, to read successive editions of the *Annuaire diplomatique et consulaire*, with their handwritten amendments and scribbled *révoqués*, is to be poignantly reminded of the insecurity and fragility of diplomatic life in wartime.

But out of this unsettled climate certain permanent features emerged with undeniable clarity. Like all servants of Vichy, Henry-Haye liked to flaunt his devotion to the venerated figure of Marshal Pétain, and, unlike some of them, he had a plausible historical justification. In March 1939, wanting to see for once a strong president in France, Senator Henry-Haye led a movement to make Pétain a candidate. That premature attempt failed in part through Pétain's reluctance to stand, and incidentally incurred the marked opposition of Laval.[28] Nevertheless, if one thing is clear it is that Henry-Haye belonged far more in Laval's camp than Pétain's. Both were parliamentarians, unlike the politically aloof Pétain; and they were parliamentarians who disparaged formal party loyalty in the name of a higher, if elusive, patriotism. Henry-Haye first ran as a deputy on behalf of veterans' organizations, and immediately joined the Foreign Affairs Committee. Both men came to have a profound contempt for the French democratic process, and indeed helped to secure that critical vote of 10 July 1940 for the new regime.[29] They had both worked for a rapprochement with Germany in the 1930s, despised the Popular Front, and opposed the drift to war from within the Senate.[30] Henry-Haye's appointment to the Washington embassy dated from that period in 1940 when Laval was briefly in power, and was renewed for the last time early in March 1942, when Laval was moving back; and he was one of the few senior Vichy officials who remained active in the United States after Laval's return.[31] Long after the war, and Laval's execution, Henry-Haye would deliver a sentimental encomium to Laval's services to France.[32]

The two men also held strikingly similar views about the United States. Henry-Haye's association with the country dated back a long time. In 1908, at the age of sixteen, he had been a lift attendant in a large New York hotel;[33] during the First World War he had been part of a French military mission sent to the United States to prepare American soldiers for wartime conditions in France;[34] and in 1931 "le candidat américain" (as he had come to be known during his successful election campaign to the Chamber of Deputies from Versailles) accompanied Laval to the United States as an interpreter in the negotiations over the Hoover moratorium on war debts. There he heard and applauded Laval telling Senator William Borah, then chairman of the Committee on Foreign Relations, that the best way to ensure European calm was for the United States to lend its active moral support.[35] Both men, Laval and Henry-Haye, retained an affection for the United States as an important component of their international vision, long after the United States was actually in the war, issuing stern rebukes in the direction of the reemergent Laval. On 27 April 1942 Laval told Leahy that "neither by word nor act would his government make any unfriendly gesture to the United States," a sentiment he often repeated;[36] and for his part, Henry-Haye was moved to complain about the misrepresentation of Laval's notorious speech of 22 June 1942. Laval had actually said, "I desire the victory of Germany, for without it bolshevism would tomorrow install itself everywhere." But with the excision of the subordinate clause by both German and Gaullist propagandists (their common strategy being yet another irony), the speech was made to appear a declaration of open hostility toward the United States, an anti-American rather than an anti-Communist statement.[37]

Thus within the spectrum of competing tendencies at Vichy—neutralism, *attentisme*, collaborationism, associated, at various junctures, with the figures of Pétain, Darlan, and Laval—Henry-Haye belonged enthusiastically to the Laval persuasion. He bore, as Cordell Hull later recalled, "the taint of association with Laval and his group."[38] This alone accounts for some of the more peculiar features of Henry-Haye's tenure of office. It explains, for example, the curious position within the United States of Camille Chautemps. Chautemps had long been, in many eyes, the epitome of the scheming, opportunist politician, who made the transition from service in the Third Republic to service in the Vichy regime with untoward ease. He had been the subtle author, on 16 June 1940, of the proposal in the French cabinet to ask the Germans what the terms of a possible armistice might be; and he had told Bullitt that a dictatorial regime would get better treatment at German hands than a democratic one. He added that he himself however was "gradually being shoved aside as an adviser of Pétain by Laval."[39] Sir Robert Vansittart, permanent head of the British Foreign Office, called Chautemps "among other things, a coward and a crook. He has very dirty hands."[40] Much later, de Gaulle treated with scorn his attempt to join the Free French.[41]

Yet to others he evidently had his uses, as a counterweight, perhaps, to Laval. Churchill, for example, did not want "this poor wretched old Chautemps . . . to be treated as a pariah," when there were so many worse tendencies at Pétain's court.[42] In any event, Chautemps arrived in the United States late in 1940 on a mission from Pétain that was personal, unofficial, and extremely vague. Its purpose has been variously described as to explain to the French diplomatic corps, and the exiles, the true reasons for the armistice, to reassure American public opinion about Vichy's treatment of Jews and Freemasons, to gather support for sending supplies to unoccupied France, to win the confidence of Roosevelt and the State Department, and to discredit de Gaulle as a fascist.[43] Conceivably it was all of those. But certainly the American administration did also use Chautemps to transmit messages to Pétain;[44] and Chautemps did gain, though imperfectly, access to Roosevelt.[45] Henry-Haye was naturally aggrieved at such an undermining of the official ambassador's position, by Pétain as much as by the American administration, and so there arose the bitter feud between him and Chautemps, each trying to have the other recalled. Henry-Haye emerged the victor in August 1941, when Chautemps's monthly salary, paid out of embassy funds, was terminated.[46] Thereafter Chautemps was cut loose, free to drift slowly in a Gaullist direction, although throughout the existence of the Vichy regime he tried to maintain contact with Pétain, and kept up a forlorn, self-serving correspondence with his supposed friend Sumner Welles.[47]

This episode, trivial in itself, perfectly captures the essence of Henry-Haye's position in Washington. The basic American strategy was to cling to Pétain, and restrain Laval. Henry-Haye, though the official ambassador, was Laval's man; Chautemps, though lacking official status, was at least arguably Pétainist. But just as in Vichy Admiral Leahy could not prevent Laval's return, so in Washington the State Department could not bypass Laval's associate. And there was a further objection to Henry-Haye, aside from his inclinations toward Laval. The Vichy regime, which departed from Third Republic customs to the extent of employing rather more politicians as ambassadors, may not always have received the quality of service to which it felt entitled.

Certainly on one occasion even Laval was moved to complain that Henry-Haye sent him nothing of importance.[48] More seriously, even when Laval was out of office, Henry-Haye persisted, it seems, in sending back reports to Vichy slanted according to the Laval school. In particular, he encouraged a belief in continued American neutrality. On the one hand, he forwarded to Vichy complete transcripts of every non-interventionist statement or speech by Charles Lindbergh and the isolationist bloc in Congress, Senators Burton Wheeler, Gerald Nye, Arthur Vandenberg, Robert Taft, and Ernest Lundeen, and Representative Hamilton Fish. On the other hand, he derided the American national defense effort by sending newspaper dispatches on labor disputes, strikes, and lockouts, and by quoting the gloomy articles and speeches on industrial productivity of Senator Claude Pepper, Representative Sol Bloom, Dorothy Thompson, and Walter Lippmann.[49]

Such articles and speeches were, in the United States, designed to stimulate greater effort; in Vichy, they could seem perilously close to defeatism. Henry-Haye thereby earned himself a lecture from Sumner Welles on the state of American public opinion. The ambassador "undoubtedly knew," Welles said, "that when the average American was determined and resolute and solidly behind his Government in the policies which it was following, he did not shout his opinions from the housetops but rather remained cool and silent." Welles admitted that there was a vocal minority in the United States, "of the kind which Colonel Lindbergh represented." But, he went on, "anyone who knew American public opinion recognized that usually the smaller a minority, the more vocal it became." On a related topic, Welles noted that American production statistics "were far more gratifying than had been anticipated." He was rather amused "at the distorted interpretation which the Germans and the Italians were trying to give to the occasional strikes." Those were in fact on the way to being solved, and in any case bore no resemblance to "the kind of revolutionary strike which had taken place in European countries in recent years." Henry-Haye of course welcomed these reassurances.[50]

In Vichy there was Leahy to counteract false impressions on the state of American affairs. But however strenuously he engaged in the task, a useful supplement would certainly have been reports from America by trusted French officials; and this the State Department, moving with extreme delicacy, sought to encourage, hoping to acquire, in the process, a helpful ally in the British government. Early in 1941 Cordell Hull suggested to the British ambassador, Lord Halifax, that they might set up a program of meetings of three people, unofficial representatives who might still enjoy the complete confidence of the British and American governments and of Vichy. Such discreet meetings might lubricate diplomatic exchanges, without disturbing official channels. Halifax replied on 19 February, to Sumner Welles, that the real difficulty was that the British could "think of no place where there are at present three suitable persons." There was, for example, "no French representative at any convenient capital in whom we have any confidence." Welles suggested Washington as an acceptable meeting ground; if Henry-Haye was not "an appropriate confidential representative of the French government," then perhaps Chautemps would serve, a suggestion that can hardly have gone down well in the British Foreign Office.[51] The most the British could contribute, in early May, was the proposal that a "prominent, reliable, and influential" Frenchman be invited to tour the "Anglo-Saxon" countries to examine opinion outside on the matter of Vichy, since Pétain and Vichy circles generally seemed ignorant of attitudes abroad. The favored candidate was Pastor Marc Boegner, president of the French Protestant Federation, a "universally respected man." The invitation could be issued through the American Council of Churches.[52] But no action was taken on what would have been, at best, a very minor corrective.

There the matter rested until midsummer when, out of Africa, a plan emerged. On 12 August Robert Murphy, then on special assignment from Roosevelt to explore North African conditions, cabled Welles about a recent conversation with General Weygand, then governor general of Algeria and a possible anticollaborationist. It developed that Weygand, on his latest visit to Vichy, had discussed with Pétain and Darlan the desirability of replacing Henry-Haye at Washington. Weygand now wanted "a personal and unofficial suggestion of the name of someone who under present circumstances might be acceptable and enjoy the confidence of the President, the Secretary, and Welles," since Henry-Haye "unfortunately did not enjoy that advantage." Having reflected on the matter, Murphy offered Welles the names of four men, all of pronounced anti-Laval convictions: François Charles-Roux, "outspokenly Americanophile," who had resigned as secretary general of the French Foreign Office, supposedly over differences with Laval; André Charles Corbin, a former ambassador to Britain, then in retirement in the south of France; Admiral Jean Pierre Esteva, resident general of Tunisia, who had over the summer apparently undergone a conversion from collaborationism to hostility to Germany; and Emmanuel Monick, secretary general of French Morocco, a man whose known Allied sympathies were in due course to get him dismissed.[53]

None of those men entirely suited Welles. He wired back an order of preference in which a new name came first, General Edmond Requin, an energetic anti-German soldier who was actually Leahy's candidate for the post, followed by Monick, Charles-Roux, and Corbin. But, added Welles, that information was to be given solely to Weygand; no American initiative should appear.[54] Murphy replied that Weygand, who thought "that it would be better to have no representative in Washington than the present one," was delighted at the suggestion of Requin. While Weygand's own candidate had been Charles-Roux, Darlan had told him that the Germans would unhesitatingly block such an appointment.[55] As it turned out, the Germans would oppose any new appointment to the Washington embassy. Leahy soon gathered from the French

Foreign Office that any move to replace Henry-Haye would meet severe German displeasure. The Germans apparently felt, with no little justification, that Henry-Haye was a source of irritation to the American administration and public opinion; and "anyone who, however unwittingly, may serve to keep relations between Vichy and Washington strained, is an asset in German eyes."[56] Henry-Haye's vices were his assets.

There remained one last hope. Pétain and Darlan did admit, according to Leahy, that no improvement could be expected in Franco-American relations while Henry-Haye served as the main intermediary. And if he could not be replaced outright then perhaps he could be gradually subverted. The person most frequently mentioned in this context was Professor Charles Rist, the distinguished economist and banker then acting as an adviser in North Africa. There was, it seemed, a proposal ready "to send Rist to the United States on some 'special mission' with rather broad powers and to appoint him as ambassador some two months hence."[57] For while there was little realization in Vichy of the true nature of American public opinion, there was at least a growing appreciation of the urgent need to improve relations. Rist, a close associate of Weygand and apparently a conscientious man, arrived in Vichy on 19 October, there to have extensive conversations with Pétain and Darlan. From them he sought an understanding that the Weygand policy of neutralism would prevail at Vichy; thus reassured, he would be able faithfully to represent his government in Washington, although nominally he was only to be dealing with the various pending economic questions, like the blocked French accounts in the United States. But he would have there the use of the French naval code and a cipher clerk, and full freedom of communication with Vichy "without any hindrance from Henry-Haye."[58] Yet once again the initiative came to nothing. Within a few weeks Weygand himself had, as feared, been dismissed from North Africa, under German pressure, and the project did not survive his fall. In any event the renewal of Henry-Haye's appointment for a further six months had been announced in Vichy in early November.[59]

It is in this context that the American program of domestic espionage, aided to some extent by British services, may be most charitably viewed. It was not designed to expose him as a spy, though, as will be seen, the British came to feel an interest in thus embarrassing Vichy-American relations. Nor was there any real prospect of securing intelligence directly related to the war effort. But before 1941 was out all the sympathetic, or manageable, channels of communication between the two governments had been effectively closed; and so the American administration began to cast about within the United States for alternatives to Henry-Haye. That is, it mounted its surveillance on the French embassy and consulates in order to discern differences of opinion and to locate individuals who might prove useful counterweights to the Laval influence coming from above.

This search was performed, in a manner entirely characteristic of the Roosevelt administration, by a whole array of government agencies, the OSS, the FBI, and the Office of Naval Intelligence (ONI). But essentially the material thus gathered fell into two parts. There was the straightforward intercepting of telegrams between the embassy and Vichy, which exposed the particular concerns of Henry-Haye. That evidence, collected by the OSS, was passed straight to Roosevelt.[60] A larger, and more diffuse, body of material purported to chronicle the goings on within the French diplomatic community, the factions, the feuds, the indiscretions, even—perhaps to lighten the reader's burden—the affairs.

This dauntingly large body of evidence and speculation came under the scrutiny of Adolf Berle, assistant secretary of state, the senior State Department official most concerned with domestic intelligence and the activities of foreign nationality groups. A sophisticated and highly intelligent man, he retained a deep skepticism about the intrusion of foreign controversies, and personalities, into American life, fearing that their ultimate effect would be simply to "Balkanize the United States."[61] Nor was he much impressed by the supposed virtues of those who served as informants. Thus he told J. Edgar Hoover, who had sent him a factually inaccurate report on Alexis Leger, that "in the entire French community the partisans of each group are endeavoring to discredit the members of all other groups, and too much credence cannot be placed in evidence thus obtained."[62] All the same, the material kept pouring in: now a leak via the House Un-American Activities Committee concerning the pro-Nazi inclination of the French consulate staff in Chicago;[63] now a report from the Military Intelligence Division of the War Department on the arrival in the United States of French "technicians";[64] now a Justice Department memorandum on the currency manipulations of Laval's agents in the United States;[65] now an ONI dossier on the Vichy propaganda coming from the consulate in Los Angeles;[66] now an FBI record of the extramural interests of the embassy personnel.[67]

So much enterprise; and yet, from the perspective of the State Department, the pickings were meager indeed. The rift within the French diplomatic community was in fact something of an open secret.[68] In general this division can be viewed as one between the political, Vichy appointees and the career diplomats; or, to put it another way, between those who, within France, had hailed the armistice, and those who, outside France, had deplored it. The first group consisted of Henry-Haye and his two personal assistants, Colonel Bertrand Vigne, the counselor of the embassy, and Charles Brousse, the press attaché (sometimes referred to behind their backs as Bouvard and Pécuchet). The second included, it seemed, the air and naval attachés, the assistant military and naval attachés, and the first secretary, Baron James Baeyens. Their guiding light appeared to be Jacques Dumaine, the former counselor, who had quarreled violently with Henry-Haye over the proposed withdrawal of

French citizenship from Raoul de Roussy de Sales, and had been transferred to Rio de Janeiro. There he was able to maintain contact with his old colleagues and to reassure them that their views were echoed in the Latin American embassy staffs.[69]

The evidence thus accumulated gave abundant testimony to the seriousness of the split. Out of this large corpus of material one report in particular commands interest, as its very title exposes the intentions of the American administration: "Report on a possible 'middle party' of opinion in the French diplomatic corps." The search, which was to occupy the next two years, was on for a "third force," neither offensively Vichyite nor embarrassingly Gaullist. The report's conclusions about the members of this group were that, while they did not carry much weight in international politics at the present moment, "after the war they might well prove to be a useful link between the democracies and the Germanophobe body of opinion in France which will never wholeheartedly support General de Gaulle."[70]

That fairly reflected the strengths and limitations of the American hope in a "middle party." Undeniably such a group existed, and, given the continuity in some quarters of the professional diplomatic corps from Vichy to the Fourth Republic, some of its members did subsequently become prominent figures.[71] But during the war it was the experience of all Frenchmen in the United States, and not only the diplomats, that a positive choice had to be made among the available leaders, Pétain and de Gaulle in the Vichy years, de Gaulle and General Giraud subsequently. One member of the group, Henri Hoppenot, more agile than most, managed to choose all three in succession. He passed from being Vichy's minister in Uruguay in 1941 to de Gaulle's delegate in the United States in 1944 via a short spell with Giraud's military mission in the United States in 1943.[72] As a whole, the "middle party" only had the option of working for Vichy or of resigning, as did Maurice Garreau-Dombasle, the commercial attaché in 1940, and Hervé Alphand, the financial attaché in 1941 (he became ambassador to the United States in 1956), and as did virtually the entire group, including Léon Marchal, the new counselor of the embassy, when Laval returned to power in April 1942.[73] Garreau-Dombasle and Alphand enthusiastically embraced Gaullism; Marchal, more befitting a member of a "middle party," did so rather more hesitantly; and Baeyens simply enrolled in the American army.

That only left, once again, Henry-Haye. In the light of all this it is easy to imagine the exasperation with which Hull and Welles confronted him, presiding over a rump embassy, and the embarrassment with which, undislodged, he faced them. Once again the familiar litany of accusation, indignation, and scorn—in a parallel recital of which Leahy had participated in Vichy—was played out. In April 1942 Welles told Henry-Haye that the United States would, whenever it saw fit, deal with the local authorities in effective control of any part of the French empire, such as the Free French in Brazzaville.[74] In

May Hull told him that the United States would never enter into any negotiations with Laval over the French possessions in the Caribbean.[75] In August Welles told him that it was "only human and reasonable" for the American people to harbor grave suspicions about the activities of the French embassy.[76] Finally, on 29 October Welles told him, in connection with a report Henry-Haye had received about an imminent American invasion of North Africa that he could hardly be expected to pay attention to every little rumor that was circulating at such a time.[77] When the invasion did take place, Franco-American relations were sundered, the Germans occupied the whole of France, and for the first time Henry-Haye and his associates were treated as enemy aliens, partly by way of reprisal for the German capture of American officials at Vichy (which, Henry-Haye notes as the crowning irony of his mission, would not have occurred had the American government given Pétain enough notice for him to take precautions).[78]

There now opened the most dispiriting episode of Henry-Haye's entire stay in the United States. For over a year he and his associates were interned in Hershey, Pennsylvania: a humiliating transfer, since the town was little more than a memorial to a great American chocolate manufacturer.[79] In its leisured pace of life, its detachment from the political world, its hotels, its popularity as a resort, this quaint little town bore a curious resemblance to prewar Vichy. But it did not thereby prove any more pleasing to Henry-Haye who tried, through his supposed friends the Spanish ambassador, the Swiss minister, and William Bullitt, to secure from the State Department some alleviation of conditions, fewer guards, perhaps, or more rounds of golf. However, the responsible official, Assistant Secretary of State Breckinridge Long, remained deaf to most of those pleas, arguing that the American diplomats now interned by the Germans lived under rather more straitened circumstances.[80] Subsequent visitors to Hershey remarked on the advancing demoralization among the "guests," the quarrels, the fights, the broken marriages, as well as various other "sordid" and "lurid" details of life there that could not, it seemed, be decently put down on paper.[81] Meanwhile, Charles Brousse, the former press attaché, though once Henry-Haye's closest collaborator, was now conducting his own campaign against him, compiling memoranda, for eventual delivery to the French authorities, that documented Henry-Haye's "traitorous" and "pro-American" activities.[82] Those memoranda which, now as then, would have made most interesting reading have unfortunately not survived. They were in any case only one item in a long catalog of misfortunes ensuring that Henry-Haye ended the war in the surprising condition of being unwelcome in both France and the United States.

He was returned to France in February 1944; but in December, with an American army on French soil, he sent a plaintive message to the American administration, begging to be allowed back into the United States, "in recognition of his irreproachable attitude during the most difficult period of Franco-

American relations when carrying out the thankless mission of French ambassador to the United States."[83]

Henry-Haye's problems in the United States ranged far beyond diplomacy. There was also the matter of his public image. For the American public he was an object of suspicion not merely on account of the regime he represented but also through his own personal contributions. He might well have been expected to enter the lists on behalf of his government's policies and to advocate sending American relief supplies to the unoccupied zone of France. But sometimes his enthusiasm deflected his judgment. He had the misfortune publicly to assert that such supplies would never be taken across the demarcation line into the occupied zone of France[84] only a short time after the publication of a dispatch from Vichy to the effect that that was precisely what was happening: food was being requisitioned to be sent to Paris.[85]

More seriously, on 5 December 1940, he directly criticized American behavior in a speech in New York. He attacked the suggestion that diplomatic relations should be broken off between Vichy and the United States, and went on to complain that Vichy was not being properly understood by most Americans. Pétain, he went on, was being vilified by the Germans, Italians, and British, and the American press was following suit. He then added the gratuitous comment that the French defeat of 1940 had been partly caused by American policy in the 1920s—the abandonment of the League of Nations, the indifference toward French security at the Washington Naval Conference, and the opposition to France's occupation of the Ruhr.[86] This drew forth an angry rebuke from the *New York Sun*, which editorialized, not entirely justly, that such criticism was singularly inappropriate from one who had himself opposed the League of Nations and had sought to maintain peace through a rapprochement with Germany, rather than through collective security.[87]

Finally, Henry-Haye appeared to wish to drive a wedge between Britain and the United States. When the RAF bombed munitions factories in the Paris area, he made, according to the *Washington Post*, a great display of his anguish "inside and outside the State Department."[88] He thus secured wide publicity for his indignation, even though the department, like most of the press, understood and approved of the bombing. And that publicity could prove dangerous, as Arthur Krock, then a greatly favored Washington correspondent, pointed out in his column in the *New York Times*. For he had detected signs, "even among strong supporters of the anti-Axis war," of regret and disapproval of the bombing that threatened "to destroy the effects of this government's policy towards Vichy." Without sharing those feelings himself, he added that they merited consideration, "because it is of the utmost importance that no division be created between this country and Great Britain."[89]

Henry-Haye's lack of caution might nonetheless still have been tolerated as the defensive response of a beleaguered ambassador. More alarming, because more sinister, were some allegations, made within a month of his arrival, that he was at the center of an espionage ring. These allegations arose initially from the tension between the Vichy embassy and the Gaullist or uncommited exiles.[90] The evidence of sour relations between the two, and of improper Vichyite efforts to bring dissenters into line (by, for example, threats of reprisals against their families in France), served at this juncture only to fortify an already widespread American distrust of foreigners in general, who were revealed to be subversive, and of Frenchmen in particular, who seemed only to quarrel among themselves. So the isolationist press abused the French exiles as harbingers of disorder,[91] while the interventionist press vilified Vichy's officials as Hitler's mannequins.[92]

In 1940 and early 1941 that was as far as the allegations went. Henry-Haye was not yet associated in the public mind with anything actually illegal. On the contrary, it was a perfectly legitimate diplomatic enterprise to attempt to get food supplies sent in to Vichy, although they might finish up in German hands, as it was to try to unblock the frozen French funds, although they too might be misused. True, the break-ins at the headquarters of France Forever and the British-American Ambulance Corps, like the threats and intimidation directed at individual Frenchmen, had suggested a more unconventional approach; and the Gaullists and their sympathizers were quick to advertise their suspicions.[93] Jacques de Sieyès, de Gaulle's personal representative in the United States, when in London on a visit to report progress, told newspapermen that Nazi agents were doing their level best to halt the flow of Frenchmen, Americans, and French-Americans to the Free French forces in Africa: "Their favourite method," he observed, "is to bring pressure to bear on the Vichy Embassy to make it take the matter up with the United States Government, which does not recognize the Free French force officially."[94] A week later Edgar Ansel Mowrer assured readers of the *Chicago Daily News* that "the attempt of the Vichy Fascists to 'control' the activities of such eminent French people as Eve Curie, Jules Romains, André Géraud (Pertinax) and Raoul [de] Roussy de Sales, would find most Americans ready to rise in their defense."[95] One such eminent Frenchman, not yet himself a Gaullist, de Roussy de Sales, was moved to write a letter to the *New York Herald Tribune*, where he outlined his fears that he and others might "be required to join a French *bund* in America to prove our loyalty . . . The project opens curious possibilities not the least unpleasant of which will be . . . to make all Frenchmen automatically suspicious to the Americans and suspicious to one another."[96]

Yet for all its high drama, this was still really only an émigrés' argument. The fiercest polemics were conducted by Frenchmen themselves, or by their colleagues in the American literary community. Thus a statement was released on 27 October 1940 signed by, among others, Robert Sherwood, Elmer Rice, Edna St. Vincent Millay, Lewis Mumford, Van Wyck Brooks, and Maxwell Anderson, calling on their countrymen "to beware of the men of Vichy who now spread the virus of totalitarianism in America." Its theme was that an unbearable strain was being placed upon the traditional, sentimental bonds between France and the United States, once both members of "the worldwide free republic of letters." Now, however, "a new kind of Frenchman has appeared in our midst to play upon our traditional loyalties and friendships . . . He possesses the charm, the skill, the subtlety, the finesse of his predecessors: but he no longer speaks for France. He speaks for his German masters and for those politicians who have sought to cover up their weakness, degradation, and even disloyalty by accepting the doctrine and policy of their masters."[97]

While the intellectuals thus engaged themselves, stressing the grander spiritual cause at stake, the more particular debate over Henry-Haye's activities in the United States proceeded apace. The indignant denials were issued: according to de Roussy de Sales, Henry-Haye sent word "that he understood my feelings perfectly, that he knew I was a good patriot, and that if he received instructions for the 'effective control' of Frenchmen over here, he had neither the means nor the intention of applying them."[98] Counteraccusations were filed, and most of the relevant issues were rapidly submerged in a mass of conflicting evidence and scholastic debate about the identity of Henry-Haye's supposed agents. The original story named one of them as Mussard, a former head of the Versailles police, but it turned out that Henry-Haye did not know him, and that the man in question was Jean Musa, a Swiss-born engineer who was in fact a recently naturalized American citizen. Similarly, another had been named as Paul Guichard, a legendary and, to some, sinister head of the Paris municipal police, but that man, it turned out, was almost seventy, had never visited the United States, and was living in peaceful retirement in France; the man in question was his son, Xavier.[99]

But at the end of August 1941 these rumors moved far beyond the insular world of French émigrés. The *New York Herald Tribune* now began to publish a series of page-long articles based, it said, on months of research by its reporter, Ansel E. Talbert; those articles, it also said, broke entirely fresh ground. Vichy's activities seemed now directly to threaten American individuals and institutions, and indeed the British war effort. In fact those articles had been planted with the *Herald Tribune* by Sir William Stephenson, the head of the British Security Coordination Service in New York, and were based not on months of journalistic investigation, but on a number of highly dangerous espionage operations undertaken by the fabled agent CYNTHIA, an American-born woman whose physical attractiveness, combined with her sharp intelligence, had been fashioned into a formidable Allied secret weapon.[100] Thus the articles had a marked propagandist design; and, like the rumors that had circulated the previous autumn, they appeared precisely when Britain's need for American involvement in the war was at its most acute. To discredit Vichy in the United States was to entice Americans still further toward the anti-Nazi cause.

The articles then are worth reviewing not so much for the "facts" that they disclosed, but for their calculated effect on American public opinion. On 31 August the *Herald Tribune* asserted that "advance plans of General Charles de Gaulle's ill-fated Dakar expedition were smuggled into the United States for transmission to Vichy last August in the gasoline tank of an automobile shipped from London to Hoboken aboard the Greek steamer, *Nea Hellas*. Also in the tank were lists of French officers and pilots under arms against Germany as part of the Free French Movement." Henry-Haye pointed out in rebuttal that he at least was not in the United States when the Dakar assault took place, but added, "I recall that Dakar is still French and will remain so. Any project about Dakar is not in connection with Germany but with France." On 1 September, the *Herald Tribune* accused him of an attempt to persuade the Western Union Telegraph Company to erect a radio station on St. Pierre, the tiny French colony off Newfoundland, and of offering the company a long-term concession to do so; Henry-Haye replied that the initiative had come from Western Union and the rejection from the embassy, not vice versa. On 2 September, the *Herald Tribune* reported an unsuccessful attempt by Vichy agents, including Musa, "to gain possession of blueprints and plans of the improved Bren gun, mainstay of British invasion defenses." Henry-Haye blustered and claimed that the Bren gun specifications were "known all over the world," while Musa, on the other hand, admitted that he had sought the rights to the gun, but for American manufacture, and that "instead of blocking the production of them here, he had tried every way he knew to achieve that end, for the American and British governments."[101]

How easy it now became for those who believed the *Herald Tribune*'s charges to conclude that the maintenance of American relations with Vichy was not only worthless, but actually damaging. The *New Republic*, which had earlier called Henry-Haye the "spiritual leader of the Fifth Column" in the United States, seemed vindicated.[102] Drew Pearson, scooped for once, responded within ten days by announcing that certain consulates of Vichy (and Hungary) had taken on Fifth-Column work, and even some of the staff engaged in it, from the expelled Nazi consulates.[103] A group of former American residents in France, veterans of the First World War, addressed a protest to Henry-Haye that distinguished Vichy from the real France, "France who was betrayed, France who suffers."[104] Henry Torrès, the French criminal lawyer, arrived in the United States to declare that he was "greatly surprised to find already operating in the Western hemisphere, with the aid of Vichy passports and diplomatic officers, men who were revealed by my investigations in Europe as more to blame than the German army for the fall of France."[105] Thus the "lessons of France" were hammered home once again. But it was the *Herald Tribune* itself that expressed most clearly the connection between the accusations leveled at Henry-Haye and the American administration's policy toward Vichy:

The ambassador speaks as representative of the French people, a
friendly power; yet the government he represents has repeatedly done
everything it could to promote the German victory which the United
States has declared to be profoundly inimical to its vital interest, and to
embarrass the British resistance to which the United States is pledged to
render every aid in its power . . . The basic ambiguities of Vichy itself
magnify many times every seeming ambiguity in the activities of its
agents abroad. Vichy does not occupy the position of a sovereign government with a defined policy, and it is only dangerous for others so to
regard it.[106]

Therein lies the real significance of Henry-Haye's mission to the United
States. Even down to the ambiguities he was an ambassador relentlessly
faithful to his government, and that fidelity was to be the source of his own
personal tragedy. For many of the mere functionaries of the Vichy regime
would survive its demise; none of the true believers did. As Alexis Leger, a
former permanent secretary general of the French Foreign Office, then in exile
in the United States, commented, on the news of Henry-Haye's appointment:
"The Vichy government has been perfectly honest with the United States
government in sending M. Henry-Haye as its representative. This man typifies
all the tendencies, the ideals, and the methods of working of his Government."[107] Thus the American administration, laboring to maintain an increasingly artificial distinction between the tendencies of Laval and of Pétain, found
itself inescapably bound to deal with a representative of Laval as Vichy's
ambassador, even as Pétain found himself bound to readmit Laval to his
cabinet. But at the same time, to a growing body of American opinion, the
meaningful distinction was not between Pétain and Laval, or even between
Vichy and Germany, but between Vichy and the Allies; and Henry-Haye with
his alleged circle of acquaintances, seemed to justify this view. Indeed, by one
irony upon which he does not dwell in his memoirs, he served to strengthen the
appeal of Gaullism.

CHAPTER 5

FRENCH CURRENTS IN
THE UNITED STATES,
1940–1941

Whatever else he may have been, Henry-Haye was never the super-intendent of French intellectual and cultural life in the United States. That office was entrusted to others, many of whom vied with one another for the post; and since their struggles had political and, more distantly, diplomatic consequences, they require some consideration here, outside the specialist fields in which they were conducted. To kindle interest in French culture was also to arouse sympathy for France, and that sympathy might be translated into political action.

But in 1940 the United States must have seemed barren soil indeed for the cultivation of any partiality for France. The French defeat, as assimilated into instant propaganda, did its work. French writers of such diverse persuasions as André Maurois, Jules Romains, René de Chambrun, "André Simon," Henri Torrès, "Pertinax," Robert de Saint-Jean, Jacques Maritain, and Albert Gué-rard, seemed for a time to be joining that insistent chorus that explained the event by reference to internal flaws.[1] The military defeat itself, the defection from the British alliance, and, still more damaging from the American per-spective, the eager embrace of alien, if neighboring, political forms, all these suggested a culture that had lost its vitality.

The unhappy evolution of 1940 was the final justification for a dwindling interest in French culture that had started long ago. One, perhaps the only, reliable index of American "isolationism" was the steady reduction in the teaching of foreign languages in American schools. Between the wars Ameri-can education acquired a more practical bent, emphasizing the social and engineering sciences to the exclusion of linguistic or literary skills, and fewer and fewer young Americans acquired the rudiments of any foreign language, with, however, one notable exception. In 1940–41, no doubt as a gesture of hemispheric solidarity, teachers of French at various state colleges were being offered six months' paid leave of absence, to go to Mexico, there to acquire the facility to teach their pupils a rather more useful language, Spanish.[2]

The French language, like French culture, never entirely died out. There were in the United States, according to one estimate, 135,000 people born in France, 340,000 with at least one French parent, and a further million of French descent. But neither their situation nor their acquired tastes prompted any concern with French political life. The oldest French communities, in Louisiana and California, nourished a sentimental pride in their origins, but shared the prevailing confusion about French politics. Their newspapers, *Le Courier de la Nouvelle Orleans*, or *Le Courrier du Pacifique*, tended to adjust their political allegiances to whatever could be seen, at that distance, as the dominant political force. Thus evading the most heated political questions, they could reserve their attention for local themes, the arts, and popular science.

France was even more remote from the thoughts of the French-speaking communities of New England, whose overriding loyalty was to their Canadian heritage. Their energies were devoted, as they had been for a century, to supporting the Catholic church and preserving their linguistic and cultural traditions from Anglo-Saxon encroachment. From Nashua, New Hampshire, and Woonsocket, Rhode Island, thunderbolts were hurled against any criticism of the Catholic church, any step toward assimilation, and, in time, against both of America's allies in the Second World War, Britain and Russia.[3] As for the rest of the country, while each major town could boast its French Chamber of Commerce and its French Veterans' Association, its *amicales* and its *mutuelles*, these cemented American, not French, loyalties. In 1939, when the French consulates summoned all those required for military service in the homeland, only 5 percent responded, the remainder placing themselves, a contemporary noted, "in an improper military position."[4]

Into this world, where French culture had been reduced to protective clothing, tourist attraction, or harmless pursuit, there now fled some real specimens of a still lively metropolitan culture: Antoine de Saint-Exupéry and Henri Bernstein, Geneviève Tabouis and Eve Curie, Alexis Leger and Fernand Léger. Old ties were renewed, with the appearance in Hollywood of Charles Boyer, Claudette Colbert, Jean Gabin, Michelle Morgan, René Clair, and Jean Renoir.[5] New ones were established, with the foundation in New York in February 1942 of the Ecole Libre des Hautes Etudes (affiliated with the New School of Social Research), a university in exile whose permanent faculty included Jacques Maritain and Claude Lévi-Strauss.[6] These men and women did not, all of them, agree on every contemporary issue; nor did they all relish public attention. Some, like the diplomat Alexis Leger, preferred relative anonymity, which in his case was accentuated by the pseudonymity of his poetic persona, Saint-John Perse.[7] But their mere presence on America soil, whatever else it said about French political life, did testify to the vitality of their beleaguered homeland's culture, even if that vitality was occasionally expended in harrowing political controversies, as it had been before the war and might be again once transplanted to the United States. Here the exiles did encounter barriers rather more formidable, if more hastily constructed, than the English language. Henry-Haye, and many lesser figures, had discovered quite early that to speak favorably of Pétain was to incur the charge of pro-

Nazism. An equivalent danger was presented to spokesmen for de Gaulle. For with a sovereign French government no longer in the war, what else could de Gaulle's movement be but the spearhead of a British assault on American neutrality, an interventionist Fifth Column?

These doubts were not confined to isolationists. An assistant secretary of state, Adolf Berle, saw in the exposure of Henry-Haye's entourage a carefully wrought British plot to secure American recognition of de Gaulle's movement (inveigling the FBI in the process) and thus precipitate the United States still further into the European cauldron, though he was uncertain whether it was "the settled policy of the British government or merely of some rather enthusiastic elements."[8] As the State Department official most in touch with both intelligence matters and foreign nationality groups, Berle was naturally suspicious. But his misgivings, widely shared and intensified as the war progressed, rested nonetheless upon a curious misapprehension. The British, we have seen, initially welcomed the American presence at Vichy and, cut off themselves from any official contact there, would actually have suffered from any reversal of American policy. The Free French, for their part, were hardly the creatures of the British war effort, and a great deal of British energy was spent on restraining, rather than sustaining, their impetuous actions. In 1941 in particular it seemed as if they were the true heirs of the Third Republic in bewildering and even hampering their formal ally. No more than the earlier Anglo-French Supreme War Council did the British recognition of de Gaulle's movement as representative of French wartime interests or the mission of General Edward Spears to de Gaulle's headquarters in London smooth the path of Anglo-French relations. Before turning to Gaullist activities within the United States, it will be useful to consider Gaullist relations with Britain.

By 1941 the initial honeymoon between de Gaulle and the British was plainly at an end. The Syrian campaign of June and July, involving British and Free French troops, had removed that area from Vichy's control, but also, foreseeably, from France's. De Gaulle was unhappy at the leniency of the armistice as well as the suggestion that the Syrians be awarded their independence.[9] Although his delegate general, Georges Catroux, did issue just such a proclamation at the end of September, de Gaulle had in the meantime responded with characteristic vigor to the British intrusion into French domestic arrangements. While on a tour of inspection of various Free French outposts he took the occasion to publicize his disagreements with the British, leaving, as Churchill commented, a "trail of Anglophobia behind him."[10] Then, on 26 August, de Gaulle gave an exclusive interview to the *Chicago Daily News* in which he made a number of startling observations calculated to dismay the British and, incidentally, irritate Anglo-American relations. He declared that he had offered the Americans the use by their aircraft of French bases in the Cameroons, Chad, and the Congo, adding, with impish Gallic wit, "and we shall not ask for any destroyers in return." He announced that the British were afraid of the French fleet, that they and the Americans had been badly compromised over the Indochina surrender, and that Britain was keeping open the lines of communication with Vichy to pave the way for an ultimate deal with Germany.[11]

This proved too much for Churchill. If the interview was authentic, he wrote to Eden, de Gaulle "has clearly gone off his head. This would be a very good riddance and will simplify our further course."[12] Although the *Daily Telegraph*, which received the interview, omitted the more offensive passages, nothing could be done to repair the immediate damage, and Churchill merely raged.[13] He refused to see de Gaulle before receiving an explanation for the interview.[14] He investigated the extent of the British subsidy to de Gaulle's movement and may have contemplated reducing it.[15] But, as would happen so often in these disputes, a tactful solution was found. De Gaulle insisted that the interview was full of misrepresentations and courteously listened to Churchill's sage advice to deal more cautiously with the press.[16] The independence of Syria and Lebanon was proclaimed, although de Gaulle characteristically suggested that it might only be provisional; and Churchill was forced to avow that, contrary to de Gaulle's suspicions, the British did not in fact covet those territories.[17]

Beyond these temporary diplomatic adjustments, however, a more fundamental issue had been raised: what was the administrative structure of de Gaulle's movement? Who was shaping Free French policy—politicians, generals, de Gaulle himself? How could it be shown to be properly representative of French democratic sentiment? A constitutional rearrangement in London was clearly required, and one was soon implemented with the establishment of the French National Committee in September, which had an intentionally conciliar rather than presidential composition.[18] But equally desirable, as an adjunct of this, was a respectable and responsible Gaullist presence in the United States, a need more pressing as the critical year of 1941 wore on, transforming an initially European conflict into a demonstrably global war.

The Free French in the United States provide an eerie reflection of their Vichy counterparts. Both groups had their internal wrangles; both labored under the same suspicion of subversion; both lacked, in American eyes, qualified, respectable leadership, and assumed, rather too easily, that once such a leader were found smooth relations with the American administration would automatically follow. The crucial difference between the two was that while it was the American government that sought to influence the composition of Vichy's representation, it was the British government that attempted to manipulate the Gaullists. The crucial similarity is that in both cases French realities ultimately asserted themselves against Anglo-Saxon management.

At the onset of 1941 the prospects of the Free French in the United States did not seem particularly bleak. France Forever, directed by the irrepressible

Eugene Houdry in Philadelphia, claimed to have attracted 4,000 subscribing members. Its organizers showed a certain flair for publicity by, for example, calling a meeting to protest against Vichy's anti-Semitic legislation,[19] and announcing that if Martinique were rallied by the Free French a naval base would at once be leased to the United States.[20] Beginning on Armistice Day, 1940, a Boston radio station, WRUC, made shortwave broadcasts, designed to counteract the effects of German and Vichy propaganda, and, according to Houdry, they were being heard all over France.[21] Reports soon appeared in newspapers that sympathy for the Free French was growing both in France and her empire.[22] And on 9 January 1941 de Gaulle attempted to weld his representation in the United States into a coherent force, giving his lieutenants responsibilities appropriate to their talents: Houdry would remain in charge of social functions; Maurice Garreau-Dombasle, the former commecial attaché at the Washington embassy, would deal with political, economic, and financial matters; and Jacques de Sieyès, the New York perfumery executive who had been de Gaulle's "personal representative" in the United States since July, would handle recruiting.[23]

But below the surface all manner of discontents simmered. However much enthusiasm the Free French might arouse in certain quarters, simply by virtue of their opposition to Vichy, there remained the bad odor of the Dakar debacle, only faintly dispelled by later triumphs in Equatorial Africa. The American administration stayed committed to Vichy, or several "Vichys," and thus unable, or reluctant, to enter into any engagements with what was, by design, a revolutionary body. And, more tellingly, there were increasingly visible signs of dissension within the French émigré community, which grew in importance insofar as they reflected upon de Gaulle's claim to speak for all of France. These divisions were later invoked by American officials as a reason for withholding a greater degree of recognition from the Free French; and it is as well, therefore, to cite the testimony, on this score, of more sympathetic observers. For example, Raoul de Roussy de Sales, the journalist and commentator who actually joined the Free French delegation in September 1941, though without any real devotion to the figure of de Gaulle, had earlier confided his misgivings in his diary. "The crux of the matter," he noted, "remains ideological, but even the most clear-sighted French do not want to admit this, and while denying the ideology they continue nevertheless to act ideologically." They remained "on the Right or on the Left, Monarchist or Communist." There could be, he concluded, "no grouping under such conditions, but only individual action."[24]

Henri de Kérillis, a former conservative deputy and editor of *L'Epoque*, moved in the opposite direction, but with similar reservations. He had begun as an ardent campaigner for de Gaulle in Canada and the United States. In 1943 he was to prove one of his most relentless critics, with the emergence of the rival figure of General Giraud.[25] But long before embarking on his odyssey, in a letter to de Gaulle on 17 February 1941, he had reflected, no less mournfully than de Roussy de Sales, on the disharmony within the French community, "the same, with but a shade of difference, as those we observed in our country."

> The little far off cells of the French family are suffering—one after the other or all together—from the terrible disease which wrought such havoc to the body and soul of the central family. Wherever there are twenty Frenchmen they fight between themselves. There are those for de Gaulle and those against him, those for him and against the British, those for the British and against him, those for Pétain, those for Weygand, and those for Laval. There are also the fools, the cowards, and those who are afraid. There is all and everything. The terrible tragedy has taught them nothing and has changed nothing.[26]

Such was the evidence from sympathetic observers. And de Gaulle himself was perfectly well aware of the centrifugal forces at work on the French nation. These ideological disputes were to him only the equivalent, on American soil, of the coincidental, German-imposed division of French territory, the assault on the empire, the fresh stimulus given to rival provincial loyalties, Basque, Breton, Fleming, all of them facets of a dwindling national ardor, "the willed disintegration of the homeland," as he wrote to de Roussy de Sales.[27] For what else had impelled him to define so precisely the authority of his henchmen at the beginning of the year but the internecine feud that persisted among them? Even then de Gaulle in London could not muster sufficient authority to control the Gaullists in New York. Within two days of each other, two of the parties to the internal Gaullist dispute, Garreau-Dombasle and de Sieyès, each sent messages to de Gaulle complaining about the activities of the other. On 19 May Garreau-Dombasle wired complaining that since de Sieyès's return from London, where he had conferred with de Gaulle, he now "declares everywhere that he is the only representative of Free France here and I am his employee."[28] On 21 May de Sieyès wired, complaining for his part that it was impossible to combine with Garreau-Dombasle "due to [his] personal ambition and [the] general lack of confidence in him."[29] A new recruit to Free France would arrive in New York in February 1941, not knowing under whose orders, de Sieyès's or Garreau-Dombasle's, to place himself.[30]

There is an evident parallel here with the exactly contemporary feud between Chautemps and Henry-Haye.[31] Like the internal Vichyite dispute, the internal Gaullist dispute was not merely a matter, as Lord Hankey thought, of "harmful squabbling."[32] Rather, it reflected different priorities. Garreau-Dombasle's field of operations was broadly in the public view, gathering support among Americans for the Gaullist cause and working closely with such American organizations as France Forever; that of de Sieyès, though seemingly more narrow, dealing as he was largely with matters of recruitment, was in fact more directly bound up with France's future in the outside world. The personal antagonism stemmed from a prior distribution of responsibility. As for the third partner in the Gaullist enterprise, Eugene Houdry, he too had his troubles. His creation, France Forever, was an American organization, largely composed of American citizens, and thus subject to all the constraints of the Neutrality Act, which forbade the contribution of funds for foreign belligerent purposes. That only left propaganda and relief (the purchase of ambulances, etc.) as outlets for American funds. Furthermore, those were, under American law, sharply distinct activities. As a member of the British embassy commented, surveying the whole situation: ". . . the State Department regard the General as an agency of His Majesty's Government. It is therefore illegal to solicit or receive money on his behalf but not illegal to give it to him if it is not solicited and not received on his behalf."[33] The effect of all this was to promote a proliferation of agencies and a dissipation of energies that actually hampered collective action. There was France Forever, which engaged in publicity and propaganda (here a Renoir exhibition, there boosting the sale of de Gaulle's writings); there was the Free French Relief Committee, which received funds from various sources, including France Forever, and sent ambulances and ambulance planes to the Free French forces in Africa,[34] or rather to a specially designated, supposedly independent body qualified to receive them.[35] But there was also, after the beginning of 1941, a dissident group that left France Forever to found United Free France, with the intention of concentrating less on spending money on propaganda and more on sending funds to de Gaulle, though how this was to be done without either rivaling the Free French Relief Committee or breaking the law was not immediately obvious.[36]

This was the state of affairs when, in early summer, de Gaulle launched a thorough reorganization. Opposition to Vichy had nowhere crystallized into wholehearted support of de Gaulle; what support he had remained splintered and rancorous. There coexisted rival anti-Vichy organizations and rival Gaullist ones. The respectable Francophile centers—La Chambre de commerce, L'Association des anciens combattants, l'Hôpital français, la Légion d'honneur, l'Alliance française, l'Institut français—were stubbornly immune to Gaullist penetration.[37] The intellectual exiles—Romains, Saint-Exupéry, Maritain—were as yet unorganized and jealously guarding their political independence. Confronted with this disorder, de Gaulle's response was swift and emphatic. He chose, in effect, to subordinate social to diplomatic activities, to press his claims on the American administration rather than the American public. He had earlier tried a different approach. In February 1941 he had sent Lieutenant Gérard de Saint-André, who had worked in his press office in London, to New York to work with Garreau-Dombasle and France Forever, studying "what could be done to improve our relations with the United States press, to furnish it with photographs . . . and to organise our cinema propaganda."[38] But despite a certain exposure to the media,[39] his mission bore little fruit. So in May de Gaulle chose another tactic.

He first detached the social activities of France Forever, guided from Philadelphia, from the political agitation of a transformed Free French delegation, based in New York. He did so, however, with due concern for Houdry's feelings. France Forever remained the only Gaullist organization officially recognized by de Gaulle. As he wired to de Sieyès, "we should remember Houdry's sincere and disinterested effort, and we do not wish to give the impression that we disavow him when making the new arrangements which are necessary." De Gaulle merely wished that newly composed committees be composed solely of Frenchmen. It was, he declared, "of utmost importance that all Frenchmen who refuse to be collaborators be united."[40]

Along with the victory of New York over Philadelphia went that of de Sieyès over Garreau-Dombasle. Acting on instructions from de Gaulle, de Sieyès resigned in early June from the executive committee of France Forever (though remaining an ordinary member), while Garreau-Dombasle resigned from the Free French delegation. The instructions to Garreau-Dombasle reveal precisely what was in de Gaulle's mind: first, he was disappointed that the many important French personalities on American soil had not rallied to the Free French banner; second, the current Free French representation had had markedly little impact, and key American decisions—like the breaking of the British blockade of continental France, and the internment of French ships in American harbors—had been made without consultation, thus reflecting on Free France's claim to represent French resistance. Though de Gaulle had other criticisms, of, for example, the poor showing in fund-raising and recruitment, those initial complaints remained of primary significance, illustrating equally his nationalist fervor and his political judgment.[41] He did not have a great deal of interest in American public opinion, whose influence on governmental policy he correctly regarded as slight; and cultural and propaganda activities could for the most part be safely entrusted to the gentleman and lady amateurs of France Forever. But if he could command the support of all the influential and respected French figures, then, having made good his claim to represent all the forces of resistance, he would have a solid base from which to influence policy-making.

This primarily political effort required a more professional approach than had hitherto been adopted, and de Sieyès's victory over Garreau-Dombasle was to prove unrewarding. For in the same period that that feud was going on, and influenced no doubt by its persistent acrimony, de Gaulle decided to send a special mission to the United States to organize a new delegation. In the second week in June he wired both Garreau-Dombasle and de Sieyès that they were on no account to publicize their personal disagreements, or the resolution that had been found, but were instead to await the arrival with fresh instructions of René Pleven, a businessman based before the war in England, an associate of Jean Monnet, and one of the earliest recruits to Free France.[42]

Pleven's mission was, in part, the fruit of de Gaulle's disturbed reflections upon the limited achievements of his American outpost. But it was also, in part, the result of British pressure. British officials had, from the very beginning, been monitoring Free French activities, and, providing the facilities for communication between Carlton Gardens and New York, they were equally well informed about the damaging internal rifts. They had in addition reports from Washington about the unenthusiastic American response, and indeed the misgivings of British embassy officials themselves about the current Free French representation. May 1941 was, here as elsewhere, a critical period, when the collaborationist tendencies of Vichy, even in Laval's absence, began to appear;[43] and the British and Free French alike sought to exploit the American administration's temporary disenchantment with Vichy.

The British feared that they would be dragged along in the wake of American policy, unable to pursue an independent line. On 9 May Major Desmond Morton, of Churchill's personal entourage, wrote a long letter to W. H. B. Mack at the Foreign Office outlining his fear that, having once had a distinctive policy toward Vichy, "now . . . we are apparently committed to follow U.S.A. policy, whatever that might be"; and he observed that "the State Department may indeed be helping Weygand and Pétain to achieve their heart's desire, to avoid further armed action and to live as comfortably as possible until the war is won by someone else."[44] A week later Herbert Somerville-Smith of the Foreign Office noted that "if the Americans attempt to supply . . . Vichy territories . . . without doing something on the same scale for the Free French colonies, the de Gaulle movement may well be killed."[45] Finally, in a discussion at the State Department on 21 May, Lord Halifax learned that Hull "thought it was better for the United States to walk down one side of the street while we walked on the other."[46] That, commented one Foreign Office official, seemed "the sheerest balderdash, meaningless, unreal, and evasive. The State Department can perfectly well find a way of walking on both sides if they really try, and I hope we will use present opportunities to get on their tails about it."[47]

Thus did British and Gaullist aims converge. Pleven's mission had its lighter moments, its interludes of *opéra bouffe*, but even those had some serious implications. One in particular threatened the reputation of the entire enterprise. It concerned the activities of a New York businessman and banker, Alfred Bergman, an extraordinarily gifted self-publicist with pretensions as an intelligence agent. His vaunted contacts in the European chancelleries enabled him to write, under the name "Peter Markham," a book on the impending crisis that reeked of "inside information."[48] Thereafter he kept up a vigorous, if one-sided, correspondence with leading figures in the British and American governments and, through Henri de Kérillis, the Free French movement. He was therefore in 1941 one of the most active, though unofficial and amateur, Gaullist propagandists. In June he wrote to Eden, with whom he claimed great intimacy, advising him to recognize the Free French as the government of France and install de Gaulle in Syria, "as that would probably be followed by recognition from the United States."[49] In July he wrote to Churchill warning him of the great mistake he was making in not recognizing de Gaulle.[50] Through Harold Ickes and Eleanor Roosevelt he sent a continuous stream of information and advice to Roosevelt, most of it along the lines of his belief in June 1940 that Russia would shortly be entering the war on the side of the Allies, or his recommendation in February 1941 that the United States should occupy Morocco.[51]

An innocent diversion, it might seem. But no sooner had René Pleven arrived in the United States than he discovered that more devious means, of questionable legality, were being employed. In April Bergman had made an agreement with de Gaulle's previous emissary, Lieutenant de Saint-André, under which if any French assets were unfrozen by the American Treasury, a commission would be paid to Bergman.[52] The Free French headquarters in London had not been informed of this, though it turned out that de Sieyès had lent his approval, influenced no doubt by Bergman's insistence that American recognition of Free France was just around the corner.[53] Pleven moved swiftly, and within a month de Saint-André was ordered to active service in Africa (and shortly afterwards died in action in Syria).[54] De Sieyès was soon relegated to a comparatively lowly position in the Free French hierarchy. And Bergman was thereafter ostracized by the Free French, though he continued to make a nuisance of himself to higher officials. "Pleven represents big business," he warned Ickes, "I feel we should go a bit slow on him. He is seeing Lord Halifax which is very much up his alley."[55] Although Bergman declined to explain why a Free French representative should not consult the British ambassador, Ickes nonetheless passed that ominous signal on to Dean Acheson at the State Department.[56] On 1 August Bergman wrote to Eden ("My dear Captain Eden") threatening to take legal action against the Free French on a charge of fraud, insisting that Pleven be recalled, and concluding, "Stupidity and personal ambition by small men has gotten the World to where it is today. Pleven may get away with such methods in Africa but not here."[57] On 4 December, by now desperate, he wrote a confidential letter to Roosevelt, again attacking Pleven, a "great snake in our midst," and claiming that "the Gestapo now knows all [and] . . . is . . . in control of the de Gaulle movement here." That insight he had, he claimed, from de Kérillis, "the Churchill of France."[58]

Such episodes, trivial in themselves, certainly made Pleven's task in the United States more difficult. They also shed some light on the nature of the Gaullist movement there. Personal rivalries, political ambitions, and sheer economic greed were fascinatingly intertwined in a movement that commanded respect even as it aroused suspicion. Pleven's assignment was thus twofold: to mend the cracks in the Gaullist delegation and then to secure a greater degree of recognition and support from the American administration. Questions of personnel had to be resolved before the question of function could be tackled. As a result there was a remarkable contrast between the Gaullist representatives at the beginning and end of 1941. Gone by the end of the year were the individual, excitable enthusiasts, who had virtually appointed themselves after the French armistice, Garreau-Dombasle, de Sieyès, de Kérillis, and above all Bergman. They had either resigned, been dismissed, sent abroad, or invited to use their talents in journalism rather than politics. In their place stood a disciplined, semiprofessional corps of politicians, administrators, and public figures: Adrien Tixier, the chairman of the delegation; Professor Raoul Aglion, the secretary; Etienne Boegner, originally titular head, then—with Tixier—joint negotiator with the American government; and Raoul de Roussy de Sales, in charge of information. The choice reflected a concern for professionalism, and, as important, a desire to avoid any taint of association with the Third Republic.[59] Boegner, the son of the pastor, was a businessman with international contacts, most recently the representative in the United States of Optique et Précision de Navallois. Tixier by contrast was a Catholic trade unionist, who had risen to prominence as Albert Thomas's adviser in the International Labor Organization: his appointment was aimed in part at those who saw in Gaullism a reactionary force, as Tixier's less cordial associates suspected.[60] De Roussy de Sales joined only with grave misgivings. As he told Pleven, "I am not a Gaullist and I will probably never be one."[61] Why then did he join? His reasons speak volumes about the limited options open to Frenchmen in the United States: "A combination of facts brought me to this decision: the difficulty of continually refusing to associate myself with anything; the vague hope that the present orientation of the de Gaulle movement, which does not particularly attract me, can be slightly modified; the even vaguer hope of being of some service to the cause of that sad firm called France."[62]

De Gaulle now had at his disposal a carefully composed team with, to him at least, many desirable features. They lacked any intimate association with the defunct Third Republic: thus Pierre Cot, air minister under the Popular Front, was confined to an unpublicized role in France Forever, and kept out of the Gaullist delegation.[63] They were free also of any tie, however short lived, with Vichy: thus no more than Garreau-Dombasle did Hervé Alphand, late of the Washington embassy, appear in the lists. As de Gaulle cabled Pleven, Alphand "is brilliant but lacks perseverence. [An] intimate of Bonnet, he is the type whose one anxiety is a rapid career."[64] Most important of all, the delegates did not represent the exact choice of the British government, which, however closely it followed Pleven's progress, had still to remain discreet in volunteering its aid. As Morton wrote to Robert Speaight, of the Foreign Office's

French department, if de Gaulle ever "knew Pleven had discussed with the British the possible composition of the Free French agency in America he would have one of those hysterical outbursts."[65] Lord Hankey went further, arguing that de Gaulle would "certainly refuse to listen to our advice on the subject out of pique, so much so, in fact, that if there is anyone whom we think would be particularly unsuitable it might almost be worthwhile deliberately putting his name forward."[66]

Only on one issue were all parties, including the State Department, in complete agreement: it was crucial to avoid all those who had been part of the quarrelsome and self-defeating New York clique.[67] De Roussy de Sales, who stood aloof, and Tixier, who stood apart, evidently qualified. But aside from such an obvious prerequisite, other goals were more controversial. Those of the Foreign Office were to neutralize Gaullism as a politically distinct force. If the Free French were to make any headway with the State Department, so the British argument ran, they should import into the United States figures of reputable, if not exalted, standing, early supporters of de Gaulle, who had worked, and preferably fought, with him in Africa or the Near East.[68] The impression to convey was of military expertise, not doctrinal rectitude.

But a glance at de Gaulle's entourage served only to reveal the aridness of the land. All the leading figures had to be set aside. General Catroux spoke no English (and had a German wife); Admiral Muselier could not be spared from his fleet and was already suspected by de Gaulle of less than absolute loyalty to him; and Admiral Georges Thierry d'Argenlieu was always required by de Gaulle for special missions.[69] Some younger men, like Captains Philippe Auboyneau and Jean Gayral, might have served, but de Gaulle was reluctant to let junior naval officers undertake a mission of such delicacy as heading the Gaullist delegation in the United States.[70] As Morton, that astute observer of Gaullism, noted: "No doubt it would be admirable if we could get several young, sincere, and clever enthusiasts to back up the head of the mission in America. It would be even more admirable if we could find two or three persons answering to this description who could be used by de Gaulle anywhere. De Gaulle's great difficulty apart from his own temperament, [which is] partly the cause of [it], is his lack of adequate recruits for the higher places."[71]

Pleven had hoped, in the United States, "to find a Phoenix."[72] But that fabulous creature was ever elusive; and so it was with a distinct air of resignation that the British learned of de Gaulle's final selection. De Roussy de Sales seemed to them a recruit of doubtful merit since, as Nevile Butler wrote from Washington, he "has sat on the fence for so long that his reputation here has rather suffered."[73] As for Tixier and Boegner, their relative positions, as chairman and deputy, seemed the reverse of what was desirable. Boegner, according to Sir Robert Campbell, was strongly Anglophile, and had established good working relations with the British embassy and the State Department. Tixier, however, though "an able administrator and a forceful character . . . may be lacking in some of the diplomatic qualities . . . for such a position." His previous political affiliations and markedly left-wing views would not help him at the State Department; and, moreover, when in Geneva with the ILO, Tixier "was apt to view problems from a purely French point of view and I doubt whether we could collaborate so cordially and confidentially with him as we could with Boegner."[74] But, as W. H. B. Mack pointed out, those supposed flaws in Tixier's character were "just the qualities which appeal to General de Gaulle." Boegner had, by contrast, "two demerits in the General's eyes." He was "anglophile," and he had "spoken strongly and independently to de Gaulle."[75]

It came as no surprise to the British when the French delegation, and Tixier in particular, began to prove intractable. "I fear," wrote R. E. Barclay of the British embassy, "that at the present moment there is a good deal of friction. What we should like is that Tixier should stay at New York, run the office and deal with his compatriots who will certainly cause him plenty of trouble, and that Boegner should spend most of his time here and be the link with the State Department and ourselves. This would also suit the State Department who much prefer Boegner to Tixier."[76] R. M. Makins, back from a short visit to the United States, had similar misgivings. Boegner had confided to him his doubts about some of de Gaulle's advisers, and indeed about his own position in the Free French movement. Tixier, on the other hand, had come across as a "clever and perfectly sincere man, with strong ideological views and a talent for intrigue"; and Makins questioned whether either of them was capable of pulling together the rather disparate Gaullist threads in the United States.[77] But already by the beginning of December, it seemed too late for the British to exert any further influence. Tixier, now free of the International Labor Conference in New York, arrived in Washington ready to take over all negotiations with the State Department, although these had, in his absence, been conducted by Boegner and de Roussy de Sales with a certain measure of success.[78]

So much then for quesions of personnel. In this rather limited sense, one may well speak of de Gaulle's personal authority over the Free French community in the United States. It was not, as it later became popular to assert, dictatorial or arbitrary control; in this instance Pleven himself exercised some influence of his own. But it was personal, inasmuch as it reflected those distinctive concerns of de Gaulle that transcended the more pressing objective of defeating Germany: to cut himself free of any association with past and present French regimes, and to advertise his independence of the Anglo-Saxon powers. It therefore enabled the American administration to generalize from its experience of the Gaullists in the United States about the characteristics of their movement as a whole; and that experience, beginning with Pleven's initial efforts, was not a particularly happy one.

One of the surprising features of Pleven's mission to the United States was that the very assets that had commended him to de Gaulle and the British worked against him. He had been appointed largely because his term of duty with Monnet at the Anglo-French Purchasing Commission in New York had given him a reputation for decency, patriotism, and administrative skills. He therefore returned in June 1941 with an entrée into American official circles. Already from London Anthony Biddle, then on liaison with the governments in exile, had written several letters to Roosevelt commending Pleven, "a serious, sincere, courageous, and intelligent patriot," and hoping that the president would receive him.[79] Now Pleven's friend, the under secretary of war, John J. McCloy, brought him in to meet Stimson, who was deeply impressed with him: "a man whose attitude tended strongly to restore one's faith in the French people. . . . [H]is description of how universal the loyalty of the French people was towards the victory of Great Britain was very encouraging."[80] At the Treasury Henry Morgenthau was also greatly taken with Pleven, and spoke warmly of him to all his friends and colleagues. To Felix Frankfurter, for example, he described him as "a very able, charming Frenchman," to talk to whom "was like a breath of fresh air."[81] Morgenthau also secured an appointment for Pleven with Harry Hopkins,[82] and wrote to Roosevelt advising him to meet Pleven on the grounds that he was an authority on French Equatorial Africa, and had some "ideas about how Dakar could be taken."[83] Pleven had in addition extensive talks with the secretary of the navy, Colonel Knox, Vice-President Henry Wallace, and Senator Claude Pepper of Florida, of the Foreign Relations Committee.[84] He took a brief holiday at Walter Lippmann's summer home in Maine.[85]

From this catalog of the well-disposed there was one notable absence, the State Department; and within it one conspicuous demurral—from Roosevelt: "I cannot see Pleven. The matter has been taken up before," he curtly wrote to Morgenthau.[86] The faults were on all sides. There was a guarded conservatism about the State Department at that time, which made it an object of suspicion elsewhere in the administration. Hence Morgenthau's sarcastic description of the European Desk officer who had interviewed Pleven as "that great liberal democrat Ray Atherton,"[87] or Pleven's own complaint that "Welles is always very cold."[88] But it is also worthwhile to explore the shortcomings of Pleven himself, a man widely believed to be demanding American recognition of the Free French, and who did announce that he was in the United States "to fight the State Department."[89] Pleven's very popularity in circles outside the State Department, among people like Morgenthau who had their own grudges against it, only reinforced its isolation within the administration as a whole.

Even the British were prepared to admit that Pleven had not made a very good impression on his first visit to the department.[90] Atherton had merely announced that the American government had to give priority to requests for aid from Britain, China, Greece, among others, and stressed the value to the United States of preserving relations with Vichy; even a relatively sympathetic official like J. C. Dunn, the adviser on political relations, opposed Pleven's visit to the State Department because the Free French were too well known for playing politics.[91] That was why Welles also initially refused to see him, consenting only to receive a memorandum delivered by the British ambassador; and he communicated, back through Halifax, his reluctance to jeopardize the delicate American rapport with Vichy and North Africa by extending "anything in the nature of official recognition" to the Free French.[92] When in early October, just before he left the United States, Pleven did finally break through and see Welles, he was told that grave local difficulties prevented the United States from proffering Lend-Lease aid to the Free French as distinct from the British government.[93] Hull, whom he finally met on 7 October, only spoke in his accustomed fashion, bland, sweeping generalities.[94]

But the strongest evidence of Pleven's own responsibility for the lack of rapport with the State Department is very simply that under his successors there was some fitful improvement. General Robert-Jean-Claude-Roger Odic, formerly commanding general of the French Air Forces in Africa, resigned, joined the Free French, and engaged in some fruitful military talks in Washington;[95] formal Lend-Lease arrangements were instituted in November;[96] and under Boegner and de Roussy de Sales the whole tone of the discussions with the State Department became markedly more cordial. On 26 November they had a meeting that seemed to the Foreign Office "the most important step forward which the Free French delegation have yet made in their relations with the State Department." De Roussy de Sales assured Welles that "the Free French Delegation have no desire to intervene directly or indirectly in the relations between Washington and Vichy." Acting upon this opening, Boegner formally asked Welles if he agreed with the Free French argument that it was vital, to avoid future misunderstandings, for the American government to give its full public support to the course of action followed by de Gaulle for over a year. Welles replied emphatically that he did indeed agree, and in return he invited the Free French, "for the sake of American public opinion and for the United States government," to continue to assert their democratic spirit.[97] By early December, however, Tixier was moving to assume control of the negotiations, and thereafter, relations once again deteriorated. On 19 December a worried British consul general in New York sent a cable to London observing that the entry of the United States into the war had produced no change in relations between Washington and Vichy, and blaming the official lack of sympathy with the Free French primarily on the aura of uncertainty still surrounding the ability, probity, and democratic fidelity of its members.[98]

There is an obvious contrast between the tortuously slow progress, full of reversals and detours, of the Free French into the inner circles of Washington, and the comparative ease with which they won public acclaim. A Gallup poll, taken in late August, showed the vast majority, 74 percent, favoring Lend-Lease aid to the Free French on the grounds, first, that they "were trying to combat Nazism," and, second, that they were "the real souls of France";[99] a resolution was introduced into the House of Representatives by a Republican, Foster Stearns of New Hampshire, calling for American recognition of the Free French "government" of General de Gaulle (it was thereupon referred to the Committee on Foreign Affairs and tabled);[100] and there was a mounting press campaign for closer American dealings with the Free French, spearheaded among daily newspapers by the *Washington Post* and the *New York Herald Tribune*, among weekly journals by the *New Republic* and the *Nation*.[101]

Yet how did the American administration publicly treat the Free French? Four examples of official disdain can be noted. In August, after de Gaulle's unfortunate interview with the *Chicago Daily News*, Hull vigorously denied all knowledge of the Free French offer of bases in French Equatorial Africa, thus emphasizing the movement's lack of standing in Washington[102] (the offer had been made on 8 June).[103] In October an initial de facto relationship was supposed to have been established in Brazzaville by observers from the American army and navy, as well as the State Department. But as the *New York Post* observed, the natives of the Middle Congo might well have been baffled by the complications in protocol, which did in the end prove quite daunting.[104] In mid-December Colonel Harry F. Cunningham, who had headed that mission, was ordered back to Washington, having been rebuked once for giving a press interview, again for asking to be made liaison officer, and a third time for giving some military and diplomatic advice to the Free French. The mission was then terminated.[105] Then, although the decision to grant Lend-Lease aid was made on 11 November, it was not publicly announced till a fortnight later, after Stearns's House resolution, thus enabling public opinion to be further aroused by American inaction after the dismissal of Weygand.[106] And finally the year ended with the revamped French National Committee failing, despite British entreaties, to be invited to a meeting called by Roosevelt at the White House of representatives of all the anti-Axis powers, including the governments in exile.[107]

Why was this so? The slow ascent to official recognition as compared with the rapid public acclaim was exactly the reverse of what de Gaulle had intended by reorganizing his delegation. He had hoped, through his instrument Pleven, to fashion a sharp political cutting edge to slice through the diplomatic and bureaucratic inertia of Washington, while leaving propaganda and the cultivation of public support to amateur organizations like France Forever. Instead, there had arisen a widespread and spontaneous movement of sympathy for de Gaulle,[108] based on only the loosest understanding of the Free French as an anti-Axis force; the delegation itself was thwarted at every turn.

Part of the explanation certainly lies in the brute facts of international diplomacy. The seeming fixity of American policy, the recognition of Vichy

France, was a large—although, as the Lend-Lease agreement and the Brazzaville mission showed, not insuperable—obstacle to more cordial relations with the Free French. But it did have the further consequence, within the United States, of fostering resistance to Gaullist claims. The French-speaking communities in New England, for example, were enabled to retain their cherished isolationism and their Vichyssois sentiments: de Gaulle could be safely regarded as a traitor to France, and Pétain its Catholic savior.[109] Wherever the Free French raised their banner—in New York, Los Angeles, Washington, D.C., Denver, New Orleans, Boston, Detroit—there, as the fruit of American diplomacy, was the Vichy embassy or a Vichy consulate to hurl anathemas, to blackguard reputations, and to threaten families left in France.[110]

These harsh conditions brought about a particular form of émigré isolation, that aura of loneliness but also of heightened personal integrity that pervades all the memoirs published since, even as it then stirred up individual resentments. All the public and private feuds that took place in émigré circles stemmed precisely from this prior loss of any effective sense of communal loyalty. At the beginning of 1941 it was de Sieyès versus Garreau-Dombasle; at the end, Boegner versus Tixier; in New York, Jules Romains versus Henry Bernstein; in Hollywood, Jean Gabin versus Charles Boyer.[111] Viewed in isolation, these arguments might seem to be distractions, interesting only to the participants. For the most part they consisted of accusations of treason and disloyalty, followed by countercharges, leaks, rumors, secret threats, and public denunciations. As such, their actual content—usually, among the celebrities, suspicions of pro-Nazi loyalties—is less significant than the impression they conveyed: exercises, it might appear, of a virtuoso French talent for intrigue and vendetta.

But when set in the context of the siege warfare into which the émigrés had stepped, the debates appear a great deal less frivolous. Though framed in personal terms, their real subject was the past and future of the French nation. Though conducted very often by writers and actors, they did not stray far from politics. And that was why news, for example, of the rift in Hollywood circles was gathered with equal energy by the American interventionist group, Fight for Freedom,[112] and by the FBI.[113] For this was precisely the period, the months leading up to Pearl Harbor, when Americans, including men of letters, were themselves engaged in lively exchanges about the future of their country in the world, however ill-served some of them might have been by the discreet and secretive nature of American diplomacy; and in the more private reflections of their guests there may be detected echoes, albeit in a French idiom imperfectly attuned to American realities, of that wider argument.

The unpublished diaries of Raoul de Roussy de Sales afford one route of access into this enclosed world.[114] They are the deposit of someone who, like the émigrés as a whole, straddled the fields of journalism, literature, and politics; someone who was not a true member of the émigré community (he had already lived for some years as a journalist in the United States), but who did become its wry chronicler, casting ironic glances at the posturings of his compatriots. It was not all levity, however. Mortified by the French defeat, and himself desperately ill with tuberculosis, fated to die before the war was over, he soon allowed the more somber side of his personality to control his moods. A debilitating sickness, a national trauma, an international convulsion divide the lighthearted author of "Love in America"[115] from the unflinching political realist and mordantly skeptical diarist who doubted that the *Atlantic Monthly* would accept his piece on the current French state of mind "because it is not altogether in my usual light vein."[116] To view again the events of the critical year 1941 through his eyes, wide open and at times cold, is to gain fresh insights into that sad, lonely, disillusioned, morbidly suspicious group of exiles who were at once the victims and the agents of their country's fallen glory.

His profession, and his ability, had already made de Roussy de Sales the object of much respectful attention. Dorothy Thompson found in his deep appreciation of the French democratic tradition a useful corrective to her "inordinate love for Germany."[117] And when the great diaspora of 1940 arrived he was, as a veteran observer of the American scene unscarred by any previous polemics, to receive numerous intimate confidences, though he attended most to those that avoided the tediously conventional partisan and ideological judgments. From the usually withdrawn Alexis Leger, for example, he learned a view of the French defeat that he soon adopted as his own: that it had been caused by France adopting the doctrines of "the German school," which consisted of "measuring exactly the material forces present and considering the moral factors as unreal." Such a calculation, in the wake of the blitzkrieg, conceived the armistice, whereas, Leger suggested, hitherto "the French school" had "always taught the predominance of the moral factor over material forces: . . . It is the English who are today demonstrating the validity of the French doctrine. They ought to have given up the fight at the same time we did but on account of Churchill they kept on against all common sense and they are still holding out."[118]

De Roussy de Sales learned the rival view from Antoine de Saint-Exupéry, the argument from "rational defeatism," or "mechanical realism": "We did not go on fighting," he said, "because the whole army knew instinctively that it was no use . . . there would be just two million more dead and nothing else." So he was left bored and resentful. "I want to do some bombing," he told de Roussy de Sales, ". . . but what use is it to fight for a negotiated Anglo-German peace? How would that help France?" Such, de Roussy de Sales noted, were "the ravages of realism even in the mind of so generous and adventurous a person as Saint-Exupéry."[119] Actually, in the United States, those sentiments were a commonplace. In his personal anguish and philosophical despair, as well as in his mental habits—the deriving of political truths from technical facts—Saint-Exupéry resembled no one so much as that other disenchanted aviator, his counterpart in so many ways, Charles Lindbergh.

These divergent, but equally depressing, sentiments were well suited to de Roussy de Sales's state of mind. He was much less responsive to the straightforwardly partisan advocates. He viewed with distinct suspicion the activities of the playwright Henry Bernstein, the scourge of Pétain, the hounder of Romains, the accuser of Gabin (and, in all likelihood, the unnamed adversary who appears in André Maurois's memoirs).[120] Such verbal duels (and on one occasion a challenge to the real thing)[121] had, in de Roussy de Sales's view, only a very slight connection with the war; the tendency to dramatize everything, so natural anyway in a playwright, was "part of the disease of being a refugee."[122] And Bernstein's own way of life, with his apartment at the Waldorf Astoria, his cocktail parties for Charlie Chaplin, bore a similarly tenuous resemblance to that of his compatriots at home: "The world which I encountered at Henri Bernstein's," de Roussy de Sales observed, "has its own geography. It moves between certain fixed points—Paris, Cannes, Palm Beach, London—but the center, the pivot, was Paris. Now it is driven toward America, toward New York, which for a time will give it the illusion of being able to continue its bizarre life, yet it will be only an illusion." For there, hanging on the wall, was one treasure that Bernstein had been able to take with him from Paris, Manet's portrait of him as a child in a sailor's suit, and as de Roussy de Sales noted, "no matter what a Manet may be in itself, when it is hung on the wall of a room at the Waldorf it is no longer the same thing."[123]

The question was not primarily of political allegiance but of moral honesty. De Roussy de Sales was no less implacably opposed than Bernstein to Vichy, which "on the plane of morality and 'honor' " was "without excuse."[124] France was, he thought, "more profoundly fascisized than is generally admitted."[125] Pétain was becoming "a mere Quisling, a tyrant";[126] Darlan's "hatred for the British" was a handy tool for the Germans;[127] Laval, waiting in the wings, was a potential "Gauleiter";[128] and all the while Washington was being hood-winked into behaving as if "all the men of Vichy [were] not of the same stripe."[129] Roosevelt was thus "beginning again with Vichy the same vain juggling he once tried with Mussolini."[130] A case in point was the attention given to the proposal, put forward by Herbert Hoover among others, to send relief supplies to the civilian population of unoccupied France, an issue that greatly vexed the French community in the United States, dividing it, as de Roussy de Sales noted, into two warring groups, "those working to break the British blockade and those supposedly against the feeding of France and who want to starve their compatriots."[131] In support of the British war effort de Roussy de Sales belonged to the second group, while admitting that "one hypnotizes one's self on questions of relief: not to let the French die of hunger, etc. . . . France the perennial beggar, alas."[132] So he saw in the eventual sending of two shiploads of grain to unoccupied France a transparent attempt by Roosevelt "to appease at the same time Pétain and Hoover."[133]

But de Roussy de Sales was not thereby led into the Gaullist embrace. He came by a more indirect route. He had, as it happened, rival sources of information about popular sentiment in France, and he did not greatly like what he discovered from them, so far removed from the joyous democratic crusade that spokesmen for de Gaulle and the resistance were describing. He was, in the company of Eve Curie and Philippe Barrès, editing for publication a collection of letters from private individuals in France.[134] There he learned, among other things, that most of the writers welcomed the relief supplies and did not adopt a heroic, self-denying, pro-British stance. More important, he detected in the letters what his coeditors overlooked, the emergence of an unthinking, sentimental patriotism of little practical or political use. "Most of the time," he wrote, the letters were "pearls of pompousness, but neither of my collaborators is in a mood to laugh at this sort of thing. The stupidity produced by the war is a great levelling force. One admires what would have made a Flaubert howl with laughter."[135] This, to de Roussy de Sales, was not the voice of democratic resistance; it was only the reverse side of the coin of Pétainist defeatism. Already he had detected in the cult of Pétain a species of "infantism," of "masochism."[136] He abhorred Vichy's "opportunism, its lack of dignity, its hateful spirit of so called realistic calculation to which we owe the armistice and which continues to prevail."[137] Now he further despised the supine French attitude that made this all possible, and which also made a mockery out of American efforts to promote democratic values: "America has a normal political system and cannot understand a country which is in the state that France is. I think of all those here who preach the democratic Gospel, liberty, etc. I do not know what will replace this, but it is finished. The Americans are mistaken and so are many others who believe in orthodox restorations. Unfortunately if one mentions this, one passes for fascist or communist or Heaven knows what."[138]

De Roussy de Sales was unquestionably a democrat; but where was democracy to be found? Certainly not at Vichy, nor yet among its dormant subjects or the comfortable émigrés of New York. Was it not an American delusion to locate democratic seeds in those unlikely quarters? And de Gaulle? There de Roussy de Sales's misgivings were even more pronounced. He instantly acknowledged that de Gaulle had made "a fine gesture," but "that is all." He lacked "political sense."[139] One obstacle to breathing democracy into the inert masses of metropolitan France was that "they no longer know what it means, lost as they are in the aberrations of the day." Another was that de Gaulle himself "set no great store by it."[140] One of de Roussy de Sales's informants, the journalist Michel Pobers, who himself had rather shaky democratic credentials,[141] gladly proclaimed that de Gaulle's support in France came from such prewar rightist groups as the Cagoulards and the Camelots du Roi.[142] And neither the Brazzaville interview nor the Syrian campaign showed the general to be a master of political or diplomatic tact.

Yet, after months of hesitation and soul-searching, de Roussy de Sales was indeed recruited by Pleven into the Gaullist delegation; and this capitulation makes sense only in terms of his prior suspicion, rather than any new enthusiasm for the movement.[143] Originally he had proposed to serve, within an American organization, Fight for Freedom, in a French Advisory Committee, at first composed of intellectuals, journalists, and clergymen—Gilbert Chinard, Father Joseph Ducatillon, "Pertinax," André Istel, Jacques Maritain, Robert Valeur, Paul Vaucher—later diluted with celebrities, Eve Curie, Henri Bernstein, Charles Boyer.[144] But eventually the tug of patriotic loyalties impelled him toward a more open attachment to Gaullism. He already knew that his work for Fight for Freedom had aroused resentment against him, lest he become, above all the rest, the official representative of de Gaulle.[145] Now he frankly took on the challenge, not in order to join, but to neutralize, such aggravating intrigues. He still distrusted his confreres: Pleven had "done nothing except to throw everything in our laps"; Tixier was "a weakling, mentality of a functionary"; only Boegner was "capable of succeeding."[146]

But de Roussy de Sales had a more ambitious goal than merely resolving the perplexities of his own team. He had the rare opportunity, which he grasped with a becoming modesty, of easing both Franco-American relations and Anglo-American difficulties over France. To the Gaullists he might well have seemed an eloquent and respectable spokesman. But to Sumner Welles at the State Department he was also a counterweight to the excitable and unacceptable Pleven, and an antibody within the factional strivings of Free France; and to the British he was equally someone who could educate the State Department about Gaullism, and educate de Gaulle about diplomacy and democracy.[147] In this complex, mediating role de Roussy de Sales might possibly, over the next few years, have exerted some slight restraining influence upon the more agitated parties to the various disputes. His honesty and his independence certainly offered him the chance. But it was not to be. This was partly due to personal factors: his own steadily deteriorating state of health, and the appearance of Adrien Tixier in a commanding, not to say dictatorial, position within the delegation. It was also because there took place, at the end of 1941, an incident that immeasurably set back the cause of Free France in the United States. After all the personal differences, the administrative reshuffles, and the doctrinal disputes had seemed to have run their course, a major diplomatic incident finally occurred, the St. Pierre-and-Miquelon affair.

CHAPTER 6
ST. PIERRE AND MIQUELON
REVISITED: THE PERILS
OF HIGHER DIPLOMACY

The Japanese bombing of Pearl Harbor sent surprisingly few tremors through Franco-American relations, which were actually more disturbed by a comparatively minor engagement, less than three weeks later, on two tiny islands off the coast of Newfoundland. The St. Pierre-and-Miquelon incident—itself a "little diplomatic [or "political"] Pearl Harbor,"[1] a "teapot tempest,"[2] a "fleabite [that] developed into a persistent, festering sore"[3]—presents, forty-five years later, a conundrum. The outraged reactions and violent controversies, the amount of time given over to it, appear out of all proportion to the action taken. On Christmas Eve, 1941, a small Free French naval force liberated the tiny French colony from the rule of its Vichy governor, and, in accordance with the almost unanimous verdict of a plebiscite the following day, announced the islands' adherence to the Free French cause. The strategic importance of the islands lay only in their possession of a shortwave radio transmitter; and it might have seemed as if the matter should have rested there, an episode to be considered, albeit in a minor way, as a successful Dakar expedition or a bloodless Syrian campaign. Why did it not so remain?

A brief answer would be that the episode took place at the junction of various distinct developments—American-Vichy relations, Anglo-American relations, the changing status of the Free French, and the changing mood of the American public—none of which ever proceeded calmly. Thus, barely a fortnight before, the American administration had renewed its 1940 agreement with Admiral Georges Robert, Vichy's governor of the West Indies and supreme commander of all French islands in the Western Hemisphere, under which all French vessels would be neutralized in return for an American guarantee of the status quo throughout the hemisphere;[4] only now the whole delicate structure of America's Vichy policy seemed to have been brought crashing down. Similarly, some equally complex negotiations had been going on for some time between the United States, Canada, Great Britain, and the Free French about the colony; and the last the Americans had heard was that the Free French naval commander, Admiral Muselier, then in Canada, had given his word not to proceed with the operation.[5] So now the diplomatic and moral standing of the Free French in Washington plummeted once again, and was hardly restored when it emerged that Muselier too felt betrayed, having been overruled by de Gaulle, and shortly resigned from the French National Committee.[6] Furthermore Churchill was at that very moment in Washington for his first conference with Roosevelt at which the two were formal co-belligerents; only now a Frenchman threatened to come between them. And finally, Muselier's forces had, almost by chance, taken on board a journalist, Ira Wolfert, whose enthusiastic, blow-by-blow dispatches to the *New York Times*[7] stirred up a wave of approval for the action from an American public newly at war; and so, within weeks of Pearl Harbor, there was exposed to view a deep rift between the policies of the administration and the desires of a vocal element of the public.

That journalistic coup makes the event especially illuminating about domestic American affairs, in particular the strained relationship between public opinion and foreign policy. This was of course primarily an episode in the history of St. Pierre and Miquelon itself; and as William A. Christian has shown, employing the most advanced techniques of the social anthropologist, the division within the colony between Pétainists and Gaullists was a revival of an ancient feud between a traditional commercial and political elite and the broad mass of younger, more radical professionals and intellectuals.[8] It was also, for a short while, an event of some importance in the international diplomacy of the war; and in that light Douglas Anglin has concluded, after an analysis of all parties to the dispute—Free France, the United States, Canada, Great Britain—that while there were legitimate "conflicting conceptions of the common interest . . . it was the personalities who participated in the drama who turned it into an affaire," especially de Gaulle and Cordell Hull.[9] These perspectives are undoubtedly revealing. But the conclusions they suggest may be further amplified by setting the event in its American context, and taking a closer look at the American public's response. Then it may be possible to see how, even in an age of bureaucratic government, international storms can appear to be caused by the vagaries of individual personalities.

Interestingly, what provoked the controversy within the United States was not the event itself but the State Department's instantly released statement, which should therefore be considered in some detail: "Our preliminary reports show that the action taken by three so-called Free French ships was an arbitrary action contrary to the agreement of all parties concerned and certainly without the prior knowledge or consent in any sense of the United States Government. This Government has inquired of the Canadian Government as to the steps that Government is prepared to take to restore the status quo of these islands."[10] It is a measure of the distance between the State Department and its critics that while officials were most concerned about agreements violated and protocol unobserved, their critics fastened on the insulting implications of one particular phrase, "so-called Free French ships." Letters and telegrams of protest were addressed to the "so-called Secretary of State" at the "so-called State Department." The *New Republic* commented that the department had by implication slurred not only the Free French but the free forces in all occupied countries.[11] Nor did Hull greatly improve the situation when, three weeks later, he offered an *amende honorable* by invoking the transferred epithet and claiming that "so-called" applied to the ships, not the Free French. "Perhaps they were actually pink elephants," suggested the *New York Herald Tribune*.[12] "Unless it turns out," warned the *Nation*, "that the Admiral and his crew approached the islands on surf boards, this quaint expression will save very little face."[13]

Why did Hull use such an unfortunate phrase? There would seem to be two possible explanations: either, as part of the press believed, it was a gratuitous insult from a badly shaken man, or, as he later claimed, it did reflect real doubts about the authorization of the ships' mission. There is evidence to support both views. Hull, still fuming over the recent conduct of the Japanese diplomats whom he frequently described in colorful Tennessee slang, would, three weeks later, scribble out a letter of resignation to the president, and was plainly not in the best of moods.[14] On the other hand it is just possible to interpret the first telegram from the American minister in Canada informing the department of the expedition as implying that Muselier had acted without consulting de Gaulle, and that therefore it was in some sense not a Free French engagement.[15] As an assistant secretary of state, Breckinridge Long, observed, "Solemn statements made to this Government by Free French representatives . . . led the State Department to doubt that the ships used in the seizure were Free French ships acting under authority of the Free French committee."[16] And yet neither explanation is wholly satisfactory. As a deliberate insult, the statement just seems rather childish; as an expression of uncertainty about the ships' origins, it is simply bad English.

In fact there is a third possibility. American entry into the war coincided with the fruition of the State Department's long-awaited policy toward all the "free" movements. These were organizations that, in contrast to de Gaulle's Free French, took little active part in the war. They consisted mostly of exiles and refugees from occupied countries, including such illuminati of the prewar European social order as Carlo Sforza, Otto Strasser, King Carol II of Rumania, Tibor Eckhardt, and Otto von Habsburg. They designed, within the United States, extensive plans for the postwar world. Not surprisingly, the American administration did not seek an intimate relationship with these organizations, which were watched by the appropriate agencies with the same intensity, and the same suspicion, as were the various French groupings. Then on 10 December a State Department release clearly set forth American policy: "The State Department is glad to be informed of the plans and proposed activities of such 'free movements' [but] it does not favor 'free movements' . . . which carry on activities contrary to the established policies, domestic or foreign, of the government of the United States; and prefers that the governing committees of such movements shall be composed of citizens of the foreign country, rather than of American sympathizers."[17] Some question arose, when the Declaration of the United Nations was being published, about whether representatives of such movements would be eligible to "adhere"; and although Roosevelt actually overruled the State Department and allowed for the signature of "appropriate authorities which are not governments," de Gaulle declined to join on such terms.[18]

The generally disparaging attitude of the State Department was more frankly exposed in private remarks by senior officials. Breckinridge Long was deeply concerned about the "movement on to glorify Russia, part of the activities of the Communists in this country who aim at control of our Government and whose ambitions the recent developments in Europe are helping immeasurably";[19] and he was aware that he personally had "incurred the enmity of various powerful and vengeful elements; the Communists, extreme radicals, Jewish professional agitators, refugee enthusiasts who blindly seek the admission of persons under the guise of refugees, and their sympathetic agents in the Government service who are their spokesmen and agents."[20] Rather more urbane were the comments of the official most directly concerned, Adolf Berle, another assistant secretary of state: "This is all very amusing, this picking of Prime Ministers and Emperors, and so forth, from the angle of Washington . . . but . . . there are not many Masaryks to be seen among the exiles here."[21] With regard to the United Nations Declaration the situation seemed to Berle to be bordering on the ridiculous: ". . . we have had everyone except the South Tyrol Yodellers' League sending in an 'adherence.' "[22]

Then, finally, on 24 January Berle made his views explicit: the problem for American policymakers was, "can we steer our way through the so-called 'free movements' in the United States, which are developing all the eccentricities of foreign politics?"[23] The use of the identical epithet, a month after it had been nationally ridiculed, would seem to indicate that the earlier use of it by Hull, at the time of the St. Pierre-and-Miquelon affair, was neither a temporary aberration, nor an expression of doubt about the nationality of the ships. Undeniably Hull felt aggrieved, but in rebuking the Free French he only employed what may have been a State Department commonplace. Used privately to refer to the gatherings of refugees in America, it naturally caused a furor when applied to the Free French movement of General de Gaulle.

Rather more oblique even than the reference to the "so-called Free French ships" was the comment, further on in the State Department's release, that the Free French action was "contrary to the agreement of all parties concerned." For there were three possible agreements that might have been intended here: the Act of Havana of 1940, which reaffirmed, with Latin American support, the United States' determination to uphold the Monroe Doctrine and prevent a transfer of the sovereignty of any European possession in the Western Hemisphere from one non-American state to another; second, the American agreement just then concluded with Admiral Robert, designed to ensure the continued neutrality of French possessions throughout the hemisphere; and finally, the undertaking given by the Free French, in London and Ottawa, not to proceed with the liberation of St. Pierre and Miquelon. Since the Free French were not a party to the first two agreements, it may seem rather perverse to accuse them of any violations; and since the third was an oral rather than a formal commitment, the department's response might seem extreme. But, as will be seen, what mattered to Hull was not so much the letter of the agreements, or the manner in which they had been formulated, as the network of relationships that they implied.

Consider first the Act of Havana. It is highly doubtful if this could ever have applied. Canada, the country closest to St. Pierre and Miquelon, was not a party to the act. Moreover, what had taken place was a transfer not of sovereignty but of government, of administration; the islands remained French. In any case the American administration chose not to enforce the Monroe Doctrine from sound tactical considerations, rather than any theoretical misgivings. Although on 13 February 1942, while Hull was on leave, Sumner Welles publicly admitted that the Monroe Doctrine did not apply to St. Pierre and Miquelon,[24] the critical decision had actually been made over a month earlier, when Hull was in full control. For there had been a group within the State Department, led by Long, who proposed to invoke, but not enforce, the Monroe Doctrine. An awkward position to adopt, it meant in effect that the American government would enter into negotiations with all interested parties, using the Monroe Doctrine as a fundamental premise, while at the same time refraining from any commitment to restore by force the status quo, since the doctrine was, in practice, unenforceable. To have implemented it in St. Pierre and Miquelon would have set a precedent for the French West Indies, French and Dutch Guiana, British Honduras, and elsewhere, dangerously stretching American resources. As Long was informed, a month after Pearl Harbor, "the Navy is busy in other ways."[25] But the curious idea of adopting, for negotiating purposes, a position that was untenable in practice was not welcomed by Long's colleagues; and the Monroe Doctrine was, if not forgotten, at least omitted. Although draft proposals to settle the dispute by using the doctrine did circulate within the State Department, none of the more formal documents that were presented to Canadian or British officials so much as mentioned it.

The situation with regard to the American agreement with Admiral Robert was, if anything, even stranger. To some extent the same practical considerations applied: if it was strategically unwise to enforce an act authorized by all the Latin American states, then it would have been equally unwise, and rather more unpopular, to uphold a bilateral agreement with a Vichy governor. But in fact the question did not arise. If the Free French could hardly have violated an agreement concluded by the American administration with their mortal enemies, still less could they have done so when they did not even know it existed.

The terms were simply not published during the war; and the British, shuttling between the Navy and State Departments, met only glacial resistance in trying to uncover what the terms were, before, in February, virtually giving up.[26] All they could discern was that the agreement did not refer to St. Pierre and Miquelon.[27] That was actually the view of the Vichy government itself, to whom the new agreement was only a confirmation of the 1940 arrangement that, equally, did not mention St. Pierre and Miquelon and essentially concerned only Martinique.[28] In short, the United States was in no formal sense bound by any existing agreement to uphold the status quo on St. Pierre and Miquelon. What did exist, however, was a voluntary, additional moral commitment made at the conclusion of the agreement with Robert. On 13 December 1941, Roosevelt sent word to Pétain that he could "rest assured that the Government of the United States . . . will continue to give full recognition to the agreement reached by our two governments involving the maintenance of the status quo of the French possessions in the Western hemisphere."[29] There certainly was a significant broadening of the American mandate.

All that now remain for consideration are the assurances given by both de Gaulle and Admiral Muselier that the proposed expedition would not take place. Here surely, it may be supposed, a breach of faith by the Free French did occur. And indeed it did. The assurances, given the same day, 17 December, by de Gaulle to the Foreign Office and by Muselier to the American minister in Canada, were unequivocal: the mission would not proceed without prior American approval.[30] Of the two, Muselier was by far the more committed to confer with other powers; and de Gaulle's insistence, later the very same day, that Muselier in fact proceed without that consultation, precipitated the long-expected rift within the ranks of the Free French, although Muselier's code of honor still required him to obey the order.[31]

De Gaulle later offered two explanations for his volte-face. The first was a mischievous desire "to stir up the bottom of things, as one throws a stone into a pond."[32] The second was a leak from the British Foreign Office, according to which the Canadians were, with American approval, about to land on St. Pierre themselves—a leak that de Gaulle appeared to believe was intended to sanction the subsequent Free French action.[33] Whichever was the stronger motive, neither could excuse de Gaulle's precipate action. But it is important to understand his change of mind within a single day. For his original plan, formulated when he first learned of the renewed American negotiations with Admiral Robert, had foreseen no consultation whatsoever, only unilateral Free French action. And he had only been forced to give his undertaking of 17 December by Muselier's own independent decision, once in Newfoundland on 9 December, to secure American and Canadian approval in the "new situation" created by Pearl Harbor.[34] That is, while de Gaulle may fairly be accused, in this single instance, of violating an agreement, it was one to which he had reluctantly and uncharacteristically given his assent.

The more the State Department release is probed, the longer the puzzle remains, of scarcely justified, but vigorously proclaimed, American outrage. The explanation for this can only be sought outside the terms of official diplomacy, and instead in the ideals that diplomacy is expected to enshrine, the ulterior moral stands that are imperfectly reflected in diplomatic dealings. The Act of Havana is a case in point. For practical reasons the Monroe Doctrine, the premise of the act, was rapidly dropped as a pretext for American action. But it did not thereby lose its force as a guiding principle of American diplomacy. For the Monroe Doctrine is, precisely, a doctrine. Far more than a diplomatic instrument, it sanctions a permanent, American involvement in the affairs of the poorer, weaker nations of Latin America, an approach that under Theodore Roosevelt might be ruthlessly intrusive, under his cousin Franklin rather more conciliatory, and at a time of world crisis still more ostensibly protective. Adolf Berle tried to explain this to two French émigrés, Alexis Leger and Jacques Maritain, who were, so he believed, overly sympathetic to the Free French cause. The events on St. Pierre and Miquelon had, he said, "raised an issue which was fundamental in the American system." For many years the United States had been insisting "that no forcible movement directed from outside could be permitted to take place in this hemisphere. If we ever allowed that kind of thing to get started, there would be endless sore spots which would be taken advantage of by somebody."

When the argument was pressed that a strict construction of the Monroe Doctrine, by which it referred solely to changes of sovereignty, removed it from consideration, Berle replied that "Hitler and everyone else had been rigging up 'national' parties which were really their puppets; any such movement would always masquerade as a true 'national' movement." By adhering to a broad construction of the Monroe Doctrine, Berle argued, the United States ensured that Haiti would feel as safe as the most powerful of nations (to which point the Haitian minister, present at the dinner, roundly agreed). When the argument was pressed that the plebiscite on St. Pierre and Miquelon seemed to settle everything, Berle replied that "no one would give much credence to a plebiscite conducted twenty-four hours after a military occupation under the guns of a commanding military force."[35] To a great extent, therefore, the ideals that the Monroe Doctrine represented—and which, suitably expanded, the United States was newly committed to uphold in the Second World War—overruled every other consideration: the formal claim to sovereignty of the Free French, the formal plebiscite on St. Pierre and Miquelon, the formal language of the doctrine itself, as well as the plain fact that the only outside power that could conceivably be directing the actions of the Free French was Great Britain, the United States' ally. American official anger with the Free French thus stemmed from a prior attachment to a higher diplomacy.

Much the same can be said of the American agreement with Admiral

Robert. If the Act of Havana reflected profound American feelings toward the other nations of the Western Hemisphere, the negotiations with Robert were no less integral a part of the whole shifting, delicate structure of America's Vichy policy. That policy, we have seen, stemmed from an initial commitment to Marshal Pétain that was moral in its implications and that, though designed to yield distinct diplomatic and strategic benefits, had already by the end of 1941 become difficult to execute. Yet, despite the impediments that the Germans cast up, and the deception in which the Vichy French engaged, the American government proceeded in its course; and it is entirely characteristic of this course that the assurances that the Americans proffered the French should far outweigh any practical benefits that would be received in return. The most recent of these assurances was Roosevelt's promise to guarantee "the maintenance of the status quo of the possessions in the Western hemisphere"—a promise that could hardly be redeemed without positive, purposive American action. But long before that the more hardheaded realists of the British Foreign Office had grown skeptical of the high-sounding guarantees about the shape of the postwar world so freely available from the American government. On 8 October, W. H. B. Mack, of the French Department, observed that a recent statement of Sumner Welles "that it is the policy of the United States Government to restore the independence and *integrity* of France goes further than His Majesty's Government's undertaking to 'secure the full restoration of the independence and greatness of France' with the qualification that this did not refer to territorial frontiers";[36] and the same point was noted by William Strang on 28 November.[37] That is to say, the undertakings given by the American administration to Vichy France, at best a neutral power, were easily more far-reaching than those given by the British government to the Free French, who were cobelligerents.

It is now possible to explain the row over St. Pierre and Miquelon without reference to personal foibles. The indisputable fact that de Gaulle and Muselier had broken their word to American and British officials counted for far less than the uncomfortable results of their action: they had propelled the American administration into an embarassing situation and might force it, in turn, to renege on its own freely given, grandiose assurances to Vichy France and the countries of Latin America. That is also why the controversy proved so difficult to resolve. A treaty, or any purely formal arrangement between sovereign states, may be coolly and rationally reconsidered under the impact of pressing new developments; a commitment in which a government has invested its extensive moral capital is not so easily breached. And there are further complications. The incident provoked a vast outpouring of domestic criticism of the official stance: criticism of the policy and of those who framed it. The American administration was thus searching for a resolution to the conflict not only in an uneasy international climate but also against the background of a restless public opinion. If American policymakers had hoped that

the onset of war would supply them with docile public support, they were to be
quickly disillusioned.

It was, to be sure, only a minority which was greatly exercised over the
affair. While no public opinion polls were taken on the incident itself, it would
seem that the majority, as so often in foreign policy, tended to follow the
government's lead. According to one press survey, though the first reaction
was pleasure at the initiative finally taken by the Free French, that quickly
yielded to concern at the embarrassment into which the United States had been
plunged, followed by open condemnation of de Gaulle by 71 percent of the
press, with only 21 percent critical of the government's stand.[38]

The majority, or deferential, view was soon evident. The *Christian Science Monitor* observed that "war is a practical business. Practical considerations could have been pointed out to the Free French zealots which might
have deterred them from this adventure."[39] The *Atlanta Constitution* thought
de Gaulle's action "ill advised," since he threatened to make the American
government seem deceitful in its promise to the Vichy French to respect
France's territorial integrity.[40] The *Philadelphia Bulletin* regarded the Free
French action as "in the highest degree reckless and irresponsible. . . . The
rashness of the Free French is likely seriously to damage the prospect of their
getting any recognition and aid from Washington."[41] Deference was carried to
a high degree by the *Baltimore Evening Sun* in an editorial titled "A Matter for
the Professionals," which argued that although the Free French action might
look at first like a good, bold stroke, diplomacy must be left to the State
Department: there ". . . are deals and psychological minutiae which the lay-
man can hardly expect to judge as competently as the State Department—
which is, after all, in constant contact with these difficult realities."[42]

The supporters of the government's policy did not furnish any new arguments. They either counselled unquestioning loyalty to the government, or
they developed the implications of that original State Department release on
the incident. Thus Mark Sullivan, a columnist in the *New York Herald Tribune*
(and at odds with that paper's Gaullist stand), argued that the government's
policy stemmed from the fact that it was engaged in a worldwide conflict
between "one group of nations which try to live up to agreements, abide
by international law, preserve international morals . . . [and] another group
of nations which flagrantly ignore and defy these considerations."[43] Arthur
Krock, a good and loyal friend of Cordell Hull, did attempt to construct a positive case for the government's policy; but he made the error of resting it upon
the Monroe Doctrine, itself rapidly jettisoned as a possible justification even
by the State Department. Claiming that Hull's protest at the Free French action
had been "obligatory," Krock found himself putting forth arguments that the
critics had no difficulty in refuting: on the legal side he had to assert that the
Free French seizure of the islands had in fact "transferred the sovereignty of

one non-American state (France) to another (the Free French)"; and in practical terms he had to argue that if that were tolerated, Admiral Robert "could have found justification in attacking the Free French on St. Pierre–Miquelon, and they in turn could have found cause to invade French Guiana, Martinique, and Guadeloupe," with disastrous consequences for Latin America.[44]

A final instance of the widespread deference exhibited before the American government may be found in a rather surprising quarter, that organ of stern, unbending midwestern isolationism, the *Chicago Tribune*. Step by step, as the United States crept into the world conflict, the *Chicago Tribune* had thundered against the irresponsibility, the deceitfulness, and the folly of the government's course. But with the United States now in the war, fully engaged as a co-belligerent, the *Chicago Tribune* evidently decided to close ranks and lend at least temporary support to the government's military and diplomatic, if not its political, activities. So, in regard to St. Pierre and Miquelon, having dutifully repeated the official line, it concluded that the Free French action "would seem to be without any point, to be useless both militarily and morally, and to be dangerously provocative." Even then, however, the old isolationism lingered on. For the problem had only arisen, the *Chicago Tribune* continued, because the French had insisted on retaining two islands as fishing bases, "vestigial survivals of European empire in the Western hemisphere."[45]

There is no question that the critics of the government's policy constituted a minority, of the press and of the public: a minority, moreover, with all the characteristics of a defensive, exclusive coterie. What they lacked in numbers they made up for in publicity. At times the reader is reminded of the militant prewar isolationists, by the same strident rhetoric, the same moral self-assurance, the same explicit fear that the loyalties of American officials lie beyond American borders. But while most isolationists had, like the *Chicago Tribune*, rallied to the flag, their opposite number, the equally militant prewar interventionists felt still excluded from effective participation. No more than the 1940 election had the attack on Pearl Harbor conferred on them moral leadership in the nation's affairs. These people were, in short, the interventionist elements in both the Republican and Democratic parties, supplemented by a more radical internationalist left wing; and they contended, in this particular case, that if the Free French had violated the Act of Havana, they had nonetheless obeyed the spirit of the Atlantic Charter.

A few examples will show the bipartisan, heterogeneous nature of this opposition. Samuel Grafton, who considerd himself a socialist, wrote in his newspaper column that "if Wendell Willkie were Secretary of State, we could be assured that it was the Fascists who were being hoodwinked, and not the American people."[46] Dorothy Thompson, hardly a figure of the left, interpreted the incident from the viewpoint of an extreme democrat, almost a populist—it was "a revolt against fascism by people"—and she attacked State Department officials for being a well-dressed clique: the "striped pants" were ignoring that it was a "peoples' war"; they had given "notice to the world that anti-fascist movements must be suppressed. That is the way the people everywhere will interpret what we did, and the repercussions on freedom-loving people in every occupied country will be awful." Those conservative elements in the State Department, she went on, "have been a calamity to the United States for a long time," and "can cost us the greatest asset we have—*the revolutionary spirit for freedom among the masses of the people of the world*."[47]

The event that made Samuel Grafton sound like a Republican, and Dorothy Thompson like a Communist, did not leave the *Nation* or the *New Republic* untouched. They both issued denunciations of American officials in terms reminiscent of the old isolationists' attacks on Roosevelt's foreign policies, or the Liberty League's attacks on his domestic policies. The *Nation* demanded the resignation of Cordell Hull, and a purge of all disloyal officials from the State Department, and it cabled Admiral Muselier that he could count on the support of all patriotic Americans.[48] The *New Republic* demanded a public inquiry into the conduct of the State Department, analogous to the one to be held concerning Pearl Harbor, to discern any official malfeasance.[49]

There was no discussion here about the diplomatic or, some would say, legalistic issues raised. Instead, there was alarm that the official American reaction, concerned with those issues, strangely echoed the reaction from Vichy. For Henry-Haye, never at a loss for a statement to the press, had emerged from a meeting at the State Department flushed with the news that that incident had brought about a rapprochement between the United States and Vichy[50]—a travesty, as it happens, of what had passed between him and Cordell Hull, who remarked, "the Ambassador always talks considerably when he emerges from my office and meets the press, and I do not know what he has said today relative to our conversation."[51] As the Charleston *News and Courier* stated, the Free French move "was not authorized by American and British agents, and the Vichy government is reported to look upon it as a highhanded enterprise by irresponsible persons, but that would be the official viewpoint on anything General de Gaulle ordered."[52] More directly, the Cleveland *Plain Dealer* commented in an editorial titled "So What?" that "we are out to win a war today, not a point in academic legal interpretation."[53] On the West Coast, the problems of St. Pierre and Miquelon seemed remote indeed. "In the mind of officialdom," remarked the *Los Angeles Times*, "the situation appeared to be of more interest than the surrender of Hong Kong by the British, the capture of Bengazi in Libya, the continued pursuit of Nazis by Russians, the hot battle in Malaya, the fate of the Philippines, the destruction of a Japanese submarine off the California coast, or more good work by the Fighting Dutch. . . . Certainly, if Vichy could be turned Axis-ward by so trifling an incident, there is not much hope of holding that government in line."[54] And finally an editorial in the *Philadelphia Record* noted (correctly) that the State Department's reaction must be taken as a sign that officials still believed that they could do business with Vichy, and, it went on: "But if the French fleet goes to Hitler in spite of our scrupulous observance of friendly relations with Vichy, it will be small, cold comfort to remember that we have always acted in accordance with 'existing agreements' instead of existing realities."[55]

Not the diplomatic niceties, therefore, but the broad moral issues exercised the critics, who started from a premise entirely different from that of the government: the plain fact that the island of St. Pierre did have a radio transmitter that had broadcast shipping and weather reports to German submarines. Upon that undeniable but slender factual basis they constructed an imposing polemical edifice. For that fact defined the Gaullist action as anti-fascist, and those who presumed to interpose themselves between the Free French and the consummation of their coup, as appeasers. And appeasement, discredited in Britain after the French defeat, in the United States after Pearl Harbor, was once again a live issue. The *New Republic* argued that the incident illustrated the fatal weakness of the State Department's policy, the belief that the Vichy regime could and must be "appeased" at all costs.[56]

It was characteristic of the critics to lump great things with small, Munich with St. Pierre and Miquelon: "Appeasement," commented the *New Orleans Times-Picayune*, "has turned out badly for the appeasers, whether British or American, in this war. . . . Let it be earnestly hoped that the statesmen who are running our part of the show never find it necessary to repent, in humility and bitterness, an error whose repair cost us heavily in blood and treasure."[57] It was equally characteristic of them to couple a critique of appeasement with an assault on the appeasers, in this case the State Department: thus the journalist I. F. Stone, addressing the foreign policy section of the American Political Science Association, announced that "we cannot fight a democratic war with an undemocratic State Department, and we cannot make a democratic peace after the war as long as we have an undemocratic State Department";[58] and the *New York Post* declared that "the time has come for house cleaning at the State Department," whose bureaucrats "obviously are not enlisted" in the present war.[59]

There is, in this grievance, a familiar populist element: on the one hand there is "the people," being kept in ignorance, and on the other hand a secretive, powerful elite, in this case the State Department. "Why," inquired the *St. Louis Post-Dispatch*, "is it considered vital policy to give these islands back to Vichy, after their people have voted democratically for Free France? How does that agree with the Four Freedoms proclaimed by Mr. Roosevelt? The people would like to know."[60] More than a month after the incident the chief complaint of the *New York Post* was still that the attitude of the State Department had never been either explained or retracted.[61] Even the *New York Herald Tribune* temporarily acquired a populist rhetoric, albeit a refined one;

on 28 December it observed: "With all due respect for the difficult and delicate nature of the Department's task . . . it is the right—indeed the duty—of American public opinion to assert its trust in the people of France and to ask that any course which is adopted in the name of the United States display that trust. If the plebiscite on St. Pierre and Miquelon is any criterion (and what other has been produced?) the cause of freedom emphatically will not suffer thereby." But of course this was not in substance populism, which was a popular movement for domestic reform, hardly a sophisticated, cosmopolitan concern with the welfare of other nations. Far from being a mass movement, the campaign to reverse the policy of the State Department was largely conducted by national celebrities, though of a distinct political persuasion.

On 30 December 1941 a telegram was sent to Roosevelt (and simultaneously released to the press) condemning the State Department's policy over St. Pierre and Miquelon, which it called "a culmination of the State Department's policy of neglecting our friends and conciliating our enemies which has resulted in failure after failure, from Spain to Pearl Harbor." It was signed by fifty-five prominent citizens who claimed to be consistent supporters of the administration's foreign policy, and who were drawn in large measure from literary, journalistic, academic, and religious quarters; they included Carl Sandburg, William Agar, Maxwell Anderson, Walter Millis, Stephen Vincent Benét, Rex Stout, and Van Wyck Brooks. Yet despite such endorsement it too had a populist tinge; the appeal to an idealistic chief executive to right the wrongs committed by one of his departments. Although the signers professed their faith in the president's leadership and their reluctance to criticize any act of the government in time of war, they could not, they said, remain silent when the State Department branded America's Free French allies as "the so-called Free French," and then tried to force Canada to reestablish Vichy's rule against the express wish of the local population. Therefore, it concluded, "we appeal . . . for a review of the whole attitude of the State Department which has often seemed unwilling or unable to understand the ideals you have expressed, for which the world is fighting." The telegram also engaged in the now ritualistic denunciation of "appeasement": "We understand, though we deeply regret, considerations which have prompted you to continue dealing with the discredited Vichy regime, but surely appeasement cannot go so far as to guarantee Vichy's rule in places where the local French population wishes to join us in the fight for freedom."[62]

Those last three words must have struck a discordant echo around the State Department. Fight for Freedom had emerged, long before Pearl Harbor, as the most militant of the interventionist pressure groups, and its association with the far left had not escaped notice. When, later in 1942, a State Department official composed a lengthy analysis of the "Campaign to undermine the State Department," he fastened on that telegram as the *locus classicus* of the campaign, "a singularly apt illustration of the manner, personnel, and objectives of all petitions of this character. . . . There is no indication that the persons who signed this telegram are essentially interested in the Free French, and it appears that the action taken was merely a pretext for an attack against the Department itself."

What then were they interested in? After a close scrutiny of *Who's Who*, the editorial mastheads (and editorial content) of such left-wing publications as the *Daily Worker*, the *New Masses*, *Soviet Russia Today*, and the *Liberator*, and lists of signatories to various other petitions on such matters as the Spanish Civil War and American immigration policy, the author arrived at a very precise conclusion. He assumed that the critics had perpetuated a deliberate falsehood: "To be charitable one could attribute their criticism of the Department on the St. Pierre–Miquelon incident to careless press releases when they claim that the Department maligned the Free French movement by the use of the phrase 'so-called Free French.' [But] on close examination, it is believed that the omission of the word 'ships' by this group, which would have changed the meaning entirely and represented what actually was said, was no accident." For the author recalled a similar campaign, four years before, mounted against the House Un-American Activities Committee. Then, its chairman, Martin Dies, who had been seeking only to draw attention to the ease with which Communist publications were able deceptively to secure the endorsement of American celebrities, was accused of calling that unlikely radical, Shirley Temple, a Communist. The combination of similar tactics and associations led the author to only one possible conclusion, which he outlined in measured State Department prose: "It is . . . ridiculous to label these signers as Communists, but the fact that they are not Communists does not exculpate them from charges that they are seeking to undermine our Government because Communists constitute only one of many groups in the United States desirous of changing our form of government. . . . [T]he Communists together with the groups with which these signers have been identified compose a great body of Marxian revolutionaries in the United States desirous of substituting proletarian dictatorship for our democratic form of government."[63]

That conclusion is not self-evident. Indeed it seems to reflect, more than any accurate perception of the public mood, an interesting obsession on the part of the State Department. The "campaign" against the department, despite all the rhetoric, was by no means a Communist, or Communist-inspired, movement, as the *Nation* itself sourly observed.[64] This was not yet the stage in the war in which Russian-American differences had surfaced. On the contrary it was a period, critical for Russian survival, during which Soviet leaders were most anxious for good working relations with the American administration, as well as the military and economic aid that accompanied them. Hence an editorial in the party's organ, the New York *Daily Worker*, titled "Unity to Beat Hitler," concluded that the episode showed only the "urgent need for a unified strategy based on a strong coalition of all the anti-Hitler forces to most

effectively achieve the defeat of the Axis."[65] Behind that, the official Communist view, dwelt a sympathy with the notion of big-power diplomacy somewhat
at odds with the attitude of the signatories to the telegram, who saw the war as
a popular, democratic crusade. In any case, there is a plain distinction to be
made between active proponents of a Communist or Marxist position on
international affairs, and their temporary, perhaps innocent associates; and it is
doubtful if some of the signers, like William Agar or Norman Cousins, fit into
either category. Even the author of the analysis allowed that no record of active
radical or left wing activities could be attributed to twenty of the signatories.
Rather than viewing the critics, as the American administration tended to, as
inspired by radical motives of a Communist nature, it would be fairer and more
accurate to see them as adopting an adversary relationship to all the great
powers, Russia and the United States alike.

But whichever of the possible interpretations of the criticisms one chooses
—a popular campaign on behalf of the Free French similar to the press
campaign for Cuban independence in the 1890s, or an impulsive critique of a
perceived policy of appeasement as had crystallized in Great Britain after
Munich, or a Communist front, *tout court*—they had an intense effect upon
the State Department. In particular the impact upon Cordell Hull was heavy:
he was tempted toward retirement. On 16 January he scribbled out a note of
resignation to Roosevelt, never actually sent. Though it consisted, for the most
part, of formalities and graceful compliments, there was one sentence, subsequently crossed out, that indicated precisely what was on Hull's mind: "There
has, as you know, been a constant incession [sic] of difficulties, mainly of an
interfering nature."[66] The *Nation*, which less than a fortnight previously had
called for Hull's resignation,[67] had come very close to achieving its goal.

By "difficulties . . . of an interfering nature," Hull did not only mean the
excitable American press. On 30 December Winston Churchill had delivered
an address to the Canadian parliament in Ottawa in which he vigorously
contrasted the "men of Vichy" with those other Frenchmen "who would not
bow their knees and who, like their General de Gaulle, have continued to fight
at the side of the Allies."[68] That may well have startled certain quarters of the
Canadian administration, which had been conducting, with Churchill's active
encouragement, its own Vichy policy, with Pierre Dupuy cast in the role of
Admiral Leahy, and René Ristelhueber playing, though with more circumspection, that of Henry-Haye.[69] Equally in the United States, commented the
New York Herald Tribune, the speech served to blow "all questions of St.
Pierre and Washington's 'so-called Free French' through the dusty windows of
the State Department."[70] Hull might then upbraid Churchill for his "highly
incendiary" remarks.[71] He might beg Roosevelt to make Churchill support the
American position ("provided Churchill would be disposed to talk with you or
rather let you talk with him").[72] But he got little practical help.

An even crueler blow was struck nearer home. On 1 January Hull offered

Roosevelt a draft statement to clarify the American position while reassuring the Latin American republics. But Roosevelt only said that he thought it "inadvisable to resuscitate this question by making a statement . . . and that Sumner Welles could best handle this situation verbally when he gets to Rio," where, later in the month, a conference of American foreign ministers was to be held.[73] Hull had had his difficulties before with Welles's close relationship with the president, and he was to have them again.[74] It must have seemed as if on all sides Hull, the faithful implementer of a policy he had not designed, was under assault. He had, after all, only set forth some of the basic facts upon which the agreed policy was premised: ". . . according to all of my information and that of my associates, some 95 percent of the entire French people are anti-Hitler whereas more than 95 percent of this latter number are not de Gaullists and would not follow him."[75]

How could such a conflict ever be resolved? There were not just four parties to this dispute, each of them pursuing some explicit, deeply ingrained national interest. There were four arenas, in which intense arguments about those very national interests were being conducted at every governmental, bureaucratic, and regional level. If it accomplished nothing else, the episode at least exposed, in every quarter, the illusion of a consensual diplomacy. The restlessness of Admiral Muselier at de Gaulle's wayward and arbitrary leadership was matched by equal concern, at Free French headquarters in London, that de Gaulle had not consulted his newly instituted council before changing his orders; meanwhile, members of the Free French delegation in New York were dismayed that de Gaulle had thus undone what little they had so far accomplished.[76] In Canada the government was now more than ever acutely aware of the tensions between British and French Canadians, and inside the French Canadian population itself, with, according to one report, Gaullist Quebec an apparent oasis within a desert of Catholic, Pétainist loyalties.[77] These tensions would increase in the forthcoming debate over national conscription;[78] and they were scarcely eased by the State Department's impertinent demand of the Canadian administration to restore the status quo on St. Pierre and Miquelon—a piece, in Canadian eyes, of hemispheric arrogance similar to the failure to invite Canada to the Rio conference.[79]

The British and American positions, no less complex, were yet oddly symmetrical. Both presented the spectacle of chief executives, grandly surveying their global domain, being distracted by the particular, and sometimes personal, grievances of their subordinates. Cordell Hull, laying siege to the White House with his batteries of memoranda and resolutions, was doing battle not just for American foreign policy, but for the integrity of his department, which had hitherto always emerged unscathed from the hectic bureaucratic infighting and turbulent political controversies of New Deal Washington. That immunity had now vanished, and, as Hull confessed to Sir Robert

Campbell, it was the abuse of him personally as well as of his department that worried him most.[80] On another flank Colonel Donovan of the OSS, relying on his own distinct sources, had already pressed Roosevelt to seize the opportunity of Churchill's presence in Washington to take up with him "the deplorable condition of the whole Free French movement in this country and inquire into the advisability and possibility of getting out of France some leader, perhaps like Herriot."[81]

Meanwhile, from British officials different, and to some extent countervailing, pressures were being directed at Churchill. Halifax defended the Free French delegation, "a good crowd," and did not want it "treated as nonexistent," or "allowed to wither."[82] The Foreign Office and indeed most of the cabinet were reluctant to permit American hemispheric obligations, however honorable, to determine Anglo-French relations, and urged Churchill not to drop de Gaulle so precipitately. As Eden observed, this was neither the time nor the issue.[83] De Gaulle himself warned Churchill of the effects on "the spirit of resistance in France" of the State Department's stand, and invited him to intercede on behalf of the Free French "because you are the only one who can explain it in the right way."[84] But closer to the center of power, among Churchill's personal advisers, the mood was more hostile. In Desmond Morton's view, de Gaulle was "anti-British, antidemocratic, and vain"; he was, moreover, "disloyal to Winston personally."[85]

But the plain fact was that the St. Pierre-and-Miquelon matter was not what Churchill was in Washington to discuss. He could hardly exert himself for de Gaulle, nor could Roosevelt for Hull, when larger issues—the balance to be struck between the European and Far Eastern theaters of war, the formation of a unified command, the proposed move into North Africa—intruded. As Churchill cabled to Eden, "it is intolerable that the great movement of events should be obstructed, and I shall certainly not intervene to save de Gaulle or other Free French from the consequences";[86] or, as Roosevelt told Churchill, "two tiny islands cannot be made an issue in the great effort to save the world."[87] The story of the resolution of the St. Pierre-and-Miquelon controversy is therefore very largely the story of the progressive isolation of the State Department and in particular of its chief.

In fact the dispute was not to be settled; there was merely a resigned acquiescence in the Free French coup. Day after day, in customary State Department fashion, the draft communiqués, the proposed joint statements, were sent back and forth, always for one reason or another unacceptable; and as time wore on it became clearer that only the department itself had anything very significant to lose by a capitulation to the Free French. And that was face. However well grounded its suspicions of the entire Gaullist enterprise, however widely shared they were in the administration or by other governments, only the American State Department had gambled its prestige upon victory in this particular conflict. The other parties to the dispute were less heavily engaged: the Canadians had been relieved of a minor trouble spot within their sphere of influence, governed, until the coup, by an Axis sympathizer;[88] Roosevelt and Churchill were busy plotting strategy for the remainder of the year; and as for the Vichy French, after attempting for a while to make diplomatic capital out of the incident, invoking it as an excuse for making further concessions to Germany, they too let the matter subside.[89]

It is idle therefore to pursue in detail the course of these negotiations since, for all their secret reservations and unconditional demands, their tacit concessions and their veiled threats, they proved fruitless.[90] Finally, on 2 February 1942, even Hull yielded. He sent a memorandum to Roosevelt that concluded: "In view of the failure to achieve a generally satisfactory settlement which would conform with the policies and obligations of this Government on both sides of the Atlantic, and in view of the paramount importance of furthering unity and harmony in the maximum cooperative war effort with Great Britain, Canada, and the other United Nations, I recommend that further negotiations or discussions of the matter be postponed for the period of the war."[91] A noble and selfless proposal indeed. But Hull's covering letter showed that he was still unhappy at the outcome, and unreconciled to those whom he felt had betrayed him. He expressed his disquiet at "the probable repercussions from Vichy when this matter is made public a few days hence, either by the British Foreign Office or by de Gaulle, regardless of whether privacy is urged by us or not. . . . I feel that I should call to your attention the real probabilities of serious deteriorations . . . in relation to the French Navy, Mediterranean bases, North Africa, etc. And yet there is no other course that we can take at this time."[92]

So the St. Pierre-and-Miquelon episode may have been minor, but it was not trivial. It exposed, as through a microscope, the veins and arteries of American foreign policy. The position adopted by the State Department was a faithful interpretation of the Vichy policy whose chief architect had been Roosevelt himself. But it had been a scrupulously exact interpretation of an essentially moralistic policy. That is, the kind of commitment to which Roosevelt had pledged the United States had been a moral one, giving advice, counseling resistance, delivering rebukes; and as Leahy discovered at Vichy, and Hull discovered with Henry-Haye, such a policy left very little in the way of practical sanctions to be imposed should the recipient of this moral support prove delinquent. Moreover, and this is the real lesson of the affair, such a policy, if relentlessly pursued to its logical conclusions, left its exponent vulnerable on two counts. First, a practical implementation of a moral commitment may prove unrealistic, and collide with other, more urgent considerations within an overall strategy. This was, of course, precisely what happened during the diplomatic negotiations after the coup, and it explains why the State Department, uninvolved in the grander strategic planning, was the last to concede victory to de Gaulle. Second, if this stance is seen to be unrealistic, then it invites criticism not only of a practical kind but, once suspicions are roused, of a speculative nature, imputing base motives; hence those cries of "appeasement" and the attacks on the State Department as a bastion of reaction. Such attacks may have been unjust, but they were the almost inevitable response to a policy that, by sacrificing prudence to moralism, had awakened domestic grievances that would persist at least for the life of the Vichy regime.

CHAPTER 7
THE ROOTS OF AMERICAN ATTITUDES TOWARD FRANCE, 1941–1942

The principal battleground of this war is not the South Pacific, or the Middle East; it is not England or Norway or the Russian Steppes. It is American opinion. Specifically, it is the individual opinion of individual Americans.
—Archibald MacLeish, Rede Lecture,
   Cambridge University, 1942

The words quoted above were addressed to a British audience by the Librarian of Congress, a sophisticated and cosmopolitan poet, a future assistant secretary of state and professor at Harvard, a former expatriate in Europe, member of an international fellowship of writers and artists, a friend to French poets and German scholars. Nevertheless, the view expressed by Archibald MacLeish serves to show how securely American isolationism was embedded within the very heart of its supposed opposite, internationalism.

By so disparaging the military effort, and foreign battlefields ("No reverse anywhere in the world can be more than a temporary setback"), MacLeish meant only to direct attention to the American public, and its apparent confusion about a war now four months old. The St. Pierre-and-Miquelon incident had already shown that American wartime diplomacy would not be conducted before a complaisant American public. Rather, it would be continuously measured against expectations and ideals that, very often, derived from prior official undertakings. MacLeish himself, as part of that personal campaign for public education which had opened with *America Was Promises* (1939) and that provocative essay, "The Irresponsibles,"[1] would spend the war years drifting from one government agency to another, the Office of Facts and Figures, the Office of War Information, the State Department itself.

Meanwhile, St. Pierre and Miquelon would be remembered if only because within a year there took place a reenactment, albeit on a grander scale: the Allied landings in North Africa and the "deal" with Admiral Darlan. Again there was the official slighting of de Gaulle, and a preference, if not for Vichy itself, at least for an erstwhile Vichyite, Darlan. Again there was, within the

139

United States, a vigorous outburst, by the same people as before, against the architect of the policy, identified, again incorrectly, as the State Department. But just as these events, the St. Pierre-and-Miquelon incident and the Darlan deal, were only the practical consequences of the long-standing American commitment to Vichy, so too the public response to them was no fleeting phenomenon. It was the product of an equally long-standing public debate over the nature of the Vichy regime and the correct posture for Americans to adopt toward it. That debate was only sharpened by acts of diplomacy. It had already been opened by the spectacle of the Vichy regime itself, variously perceived. To some observers the regime meant the restoration of order, the semblance (at least) of piety, and doctrinaire anti-Communism; to others, the repudiation of democracy, the conscription of labor, and deference toward Nazi Germany. These views, and the American context in which they were formed, help to explain the specific controversies sparked by more particular, isolated acts of American foreign policy.

Public opinion polls by themselves, however quantified and calibrated, do not greatly advance an understanding of the climate of opinion, though they may be revealing about sheer matters of fact. In November 1941, only 47 percent of one sample knew anything at all about the Vichy regime, while only 45 percent could identify Pétain as its head.[2] In July 1941, 36 percent could recognize de Gaulle, in August 38 percent. By the following July that figure had risen to 51 percent; but of that total nearly a third believed that the American administration actually negotiated with the Free French rather than Vichy when it wanted to deal with the French.[3] However, that select group with any knowledge of French affairs, a minority in 1941, a bare majority in 1942, evidently held pronounced views. In July 1941, 73 percent of it considered that the Free French came closer than Vichy "to representing the opinion of the French people as a whole." In August, 77 percent thought that Vichy was helping Germany. In September, 74 percent wanted the American administration to extend Lend-Lease aid to the Free French. In November, although only 36 percent favored full American recognition of the Free French, 81 percent still held a very unfavorable opinion of Vichy: 65 percent thought Vichy would let Germany use the French fleet against Britain, and 76 percent thought Vichy would let Germany likewise use the French bases in Africa. By July 1942, 74 percent thought that the United States should recognize the Free French.[4]

Those raw data suggest a keen, but scattered concern with France among the American public. Such interest as can be found was overwhelmingly critical of Vichy, although there was, as there always would be, a devout minority that was not. What the polls do not and cannot show are the various sources of these views. In particular they cannot measure the relative weight thus given to French and American considerations, to foreign affairs and foreign policy. That is, they do not distinguish between "France," a society undergoing certain experiences that foreign observers may have wished to scrutinize, and France, a country on the receiving end of an American foreign policy. It is, however, a commonplace of wartime public opinion, in the United States as elsewhere, that it tends to follow the government's lead.[5] What is striking about the United States is that the administration did not provide any clear and consistent lead. An idealist rhetoric proposed, it seemed, but diplomacy disposed. The proliferation of official agencies of propaganda and censorship did not harvest a rich crop of sustained, vigorous public guidance. It became, instead, a typical fruit of Roosevelt's style of leadership.

For there was never any real correlation between propaganda and censorship. Roosevelt's policy was the reverse of that adopted during the First World War. Then George Creel's Committee on Public Information, established by Congress, had performed both functions. Now they were undertaken by separate government bureaus, established by executive decree. These were administered mostly by men of broadly liberal sentiments. The U.S. Office of Censorship was set up in December 1941 under a former newspaperman, Byron Price; and he strictly limited his mandate to matters of national security, invariably of a military nature. He exercised no influence on editorial opinion, and the row over St. Pierre and Miquelon, particularly the calls for Cordell Hull's resignation, showed early on a latitude of expression for which it would be difficult to find a counterpart in Great Britain. Domestic propaganda (and the related gathering of information about public opinion) was covered by four agencies, the Office of Government Reports, the Office of Facts and Figures, the Office of the Co-ordinator of Information and the Division of Information in the Office of Emergency Management, all nominally consolidated in June 1942 in the Office of War Information (OWI) under Elmer Davis, another liberal newspaperman. He too inclined toward generosity. "This is," he wrote, "a people's war, and to win it the people should know as much about it as they can."[6] That perspective was shared by the head of the Office of Facts and Figures, later assistant director of OWI, yet another liberal but one of grander intellectual and artistic accomplishments, Archibald MacLeish. Invited to distinguish between his "kind of operation and the propaganda office of a totalitarian state," he declared, borrowing a phrase from Edmond Taylor after the French collapse: "The difference is the difference between the strategy of terror and the strategy of truth. . . . Democracy is based on the proposition that the Government can trust the people and that the people are entitled to all the facts and figures necessary to make up their own minds within the limits of national security."[7]

But neither MacLeish nor Davis saw his expansive liberal dreams realized. MacLeish resigned after barely six months with OWI, disappointed at the lack of attention given his arguments for a forceful presentation of American war aims;[8] earlier at the Office of Facts and Figures he had complained to his friend, Harold Ickes, Secretary of the Interior, about how his efforts were being consistently undermined: "I am willing to give everything I possess to this cause except my reputation for basic honesty. That I will not sacrifice to anyone for any purpose, and least of all for the purpose of covering the failure of the Armed Services to make good on their commitments."[9] Elmer Davis's personal "Report to the President" at the end of the war is similarly a sad chronicle of an idealist's odyssey through interagency rivalry, obstructionism from the War, Navy, and State departments, and personality clashes.[10]

A modest censorship combined with a bland, ineffectual domestic propaganda: there were a number of reasons for this state of affairs. One was the sour impression that had been left, in the wake of the First World War, by the activities of the Creel Committee; in this, as in so much else, Roosevelt showed himself to be not so much Wilson's disciple as someone resolved to learn from his predecessor's errors. A further reason lay in the American public's more general distrust of all propaganda. Already evident in 1940 with regard to foreign propaganda,[11] that suspicion could be equally aroused by overt propaganda from government sources. "Propaganda," wrote Elmer Davis, "is a word in bad odor in this country; but there is no public hostility to the idea of education, and we regard this part of our job as education."[12] But a more fundamental explanation is to be found in Roosevelt's own conception of the task. No doubt he did desire some form of government propaganda, and the "Fireside Chats" of the New Deal had already shown his delicate understanding of the public mood. Similarly, with regard to foreign policy it is at least arguable that he was as well attuned to the eddies of public opinion as any president this century. That much is clear from the caution and hesitancy, as well as the secretiveness, of his diplomacy from 1939 to 1941.

Thus the propaganda agencies that Roosevelt eventually set up, with their overlapping jurisdictions and their slim ambitions, reflected alike the bureaucratic explosion of the New Deal era and his own uncertainty about the public's tolerance. And the typical propaganda that emerged was little more than an internationalization of the goals of the New Deal, couched in grandiose, moralistic language and taking as its basis presidential rhetoric—the Charlottesville address, the Four Freedoms, the Atlantic Charter (which Roosevelt always regarded as a propaganda exercise and once compared as an objective, and in its practical relevance, with the Ten Commandments),[13] and the Declaration of the United Nations. It was altogether characteristic of this climate that in April 1942 one liberal internationalist at the Office of Emergency Management, Edgar Ansel Mowrer, should write to another, MacLeish, at the Office of Facts and Figures in the same Executive Office Building, with the news:

> Secretary Welles asked me to tell you that he thinks the war should be made a crusade.
>
> He thinks that the White House should take the lead in proclaiming international aims, one of which should be the freedom of all peoples

. . .

He thinks that to encourage general discussion of postwar organization at this time would be definitely bad, and that the Government alone
is qualified to push public opinion in the desired direction.[14]

In short, government propaganda would only be compelling so long as government actions were applauded. The role of the liberal idealists—Davis,
MacLeish, Mowrer—was thus sharply limited from the start.

Such a governmental stance had a number of consequences, all unforeseen,
that bore directly upon the development of American attitudes toward France.
For Roosevelt was impelled by his distrust of purely verbal propaganda toward
a reliance on military success, a belief that actions would speak louder; and the
Allied landings in North Africa in November 1942 were a replacement for the
ideal Second Front in Europe, for which, however, the armed forces were as
yet unprepared.[15] But there exists no easy distinction between military and
political objectives. In seeking to gratify public opinion with military achievements, Roosevelt invited them to be measured by precisely those idealistic,
moral standards to which, in general terms, he aspired. For the remainder of
the war, and particularly with regard to France, Roosevelt was to be caught
between the doctrine of military expediency, which would assure victory, and
the ideals of the Atlantic Charter, which would make real success harder to
attain. George Creel, drawing upon his own earlier experience, wrote to Elmer
Davis in August 1942, "While you may think you have established an arrangement that will permit a free flow of the news, just wait till an issue arises." He
then went on to make a number of other comments (including an animadver-
sion upon Nelson Rockefeller, then co-ordinator of inter-American affairs),
and Davis later noted on the letter, "He was about right on all points."[16]

There was one further consequence. If such propaganda as emerged from
the administration was exceedingly, and deliberately, general, leaving the
details uncertain, then the void might well be filled by private action. That was
the task undertaken by such pressure groups as the Free World Association, the
Union for Democratic Action, Fight for Freedom, even France Forever, the
members of which conceived their responsibility as being to discern, and open
up for public debate, the practical implications of presidential rhetoric. Hence
the formation in August 1941 within Fight for Freedom of a group of eminent
anti-Vichy Frenchmen, including Jacques Maritain and Raoul de Roussy de
Sales, precisely in order "to interpret for Americans the interest of Free
Frenchmen in the survival of democracy." Their first objective, so they said,
was to "co-operate by all means in their power to [sic] the establishment of the
kind of world outlined by President Roosevelt in his 'four freedoms' program."[17] On this front too Roosevelt was to lay himself open to the charge of
failing to make performance match up to promise.

Such was the American context in which discussion of French affairs took place. And it sharply contrasts, on the French side, with a rigid censorship of American correspondents' dispatches home. Originally, after Laval's dismissal in December 1940, the prospects for a considerable relaxation seemed favorable. On 29 December Laval's successor, Paul Baudouin, told journalists that his government now recognized the need to give the fullest possible information to the United States; and the correspondent for the *New York Times* observed that the censors appeared to be "taking a broad view so far as American correspondents were concerned."[18] But the change did not survive Baudouin's own departure from the government on 3 January. A new chief of censorship complained that "much false news comes from Anglo-American sources."[19] Arrangements to film and photograph Leahy's first visit to the new foreign minister, Pierre-Etienne Flandin, were peremptorily canceled; and the *New York Times* correspondent soon reversed himself, declaring that the new control was characterized by all the severity of Laval's tenure of office.[20]

So it indeed proved for the next two years: Leahy's statement that Americans were convinced that Britain would be victorious was not only kept out of the French press but cut from dispatches back to the United States;[21] within Vichy, reports of Roosevelt's speeches were slim, and more space was given to an anti-interventionist broadcast by former ambassador Joseph Kennedy than to Roosevelt's message to Congress on the Lend-Lease bill;[22] the harassment of American reporters and the demands by Darlan and others for favorable American commentary were a familiar story at the American embassy.[23]

The effect of this combination—fluency of discourse on the American side with censorship of information on the French—was further to encourage a development already evident in 1940. If all that came out of Vichy was skeletal news, concerning the comings and goings at Pétain's court, or a bare recitaton of events—the dismissal of Weygand, the Riom trials, the return of Laval— then the interpretation of those events in terms of their significance for the United States could only be supplied editorially. Thus the combined effect of weak American and stringent French censorship was to enlarge that area in which speculation could flourish and France could be understood only in an American idiom. This process was already evident in 1940.[24] A few examples will suffice to show it at work in the later period, with the Vichy regime in full bloom.

There is the case of the Riom trials, which, first proposed in 1940 and eventually begun in February 1942, neatly epitomize the period of Vichy's effective sovereignty. They were its most famous assault on France's republican past. Two conflicting interpretations were current outside France about the purpose of the trials: either they were instigated at German insistence, "war-guilt" trials, to prove the German thesis that the Allies had forced Germany into the war; or they were a response to French public opinion, which demanded the punishment of those who had misguided the nation and brought it to disaster. Whichever explanation is correct, the trials undoubtedly also reflected the Vichy regime's desire to discredit its predecessor, and the charges leveled against the defendants would appear to have satisfied every criterion: General Gamelin and Robert Jacomet, the comptroller general of the army, were accused of unpreparedness; former air ministers Guy La Chambre and Pierre Cot (tried in absentia; he was in the United States) with negligence and sending airplanes to republican Spain; Daladier with entering the war without consulting Parliament or the army; and Blum with disrupting production by nationalizing war industries and subordinating work to leisure as a national creed.[25] The charges themselves are most revealing, and it might have been expected that the trials, held publicly, would attract considerable outside interest: Roosevelt himself privately requested a transcript.[26] What was not to be expected was that at the opening session of the trial Blum and Daladier would themselves take the offensive, with Daladier denouncing the entire proceedings as a German ploy, and Blum declaring that it was the Republic and democracy that were on trial, and that he was as proud to defend them then as he had been in the past.[27]

Naturally it was this outburst, rather than the formal procès-verbal, that gave the trials their symbolic potency; and by most of the American press it was hailed as a vindication of the traditional courage and desire for freedom of the French people.[28] But there was one significant demurral, from the Hearst press, still the voice of unbending conservative isolationism. There, in the pages of the *New York Journal-American*, the old complaints, the old arguments were once again resurrected:

> The trial of Daladier and Blum in France may be the beginning of a new era of justice and peace on this earth. . . . It is to be hoped that the guilty will be convicted in France and that their prosecution will afford an example—a precedent—which all the other outraged peoples of the world will follow. Blum . . . is blamed for coddling the communists and the anarchists when they were undermining the strength of France by strikes and sabotage and every kind of obstruction to progress and production. He is arraigned for having wasted the wealth of France in political boondoggling, in compelling the payment of preposterous increases that disloyal strikers demanded through force and violence . . . for having filled the public offices of France with political bureaucrats loyal to nothing but themselves and the regime which kept them in place and power. The point that holds a bright promise for a better future is that leaders who project their nations into the war are already being prosecuted, with fair hope of punishment for their failure in the war.[29]

For its part the *Nation* only stated the obvious when it observed that that description of the charges against Blum and Daladier fitted equally well the charges brought continuously against Roosevelt by the extreme isolationist and conservative press of Hearst, Joseph M. Patterson, and Colonel Robert R. McCormick.[30]

The Riom trials were to some extent a special case, in which politics, history, and ideology were so thoroughly entwined anyway that American commentary naturally acquired an introspective quality. But it is not difficult to find other instances where the writer's preconceptions colored his interpretation of French affairs. This is especially, though by no means exclusively, true of the traditional isolationist press. For example the mass murders of French hostages in October 1941 (by way of a reprisal for the assassination of German officers in Nantes and Bordeaux) were condemned by the whole of the American press. But the *Chicago Tribune*, even while considering the executions "revolting," declared that Roosevelt and Churchill were the ones who were responsible for murdering innocents in France, measured in thousands rather than groups of fifty, by refusing to break the blockade.[31] The following year, after Laval's return to power in April, the *Chicago Tribune* was again incensed, this time by Sumner Welles's reference to the "handful of Frenchmen" who were "sordidly and abjectly" surrendering their countrymen to the German enemy. Welles, commented the *Tribune*, "with his usual finesse was explaining the fair and honorable intentions of this country to men whom he described as first-rate scoundrels. If Mr. Welles intended to have any effect upon Pétain's ministers, his approach to the subject was peculiar even for our State Department. . . . [He] hasn't improved the situation in Vichy and he certainly hasn't outwitted Hitler by calling the dominant Vichy politicians sordid and abject."[32] On the opposite side, the far wing of the interventionist movement, Herbert Agar, a member of the Fight for Freedom committee, wrote in the *Louisville Courier-Journal*, also on the matter of the blockade: "Food or no food [Hitler] will do what seems to him expedient with the French fleet. No one will ever make a successful bargain with a country under Hitler's heel. But if we pretend that we are paying Hitler's blackmail because of humanitarian reasons (or because there is such a thing as an independent France) there is no logical ground for stopping short of Hooverizing [sic] the whole world into slavery."[33]

To accuse Roosevelt of murdering thousands of innocent French civilians, to see Herbert Hoover as willfully furthering Hitler's ambitions—such indictments convey something of the polemical flavor of the day. They were not, of course, the whole story. In private such spokesmen often adopted a more reasoned approach. Dorothy Thompson, for example, who held the most forthright views, sent a carefully argued letter around to a number of her acquaintances, inside and outside the administration, such as Herbert Feis, the State Department's economic adviser, and Henry Luce, the publisher of *Life*. There she proposed in the most persuasive and rational way that the American administration actually send food and medical supplies "as a political weapon" to Vichy France, thus robbing the Germans of a propaganda coup, although she appended to her proposal a list of the most unlikely conditions for Vichy to accept in advance, which would have amounted to curbing its already limited sovereignty over unoccupied France.[34] Certainly by fastening attention on the extreme wings of the interventionist and isolationist press only a partial and distorted picture will appear. In other quarters the debate was being conducted in more refined and sedate terms.

The *New York Times*, for example, maintained in its editorials its then-characteristic standards of journalistic equipoise, even while granting space to "Pertinax" to publish his misgivings on the whole subject of Vichy.[35] The *Wall Street Journal* published the sober, conservative reflections of Felix Morley and Thomas F. Woodlock (whose column was appropriately entitled "Thinking It Over"), who argued in favor of granting a considerable measure of indulgence to Pétain, Darlan, and even Laval, always in the most moderate and reasoned of terms. Woodlock concluded one column on the subject by wistfully observing: "Some day, perhaps, when we are no longer under the spell of our own over-simplified generalizations, and the vociferations of discredited Third Republic propagandists, some of us may feel a little ashamed of the judgments we have so confidently passed in the last two years."[36] Walter Lippmann in his thrice-weekly column regularly expressed his unease at the American commitment to Vichy; and although his criticism often merged with those from more outspokenly liberal quarters—especially in his stress on the role of the State Department—his were always advanced in that tutorial mode of address which was his distinctive journalistic idiom, ever seeking to reform by precept rather than abuse.[37]

If, to take one last example, one turns to *Commonweal*, an influential journal of moderate Catholic opinion, there is a discussion of the "new French regime" in the most scrupulously dignified, even academic terms. One writer, Professor Louis Mercier of Harvard, rather enamored of the regime, concluded: "That many difficulties will be encountered, and even mistakes made, in the substitutions of this [i.e., Vichy's] realistic democracy to [i.e., for] the pseudo-democracy of social irresponsibility there is no doubt. It is, in any case, startling to note that only a few weeks after her defeat France was courageously re-organizing on the basis of formulas which *every democracy* may well have to take into account if it would survive."[38] Similarly, a writer who disagreed with Mercier, Professor Yves Simon of Notre Dame University, given equal space by the editors of *Commonweal*, stated: "It is not possible to carry on any propaganda in favor of the 'new French regime' without weakening the resolution on which depend the liberation of France and the liberation of the world. . . . [M]y disagreement with Professor Mercier is mostly concerned with the interpretation of the political history of contemporary France. It is my conviction that Professor Mercier has missed the historical meaning of the Vichy government."[39]

The same central issues were being raised in these quarters: the moral dimension to America's Vichy policy, and the universal validity of the French experience. Those were in fact the foundations of all American commentary on France, and the prerequisite of any public discussion of American policy. But there was, undeniably, a difference in tone, which raises certain questions: why did the problem of Vichy France matter so much more in some areas of American opinion than in others? why was it possible for some to engage temperately in honest differences of opinion, while others were prompted to make the most far-reaching assaults on their opponents?

The distinction is in part one of timing. Those who engaged in moderate discussion tended to be confident of an Allied victory in due course and thus interested, in a leisurely way, in formulating postwar plans. The period of America's Vichy policy, precisely because it was one of limited military activity, encouraged such speculation. It was a time of important books, articles, and speeches by Henry Luce, Henry Wallace, Sumner Welles, Wendell Willkie, Herbert Hoover, Clarence Streit, and Nicholas Spykman;[40] these were in direct succession to the earlier, wide-ranging public discussion of the fall of France in the summer and autumn of 1940, though they took a broader canvas. There were obvious differences among the various viewpoints, from the economic Wilsonianism of Wallace and the imperialist idealism of Luce to the world federalism of Streit and the geopolitics of Spykman. But there were also common preoccupations, chief of which was a suspicion of all forms of European nationalism, especially of its dangerous outgrowth, European imperialism. The point was not lost on a non-American readership. Churchill received from Desmond Morton in due course a commentary on Willkie's book, *One World*, which concluded that the work aimed "at founding an American policy against all Empires and is therefore subtly anti-British."[41] Similarly Raoul de Roussy de Sales noted of Spykman's book *America's Strategy in World Politics* that as a result of the author's supposed "realism" about power politics he engaged in "no discussion other than in the past": "This is also true of most of the books and articles which one reads about the world of the future. France, whatever happens, is relegated to the rank of Spain or even lower."[42]

The eviction of European nationalism from international affairs could be accomplished by a variety of means, and it was these distant goals that determined much of the intermediate debate on wartime policy toward France. To Walter Lippmann, any postwar plans should be premised upon insistent, but friendly, Great Power action to combat the perils of nationalist rivalries in Europe; and in the meantime support should be extended to those who resisted, not those who capitulated before, their oppressors.[43] To the columnists of the *Wall Street Journal*, by contrast, hope lay in the promise of a stable, anti-Communist, and conservative bloc, of which Pétain also dreamed. Thomas Woodlock's conclusions are worth quoting in full, since they illustrate both his long-term fears and his immediate perception of parallels between France and the United States:

> The conditions in France today seem to favor the emergence of a new Front to succeed the suppression of anarchy, because it is sufficiently capacious to house the elements of the discontented, the dispossessed, and spiritually uprooted masses that are concentrated in the cities, to whom it holds out promise of material benefits and—equally alluring—revenge upon the "classes" which have oppressed them. It can in fact offer them a "New Deal" and one to which in strict justice they are in no small means entitled. It would, of course, be strictly "democratic" in forms. In both these respects it would strongly commend itself to American "opinion," especially in its forms. Nor would its laic principles offend much; to many indeed they would offer a positive attraction, for we have not yet learned that Rousseauist "democracy" (the Front would of course be Rousseauist) and our own are at opposite poles in this respect and that the end of any Rousseauist "democracy" (and of any despiritualized "democracy") is totalitarianism and the death of liberty.
>
> Thus the question of great importance to Europe is whether France will or will not go Rousseauist, for if it does a vital stronghold of the Western culture will go down.[44]

Doubtless too, Catholic loyalties, and Christian charity, played some part in *Commonweal*'s ongoing forbearance toward Pétain.[45]

But a large gulf divides these far-reaching considerations from the more immediate objectives of more radical organs. For the *Chicago Tribune* and its isolationist sympathizers the wartime transition from "America First" to "Asia First," the belief in the primacy of the Far Eastern theater, was an easy one. Both viewpoints were based upon at least an indifference toward Europe, the status quo of which would be more readily assured by the conservative Pétain than by the restless de Gaulle. For the same reason the *Chicago Tribune* later gravitated toward the camp of General Giraud.[46] On the other side, the chief concern of the more committed American supporters of the Free French was with sustaining the radical, anti-fascist movements of occupied Europe, in other words, with a second front; and Roosevelt was to grow just as impatient with their insistent pressure as with his earlier isolationist critics. "Sometimes," he wrote to his vice-president, Henry Wallace, "writers of articles forget that troops cannot be sent to a nice, peaceful wharf in France, nor have troops yet acquired the divine power of walking on the water."[47]

A second front in Europe or "Asia First": these most pressing of aims, so unalterably opposed, account in part for the virulence and extremism of their adherents' campaigns. But while they may explain the style of the argument, they still do not effectively explain its content, the pivotal role ascribed to

France. For the accusations that were made always involved a presumed allegiance owed to a foreign country. The *Chicago Tribune* believed that the State Department automatically followed the lead of the British Foreign Office;[48] the *New Republic* asserted that the State Department "likes the men of Vichy . . . [and] is trying to save their prestige until victory is won, in order to install them as the postwar rulers of France";[49] and the editor of the *Nation* wrote of the State Department, "Its spirit is un-American, its atmosphere is pseudo-aristocratic, its ways are secret. . . . A large section of its permanent bureaucracy are [sic] if not sympathetic to fascism, at least unsympathetic to democracy."[50] Nor do the differing strategic goals adequately explain the fact that one group, the opposition to Vichy and to America's support of Vichy, steadily grew until there was a major eruption at the time of the Darlan deal. At the very moment, that is, when a bridgehead was being built into occupied Europe, the distinction between the moderate and the extreme opposition to Vichy was erased, and both vented their fury, once again, on the hapless State Department.

If these features are to be explained, and the later storm over the Darlan deal understood, certain other elements will have to be introduced. Three in particular suggest themselves: the subjective claim on American loyalties of the Free French and the parallel loss in prestige of Vichy, largely as a result of particular events; second, the growth of broadly based organizations and pressure groups, forums for all varieties of liberal and left-wing dissent from American foreign policy; and finally the curious position of the State Department, vulnerable to domestic criticism while powerless to direct foreign policy.

The pressure for increased American support for de Gaulle did not come from a mass movement, nor was it especially well organized. The letters sent to the State Department, and preserved in its archives, complaining of American policy, came mostly, as might be expected, from literate, professional, middle-class individuals, particularly lawyers and teachers, the same milieu in fact out of which letters of support tended to come. Newspaper clippings were enclosed and demands were made that something be done.[51] France Forever, the organization of enthusiastic amateurs, had, for all its good intentions, gained only 15,000 members in the United States by the end of 1942. A typical function, a Fête Champêtre, held by one of the largest chapters—the one in Chicago with nearly a thousand members—raised less than five hundred dollars. The chairman of the membership committee, Mrs. Walter Brewster, observed morosely in a letter to the treasurer that ". . . it is very unfortunate that there is no [illegible] agreement among the French people of Chicago. On the subject of Vichy there can be no compromise but so many criticisms and enmities have come to me since I undertook to re-organize 'France Forever' that I have been thoroughly discouraged."[52] The office in New York was similarly in the grip of a financial and administrative crisis, from which it only gradually recovered.[53]

Nor was the official Free French delegation in any better state. Throughout 1942 Adrien Tixier continued to quarrel with de Roussy de Sales and Etienne Boegner, and their disputes were never conducted discreetly. De Roussy de Sales's disillusionment with the Gaullist enterprise steadily deepened, until by August 1942 he was "convinced of the purely episodic character of this enterprise."[54] Boegner for his part, after a number of furious arguments with Tixier and with de Gaulle over the course of Free French policy, decided to withdraw from the movement. Already in April he had apologized to Adolf Berle for another provocative speech by de Gaulle and insisted that it in no way represented his own or de Roussy de Sales's views. "The French colony here," he added, "was, in the main, bad, representing the worst of France—just as the expatriate colony of Americans in Paris did not always represent the best of American types."[55] Now, in October, he explained to Berle his reasons for resigning, and they chiefly concerned the Gaullists' behavior toward the United States: "The whole atmosphere, both with the General and with his supporters, was anti-American. They accused the U.S. of trying to set up a world octopus; of trying to fragmentize the old French Empire; in the hope of seizing it for themselves."[56]

Tixier's nominal control of the delegation made it unlikely that the respectability of the Free French in official circles would ever rise from the low point to which it had sunk after the St. Pierre-and-Miquelon affair. Berle detected in him "a curious combination of sincerity and ambition"[57] and throughout 1942 could only give him the vaguest encouragement.[58] Since, moreover, the delegation had been as effectively penetrated as the Vichy embassy, by all manner of intelligence agencies from the OSS to a private operation under the direction of the journalist John Franklin Carter,[59] the American administration was perfectly well aware of the internal discord. It knew, for example, that Tixier himself, showing a breadth of experience far beyond his obvious trade-union qualifications, had compared the Gaullist movement in New York to a poorly run brothel.[60] It also heard the more startling, if less credible, rumor that Tixier was engaged in an intrigue with a fellow trade unionist, John L. Lewis of the Congress of Industrial Organizations, "looking to the overthrow of the Administration by means of a workmen's revolt which will make Lewis all-powerful."[61]

Finally evidence appeared of considerable unrest within the émigré journalist community. There did exist an ostensibly Gaullist publication, *Pour la victoire*, edited by the lively and independent-minded Geneviève Tabouis, with contributions from Henry de Kérillis, Jacques Maritain, and Philippe Barrès. But it had run into difficulties, both financial and ideological. It needed a subsidy, but it was also beginning to dissent from the official, at times intolerant, line of the Gaullists in London. The differences had been over such issues as the appropriate attitude to adopt toward recent right-wing arrivals in England like Charles Vallin, as well as toward political figures still in France like Edouard Herriot and Jules Jeanneney, the last presidents of the Senate and Chamber of Deputies respectively.[62] Other issues were personal as well as political, Mme Tabouis going to great lengths to defend her vaunted, and deserved, reputation for journalistic integrity; she rejected de Gaulle's demand that her journal become the official Gaullist organ.[63] The crisis would come to a head in 1943 when the appearance of General Giraud threatened to split the émigré community into partisans of one general or the other. In the meantime an uneasy compromise was reached. *Pour la victoire* did receive a Gaullist subsidy in return for reprinting articles from *La Marseillaise*, the London Gaullist journal. But the result was that the differences were now there to be seen between *Pour la victoire* and *La Marseillaise*, and they may at this stage be crudely summarized as between pro- and anti-American Gaullism.[64]

Gaullism in America was not advanced so much by Gaullists in America as by the pressure of events. This was true of the revelation of Henry-Haye's alleged activities, the St. Pierre-and-Miquelon affair, and the Riom trials. The last incident of that dimension was the return to power in April 1942 of Pierre Laval, back to replace as prime minister Pétain, who henceforth retained only the title of head of state. It would be hard to overestimate the significance of this act. More than just prompting the recall of Admiral Leahy, it invited a whole reconsideration of the Vichy regime and, a fortiori, the American policy toward it, an enterprise rather more willingly undertaken by the American press than the American administration. It was only the very rare commentator, like Arthur Krock of the *New York Times*, who argued that the event vindicated the entire American approach to French affairs: Leahy's mission, he wrote, had "exceeded the most optimistic hopes . . . by holding Vichy within the terms of the armistice for more than two years [sic] simultaneously and in surprisingly strong degree a restraining force against collaborationists in France, as well as a symbol of our 'ancient and loyal friendship' towards the French people and of the 'armed might of this nation.' "[65] For most of the rest of the press, including the *New York Times* itself, Laval was equated with Hitler, and the question of American success was at best a moot point.[66] "On the face of the facts," remarked the *New Republic*, "the State Department policy toward Vichy looks to be as great a failure as its policy toward Spain, Italy, or Japan."[67] The accession to power of Laval was, said the *Nation*, "a minor Pearl Harbor."[68]

Worse news was to follow. In June Laval announced that he was negotiating with Germany for the release of French prisoners in return for the dispatch of French workers, and he openly avowed his hope for a German victory. That provoked the *New York Herald Tribune* to comment on the "split personality" of the State Department, which "does not like Laval but refers in kindly fashion to an elderly Marshal of France who bears the title of Chief of the

French State";[69] Samuel Grafton was led to attack the "obscurantists . . . muttering that Vichy, established by Hitler to keep the French from helping us, is the device by which we shall get the French to help us";[70] and the *Chicago Sun* concluded that "American recognition of the puppet Government at Vichy . . . [is] a prop to keep it in power. We can scarcely expect the French people to revolt against it as long as they are obliged to reflect that we defer to it."[71] In July Vichy refused to permit any transfer of the demilitarized French vessels in Alexandria during the German advances on Egypt, and Sumner Welles himself attributed that rejection to the influence of "pro-German elements in Vichy."[72]

Laval's return also marked the beginning of serious congressional discussion of American policy. Previously concern had only been expressed sporadically: the occasional insertion into the *Congressional Record* of an apposite newspaper editorial,[73] Representative Foster Stearns's resolution that the United States recognize the Free French (defeated in committee),[74] and Senator James Mead of New York's proposal that the United States occupy all French possessions in the Western Hemisphere (politely rejected by Cordell Hull).[75] Now, with Laval's return, the discussion became more heated. On 14 April, Representative William R. Poage from Texas insisted that the United States "repudiate any policy of appeasement. England appeased Hitler and later Mussolini. We appeased Japan. What were the results? Stabs in the back. So it will always be. Thousands of American boys have died in the Philippines because Vichy France was ready even under Marshal Pétain to appease Japan. Laval has proved himself to be the enemy of all free people. Let America act today to aid the Free French. Let us have an end to appeasement."[76] The same day Representative Charles Faddis from Pennsylvania complained that the American hope "that France would refuse to be a party to Hitler's rape of civilization . . . has carried us much farther along the road of appeasement than can be justified by sound judgment."[77] Within a week Stearns had disinterred his earlier resolution.[78]

Later in the year a more sustained debate took place. After Admiral Leahy had appeared before the Senate Committee on Foreign Relations, meeting in executive session, its chairman, Tom Connally of Texas, professed himself satisfied with the American maintenance of relations with Vichy;[79] but his colleagues Guy Gillette of Iowa and Claude Pepper of Florida had long before expressed their misgivings.[80] By October Connally found himself virtually an administration spokesman on the floor of the Senate, pleading for caution in discussing foreign policy. Such matters as the appropriate American policy toward Vichy were, he argued, best left to the discretion of the president and the secretary of state. For Mead had renewed his call for the immediate occupation of all French possessions in the American sphere—this time in response to the arrests of American civilians in occupied France—and warned that while the United States remained the true friend of France, there was not "room for both the policies of Washington and Vichy."[81]

So far, with the exception of France Forever, we have been looking at individual responses to Vichy: the congressmen do not seem to have been trying to placate any particular constituency. But it is now necessary to consider the more collective forms of activity. For protests against American policy were also registered by the Union for Democratic Action (UDA), Fight for Freedom, the Committee to Defend America by Aiding the Allies, as well as such lesser bodies as the Greater Boston CIO, the National Maritime Union, and the New York College Teachers' Union.[82] This would suggest that the Vichy controversy gained in importance insofar as it became entwined with other concerns; and those concerns were, broadly, of two kinds: the future of Europe as a whole, and certain domestic preoccupations of liberal and left-wing American intellectuals. These more immediate issues included the immigration policy of the American administration, the question of supporting anti-fascist and resistance movements within occupied Europe, and, naturally enough, "appeasement." They had long concerned such organizations as UDA, the Free World Association (FWA), and Freedom House, where eminent American figures like Edgar Ansel Mowrer, Freda Kirchwey, Max Lerner, and William Agar (a naturalized American) cohabited with European émigrés like Julius Alvarez del Vayo, Charles Davila, Count Carlo Sforza, General Julius Deutsch, Count Ferdinand Czernin, and Professor Rustern Vanberry.[83] All drew upon the same pool of Gaullist talent: Philippe Barrès, Henri Bernstein, Eve Curie.[84]

The many links among members and organizers readily identify them as a remarkably cohesive and self-conscious clan: the treasurer of the UDA was the editor of the *Nation*, Freda Kirchwey; a vice-chairman of the UDA was the managing editor of the *Nation*, Robert Bendiner; starting in September 1942, Alvarez del Vayo edited a special "Political War" section for the *Nation*; Clark M. Eichelberger, a member of the Committee to Defend America by Aiding the Allies and of the Citizens Committee for Victory, was one of the directors of the Free World Association, along with Freda Kirchwey; in the March 1942 issue of *Free World* there appeared an article describing the work of Citizens for Victory written by the Reverend Dr. Frank Kingdon, president of the UDA; the titular president and the acting president of Freedom House, founded in January 1942 as the successor to Fight for Freedom, Inc., were Herbert and William Agar, respectively; once again Frank Kingdon was on the board; and so on.[85]

What did they all want? Obviously to influence policy, but less by shifting public opinion than by gaining access to the wielders of power. Hence, for example, the letter from the chairman of UDA, Reinhold Niebuhr, to Mrs. Roosevelt inviting her to sign an open letter to her own husband protesting his administration's French policy.[86] Such efforts did not greatly advance the anti-Vichy movement. FWA might obtain an article from Cordell Hull for the first issue of *Free World* and contributions from Sumner Welles and Adolf

Berle for the first anniversary issue; but by then its policies had already lost their charm for the State Department, which it would revile alongside those very articles. Thus it denounced the department's "anti-Semitism, its cruel, reactionary policy towards political refugees," and declared that "many thousands of honest and patriotic citizens have felt that the Department's policies these last ten years have dishonored and enfeebled the national tradition."[87] Roosevelt, when directly approached, refused on principle to send messages of encouragement to the FWA.[88] Freedom House might request the use of Eleanor Roosevelt's name in a fund-raising drive for a new Statue of Liberty to be presented to the French people after the war, but her husband intervened to forbid it, and similarly declined to give his own support to that project, under those auspices.[89] Members of the UDA might flaunt a hostile article about them in the *Daily Worker* as evidence of their independence from the Communist party line; but one State Department researcher concluded that the language of that particular editorial—which termed UDA members "broken-down 'radicals,' renegades, Hillmanites, and a sprinkling of terrified 'liberals' . . . [the] hidden hand of imperialism"—was entirely "characteristic of that reserved by Communists for those who had co-operated with them previously and then broken."[90]

But the beleaguered wartime State Department does not necessarily afford the clearest perspective upon this movement of opinion. The leading spokesmen for the cause—that intriguing combination of Protestant clerisy (Niebuhr, Kingdon), European exiles (Bernstein, Curie), and American liberals (Mowrer, Lerner)—were scarcely renowned for their Communist sympathies. Nor were all those respectable American figures who lent it their support: Eleanor Roosevelt, the honorary chairman of the FWA; Mayor Fiorello La Guardia of New York, Wendell Willkie, and Harold Ickes, all of whom were involved in Free French Week in New York in July 1942;[91] and Henry Wallace, whose address, *The Price of Free World Victory*, was delivered to the FWA.[92] No doubt there were fellow travelers to be found in the rank and file, where there were certainly also political naïfs; but these were never predominant. It would be rather more just to take into account the rhetoric of the movement as a whole, which drew largely upon that of the New Deal, suitably internationalized, and thus to shift the analysis somewhat to the right. De Gaulle himself is scarcely recognizable as a figurehead for a Communist onslaught. But it was entirely characteristic of the wartime de Gaulle to adjust at least his rhetoric, in the interest of gaining wider appeal, to the existing climate of opinion; and accordingly in June 1942 he issued a five-point declaration of the war aims of the Free French, avowedly based on the Atlantic Charter; and this prompted the *New York Times* to ask: "If we, as citizens, or our Government, must choose between Laval and de Gaulle, how can there be an instant's hesitation?"[93]

In short, the Gaullist movement in the United States, the campaign to reverse the administration's policy, was a stepchild of New Deal rhetoric. An exception proves the rule: Willkie, who had battled against the domestic programs, was now very close to being the New Deal's advocate in world affairs, as the proponent of "One World," the friend of Roosevelt.[94] Once Roosevelt had been forced to abandon the narrow economic nationalism of the early New Deal, his humanitarian liberalism shaped a broader canopy, and the resultant idealism intoxicated all his colleagues, as one example in particular reveals. "This is fundamentally a people's war," he declared in a message to Congress; "the war of the United Nations is a people's war," broadcast Adolf Berle; "our war today is a war of peoples," declared the attorney general, Francis Biddle; "Since this is in truth a people's war, it must be followed by a people's peace," announced Sumner Welles;[95] and *People's War* was the title of a journal brought out after October 1942 by the FWA, planned with the help of members of OWI, Rockefeller's office, and Wallace's office, and designed to "be slightly, but sensibly, left-of-center, in other words New Dealish."[96]

It is not necessary to probe too closely the exact meaning of a "people's war," nor to ask whether this was an accurate or distinctive label, in order to see that a shared vocabulary is in evidence. The critics of the administration borrowed its uplifting rhetoric, its idealistic language, that moralizing stance toward the outside world which it had adopted. But they also, in the absence of any clear, precise governmental propaganda, filled out the details of such a stance, just as in 1940 much the same people had, in the absence of clearly defined Allied war aims, contrived some themselves.[97] As events in North Africa and elsewhere were shortly to demonstrate, it had become one of Roosevelt's most pronounced convictions, for reasons both tactical and prudent, that the really important decisions, the political ones, should be postponed until the end of the war. Viewed in this light, the difference between the administration and its critics may simply be that the latter, free of practical responsibility, were able to pursue the logic, as they saw it, of the former's avowed ideals. But in so doing they inevitably stumbled across one particular point of contention, and this was what made the differences ultimately irreconcilable: the State Department itself.

To Roosevelt the State Department was only one possible instrument, and not always the most desirable one, for the implementation of his foreign policy (he also used personal emissaries and in wartime, naturally, the armed forces and associated intelligence agencies). But to the administration's critics, the department was the sole architect of a maladroit diplomacy, the Achilles heel of the New Deal. The polemical literature of the period is studded with denunciations of the State Department and its conservative, reactionary, even crypto-fascist proclivities. That is the theme of dozens of editorials and articles in the *Nation*[98] and the *New Republic*.[99] It was elaborated by columnists as different as Samuel Grafton and Dorothy Thompson.[100] One version of it underwent lengthy serialization in *PM* in February 1941;[101] another in the

Nation in July and August 1942.[102] It is the thesis of Robert Bendiner's *The Riddle of the State Department*,[103] and the constant refrain of Waverley Root's three-volume *Secret History of the War*.[104]

No great mystery lies behind the State Department's vulnerability to liberal criticism. Under the (never absolute) command of a Southern conservative, Cordell Hull, employing a Southern grandee like Breckinridge Long or a corporation intellectual like Adolf Berle, it no doubt appeared somewhat at odds with the reforming zeal evident elsewhere in the executive branch, just as, at an earlier date Hull's free-trade ambitions had collided, but coexisted, with Roosevelt's economic nationalism. Nor, for all that its mandate was foreign affairs where Hull was possessed of some liberal economic convictions, had the department ever been imbued with any great international spirit. As was correctly observed in an exceptionally favorable article, in *Fortune* in 1939, the department's "traditions lie behind its own oceans, with its own people, who are not an international people."[105]

The outright criticism that now came to be directed at the department, from liberal-minded internationalist quarters, thus tapped great springs of resentment. Herbert Feis, the economic adviser, termed *PM*'s piece about him "dirty . . . smart . . . sneaky. . . unreliable . . . inaccurate . . . irresponsible . . . lazy journalism."[106] Berle asked the journalist I. F. Stone whether "facts had any real interest" in a proposed series of articles in the *Nation* meant "to prove we are all Fascists." According to Berle, Stone replied "that he considered his job was to express a particular set of tensions in the complex whole which would pull in a given direction—which being translated from Marxian lingo meant that they were going to push a set of conditions irrespective of truth."[107] And Berle was similarly aware, and equally troubled, that by the autumn of 1942 an open attack had been planned on the department, and on him in particular, by the Communist party.[108]

In such a climate it was perhaps inevitable that the department should regard all this criticism as part of an extensive "campaign" and that little effort was made to draw distinctions among the various interests involved: the demands of sensational journalism (for which the editor of *PM*, Ralph Ingersoll, did offer a rather lame apology to Feis, via their mutual friend Felix Frankfurter);[109] the principled, if not always factually reliable, views of the liberal press; and the unquestioned opportunism of the *Daily Worker*. All, in the department's eyes, came to be subsumed under the general heading of the "extreme left," to be dealt with accordingly. "It is sufficiently obvious," Berle wrote to Sumner Welles after one such attack on him, "that 'appeasing' Communist groups gets nowhere; the policy must be all possible military and economic support to Soviet Russia on one hand, and on the other, not even the remotest acceptance of any right of Soviet Russia to monkey with our internal affairs. Otherwise, this Government would wind up in the wretched state of the French pre-war governments."[110]

Had abuse of the State Department come solely from outside the administration, then, conceivably, officials such as Berle might have been able publicly to refute the accusations leveled against it and to dismiss them as politically inspired or ideologically suspect. But abundant testimony exists that the department was neither united within nor supported outside. Personal feuds at the top, and bureaucratic rivalries lower down, greatly weakened its ability to mobilize against the attacks, as officials like Robert Murphy and Dean Acheson later admitted. Acheson compared the department to a feudal state, with the separate, competing fiefdoms of the regional, economic, and visa divisions, the court intrigues, and the bureaucratic inertia: "Authority fell to him . . . who could take and hold it."[111] To Murphy the appropriate comparison was with the anarchy of the economic marketplace: "The American anti-trust philosophy has been carried into the field of foreign relations, where competition is rampant enough to satisfy every disciple of the Sherman Act."[112] And it is one of the ironies of wartime Washington that the governmental department actually charged with the conduct of foreign policy was seemingly locked forever in antagonism with other domestic departments, agencies, and bureaus, from the Board of Economic Warfare[113] to the Treasury.[114] Nowhere, it seemed, could State Department officials turn for consistent support or even encouragement. As Berle confided to his diary at the time of the St. Pierre-and-Miquelon affair: "All of the bright people are saying bad things about the State Department this morning. I think sentiment is particularly rife in the Donovan organization where a lot of people whose valor is greater than their knowledge insist that the State Department is the last stronghold of the Axis."[115] Henry Morgenthau and Felix Frankfurter were scarcely more enamored of the department. Frankfurter considered that its stand on Vichy "wouldn't be the first time that the State Department is wrong";[116] Morgenthau felt that there was not a single person in the department whom he considered to be as loyal to the president as he was himself; together they plotted to have Acheson installed as assistant secretary of state.[117]

Frequent examples might be given of a lapse in cabinet solidarity with regard to the State Department, but the figure of Harold Ickes, secretary of the interior, an old midwestern progressive, has earned a distinct prominence within the gallery of Hull's detractors. Whether the issue was the embargo of arms to Loyalist Spain or the sale of scrap iron to Japan, immigration policy or "appeasement," Ickes delighted in supplementing his nominal responsibility for conservation and natural resources with the role of sharp critic of the State Department.[118] He spoke as freely to the Russian ambassador as to Herbert Hoover.[119] He positively welcomed any opportunity to tell his views to journalists such as Freda Kirchwey, I. F. Stone, and Robert Bendiner.[120] To Walter Lippmann he wrote, "Next to the affairs of my own department, I have been more interested in what has been going on in the State Department than in any other administration activity." It was always important, he went on, to keep in mind that the department was "only a ward political club dressed in spats and a morning coat."[121] To him, as to so many other critics, the Vichy policy seemed an emblem of the State Department's shortcomings, exposing its feeblemindedness, its indifference to democracy, its reluctance to enlist in the real wartime crusade. "The justification of our State Department," he wrote in his diary after the return to power of Laval, "is that we have 'bought time,' but the damned fools don't seem to realize that Hitler, with the same currency, has also 'bought time.' "[122] Ickes was thus a natural choice to address a France Forever meeting in New York; and when he was unable to attend he found a substitute speaker, the assistant attorney general, Francis Shea, possessed of the same views, who went on to deliver a speech that Sumner Welles, reading it in the State Department, found "entirely inadmissable."[123]

Yet Ickes was not the greatest obstacle between the State Department and a sympathetic public. Throughout the controversy over the Vichy policy, the critics invariably directed their fire at the convenient, familiar scapegoat of the State Department, leaving the president, who actually designed and controlled that policy all but exempt from criticism. There can be no doubt that—as the St. Pierre-and-Miquelon affair demonstrated—the department was a willing, even overzealous exponent of Roosevelt's policy, sharing the customary suspicions of the Free French. Nevertheless, the obloquy heaped upon the department alone was rather one-sided; and part of the reason for this may be detected in the following extracts from Roosevelt's press conferences, all concerned with French affairs:

25 June 1940:
Q: Is there any possibility this Government might withdraw its recognition of the French Government at Bordeaux?
FDR: I have not heard anything about it, one way or the other.
Q: Will any consideration be given to recognizing the French Government that has not surrendered?
FDR: Same thing; I have not heard anything about it.

11 February 1941:
Q: Anything you can tell us on the French situation?
FDR: No, I didn't know anything about it till I read it in the papers.

5 September 1941:
Q: Mr. President, is—are the Free French eligible for Lend-Lease assistance?
FDR: You had better ask the State Department that question, because they will reply to it in State Department language.

21 November 1941:

Q: Mr. President, is any consideration being given to breaking diplo-
    matic relations with Vichy?

                                    · · ·

FDR: Haven't heard of it.

19 December 1941:

Q: Mr. President, have there been any conversations with France in
    regard to the French islands on our northeast coast [i.e., St. Pierre
    and Miquelon]?

                                    · · ·

FDR: You will have to ask the State Department.

13 February 1942:

Q: Mr. President, have you any thoughts on the status of French-
    American relations?

FDR: Oh, you will have to ask the State Department about it.

14 April 1942:

Q: Mr. President, are our relations with Vichy going to be changed as
    a result of the difficulties there?

FDR: Oh, I think you will have to ask the State Department.[124]

Most Presidents would attempt to establish a framework for the discussion of
their policies. Roosevelt told critics whom to blame.

In drawing together the various threads from this examination, the conclusions it points toward are twofold. In the first place an interest in French
affairs, and a concern about the American policy, was indisputably a minority
taste; that much may be gleaned from public opinion polls, private letters to
the State Department, and congressional debates. Second, that minority which
gravitated toward the Gaullist camp was a self-conscious, cohesive, intellectual clan, animated by matters other than the current situation in France; that
much may be deduced from newspaper editorials, magazine articles, and a
glance at the personnel of the relevant organizations. It is similarly evident in
Bendiner's book on the State Department, where his complaint is that the
department had "the company of at least part of the Administration, of great
sections of the country, and in fact of much of western civilization."[125] Beyond
all that there is the revealing matter of Rooseveltian practice; as suggested here
it was indeed masterly. Roosevelt designed the Vichy policy. He established a
wartime propaganda program that permitted the maximum circulation of liberal, internationalist ideals, without ever falling into the trap of explicitness.

And when the ideals conflicted with the practice, he skillfully deflected critics toward the State Department. The most formidable clash was, however, still to come, precipitated not by the movement of events in France, deliberated and discussed in America, but by the first major exercise of American wartime strategy, the landings in North Africa.

CHAPTER 8
THE DARLAN DEAL
AND AFTER

Dealing with Darlan is dealing with Germany. . .
—Churchill to Roosevelt, 12 March 1941

n November 1942, after the Allied landings in North Africa, American policy toward France entered a new phase. As Germany, by way of repri-sal, seized the previously unoccupied portion of France, the Vichy govern-ment—and with it America's Vichy policy—went into liquidation. Apart from a few pathetic attempts to revive the notion of a sovereign, independent, metropolitan France,[1] no more was heard from Pétain and Laval. But the other member of the Vichy triumvirate did step forward for one last moment of glory. A few days after the landings, on 14 November, it was learned that French cooperation in North Africa had been secured by the recognition as high commissioner in Morocco and Algeria of Admiral Darlan. The event itself, and the ensuing public uproar, will now be examined in turn.

Darlan was an unlikely recruit to the Allied cause. Next to Pétain the longest serving and highest ranking official at Vichy, he had always been associated with its most abject collaborationism. He had well earned Churchill's suspi-cions of him, since a thoroughgoing Anglophobia, combined with a devotion to "his" navy, was one of the few constant principles of his career. He had scarcely needed the British attack on the fleet at Mers el-Kébir in July 1940 to seal his hatred for a rival power that had, in his eyes, connived since the previous war, in conference after conference, at the relative weakening of the French navy, most recently by the Anglo-German naval agreement of 1935.[2] Hence Darlan's inability to disguise from the American ambassador, Bullitt, his relish at the prospect of an imminent British defeat.[3] That defeat, and France's corresponding recovery, he now sought to hasten by strategically granted measures of collaboration with Germany. Thus his first task, after Laval's dismissal in December 1940, was to reassure the Germans that that event was a purely domestic affair; Laval's policies would be resumed under fresh auspices.[4]

Hence the new American ambassador, Leahy, came to find Darlan the most devious and unrelenting collaborationist at Pétain's court, the man of the Paris Protocols and the Syrian resistance. Whenever Leahy tried to beard Pétain about some new submission to Germany—the dismissal of General Weygand

162

from North Africa, or the undermining of the economic accords Weygand had previously concluded with Robert Murphy—there, at the marshal's elbow, was Darlan, offering excuses, evasions, and sometimes downright lies.[5] Indeed Darlan not only took collaborationism further than Pétain knew or desired; he also tried to push it beyond what the Germans themselves wished. For as the war took on its global dimension, with German armies stretched across Russian territory, Hitler least wanted a France whose provocative actions on his behalf would only bring forth distracting British reprisals.[6]

But there was, even in this sorry record, an element of ambivalence. If Darlan was personally ambitious, if he was truly jealous of his navy, and above all if he did possess, or seize, a certain independence of the Vichy junta, then, conceivably, he might one day turn around. His most ardent collaborationism, late in 1940 and early in 1941, occurred precisely when Hitler seemed at his most invincible, master of a continent. But later, with Germany mired in the east, careless of western strategy, Darlan began, appropriately, to send out feelers, not of course to the British but to the Americans: Leahy and Murphy, both in person and through various intermediaries like his son Alain and his friend Admiral Raymond Fenard.[7]

These tentative overtures did not preclude further collaboration with Germany. They were, rather, supplements to it. Whichever direction Darlan appeared to be taking at any given moment, it could be safely assumed that his own career and the French navy, his sole bargaining counter with the Allies and Germany, would transcend any temporary diplomatic reversals. But to succeed he needed every last measure of independent power; and his prospects were greatly jeopardized by the reinstatement of Laval, stronger than ever, in April 1942. There soon emerged some on the Allied side who were prepared to exploit what might prove to be a more permanent disaffection from Vichy. That month Colonel Donovan of the OSS wrote to Roosevelt: "Would you think it fantastic, and if not, is it feasible to have someone who is close at hand in Vichy talk with Darlan? His nose must be greatly out of joint at this moment. That being true, would it be possible to suggest something along the line of putting him in command of that particular unit of an Allied fleet? Men disappointed in their ambitions have gone much further than that."[8]

But Darlan did not glide smoothly into the Allied camp. He had lingered for a long time between the Allies and Germany, and the Allies equally hesitated before fastening upon him as their candidate in North Africa, just as they had waited before selecting North Africa as the site for their first joint operation. Although that region had been suggested by Churchill at his meeting with Roosevelt in Washington in December 1941, it was not until the following July that it was firmly chosen, when a landing there appeared to possess the manifold advantages of blocking Rommel's westward path, drawing off German troops from Russia, and serving as a bridgehead into Europe.[9]

By this time Murphy had greatly extended his contacts in a different direc-

tion, among the dissident army officers of North Africa.[10] In particular he was
in touch with the coordinating group, the Committee of Five, led by Jacques
Lemaigre-Dubreuil, a wealthy peanut-oil manufacturer. This group had taken
it upon themselves to create precisely the right circumstances for France to
reenter the war on the Allied side: economic, then military aid from the United
States to North Africa, which would lead to an uprising and the formation of a
rearmed and reconstituted French army of liberation.[11] The most taxing problem, and Lemaigre-Dubreuil's special concern, was who was to have the
eventual high command, but this appeared to have been settled after the escape
from a German prison in April of General Henri Giraud, a greatly respected
military hero. Although his first move had been to confer with Pétain at
Vichy,[12] and although de Gaulle spoke most favorably of him at a press
conference in London,[13] he was, it seemed, tainted neither with Vichy nor
Free France.

Giraud rather than Darlan was thus, to Murphy at least, the likelier candidate. This lends a superficial plausibility to the various explanations and
rationalizations that were offered in American official circles once it turned
out that Darlan rather than Giraud had taken over, and that a public outcry, in
Britain and the United States, was the result. But in fact the first step in
exploring the American context of the Darlan deal is to discount virtually
every immediate defense that was made of it. It was, said Roosevelt, a temporary, military expedient, governed exclusively by the need to save American
lives.[14] Actually the deal itself was a political arrangement.[15] Any lives that
were saved were done so by the (rather late) ceasefires that Darlan had been
persuaded to issue, in Algiers on 8 November and for the whole of North
Africa on the tenth, not by the political settlement that was concluded on the
thirteenth. Insofar as there was a military justification, it lay in releasing the
Allied command from the need to administer occupied territory and enabling it
to concentrate, with a measure of French support, upon the advance on
Tunisia. Moreover, the military view of Roosevelt's chief of staff, General
George Marshall, was that to refer to the arrangement as "temporary" was
disastrous. That conceded far too much, and gravely weakened the position of
the Americans on the spot.[16] Nor was the judgment of the secretary of war,
Stimson, that this was an improvised arrangement,[17] entirely accurate. Certainly Darlan's presence in Algiers, to visit his hospitalized son, was unforeseen; certainly the details of the extensive negotiations over the next few days
had not been predicted in every respect. But American military planners had
always intended to deal with whichever French official was available; and, as a
result of those earlier overtures, Darlan's name had frequently cropped up,
alongside Giraud's, in Anglo-American military talks in London[18] and in
exchanges between the White House and Murphy in Algiers.[19]

Finally, and strangest of all, Cordell Hull leapt forward, in an "extraordinary" press conference, to pronounce the whole affair a magnificent vindica-

tion of his and his department's policy of maintaining relations with the Vichy regime.[20] Yet the State Department had long been excluded from North African planning. Originally, when American involvement in North Africa had been primarily economic—the sending of aid to win the inhabitants' loyalty to the Allied cause—the Department had been the leading governmental agency involved; and, in a characteristic Washington feud, it had fought tenaciously, and for the most part successfully, to retain its ascendancy over Henry Wallace's Board of Economic Warfare.[21] That episode and the economic program were duly commemorated in official State Department annals.[22] But after July 1942, when the invasion plans were set, and American interest in the region was more directly military, it moved out of the State Department's orbit. Murphy, the career officer in the Foreign Service who had laid the groundwork for the program, was transferred to General Eisenhower's staff, since he was still invaluable for all his contacts in the region; and he now worked closest with Eisenhower's deputy, Mark Clark. He communicated through the Department of State with the War Department, in a War Department code; and it was not in fact until 1960 that deciphered copies of his messages were supplied to the State Department.[23] Between the Murphy-Weygand agreements of 1941 and the Clark-Darlan agreements of 1942 the State Department had fallen by the way.

There was nothing sinister about the misleading impressions conveyed by Washington officials. Such instant and favorable reactions were due partly to ignorance, partly to a prudent loyalty to the men in the field, and partly to a desire to capitalize on what promised to be a spectacularly successful venture. Stimson, for example, was greatly surprised at the news of the Darlan deal. He was also pleased at it, for he had long been skeptical of the wisdom of the proposed invasion. But he had never anticipated that Murphy and Clark would land such a handsome catch.[24] Cordell Hull for his part was glad to be able to claim credit for the seemingly successful outcome of a policy for which his department had been so often and so bitterly criticized in what he liked to call "starry-eyed circles," by "young communists."[25] This long overdue vindication was the Darlan deal's chief asset. Hull was not himself particularly enthusiastic about the specific policy. He actually told Stimson that he was opposed to going so far as to recognize Darlan as the French leader or government in North Africa.[26] Sumner Welles similarly felt that if the department had been consulted it "could have accomplished the same thing without giving the North African set-up such a Vichy tinge."[27]

In short these were not the responses, whether favorable or not, of active, informed participants. Only a week before the landings Hull had complained that Roosevelt was telling him nothing about current American diplomacy, and Stimson had commented that he too was left uninformed.[28] A more amusing exchange occurred on the morning of 16 November at the Treasury Department where a puzzled and dismayed Henry Morgenthau attempted to learn something about what the administration had now committed itself to. But his ensuing telephone inquiries yielded him nothing. At the War Department Robert Patterson told him that "the White House knows about the thing and . . . it did not pass much through the War Department. We only got some very superficial notice about it, and it was handled through the State Department by this man Murphy. . . . The route was from Murphy to Welles to the White House." Minutes later Welles at the State Department told Morgenthau that "none of us here have had the slightest knowledge of any of the negotiations that have been going on." As for Patterson's version, "that's entirely untrue . . . he probably doesn't know what he is talking about."[29]

Welles also told Morgenthau that the negotiations had been conducted jointly by the British and the Americans. But this too was an illusion. British political and military involvement was slight. It would in any case have been kept to a minimum by the known hostility to Britain of French army and navy officers. But the United States had also, through its Vichy policy, already achieved a superior negotiating position with Vichy officials. Thus more than two months before the invasion Roosevelt was able to insist to Churchill that the Free French would not participate in the operation, and that the British role would be secondary: "An American expedition led in all three phases by American troops will meet little resistance from the French Army in Africa. On the other hand, a British commanded attack in any phase or with de Gaullist co-operation would meet with determined resistance. . . . As you and I decided long ago, we were to handle the French in North Africa, while you were to handle the situation in Spain."[30] A week later Roosevelt similarly prevented the British from establishing a joint policy toward North Africa when he instructed the British ambassador in Washington to refer all questions not to the State Department, for inter-Allied discussion, but to Eisenhower, the designated joint military commander.[31] But for these preemptive moves some British hesitations might have been registered sooner. As early as March 1941 Churchill had prophetically warned Roosevelt that "dealing with Darlan is dealing with Germany";[32] and as late as 12 November 1942 a member of the British embassy in Washington, going over the possible results of the North African expedition, had concluded: "If Darlan were to declare for Allies and try to head the new French provisional government? Presumably it is agreed that he would be the worst choice of all and would command practically no allegiance inside France or outside it."[33]

Thus the arrangements caused rather more consternation in British than in American circles. Eden wanted it put on record that the British would consider "disastrous" any permanent settlement concluded with Darlan.[34] William Strang, of the Foreign Office's French department, argued that if General Montgomery instead of Eisenhower had been commanding the expedition, "the Darlan situation would not, I think, have been allowed to arise"; the British had been able to avoid equivalent dangers in Madagascar and Djibouti.[35] And as the American ambassador in London, John G. Winant, cabled to Roosevelt, there was now considerable agitation among "trade unions, Jewish organizations, and other groups, in the British press and among members of our own press."[36] A question had been proposed in the House of Commons, and another, by Lord Vansittart, in the House of Lords.[37] Yet having been for so long the junior partners in the enterprise, the British could not now commence to assert any new influence. No more than the State Department could they make their presence felt in North Africa; and just as the State Department was overruled by Marshall when it tried to intervene by instructing Murphy to work toward the liberalization of the emergent North African regime,[38] so equally the British in Washington were unable to intrude upon the discussions.[39]

Churchill, at least, acknowledged the fait accompli. Canceling, at Roosevelt's request and to Eden's dismay, a proposed, and possibly incautious, broadcast by de Gaulle, he had informed Roosevelt, "being your ardent and active lieutenant I should bow to your decision without demur."[40] No doubt Churchill was grateful that when the storm of controversy did burst over the deal British responsibility could be seen to be negligible; and he could truthfully assure the House of Commons that "neither militarily nor politically are we directly controlling the course of events."[41] On the other hand British influence was brought to bear, not on the matter of the deal, but on the manner of its presentation to the outside world. Churchill warned Roosevelt on 17 November that ". . . very deep currents of feeling are stirred by the arrangements with Darlan. . . . A permanent arrangement with Darlan or the formation of a Darlan government in French North Africa would not be understood by the great masses of ordinary people whose simple loyalties are our strength." And he employed a mystifying phrase to describe the deal, "a temporary expedient justifiable solely by the stress of battle," which found its way later the same day into Roosevelt's statement at his press conference.[42] The phrase is ambiguous because it is not instantly apparent whether the "battle" demanded a militarily correct decision, or the "stress" caused a politically unwise one.

British and American government agencies may therefore, for the moment, be left aside. Is responsibility then attributable solely to the men in the field, Eisenhower, the commander, and Murphy, the civilian adviser? Eisenhower may be most readily disposed of first. He was the soldier par excellence, and his published papers frequently disclose a professional's impatience with civilian distractions. On being informed by Murphy that Giraud needed more time to make his preparations and was making additional demands as the price of his cooperation, Eisenhower frankly observed, "It is . . . inconceivable to me that our mere failure to concede to such demands as have been made would result in having the French North African Army meet us with serious opposition."[43] Later, when the expedition was under way, he confessed, "It isn't this operation that's wearing me down—it's the petty intrigue and the necessity of dealing with little, selfish, conceited worms that call themselves men."[44] He found himself, he admitted, "getting absolutely furious with these stupid Frogs."[45] There was, in all this, an implicit criticism of America's Vichy policy, whose fruits had been so meager. Despite his genuine appreciation of Murphy, Eisenhower had not failed to observe that Murphy's best efforts had not yet produced an amenable, sympathetic French high command. Eisenhower's famous telegram of 14 November explaining the Darlan deal to his superiors, which so impressed later commentators from William Langer to Robert Sherwood, was really a severe indictment of American diplomatic action: "The actual state of existing sentiment here does not repeat not agree even remotely with some of prior calculations."[46] To Eisenhower, at least, the Darlan deal was not the triumphant outcome of America's Vichy policy, but a severe reflection upon it.

Eisenhower saw himself confronted with a situation for which, whether by negligence or intent, the civilian arm held responsibility. The preparatory work for the invasion had been of several kinds. In the spring of 1942 the Psychological Warfare Branch of Military Intelligence employed two academics to frame a questionnaire for sampling North African attitudes prior to the landings; and the conclusion of their survey had been the happy one for Roosevelt that a landing force from which the British and Gaullists were absent would encounter only token resistance.[47] On a larger scale there had been the clandestine subversive work of OSS, and the civil affairs planning, both activities nominally under the command of Robert Murphy. Concerning the former little need be said, as delay and short supplies on invasion night gravely hampered the task of the hundreds of young, pro-Allied French patriots (many of them Gaullists) who had been thus recruited, and who, after some early successes, were arrested by the Vichyite police.[48] Of more far-reaching importance was the civil-affairs planning, where an undeniably crucial part was played by Murphy.

He, if anyone, might be assumed to be the eminence grise of the Darlan deal, since he was in so many ways the pivotal figure of the entire enterprise. It was Murphy in Algiers who, after Weygand's dismissal from North Africa in November 1941, insisted, in telegram after telegram to the State Department, that there be no halt to the American economic supply program.[49] In October 1942 he again defended the program in a letter to Hull in which, as if anticipating the public criticism he would shortly undergo, he concluded: "If appeasement means support of our friends in a practical way when they need our help badly, then I am all for appeasement. It is also clear to me from what little I know of the French situation, that we do have friends in France and French North Africa."[50] And after the Darlan deal was made, Murphy duly rounded on the critics of that measure: "The ideal Frenchmen which the critics see from the heights of their ivory towers we did not find."[51] A conservative and a Catholic, who had formed his own critical understanding of French democracy in the 1930s, Murphy was easily able to achieve a satisfactory working relationship with the dissidents, rather than the outright opponents of Vichy—first Weygand, then Giraud's intermediary, Lemaigre-Dubreuil. So with a recalcitrant Giraud staying put on Gibraltar on invasion night, holding out for greater glory, it was naturally Murphy who, together with Clark, hammered out the details of the alternative arrangements with Darlan.[52]

Yet in reality how much freedom of action did Murphy possess? He had been instructed by Roosevelt to discuss plans for the North African invasion only with Eisenhower or authorized military officials, not with the State Department ("a sieve" Roosevelt called it);[53] and if he told the department little he got little in the way of advice or help in return.[54] On 22 September he was told by Roosevelt to deal with "those French nationals whom you consider reliable";[55] and on 17 October, as we have seen, Darlan was mentioned by name.[56] But that was all. Thus what seemed to Murphy to narrow his options was the situation as it arose after 8 November: the unpostponed arrival of the American armada; Giraud's insistence on a larger role for himself—Allied supreme commander, no less[57]—and greater authority after the ceasefire; and above all, the absence of any alternative leader who could rival Darlan's claim to be Pétain's representative, acting in his name, and bring into line the more hesitant and Vichyssois French officials—Pierre Boisson of West Africa, Yves Chatel of Algeria, Jean-Pierre Esteva of Tunisia, and Auguste Noguès of Morocco—who would not have yielded to Giraud. It mattered little in this context, though it was typical of Darlan's wily performance, that his claim was nugatory: he had in fact been repudiated by Pétain. But a little judicious reinterpretation of secret messages from Vichy enabled Darlan to maintain the fiction that there lay the source of his authority.[58]

So the deal was made. It was perhaps natural for the actors in this drama to view it as the outcome of an unforeseen and unpredictable chain of events, a totally unexpected occurrence. Their impressions are clear from most of the memoirs and accounts that have appeared since, rightly emphasizing the sudden and bewildering nature of the opportunity that arose.[59] Yet that is still only a partial view. Too much stress upon the contingent and the merely accidental tends to obscure the more obvious fact that these events occurred within a framework established long ago by America's Vichy policy; however they disguised the fact from themselves, the participants were only obeying the logic inscribed within a policy that, having conferred recognition upon Marshal Pétain, naturally allowed it to seep down to his lieutenant, Darlan. Such at least was the view of one American agent on the spot, Percy Winner of the Psychological Warfare Branch, who frankly observed in a letter to Robert Sherwood of OWI, "In effect we legitimized Darlan, and won the victory for him before he helped us by giving the 'cease-firing' order."[60] Once the Americans were known to be negotiating with Darlan, then his passage to power lay open: the few French officers who actually had conspired to assist the landings soon lost their influence, while the small anti-Vichy movement that had paved the way in Algiers and reduced the bloodshed there was demoralized and discouraged.[61]

To this extent, therefore, some allowance can now be made for Cordell Hull's public exultation at the fruits of the North African invasion: not because he took far too large a share of the responsibility for the State Department, but because he did at least see the thread of continuity running from the maintenance of relations with Vichy through the political disparagement of the Free French to the installation of Darlan in Algiers. In a similar fashion the Darlan deal gratified, after initially surprising, those who had actually carried out that policy, working alongside Murphy in the American embassy at Vichy. H. Freeman Matthews, for example, formerly chargé d'affaires there, then in London after a brief spell of duty in Algiers, wrote to his former superior, Leahy: "You and I have no illusions about Popeye [Darlan], and it seems strange after our many problems and unpleasant hours with him in Vichy for me to be cast somewhat in the role of his defender!" But in Matthews's view Darlan, carrying, however irregularly, the mantle of Pétain, had delivered what no one else could, and there the matter should rest. As for the public outcry, in Britain that was the result of "confusion in the public mind," itself fed "to a certain extent by deliberate Governmental propaganda policy." Darlan was being abused now not as a collaborationist but as "an American puppet" suspended over a traditional British sphere of influence, the Mediterranean: "I think," Matthews wrote, "there is a certain suspicion by British 'imperialists' . . . of American 'imperialist' intentions."[62] Leahy for his part was equally delighted at the deal and similarly dismayed at the criticism it evoked, which he found barely comprehensible, given "our full adoption of Stalin."[63] "It is my opinion," he wrote in his diary, "that if we the Allies succeed in crushing Germany, Admiral Darlan will join the centuries-old galaxy of Heroes of French History."[64]

This logic, underlying the entire policy, soon became self-evident to most of the American administration. However, it did need to be vigorously impressed upon the untutored Gaullist mind, and this was attempted by various hands. There took place on 20 November a lengthy exchange between Roosevelt, Adrien Tixier of the Gaullist delegation, and André Philip of de Gaulle's French National Committee. It was the first such meeting, but instead of being the occasion for happy reconciliation, it turned into an angry debate. The Gaullists, according to Sumner Welles, who was also present, showed an inadequate appreciation for American efforts on France's behalf, while Roosevelt, according to the Gaullists, sharply insisted upon American freedom of action, including the freedom to exercise the rights of an occupying power —now in North Africa, foreseeably in France—and to deal with whoever— Darlan, Laval, Quisling—would aid the military effort.[65] Cordell Hull similarly attempted to convince the same visitors with a characteristically homespun historical analogy: "France," he told them, "had a unique and glorious opportunity to reconstruct herself very much as the United States reconstructed herself after the American Revolution when one-half of the inhabitants almost were Tories [sic]. The reason Americans of that period lived in American history at the moment is that they were big enough to overlook differences and convince all parties that the construction of America was a great common problem outweighing sectional, factional or political differences."[66]

Much the same view was presented to Tixier by Adolf Berle, who instructed him "that all Frenchmen now had to collaborate in beating the Germans, however bitter their individual differences might be."[67] Privately, among his colleagues, Berle elaborated on his views. He could detect, he said, "a growing cleavage between those who wanted to win the war as speedily as possible irrespective of ideologies, and those who were primarily interested in 'liberalizing Europe,' irrespective of military considerations."[68] In his view, much could be gained from a correct understanding of what had taken place in North Africa:

> Probably the break-up of Europe, when it came, would be more likely the detachment of great fragments of satellite states who wished to change sides, rather than the completeness of any cataclysmic revolution such as had been imagined by some of our more hopeful publicists. In that case, we might be presented over and over again with situations in which choices might be presented to us which we did not altogether like. For that reason it seemed to me that the closest agreement on policy and the wholehearted support of the commanders in the field were necessary, as political intrigues—of which there were many— complicated things for everyone.[69]

There was audible in these pronouncements, for all their differences in tone—the confident assertions of Roosevelt, the crude historical generalizations of Hull, the more elegant disquisitions of Berle—one unmistakable accent, that of political and cultural condescension: the same, in a blunter turn of phrase, as could be heard, across the water, from Eisenhower when he called upon the French to abandon their "pettifogging struggles for personal power."[70]

Such, in brief, was the official American case for the Darlan deal. Before turning to the public reaction it is only necessary to note, finally, the real author of the policy, the chief expounder of its underlying logic. It was of course Roosevelt himself. He had chosen North Africa as the site for the first Allied move, despite the hesitations of Marshall and the War Department.[71] He had excluded both the British and the Free French from any effective participation. He had removed the State Department, and indeed all other government agencies, from any influence, leaving himself, as commander in chief, with sole responsibility. Above all, as already noted, it was America's Vichy policy, which he had formulated and in which he had maintained an active interest, that now determined that the deal should take place. Even down to the smallest detail, the style of French in his broadcast message to the French people after the landings, Roosevelt liked to have his way. As he wrote to Eve Curie: "I tried an experiment. Bill Bullitt and some of the State Department people said that my message was wholly contrary to French usage—no beautiful phrases, no oratory—and that the French people had always been accustomed to the old-fashioned flowery appeal. I thought, however, that I ought to be myself and that the French people would understand my normal simplicity better than if I did something which was not a part of me."[72]

Roosevelt did not merely assume responsibility; he relished it, as he made clear at a cabinet meeting on 20 November. There he berated his entire cabinet for attempting to interfere in civilian affairs in North Africa. Only the postmaster general, Frank Walker, was exempt from criticism, since he had not, Roosevelt said, tried to take over the telegraph lines there. It seemed, according to one observer, Harold Ickes, as if the bureaucratic struggles that had so characterized Roosevelt's Washington—and which the president had hitherto viewed with ironic detachment—were now being exported to the liberated territories; and Roosevelt was at last moving to stop them.[73] Stimson did not greatly like the implied rebuke to the War Department, particularly as he had been teased by William Bullitt earlier that day for being "a mere housekeeper of the War Department now that the President had taken over all relations with the military men." So at his turn to speak he read out a recent telegram from Eisenhower explaining the circumstances of the Darlan deal, and observed to Roosevelt that "there must have been telepathic communication between him and . . . Eisenhower for we had carried out so exactly his theory."[74]

And what, in conclusion, was this "theory"? In Eisenhower's words it amounted to little more than a disavowal of any intention to establish a government in North Africa.[75] A more extended treatment of the "theory" or theories was provided by Roosevelt himself at his press conference on 17 November when he justified the deal. Although the ingredients of that statement came from a variety of sources, from Churchill to the OWI, Roosevelt had, as was his fashion, thoroughly reworked them into an eclectic blend of his own wartime goals and ideals:[76] the elimination of the Free French from all major strategic engagements ("I wouldn't worry about it—it's all right" was his response to a question about the position of de Gaulle); the supposed primacy of military over ideological considerations (the deal was a "temporary expedient, justified solely by the stress of battle"); the postponement of all political decisions until the conclusion of the war ("No-one in our Army has any authority to discuss the future government of France or the French Empire"); and, above all, national self-determination, which may seem a curious justification for the Darlan deal but was nonetheless Roosevelt's major defense of it. Thus he spoke in emphatic Wilsonian terms: "The future French government will be established not by any individual in metropolitan France or overseas, but by the French people themselves, after they have been set free by the victory of the United Nations."

Roosevelt had long ago chosen between the rival claims of Vichy and Free France; and now the logic of that decision, grounded in the diplomacy of 1940, renewed in the military planning of 1941 and 1942, had made itself felt. As the inert body of Vichy began to expire, a serviceable limb had been detached from it. Vichy, that is, was the nearest to self-determination that the wartime French would be allowed. In view therefore of Roosevelt's direct, personal responsibility for the Darlan deal, in conception and execution, it was a remarkable display of modesty for him to begin his jovial performance at that press conference with the declaration: "I have approved General Eisenhower's acceptance for the time being of the present political arrangements in Northern and Western Africa."

On the day of his press conference Roosevelt sent a letter to Hull in which he expressed a hope that the statement he had just delivered would "take" all right.[77] It did, of course, but not in a manner Hull could be expected to appreciate. Not for the first time the effect of a public clarification by Roosevelt was to deflect criticism of his foreign policy onto the State Department. The Darlan deal would soon provide Hull with ample cause to regret his early vocal enthusiasm, which had, in its exuberance, even surprised Robert Murphy, who was far more aware of the dangerous realities from his exposed position in North Africa.[78] The deal was actually to provide Hull with some new critics, among those who might otherwise, in their international ardor, have proved his supporters, for example, Henry Luce. In early December Luce sent a memorandum to his editors at *Time* on the whole subject of America's Vichy policy and the conduct of the State Department:

> The Department's policy is all nakedly clear now—i.e. completely unprincipled expediency. Necessity knows no principles . . . we were appeasers in Europe and, until late 1941, we were appeasers in the Pacific—on the grounds of expediency. . . . Nothing has changed. The important thing now is to explain to Americans that all our policy is mere (or super) expediency. . . . There is a detail which makes the whole subject so difficult—our picture of Judge Hull as a noble man. How then can his policy have been the most unprincipled in our history? That's a long story—going back to 1933 if not further. It is easier to say now simply that he is old. He is too old to carry a revolutionary and counterrevolutionary world. He ought to have departed in peace when Chamberlain cried "Peace in our Time."[79]

So there shortly appeared in *Time* an editorial on "Expediency" that had some harsh words for "good, gray Cordell Hull."[80]

On the other hand, the Darlan deal recruited for Hull some surprising new allies among his erstwhile critics within the isolationist community. "He deserves the highest commendation for his policies with regard to Vichy, which enabled American soldiers to land in North Africa, and have brought the French African army to our side. It was the greatest military, naval and diplomatic victory of the war"—in those words he was championed by Representative Hamilton Fish, the scourge of the New Deal.[81] In the Senate a vigorous defense of the Darlan deal was mounted by Arthur Vandenberg, stepping further down the Damascan road that would lead him to postwar international fame.[82]

The Darlan deal afforded an opportunity to test public attitudes toward America's wartime policy, and OWI's Bureau of Intelligence duly undertook the work.[83] The studies plainly demonstrated that Roosevelt's statement did have the effect of soothing an uneasy public, at least as measured in newspaper comment, two-thirds of which came to favor the deal; and, moreover, that this emollient had been applied largely by Roosevelt's stress upon the temporary nature, and military justification, of the arrangement. All this would be much as expected. But the substance of the actual controversy is more usefully suggested by examining the arguments advanced, rather than simply counting the frequency of their expression. The issue was not dead merely because a majority supported the president; and this issue, not unlike others in Franco-American relations, soon touched off a score of related grievances.

Those who defended the Darlan deal, and applauded the State Department, did so, with few exceptions, on ostensibly patriotic-pragmatic grounds. A sampling of such writings was printed in the *American Foreign Service Journal*, and their importance lies not in their representative character, but in their suitability for inclusion in an official State Department publication. George E. Sokolsky, the *New York Sun* columnist, called the department "an unusually competent and efficient organization." The *New York World-Telegram*, "which always has shared the admiration of rank-and-file Americans for our great Secretary of State, congratulate[d] him on another hard job well done." "All this," commented the *Baton Rouge State-Times*, "is to the credit of Cordell Hull whom the American people congratulate and recognize as a real American and a real man."[84]

But this was more than simple folksy loyalty; a much older quarrel was being resumed. Hull in his special press conference had gloated over the supposed embarrassment of his critics;[85] Sumner Welles had invited the audience at the *New York Herald Tribune* Forum on Current Problems to evaluate the "lack of vision and knowledge" of those who criticized American policy;[86] so after them other defenders of the deal sprang up to reveal their domestic preoccupations. Thus the conservative Sokolsky began his piece: "For several months now, the glib smart boys on the Left have been conducting a violent and vicious campaign against the State Department. It was obviously a campaign rather than the expression of personal opinion because all the organs of the Left participated in it. . . . [D]ay by day and week by week, these puny-minded liberals swatted one of the most honored officials in our Government." The *New York World-Telegram* complained that Hull "has been without honor too long among the bright boys in Washington . . . the victim of slanderers inside and outside the Administration." And the *Baton Rouge State-Times* recalled that Hull "was smeared by a lot of the New Deal boys in Washington, who considered him an 'appeaser' and a 'fascist,' and insisted that the President should fire him." Arthur Krock, Hull's friend, also joined the chorus in the *New York Times*, pointing out that although Roosevelt had ultimate responsibility, the attacks had always centered on Hull and had come largely from the "New Deal left wing," whose "party line" was "that everything in Washington of which they disapproved is put over on the President and that in some mysterious way he is powerless—particularly with the State Department—to do anything about it at all."[87]

The North African invasion thus provided an invaluable opportunity to settle old scores. Once again the *Chicago Tribune*, in its detailed editorial commentary, explored, however idiosyncratically, many of the crucial issues. Isolationism is distinct from insularity; the *Tribune* displayed an affection for the French people and a concern for their colonial subjects. It recommended that the exchange of letters between Pétain and Roosevelt in the wake of the invasion be used as translation exercises at schools, to give pupils "the sense that French is a living language." It saw in Giraud a soldier whose usefulness was more than strategic: ". . . the people of France, occupied and unoccupied, can now turn to him in hope as two years ago they turned in despair to Pétain." And when, a fortnight after the invasion, the French metropolitan fleet was scuttled at Toulon, lest the invading Germans expropriate it, the *Tribune* commemorated the gesture of the "heroes of Toulon" on three separate occasions, calling it "as heroic and dramatic an incident as can be found in all military history." At last the *Tribune* had found a foreign country whose virtues justified American sacrifice, "an ally to whose liberation we can devote ourselves confident that by so doing we are advancing our own cause and our own interest." Henceforth American efforts could be directed toward furthering the cause not of Russian Communism, European monarchy, or British imperialism, but of "an ally of a different sort, a republican ally which more than any other nation shares our fundamental beliefs and opinions. . . . The terrible sacrifice at Toulon has reunited the two republics to which the world is chiefly indebted for free civilization." That feat of heroism ensured that "France will rise"; after the disintegration and confusion of the interwar years, "a miracle was needed and that seems to have been offered at Toulon."[88]

But despite this sudden access of cosmopolitanism, the old issues remained.

The *Chicago Tribune*, whose wartime heroes were General Douglas MacArthur and Captain Eddie Rickenbacker, would not brook any civilian criticism of Eisenhower. Such criticism, it said, came chiefly from two sources: "those who want to make us puppets of Russia . . . [whose] goal is not a free France but a communist France," and "those who wish to make Americans subservient to the British aristocracy. The attack on Eisenhower expresses a resentment that this American general is commanding titled British officers." Nor would the *Tribune* permit Roosevelt, flushed with the invasion's success, to assume airs. It noted that in addressing foreign statesmen, Marshal Pétain or the bey of Tunis, he had taken to referring to himself as "Chief of State" (also, though the *Tribune* did not remark on it, Pétain's title): "The executive power of the country over the span of its history has been invested in thirty-two citizens. Only one has found himself cramped by the title, President of the United States."

More seriously, the *Tribune* objected to the president's entire handling of the Darlan deal. To issue, as Roosevelt had, an announcement that the United States would make no permanent arrangement with Darlan was not, the *Tribune* argued, "the best way to win his confidence and his help"; nor would more valuable help be forthcoming, as the "bleeding hearts" appeared to believe, from "the so-called Fighting French" ("so-called" again). Finally, the *Tribune* attempted to measure the American performance in North Africa against the standards set down in Roosevelt's Four Freedoms address and the Atlantic Charter. The result was not entirely satisfactory. Even after making due allowance for the difficulty of implementing the more far-reaching of those goals in a war zone, the *Tribune* still observed that no attempt had been made to facilitate article 3 of the Atlantic Charter, "the right of all peoples to choose the form of government under which they will live." Roosevelt's insistence that the United States did not covet any of France's colonial territory appeared to recognize France's title to the lands of North Africa: "The Algerians, Tunisians, and Moroccans were not given an opportunity to express their views." In short, "It was all very well for Mr. Roosevelt to think up a few desirable freedoms on January 6, 1941, and to sit down on a boat with Mr. Churchill August 14, 1941 and toss the rhetoric around, but it is something else to translate the words into something tangible."[89]

That was a point on which many of the critics and defenders of the Darlan deal actually agreed: both saw in Hull's and Roosevelt's frank avowals of expediency as a diplomatic principle a retreat from American idealism. That was why the *Christian Century*, a journal of liberal Protestant opinion, which agreed with the *Chicago Tribune* on very little else, could make the identical complaint, that the Darlan deal and a recent reiteration by Churchill of traditional British imperialist goals were "not guideposts marking the way to a just and lasting peace."[90] Both organs, that is, opposed American toleration of an older European order, while the *Tribune*, making a more rigid distinction

between political and military objectives, advocated more wholehearted cooperation with Darlan. In one sense the *Tribune* may have had the better of the
argument. Having lost the support of the Gaullists by the Darlan deal itself, as
was shown by a recent speech by de Gaulle in Brazzaville,[91] the Americans
had not endeared themselves to Darlan by stressing the temporary nature of
their arrangement with him. As Darlan himself remarked to Milton Eisenhower, then in North Africa to advise the OWI: "I know what you Americans
think of me. Your President thinks that I am a lemon to be held until all the
juice has been squeezed out. Then the rind will be discarded. That is all right
with me. I am co-operating with you not for the benefit of the United States or
Great Britain, but for the good of France."[92]

But whatever the strategic realities, the critics of the Darlan deal had the
stronger moral case. More committed to the ideals of the Atlantic Charter and
the Four Freedoms, they were more aggrieved at the diplomatic slide into
expediency. They also, like the defenders, possessed some long-established
convictions (which were examined in chapter seven):[93] loyalty to de Gaulle,
distrust of the State Department, and a concern for the resistance movements
in occupied Europe and the democratic (as distinct from the monarchist)
governments-in-exile. "War and politics are inextricable," wrote Dorothy
Thompson; and, she went on, by attempting to manipulate Darlan, Giraud, and
de Gaulle, the United States could "produce not only rifts in France, but rifts
inside our own coalition—Britain, Russia, America. It will also create unease
among all the governments in exile, who will fear to be let down."[94] Edward
Murrow, broadcasting from London, was equally appalled: "One wonders
whether we may not stand dishonored in the eyes of the conquered people on
the continent who have been led to believe through Anglo-American propaganda that Darlan is one of the greatest living traitors."[95] In New York "Pertinax," with that circumspection which befitted an émigré journalist, expressed
similar misgivings.[96] Freda Kirchwey, in a *Nation* editorial titled "America's
First Quisling," went much further: "We can't afford new ventures in double-
dealing or in reactionary diplomacy even in the interest of military gains. The
price is too high."[97]

Even those liberals who might endorse the Darlan deal, on strictly military
grounds, were greatly alarmed at the possible politial repercussions. The *New
Republic*, for example, while admitting that the temporary acceptance of
Darlan was "probably a wise move," was concerned that the exuberant counterattack by Hull and Welles on the State Department's critics implied a more
thoroughgoing reactionary policy in foreign affairs. In an editorial titled "Liberals Be Strong," it warned that "appeasement of the fascists in Spain, Italy
and elsewhere is obviously not over. The intensity of the attack upon the critics
of appeasement by the State Department makes it clear that the purpose of the
attacks is not the negative one of discrediting the liberal movement, but the
positive purpose of preparing the way for a continuation of the appeasement

policy." And "the arguments for and against our Vichy policy . . . are being used for much larger political ends. They are being used to crush liberal agencies in Washington, to establish reaction as a permanent policy, to influence the future of all peoples."[98]

For with Darlan proclaiming himself chief of state, assuming the mantle of Pétain, and keeping intact all Vichy's legislation, including the anti-Jewish decrees and the imprisonment of Gaullist sympathizers, with Axis agents freely crossing frontiers, with French soldiers punished for desertion because they tried to support the Allied landing, and with anti-Allied propaganda still appearing in the press and on the radio[99]—with, in short, a replication in process of the Vichy regime—precisely how "temporary," or desirable, was this expedient? So the critics inquired, with a good deal of force. The *New York Post* commented: "For a 'temporary expedient' that Darlan is getting pretty big for his pants. How long is 'temporary'? . . . Who has whom? Have we got Darlan or has Darlan got us?"[100] Precisely the same point, in similar words, was made by the *Christian Science Monitor*: "The question of who was using whom in the Vichy episode has not been resolved even now, and as applied to Darlan and Eisenhower today the answer is far from clear. . . . American controls are far from complete in French Africa. . . . Certainly there should be a limit to the 'temporary expedient' and the firmest resistance to Darlan's apparent effort to cement his position by use of American power."[101] The *New Republic* demanded an end to "fascism in North Africa."[102] And the *Nation*, commenting on Hull's statement that the French, when freed, could "select their own leaders and forms of government," feared that by then there would be a de facto government of Vichy generals already recognized by the American high command and that the new government would have as its basis "men who until now have been training in Pétainist youth camps and are well inculcated with fascist theories."[103]

Such were the published criticisms, examples of which could be indefinitely multiplied. But the flavor of American debate can also be captured by recalling the more private communications that took place. Here the experiences of Walter Lippmann and Wendell Willkie, in attempting to outline their misgivings about America's French policy, are particularly revealing.

On the evening of 16 November Henry Stimson learned that Willkie was about to deliver an address to the *New York Herald Tribune* Forum on Current Problems, in which he proposed to attack the Darlan deal. Stimson had just spent part of the evening justifying the arrangement to Felix Frankfurter, Archibald MacLeish, and Henry Morgenthau (who "was almost for giving up the war which he said had lost all interest for him"). Eventually he had succeeded: "Frankfurter was all right on the matter throughout of course, and MacLeish was only puzzled and troubled. Finally after grunts and groans we got Morgenthau into line . . ." But Willkie was to prove more stubborn. When Stimson raised with him the matter of the forthcoming speech, he was called names and accused of trying to control Willkie's freedom. Stimson rehearsed all the military arguments in favor of the deal; he read out Eisenhower's telegram; he argued that a repudiation of the arrangement would have fatal consequences in North Africa; and he finally told Willkie that he had "esteemed and respected him for many years but, if he persisted in doing this, my respect for him would be gravely diminished."[104] One of those points evidently came across, because Willkie did in fact excise some passages from the speech, to Stimson's surprise and Roosevelt's delight. The objectionable passage had run:

> *Shall we in America be quiet for instance when our leaders, after promising freedom to the French people, put into control over them the very man who has helped to enslave them?* Shall we be quiet when we see our government's long appeasement of Vichy *find its logical conclusion in our collaboration with Darlan, Hitler's tool?* I tell you we cannot fight this war in silence whatever our experts say, because if we fight in silence those same experts will, in the end, even winning the war, win nothing but blood and ashes.[105] (Italics added)

As delivered at the Forum, with the exclusion of the italicized sections and the substitution in the remainder of "State Department" for "government," the speech was not an attack on the Darlan deal, but a general appeal for more popular control of American diplomacy, a complaint about censorship, and a familiar, indeed conventional, criticism of the State Department. None of Willkie's arrows found their target.

Even in its uncensored form the speech was no more hostile than much current newspaper commentary. Doubtless Willkie was even more aggrieved when the following day Roosevelt issued his press statement emphasizing the temporary nature of the Darlan deal: "People in the United States . . . would never understand the recognition of a reconstituting of the Vichy government in France or in French territory. We are opposed to Frenchmen who support Hitler and the Axis." Roosevelt then said to the assembled reporters: "I am afraid I am cutting a lot of good stuff . . . from under the feet of people who don't think things through." But the two key sentences had been added by Roosevelt himself to the suggested OWI draft.[106] It must have seemed to Willkie as if Roosevelt, notwithstanding his government's performance, was chiefly concerned about retaining his monopoly as the spokesman for liberalism, and anxious to preempt a possible usurper. Certainly the memory of the episode temporarily soured Willkie's relations with even his friends within the administration, such as MacLeish.[107]

Walter Lippmann at least tried to be more discreet in his criticisms. He wrote one column, published on 12 November, in which he drew attention to the still unresolved problem of making contact with the French population under German occupation, and argued that the first requirement, given the liquidation of Vichy, was the formation in North Africa of an independent, provisional French authority. He saw the chief obstacle to that move to be the prevalent belief within the American administration, as evinced in Hull's press conference, that it was American diplomacy that had prevented France from joining the Axis, immobilized the French fleet, and opened up North Africa. In fact, Lippmann argued, the foundation for all that had been "the increasingly organized and ever more vehement resistance of the people of France, and we must not approach the tremendous problem of France with the illusion that the tail has been wagging the dog."[108] It was a typical Lippmann tutorial, precise, courteous, and with an air of omniscient condescension.

Privately, he expressed himself more severely. In a letter to Stimson on 19 November he remarked, with reference to Hull's "confession to the world that we had maintained diplomatic relations with Vichy in order to prepare an invasion of territory governed from Vichy": "I do not know what the Axis propaganda has done with this admission but I should think it could be used most effectively against us in Spain and Portugal." A second complaint by Lippmann more directly concerned Stimson's department: the revelation from North Africa that on his secret preparatory mission General Clark had had a large amount of money at his disposal. As Lippmann pointed out, "our enemies can use this disclosure by claiming that any Frenchman who joins us has been bribed."[109] He also forwarded to the State Department and the War Department a seven-page memorandum on the situation after the Darlan deal. It started from the premise that the deal was a consequence of faulty political intelligence, and then made certain concrete recommendations: that the only obligation the Americans had incurred toward Darlan was to protect his life, not to endow him with any official status, and that after the immediate military crisis was over, when Tunisia and Dakar were in Allied hands, he should be stripped of all political authority. In the meantime, Lippmann urged, Darlan should be compelled to annul every measure of Vichy legislation then in force in North Africa. By thus repudiating the Vichy regime, the United States would, ". . . vindicate our war aims, and indeed clarify them and fortify them. What we do in the first territory liberated by American arms will obviously have the profoundest influence as an example and as a precedent upon all the other occupied territory in Europe. . . . We shall also provide the only possible platform upon which all patriotic Frenchmen can be united. For the one common denominator of all loyal factions is in the legitimate constitutional liberties of France."[110]

Such were Lippmann's confidential recommendations, which may seem unexceptionable now but which did not then, in that climate, endear him to the relevant officials. The War Department denied in effect that the political preparation had been misleading, and claimed that the only unexpected feature of the whole operation had been the presence of Darlan in Algeria. It also contested Lippmann's assertion that the intelligence services of the Fighting

French could have provided more accurate information about political senti-ment in North Africa. The response from Hull was characteristically blunt. In a brief letter to Lippmann ("Dear Sir"), with whom he had in fact personally discussed the whole affair on 14 November, he curtly regretted that Lippmann had written and published what he had on insufficient information. That evidently astonished Lippmann, who wrote back that Hull's note "should be expunged from the record." For, he went on, the memorandum had been confidential, not public, and his belief that the political planning had been weak stemmed from Eisenhower's telegram, read to him by General Marshall: "I do not see why you should resent my stating this fact since it is based on what you yourself told me, namely that the arrangement with Admiral Darlan had been made by General Eisenhower and you had no special knowledge of it. If you had no special knowledge of it, it is obvious that the arrangement with Admiral Darlan was not prepared in advance by our political officers."

It developed that Hull was not particularly interested in Lippmann's positive recommendation, only affronted at the explicit criticism of the State Depart-ment. Nor would he accept Lippmann's contention that the same criticism was explicit in Eisenhower's telegram, and implicit in Roosevelt's press statement, in which the president had indicated that he had not anticipated an arrangement with Darlan. It was that part of the memorandum which Lippmann had incor-porated in a column on 19 November. This exchange of views ended with a pained letter from Lippmann on 10 December, in which he expressed great sympathy for the department's problems and attempted to dissociate himself from those who had ever attacked the State Department for the general policy toward Vichy. But Hull may well have recalled Lippmann's column of 6 Janu-ary, "Concerning the State Department" (". . . there has long been doubt whether in some of the most critical areas of the outside world the State Department has had sufficiently astute and experienced observers and infor-mants") or his comment on 21 March that Roosevelt should put a statesman in the department capable of distinguishing friends from enemies.[111]

The different experiences of Lippmann and Willkie illustrate the same general point: the heightened sensitivity within certain quarters of the adminis-tration to domestic criticism, and the resulting closure of free discussion. Willkie, thwarted, and Lippmann, rebuked, were no radical, subversive revo-lutionaries; they had many views in common with those who cautioned them. They were nonetheless targets for official wrath, although Roosevelt was himself personally uninvolved: he did not instigate either Stimson's telephone call or Hull's letters, however much he may have approved of them. George Creel's earlier prophecy to Elmer Davis—that with the first military engage-ment the pressures would be on to tighten censorship of civilian commen-tary[112]—had been proved exactly correct; and in the absence of effective machinery and willing helpers within OWI, which had, rather like the Psycho-logical Warfare Branch, acquired within the administration something of a reputation for wayward liberalism,[113] it followed that such censorship would be undertaken on a private, informal basis. Stimson's energetic attempts to bring into line waverers within and a critic outside the administration are a case in point.

If outright censorship were not feasible, then news management might suffice to stifle criticism. Though the full dimensions of such covert activity can never be properly examined, various examples of it, extending into 1943, have survived, including one where the control was turned back upon the OWI itself. This was the case of the journalist Edgar Ansel Mowrer, who shortly resigned in protest from OWI after being refused permission, at the insistence of the War Department and Roosevelt himself, to visit North Africa.[114] At the other extreme were the favors granted to Demaree Bess, a journalist who wrote a series of laudatory articles about the North African invasion for the *Saturday Evening Post*, based on privileged access to military documents.[115] As Lippmann argued, "It is obvious that Mr. Bess did not get to North Africa without his trip being arranged in Washington, and it is equally obvious that General Eisenhower did not open his files to Mr. Bess, rather than to some other journalist or to all journalists, except on instructions from Washington. Mr. Bess has accordingly sung for his supper."[116] A number of other journalists, including Dorothy Thompson, Marquis Childs, and William Shirer, joined Lippmann in sending a telegram to Roosevelt on 4 August 1943 protesting, with specific reference to the Bess articles, the "practice of opening the secret files to individual journalists which enables them to exploit for their own advantage information that belongs to the whole nation and should be available to the profession as a whole."[117]

But the finest specimens of administration sensitivity are to be found, as always, in the State Department. There a memorandum was drawn up, the latest in a series, on the sources of the widespread criticism of American policy. The responsibility was firmly placed on British rivalry with the United States, Gaullist postwar ambitions, Soviet interference, and, within the United States, on the activities of "many persons prominent in public life and in press circles . . . who are more concerned with the ideological aspects of the war than the military and who sincerely feel that unless the struggle against Nazism and Fascism is won in its entirety the military defeat of our enemies would be of no value."[118] On a more personal level, the actual behavior of Cordell Hull is itself revealing. On 28 January 1943, after persistent questioning from I. F. Stone about the recent arrival in North Africa of Marcel Peyrouton, formerly Vichy's minister of the interior, Hull lost his control and angrily demanded of Stone whether he wrote under an assumed name. Hull had later to explain to a number of troubled inquirers that his question did not constitute an ethnic slur (Stone's original name was Feinstein).[119]

In the end the debate over the Darlan deal could not be fruitfully resolved. This was not because it was sometimes intemperately conducted, nor because the odds were unequal, the critics being outsiders and the defenders possessing the full weight of governmental prestige and the sanction of military necessity. More fundamentally it was because the two sides were talking past one another. The critics could claim, with some justification, that the record of American diplomacy, as tested by the North African invasion, was uninspiring. General Weygand had been dismissed; General Giraud had at the critical moment refused American terms; Admiral Darlan, a last-minute choice, had been of limited effectiveness, and in accepting him Americans had frankly adopted a policy of expediency. The defenders could reply, also with some justification, that under the circumstances—chiefly the absence of any significant non-Vichy elements—the best resolution had been found; American diplomats and soldiers had had to work with whatever material was available. Of more interest, in the American context, is the fact that the debate did not end there. The more extreme critics saw in the record their government's lurking sympathy with fascism; the more extreme defenders saw the critics as possessing equally undesirable loyalties. And all the while the appropriate governmental bureau, the OWI, was powerless to prevent the rift widening. Elmer Davis, who was told on the same day by Hull that the American army was not an army of occupation and by Roosevelt that it was, felt neither in control of the distribution of information nor competent to issue it. Before one press conference he privately confessed to being very worried "about what I don't know about Africa"; and at the end of the day he admitted, "maybe I did most things wrong."[120]

CHAPTER 9
THE UNITED STATES
AND GREAT BRITAIN IN
NORTH AFRICA, 1943

A single assassin, Bonnier de la Chapelle, determined that the Darlan deal should prove a great deal more temporary than its framers had intended. On Christmas Eve, 1942, he shot Darlan dead, and on Boxing Day was himself, with equal dispatch, court-martialed and executed. There thus appeared a curious symmetry about Darlan's brief North African excursion. Both his initial arrival there and his peremptory removal were events of such remarkable fortune, good or bad, that they encouraged the widest and most suspicious conjectures. Yet, on closer inspection,[1] both were what they seemed: Darlan really had gone to Algiers to visit his stricken son, and he really was killed by a solitary, though certainly inspired, Royalist fanatic.

His death sealed, finally, America's Vichy policy, which he had adventitiously extended six weeks beyond the actual severance of relations. His appointed successor, General Giraud, captured by the Germans in 1940, could in no strict sense be identified with either the Vichy policy or the Vichy regime. But his was not thereby a tranquilizing presence. On the contrary, the year 1943—from the Casablanca to the Teheran Conference—witnessed a profusion of irritations and controversies surrounding French policies that burst into the open at times to distract and confuse the entire wartime alliance. The sequence of events is clear and may seem, in retrospect, both logical and straightforward: the extension and consolidation of de Gaulle's effective control over the French Forces of Liberation, political as well as military. During this year de Gaulle and Giraud disputed control first of the North African army, then of that broad association of colonial forces, underground and resistance elements, political parties, and trade unions which came to be known after June as the French Committee of National Liberation (FCNL). In August, when de Gaulle and Giraud might have seemed coequals, this body was accorded limited administrative recognition by the American government. But by November de Gaulle had emerged as victor ludorum, with Giraud stripped of all political authority, even deprived of his seat on the committee, remaining only commander in chief of the French army.

But this was far from a smooth progression. The contest between de Gaulle and Giraud blended with the various other elements that had contributed to the uneasy passage of Franco-American relations over the previous three years. It was conducted against a background of previously submerged Anglo-American governmental differences, to the bewilderment of certain sections of the American public, amidst the outbreak of personal feuds and intrigues within the French émigré community, and in the face of an increasingly personal, at times idiosyncratic, command of American foreign policy by President Roosevelt, of which the actual appointment of Giraud, setting the train in motion, provides an early instance. Stimson at the War Department recorded his surprise at Roosevelt's swift response to the hiatus caused by Darlan's assassination. At a time when Stimson, Marshall, Eisenhower, and Hull had all been considering ways of insinuating Giraud into his post without offending French dignity,

> . . . suddenly there came news from the White House that the President quite independently was acting through Leahy to draw papers of his own and had sent a curious document to Eisenhower providing that Eisenhower should appoint the governor. I took it up with the President . . . and found that he meant, although his paper did not make it clear, that this was to be only in case the provincial governors seemed to be on the verge of appointing someone else than Giraud. Consequently I sent another telegram to Eisenhower explaining what would otherwise have been a very great puzzle to him if my explanatory telegram had not come. But the President's quick action quite took the place of what we were doing.[2]

The North African regime over which Giraud fleetingly presided can most readily be described as residual Vichyism, Vichy without Pétain. Political freedom was still absent; anti-Jewish legislation was sustained (including the abrogation of the Crémieux decree of 1870, which had bestowed citizenship upon Algerian Jews); and political prisoners were categorized as before, according to whether they were Jews, Communists, or refugee Spanish republicans. Since this was a state of affairs implicitly sanctioned by the original American arrangement with Darlan, it was naturally prolonged under Giraud. Equally striking is the general's spiritual affinity with Pétain. In a long report that he wrote for Pétain about the causes of the French defeat of 1940, he echoed the marshal's own view that they lay in a declining birth rate, in physical and moral degeneration ("the aim of all classes of society was not to create a better world but to be amused"), in anticlericalism, in the absence of authority and the disrespect for tradition, and in the Popular Front ("which taught people to be lazy").[3]

Despite superficial resemblances this is not doctrinal fascism; nor may the emergent regime be accurately described as "neofascist."[4] The guiding beliefs, like Pétain's, were those of a professional soldier uninterested in social amelioration, concerned rather with the establishment of an orderly, disciplined, and above all stable society. What Pétain had sought in order to maintain the precarious sovereignty of Vichy and hold in check the competing tendencies at his court, Giraud sought in order to maintain his authority over the French forces that had been newly brought under his command. The essential constituent element of fascism, its dynamism, was altogether lacking. The one adviser of Giraud who might have framed for his policies some ideological coherence, who did possess some distinct social and economic visions, Jacques Lemaigre-Dubreuil, was dismayed at Giraud's political innocence and resigned in March.[5] He was succeeded by the more technically minded Jean Monnet, who, by his own account, sought "no jobs and no favors."[6]

Just as the practices and, like Marcel Peyrouton, some of the personnel of Vichy were initially transplanted to North Africa, so, in their wake, were the underlying premises of America's original Vichy policy. By other means and on fresh soil, the Americans were continuing to act upon the same conviction, that they could control the evolution of French wartime policies: away from collaboration with Germany in the case of Vichy, toward an obedient cooperation with the Allies in the case of North Africa. The figure of Robert Murphy, counselor of the American embassy at Vichy, chargé d'affaires in Algiers, political adviser to Eisenhower and Roosevelt, provided an element of continuity.

But 1943 was to see the steady fading of these illusions. In helping to dispel them the British played a considerable part, although the actual differences between the two Anglo-Saxon powers were not so clear-cut as might at first appear. Too much attention to the clashes of personality can force the North African contest into an uncommonly uniform pattern, Giraud acting as the American candidate and de Gaulle as the British, with the civilian advisers, Robert Murphy and Harold Macmillan, playing complementary roles. It is true that both Roosevelt and Churchill liked to talk as if they were bringing into line two of their protégés. Each spoke of de Gaulle and Giraud as bride and groom, and claimed to be effecting some kind of marriage.[7] When at Casablanca in January that did not happen and de Gaulle at first refused even to make an appearance, Roosevelt sent word to Hull: "She has become quite high hat about the whole affair and doesn't wish to see either of us, and shows no intention of getting into bed with Giraud."[8] When in Algiers in June the FCNL was formed, with the chairmanship alternating between de Gaulle and Giraud, doubtless Churchill and Roosevelt felt like parents. That, however, suggests harmony rather than discord at the highest Anglo-American levels. In truth neither statesman considered himself to be ineluctably bound to any one particular French candidate. Roosevelt diluted his support for Giraud by stressing the provisional nature of his rule, thus robbing him of any real political weight. As Roosevelt told his cabinet on 8 January, ". . . the American army was an army of occupation in North Africa. It couldn't recognize French sovereignty or the right of Giraud or of the Governors' Council that set up Giraud. It was all right for Giraud to operate as Eisenhower's agent, if Eisenhower had designated him as his agent."[9] As for Churchill, he persisted in pressing the claims of General Alphonse Georges, the former commander of the French Northern Army, who represented, he said, "a certain continuity in Anglo-French relations which is most desirable." Despite Georges's lamentable military record, he might still serve as a support to Giraud and a counterweight to de Gaulle.[10] And with the formation of the FCNL in June, Churchill plainly considered that his "official connection with de Gaulle as leader of the Fighting French" was at an end.[11]

The real Anglo-American differences were to be found in other quarters, among those directly charged with the execution of policy. There, feelings ran deep. But, again, these were not clashes of personality or temperament. Between Murphy and Macmillan, for example, there arose, despite their very different backgrounds—the Catholic diplomat and the Tory parliamentarian— a firm bond of mutual respect, based perhaps on their shared sense of being distant appendages of their respective countries' power. As Macmillan later wrote of Murphy: "There is no man with whom I had a more pleasant relationship, often in difficult and baffling circumstances, and whose character I grew so quickly both to appreciate and to admire."[12] That did not, however, restrain Macmillan from delivering some rather tart criticisms of American policy, in a series of remarkable dispatches to London. He held the view that "the Americans have made a kind of bogey of Gaullism." But "the principal doctrine of Gaullism, namely the continuance of resistance and the constitution of a new France on Republican lines, is espoused by the great majority of Frenchmen under thirty-five years of age." As such, it contrasted sharply with Pétainism, "the principle of negation and defeat," but also with Giraudism, which "was scarcely a principle at all." The further Giraud moved away from Pétainism, the more he lost his natural support "in the *attentistes* among the Colonial Army, among the planters of North Africa, and among the few big industrial concerns who were hedging the bet." Gaullism was therefore bound to win the day, and the Americans were, at considerable risk, backing a loser.[13] "I am the last person," Macmillan wrote to Eden in October, "who can be accused of being 'anti-American.' On the contrary, my policy has always been to get their confidence and carry them with me. But I do want to save England and America from the consequences of a policy towards France which may easily leave us even more hated than Germany in years to come." "You and I are Tories," he reminded the man he was later to succeed as prime minister, "and half the strength we have against that form of radical communism which would like to bully the English people is that they have not forgotten Cromwell and the major Generals. I warn you very strongly that if you try any of this nonsense in France there will be a bitter revolt against you."[14]

De Gaulle's best friends, throughout 1943, were in the Foreign Office, whence came nearly all the pressure on Churchill to soften Roosevelt's hostility. In April Eden reported to the War Cabinet on his recent visit to Washington, where the divergencies between British and American policies toward France had been thoroughly aired. It appeared to him that while the British were working toward the creation of a single French authority, a trustee of French wartime interests, the Americans "preferred to deal with individuals, and were willing to see Giraud and de Gaulle separate." Similarly, while the British wanted to see some French authority established for civil affairs in the event of an Allied landing in France, the Americans desired an Allied administration.[15] Actually Eden and his chief adviser on French affairs, William Strang, were pleading their case as much to Churchill as to the Americans. For Churchill, like the Americans, had been growing alarmed at the gathering momentum of de Gaulle's climb to power, before he had even set foot in Algiers or there was a Committee there for him to subvert; and great efforts had been made to induce de Gaulle to postpone his arrival in Algiers until the military and political situation there was stable.[16]

Now, in conference with Roosevelt and Hull in Washington in May, Churchill was impressed by the strength of the Americans' commitment to Giraud. He therefore sent three telegrams to the War Cabinet in London, based on State Department memoranda, urging the elimination of de Gaulle and a more insistent Anglo-American control over French affairs. On 23 May, in Churchill's absence, the War Cabinet discussed these proposals at great length and rehearsed all the arguments against them: that de Gaulle was just on the point of reaching an agreement with Giraud, that any break with him would be visibly made at American prompting and would strengthen his appeal to the French, and that Gaullism, which was steadily gaining ground in North Africa, could not be separated from the figure of de Gaulle. The man was a symbol of the Republic, his movement of the Entente. "We are convinced," the reply went back to Churchill, "that the Americans are wrong in this and advocate a line which would not be understood here, with possible evil consequences to Anglo-American relations."[17]

The differences within British circles were never to be fully resolved. They were merely held in abeyance while other, then more urgent matters—the Tunisian campaign, the landings in Italy, the Burma campaign—pressed forward. The Anglo-American differences, by contrast, were never far from sight, and came into full view after June when, with a properly constituted French committee on French soil, the question of Allied recognition arose. The upshot, after weeks of discussion, was two distinct statements, from London and Washington, that laid bare the contrasting perspectives. Originally Roosevelt, affronted at de Gaulle's proposed moves against Pétainist officials like Boisson of Dakar, would not countenance anything like "recognition." He readily shared Churchill's semantic distrust of the term ("What does recognition mean? One can recognise a man as an Emperor or as a grocer"),[18] and in place of "recognise" would only accept "accept."[19] When he did come round to employ the more cordial term he did so in a lukewarm fashion. The American statement, released on 26 August, read: ". . . the Government of the United States recognizes the French Committee of National Liberation as administering those French overseas territories which acknowledge its authority."[20] That was little more than admitting the facts of the situation: the United States would recognize the authority of the FCNL only in those areas where it manifestly exercised that authority. The future of metropolitan France, and of Indochina where de Gaulle's writ did not as yet run, was left conveniently, and ambiguously, open.

The British statement, released the same day, went further on one critical issue. Noting, like the American, "with sympathy . . . the desire of the Committee to be regarded as the body qualified to ensure the administration and defence of all French interests," it went on: "It is the intention of His Majesty's Government to give effect to this request as far as possible while reserving the right to consider in consultation with the Committee the practical application of this principle in particular cases as they arise."[21] Throughout the preceding discussions Churchill had served both as the War Cabinet's spokesman with the president ("I beg you to go as far as you can in your formula because however justly founded one's misgivings may be there is no use making a gesture of this kind in a grudging form")[22] and as Roosevelt's emissary to the War Cabinet: when the deputy prime minister, Clement Attlee, observed that Washington's insistence on "the principle of collective responsibility" in the new French Committee came oddly from such a nest of bureaucratic intrigue, Churchill sharply retorted, "Nothing is easier than to find grounds of disagreement with the President, and few things would be more unhelpful."[23]

The British view—the view that Eden pressed on Churchill, and Churchill, with greater reluctance, on Roosevelt—had at least the virtue of simplicity. It was centered on Europe. It looked to the future containment of Germany, by Russia in the east and by France in the west, for which a strong France was an obvious prerequisite. It was not therefore in the British interest for any anti-American sentiment on the part of the French to be transferred to Britain; and the distinction between the two countries' policies toward France had therefore to be upheld. Where Churchill departed from this view was in his arguably more realistic sense that American policy was unlikely to be changed: Roosevelt was set in his ways and de Gaulle in his. De Gaulle's renewed assaults upon his rivals—the enlargement of the Committee so as to provide him with an effective majority, his proposed removal of Boisson—would never endear him to Roosevelt. In the meantime, Churchill argued, de Gaulle was a threat to Britain, to France (since he showed "many of the signs of a budding Führer"), to the Churchill-Roosevelt partnership, and, not least, to Franco-American relations: "I am afraid lest the anti–de Gaullism of the Washington Government may harden into a definite anti-France feeling."²⁴ British policy thus emerged as the product of these tensions.

The American policy was rather more complex, although it suffered from none of the British strains; interdepartmental disputes over France did not properly arise in the United States until 1944. In 1943 there was only an unambiguous anti-Gaullist stance and a firm backing, against all odds and to little avail, of Giraud. Yet the process by which American officials came to occupy such a position varied according to their responsibilities; and they should therefore be separately considered.

The military argument by itself was not decisive: as to who would be the more reliable commander of French forces, there may have seemed little to choose between Giraud, captured by the Germans in 1940, and de Gaulle, whose most famous exploit was still the Dakar fiasco of the same year. Evidently something more than the generals' military skills was involved. At the War Department Stimson was adamant that the United States should retain its dominant influence on any future campaigns and that, of the two Frenchmen, de Gaulle posed the more serious threat to that predominance. As Stimson expressed it, ". . . de Gaulle gave me the impression of a general who had too many press agents and was too occupied with his personal fortunes to do any fighting." The fundamental question in North Africa was of giving maximum support to Eisenhower who, in the midst of the Tunisian and then the Italian campaigns, "was being distracted by constant nagging and factional attacks from the press in this country."²⁵ In a long memorandum to Roosevelt on 1 February, Stimson argued that the Imperial Council, which had been set up in Africa by Darlan and was then headed by Giraud, was "not perfect enough or sufficiently generally acknowledged to be considered a successful general government of North Africa." That was a striking admission. Stimson cited examples from Latin America at the turn of the century, the Philippines, Puerto Rico, and Cuba, when the American army had exercised full administrative powers and when, incidentally, his own profoundest convictions had been formed.²⁶ On that basis he insisted that in North Africa (whose resemblance with those other areas may be questioned) the "delicate and dangerous" administrative and political problems ". . . must be solved by the war power of the President exercised through Eisenhower's command. . . . No matter how carefully their nature may be veiled to avoid exciting the antagonism of the French, no power exists in North Africa today except the military power under Eisenhower which is competent to deal with them without the danger of a military defeat by the Germans."²⁷ If the Imperial Council was regarded as of little use, it followed that the later, and more vigorous, FCNL could only be accorded the most modest recognition. In August, Stimson found Hull in agreement on this: "We both were afraid that the Committee might sometime fall into the hands of de Gaulle and, if it is recognized in any sense as the government of North Africa, that will give de Gaulle a platform for making trouble."[28]

Such was the argument from military necessity: fear of de Gaulle's unruly behavior, and not any military virtues detected in Giraud, determined Stimson's attitude. But that was not an unshakable conviction, precisely because it was based on military requirements. It was a tactical, not a strategic, preference. If ever sound military arguments could be adduced for recognizing the FCNL even when, after November, it had passed under de Gaulle's control, then Stimson could safely change his mind; this was indeed what happened in 1944. It was prefigured long before, in June and July of 1943, when Eisenhower began, partly at Macmillan's prodding, to consider proposing recognition of the French Committee. He was also, according to Macmillan, growing restless at Roosevelt's "autocratic instructions" issued through him to the Committee: the insistence, for example, on the retention of Boisson at Dakar, or the suggested ban on further meetings of the Committee. Such intrusions were, in Eisenhower's view as reported by Macmillan, more threatening to the stability of the region than almost any reasonable settlement concluded by de Gaulle and Giraud.[29] But Eisenhower's tentative steps toward recognition were quickly erased. Churchill wired back to Macmillan that he was shocked at the disloyalty shown by a commander in the field daring to complain of his president's policy to a British official;[30] and when he later reported to Roosevelt the substance of Macmillan's report and the recommendation of Eisenhower and Marshall, Roosevelt immediately sent a telegram to Eisenhower ordering him not to recognize the French Committee.[31] Eisenhower, baffled, merely replied that he had never contemplated doing so on his own authority.[32]

While current and prospective military needs determined the policy of the War Department, the perspective of the State Department lay both in the recent past and the more distant future. That was a measure of the Department's steady eviction from current policy-making. Though it was engaged throughout this period in a multitude of activities concerning the shape of the postwar world, these had little to do with actual diplomacy and possessed at times a markedly abstract quality. As Dean Acheson later realled, "Largely detached from the practicalities of current problems and power relations, the Department under Mr. Hull became absorbed in platonic planning of a utopia, in a sort of mechanistic idealism."[33] As an example, an assistant secretary of state, Breckinridge Long, became fascinated with the arguments around Walter Lippmann's latest book, *U.S. Foreign Policy: Shield of the Republic*.[34] He invited comments and criticism from numerous authorities, including Quincy Wright, the professor of international law, and himself wrote forty-two pages attempting to refute Lippmann's thesis. Discussion came to a close when Long sent to his colleague Stanley Hornbeck a note that contained the following wisdom: "As I understand his use of the words Quincy Wright intends to say that the *principle* is translated into *action* through the application of a *policy* and that somewhere there must be force to attain the objective which would be the successful realization of that principle through the agency of the *policy.*"[35] At a more vital level there were those regular State Department seminars, drawing upon a crowded pool of intellectual talent, inside and outside academe: Sumner Welles, Adolf Berle, the journalist Anne O'Hare McCormick, Hamilton Fish Armstrong, editor of *Foreign Affairs*, James T. Shotwell, professor of history at Columbia University, and Isaiah Bowman, president of Johns Hopkins.[36] They made many valuable recommendations concerning a future international organization and the favored American resolution to the problem of imperialism, trusteeship. There in particular the specter of Gaullism hovered over their deliberations.[37] However, at the conferences in Quebec in August and in Moscow in October, which were conducted without French participation, a broad general agreement was reached on many of the department's proposals, much to the satisfaction of its officials.[38] But in the meantime events in North Africa were moving on, and there the department had much less to contribute. It chose only to defend its past record.

For the State Department nursed a long series of grievances against de Gaulle, going back at least as far as the St. Pierre-and-Miquelon affair. To the department the Gaullists posed a dual threat: first in opposing, and sometimes obstructing, its policies abroad, and second in being the cause, and sometimes the source, of much heated criticism of the department within the United States. Both irritations were considerable, but as in the course of 1943 the department's share in making policy was even further reduced, while the criticisms of it did not let up, it was the second, domestic threat that most exercised its officials. Hull in particular was greatly affronted at the continued assault on his reputation, and Stimson, Ickes, and Eden all noted the near impossibility of getting Hull to discuss anything except his resentment at the Gaullists and their British sponsors.[39] Consequently, in order to ease its burdens the department began to counterattack and provide itself with a larger volume of favorable comment. Sometimes this was done in a perfectly open manner, as by the radio series "The State Department Speaks," broadcast on the Blue Network in late 1943 and early 1944. Murphy himself spoke on the French policy at great length on 15 January.[40] But no very great results ensued. Walter Lippmann was appalled at the inadequacy of the broadcasts and was moved to write to the new under secretary of state, Edward Stettinius: "The technique is that of the lower forms of commercial advertising. The style is vulgar. The intellectual level of the questions, and therefore of many of the answers, is low. The result is crass propaganda which can only mislead the ignorant and infuriate the well-informed. . . . I feel as if I had seen grandma tipsy in the cocktail bar of the Mayflower Hotel." When Stettinius retorted that 98 percent of the letters received at the State Department had been favorable about the broadcasts, Lippmann gave him a stern lecture on fan mail: ". . . the one almost certain rule . . . is that it does not reflect the opinion of those who in the end make opinion: they very rarely write fan letters."[41]

Of greater worth, in fact, were the more covert ways the department sought to defend its position, and a few of these have since come to light. There was the case of Dr. Harry Gideonse, president of Brooklyn College, and once a powerful critic of the department: he had publicly opposed the embargo on Republican Spain, he had signed the telegram to Roosevelt criticizing the department over St. Pierre and Miquelon, and he figured in the department's files as one of the non-Communist participants in the "Campaign to Undermine the State Department."[42] However, a visit to London in the summer of 1943, where H. Freeman Matthews, then in the American embassy, "put him in touch with some right-minded people, both French and American," rapidly convinced him of the department's rightness; and he assured Matthews that on his return to the United States he would deliver some lectures on the subject.[43] There soon followed an address to the Chicago Council on Foreign Relations, in which he observed that "the State Department has been extraordinarily well-informed and very delicate in its handling of an extremely touchy situation, full of ideological dynamite."[44] Then, in an article in the *New Leader*, a labor journal, Gideonse quoted a distinguished, but anonymous Frenchman in London who had declared to him that he "thanked Providence every day, for the restraint and wisdom of the American State Department."[45]

More direct intervention was made by the department in the matter of the Dufour case. This concerned a young Frenchman, Maurice Henri Dufour, who claimed that after he had arrived in England in April 1942, in order to enlist in the Free French, he had been severely beaten up by de Gaulle's secret agents in an effort to discover whether he was working for the British. Accordingly, he obtained a High Court writ against de Gaulle in August 1943. Though the matter was eventually dropped and Dufour was paid considerable compensation,[46] the State Department, and again Matthews in London, developed a keen interest in the case.[47] In due course, the widely read *Reader's Digest* published an article called "Spotlight on the State Department," written by Kingsbury Smith, a prominent defender of the department, who had earlier outlined "Our Government's Case for Appeasement." This latest article had many of the trademarks of a department plant, as in its reference to the "Gestapo" methods of de Gaulle's organization: "Details of these activities, including 'suicides' and brutal treatment, would shock the American people. The State Department," it added curiously, "has refrained from making these reports public."[48]

It was likewise from the embassy in London that news was spread of the personal oath that members of the Free French were allegedly required to swear to de Gaulle; and Matthews characteristically added that he had heard of Gaullist agents boasting of their success in assassinating Darlan and plotting to

assassinate Giraud.[49] And finally there came, from the same source, the text of
Churchill's confidential memorandum to the British press of 12 June in which
he had said of de Gaulle: "He has undoubtedly Fascist and dictatorial tendencies. At one time he represents himself as the sole barrier against Communism;
at another, as enjoying Communist support."[50] This too appeared in the articles of a favored journalist, Ernest K. Lindley.[51] The words were damning
enough even before they were detached from the particular context in which
Churchill had used them: his desire that in the interests of French unity the
press not play up the political rivalries then evident in Algiers.[52] But so intense
was this barrage of black propaganda, so shrill the crescendo it reached just
when the rival figure of Giraud was being fêted in Washington,[53] that the War
Cabinet was moved to register its objections.[54] When the American ambassador in London, John C. Winant, reported British misgivings, he said that
Churchill "felt that the almost verbatim quotations were an unfair use of a
confidential directive"; and Winant himself was "disturbed about the security
of our codes."[55]

There is no mistaking the relish with which Matthews in particular engaged
in this assault on the man he termed, in a letter to the State Department, "this
French Adolf";[56] nor can there be any doubt that Matthews, along with
Murphy and Leahy, was concerned to defend the record of the American
embassy at Vichy. This was, in short, retrospective propaganda, showing the
historical roots of the State Department's hostility to de Gaulle. But the
hostility was not, for that very reason, rigid: a changed climate would ease
Hull's resentment. Specifically there were two events in 1943, neither of them
directly concerning France, that may have encouraged him to adopt a more
balanced approach. The first was the resignation in August, for reasons rather
remote from foreign policy, of Sumner Welles as under secretary of state.[57]
This marked the triumph of a whispering campaign conducted by, among
others, William C. Bullitt, who had, with some assistance from J. Edgar
Hoover, communicated to all who would listen a number of unsavory details
about Welles's private life.[58] So fiercely were the rumors being spread that
Hull seized his opportunity to rid himself of someone whom he had increasingly come to regard as an undisciplined and disloyal subordinate, to whom
Roosevelt had listened more readily than to the secretary.[59]

Hull was now, for the first time in the war, master in his own house. The
second event was related to this: the Moscow conference in October, at which
Hull was the senior American delegate (a novelty for him) and could be seen to
have secured a resounding personal success, with the promise of Russian
support for the projected United Nations organization. He even received a
gracious telegram from Lippmann (which Hull equally graciously acknowledged) congratulating him on his "epoch-making work."[60] Soon there appeared a distinct mellowing in Hull's attitude, toward Lippmann of course,[61]
but also toward de Gaulle, whom he had visited on his way to Moscow.

According to Lippmann, Hull had praised de Gaulle, calling him "a greatly misunderstood man," whose "idea of democracy turned out to be singularly close to Hull's own."[62]

A comparative flexibility may have emerged in some quarters of Washington by the end of 1943, but not in the White House. There, and there alone, could be found principled, consistent, and implacable hostility to de Gaulle. Starting with the designation of Giraud to succeed Darlan, Roosevelt's personal interventions into French affairs never slackened, even when the French themselves might reasonably have claimed some autonomy. The month of June, which opened with the formation of the FCNL, witnessed a notable burst of activity. On the fifth Roosevelt vigorously complained to Churchill about the Gaullist slant of British reporting ("We receive only the bride's publicity. What is the matter with our British-American information services?"),[63] thus prompting Churchill's disastrous memorandum to the press. On the eighth Roosevelt refused to let the FCNL participate in United Nations day.[64] On the seventeenth he insisted on the retention of Boisson in office;[65] and the same day he proposed to prevent further meetings of the Committee.[66] And the year ended with his angry démarche at the Committee's arrest of three Vichyites, Boisson, Peyrouton, and Flandin, the first two of whom had been of moderate assistance to the Allies, though none of them had ever repudiated his past record.[67] This was at best a tactless intrusion, in language of a vehemence that startled even the Americans in the field,[68] and Roosevelt was persuaded to lower his demand from immunity for the three prisoners to an assurance from the Committee that their trial would be postponed till after the liberation of France.[69] It all added up, on Roosevelt's part, to a highly individual approach to coalition warfare even when, as in the last episode, he had Churchill, alone on the British side, as copartner.

The nature of Roosevelt's policy comes across most clearly in one episode that extended for most of the year, the visit of Jean Monnet to Algiers.[70] In conception the mission of this undoubted French patriot, the friend of Morgenthau, Harry Hopkins, Felix Frankfurter, and John McCloy, exactly conformed to the Rooseveltian pattern of court diplomacy. He had first come to Roosevelt's notice in the context of North Africa when a memorandum that he addressed to the White House showed a pleasing convergence with many of the president's own ideas, albeit couched in the more systematic French idiom: the urgency of reequipping the French North African army, the need to safeguard French sovereignty for the duration of the war, and, as an aspect of that, the importance of limiting the functions of any French authorities abroad to local civil and administrative matters.[71] Monnet in his writing stressed the benefits to France, Roosevelt by his actions the rewards for American strategy; but these were initially two facets of the same policy. On 16 January Roosevelt sent Hull a cable from Casablanca proposing that Monnet be sent over to assist in civilian affairs; but Hull, suspecting Monnet of Gaullist sympathies, disapproved.[72] Roosevelt believed that Monnet's worth lay in his technical and administrative abilities, divorced from any obvious political attachments while respected by all parties; and a month later he authorized the trip anyway. Monnet's ostensible brief was to handle the Lend-Lease supplies to the French army; his real task was, as he saw it, to work for the unity of all French factions in North Africa or, as Roosevelt saw it, to strengthen Giraud at the expense of de Gaulle.[73] At the outset of Monnet's visit those aims seemed nicely congruent.

But Monnet did not regard himself as Roosevelt's instrument, and the apparent coincidence of their aims was not to be prolonged in the tense atmosphere at Algiers. Strengthening Giraud meant, at first, purifying his regime, baptizing it in the waters of French (and American) liberalism. So with all the tact he could muster Monnet urged Giraud to remove those odious features of his administration which had hitherto blackened it in the eyes of the American and British public. There followed the steady repeal of Vichy's legislation, the resignation or dismissal of numerous Vichyite officials, and, above all, a speech by Giraud on 14 March, largely written by Monnet, that affirmed the democratic and republican basis of any future French government.[74] But it was a hard course for Monnet. Like almost everyone else he was struck by the obduracy and political naiveté of Giraud, although, respecting the soldier, he was more sympathetic than some to his flaws: "Do not forget," he wrote to Hopkins, "that he is a French general accustomed to operate in an orderly society and that he now is in an anarchic one."[75] In one sensitive area Giraud proved especially intractable. This was the Crémieux Law of 1872, which had conferred citizenship on North African Jews but not Moslems, and had, for anti-Semitic reasons, been repealed by Vichy. It should accordingly have now been restored by Giraud; instead, the repeal remained in force, greatly alarming liberal and Jewish opinion abroad.[76] Although Monnet did in his *Memoirs* admit the "error,"[77] he was at the time more concerned about reassuring Giraud's critics, like Frankfurter, that it was merely a housecleaning measure prior to a thoroughgoing review of the status of both Jews and Moslems.[78]

But however reformed Giraud's administration became under Monnet's tutelage, its relationship to de Gaulle's Committee in London was still undefined. This was where Monnet began to depart from Rooseveltian premises. French unity became, for him, the transcendent goal, its absence the direst threat to French recovery. He may have shared many of Roosevelt's suspicions of de Gaulle: "De Gaulle," he wrote to Hopkins, "stands for arbitrary action, with all the risks of Fascism. Giraud stands for the preservation of the right of the people and democratic process."[79] But since Monnet always preferred technical adjustments to political battles, he was content to adopt a mediating role between the two men, even though they were in an unequal combat, with de Gaulle employing every political stratagem and propaganda device while

Giraud rested on his military dignity. Nevertheless, where Roosevelt and Churchill had failed in January, Monnet succeeded in June. He in effect fathered the FCNL.

In so doing he strangely justified Hull's misgivings: not that he became a Gaullist, but because—with the Committee formed, de Gaulle, Giraud, and their respective nominees delicately balanced within it, and collective responsibility affirmed—he too began to recommend Allied recognition. His argument was in part that such recognition would not aid but hamper de Gaulle's future prospects: "I cannot emphasize too strongly," he wrote to Hopkins, "that De Gaulle's main object is to minimize committee's authority and then free himself from the ties of the committee's collective responsibility. A prompt recognition by the great powers should insure committee's survival and enable civilian members to deal with any new threat. Its non-recognition continues to facilitate De Gaulle's plans."[80] But such subtleties were not appreciated in Washington; and Monnet came to be regarded, in quarters hostile to de Gaulle, as a Gaullist.[81] Undeterred, he left Algiers for Washington in November to start work on the aid programs for a soon to be liberated France.[82]

Monnet's accommodation to the FCNL neatly exposed the limitations of Roosevelt's policy: the liberalization of Giraud's regime had only weakened Giraud; French unity would only lead to Gaullist ascendancy. Between American policy and French reality there lay a broken thread, but it had been snapped less by personal vexations than by ulterior issues of principle. Halifax, the British ambassador, was only partially correct when he observed that Roosevelt alone was "responsible for our difficulties. . . . [H]is attitude . . . seems to be a purely personal one."[83] For it was an attitude compounded of various elements, all of them the stock-in-trade of official Washington's views of wartime France. Roosevelt merely preserved and institutionalized them. He never himself systematically expounded them, although they can be found, jumbled together, in an important telegram that he sent to Churchill on 17 June, at the height of the FCNL negotiations:

> I am fed up with de Gaulle, and the secret personal and political machinations of that Committee in the last few days indicate that there is no possibility of our working with de Gaulle. If these were peace times it wouldn't make so much difference but I am absolutely convinced that he has been and is now injuring our war effort and that he is a very dangerous threat to us . . .
>
> We must divorce ourselves from de Gaulle because, first, he has proven to be unreliable, unco-operative and disloyal to both our Governments. Second, he has more recently been interested far more in political machinations than he has in the prosecution of the war, and these machinations have been carried on without our knowledge and to the detriment of our military interests . . .

Our two countries have solemnly pledged that they will liberate the French Republic and, when we drive the Germans out, return that country to the control of the sovereign French people.[84]

Though an artificial exercise, it is worth separating out the various elements that comprised Roosevelt's attitude toward France. There was, first and most famously, contempt for the arrogance of the man who, according to the stories with which Roosevelt regaled visitors, presumed to be both Joan of Arc and Clemenceau simultaneously.[85] As Roosevelt once remarked, he was reluctant to "give de Gaulle a white horse on which he could ride into France and make himself master of a government there."[86] There was, second, what Roosevelt's son Elliott recorded, disgust at the practice of colonialism, especially French colonialism, and de Gaulle was resolutely committed to retain the French empire. According to Elliott, his father said to him: "The thing is . . . the colonial system means war. Exploit the resources of an India, a Burma, a Java; take all the wealth out of those countries, but never put anything back into them, things like education, decent standards of living, minimum health requirements—all you're doing is storing up the kind of trouble that leads to war. All you're doing is negating the value of any kind of organizational structure for peace before it begins." Elliott's overall testimony can be questioned on grounds both scholarly (the unlikely exactness of such extended verbatim quotations) and political (the recollections were explicitly written to discredit the successor Truman administration),[87] but in this case it can be confirmed from other sources.[88] Churchill, for example, was familiar with Roosevelt's sentiments, but he was not unduly perturbed; he was confident that they could not matter until the peace settlement needed drafting. In the meantime Churchill could point to the more generous undertakings with respect to the French empire that had come from other quarters of the administration, notably the State Department.[89]

But far more telling than either the individual animosity or the anticolonial ardor was, third, Roosevelt's compartmentalized approach to wartime problems. He, the civilian, did believe what de Gaulle, the general, did not, that the political and military aspects of the war could be sharply distinguished, and that political issues could only be resolved after the conclusion of hostilities. The whole thrust of presidential rhetoric had been directed at outlining a postwar world that would be conjured into existence at the peace conference, not established piecemeal in the course of armed conflict. Whatever the sources of this belief—the oft-repeated Wilsonian desire for self-determination for the occupied peoples, the fear that if political decisions were made the United States could be forced to concede more in a delicate military situation than after an Allied victory, or simply a temperamental addiction to procrastinations—it was not an ignoble one. But it did have immediate political consequences. Above all it inescapably produced a series of short-term expedients, of which the French policy, more than any other, affords numerous illustrations. Even when Giraud, like every other non-Gaullist Frenchman to whom the Americans had turned—Pétain, Weygand, Darlan—proved a broken reed, Roosevelt still would not enter into any firm political relationship with the FCNL. He would only, as he continued to do throughout 1943, issue his instructions to it.

In pursuing its policy the American administration was not deflected by any sustained intervention by the American public. The Gaullists did not, in 1943, capture any large numbers of new recruits. Indeed Gaullist sentiment seemed to have reached its peak at the time of the Darlan deal; and with Darlan's assassination followed by more complex developments in French politics, it even subsided somewhat. Giraud's regime never commanded the same interest as Pétain's; the abrogation of the Crémieux Law caused only fitful concern,[90] unlike Vichy's more prolonged anti-Semitic affronts; and when a dramatic incident did occur, like the *Richelieu* affair, when French sailors in New York were at first restrained by their officers from enlisting under de Gaulle rather than Giraud, it reproduced none of the excitement of the St. Pierre-and-Miquelon affair.[91] So there was some justification for the exultance of H. Freeman Matthews, back in Washington at the State Department's European desk, when he remarked in August that, ". . . in spite of all the criticism on the part of the columnists and editorial writers of a certain section of the press during the past eight months, not one single Senator or Congressman has ever raised any questions or written any letter critical of that policy—a rather significant fact I think in view of how close they must keep their ears attuned to sentiment back home."[92] This was not, however, only because some former critics had been convinced, or cowed, by that vigorous summer propaganda campaign in which Matthews had played such an enthusiastic part.[93] For as Halifax observed in a different context, there was no French vote, no French lobby in the United States.[94] Furthermore a multitude of rival demands now pressed for the attention of both French émigrés and American sympathizers. The particular question of Franco-American relations became, more than ever, a specialist taste, as Frenchmen, with the liberation of their homeland in sight, turned to debate its future course, and Americans, with the end of the war at least partially in view, debated their own role in the postwar world.

The French community in the United States had been greatly demoralized by the Darlan deal. Raoul de Roussy de Sales sadly observed that ". . . the first result of American presence on French territory has been the confirmation of the authority of a traitor and of a Fascist regime."[95] Even those not themselves beholden to de Gaulle, like the poet and diplomat Alexis Leger, were alarmed. Leger had tenaciously refused to take part publicly in French wartime politics, although he did give his blessing to the Resistance[96] and he did offer his counsel, based on years of experience at the Quai d'Orsay, to American diplomats.[97] But he always refused any offer, from Churchill, de Gaulle, or anyone else, to join any new French authority because, given the circumstances of the 1940 defeat, he viewed such politics as illegitimate, a usurpation of the powers and functions of the Third Republic, which could only be properly restored upon liberation.[98] While applauding the military presence of the Gaullists, he would not advance what he saw as their latent political goals. He was thus led, on non-Gaullist grounds, to deplore the Darlan deal, which threatened, from a different direction, to impose a novel political system upon the French, equally disintegrative of republican traditions; and he expressed his fears to numerous officials. It was necessary, he said, for France to fight again, to "rise from the valley of humiliation," and no collaborationist should be recognized by outsiders as holding any authority over the French people.[99] For the same reason, when the Peyrouton appointment was first suggested in December 1942, Leger compiled for the State Department a list of alternative French officials who could be better trusted for their patriotic integrity and their disinterest.[100]

Leger's interventions, always consistent with that stand, were for the most part discreet and unofficial.[101] The more typical activity of his fellow émigrés was to prolong, even to advertise, the dissension within their ranks, though this was usually supplemented with pleas for unity. Before 1943, as already noted,[102] these differences could be camouflaged under a uniform anti-Vichy gloss: the few apologists for Vichy tended to remain within the French diplomatic corps. But with Darlan's removal and Giraud's appearance new and more subtle distinctions emerged. Those who, like Etienne Boegner,[103] had chafed under de Gaulle's authority could now enroll under a rival, equally anti-German banner; and the ensuing tensions could be observed at every level. An early attempt to analyze the effects on the French community of the North African landings came on 29 November in the form of "An Open Letter to Frenchmen Everywhere" by Antoine de Saint-Exupéry.[104] The author, who had thirsted for military action since the 1940 defeat,[105] now leapt at the chance to rejoin his old comrades in Tunis and urged all Frenchmen to set aside their political ambitions, which he termed merely "comic," for the service of their country's military recovery: "The only places open are soldiers' places." He likewise dismissed the previous two and a half years of vigorous émigré culture: "Our talk about sociology, politics and art will carry no weight" with Vichy's subjects, who had had to endure by far the greater measure of suffering. "They will not read our books, they will not listen to our speeches. Perhaps our ideas may make them sick." Vichy itself, now defunct, he charitably viewed as "a trustee in bankruptcy, negotiating with a greedy conqueror." He concluded by inviting all Frenchmen of military age in the United States to enlist in a reanimated French army, and to tell Cordell Hull that they would "accept in advance any organization that may be deemed suitable," asking only that it be "outside politics." For "the provisional organization of France is an affair of state. Let us leave it to Britain and to the United States to do the best they can."

A response to this was made, also in the form of "An Open Letter to Frenchmen," by Jacques Maritain in April.[106] He entered a number of reservations about Saint-Exupéry's eviction of politics from French wartime affairs. Too generous a desire for union might, he feared, "transform itself into an abandonment of the powers of judgment." Events in North Africa had served to show not so much the death of Vichy but the longevity of some of its servants. The "quarrels" that might appear trivial or damaging to an observer in New York actually concerned "that terrible split which will divide Europe, on the day of peace, between the former accomplices of the vanquished totalitarian order and the men of a new democracy." Frenchmen were therefore entitled to interest themselves in the future government of their country, and the necessary military unity required to defeat the Axis must not take the form of "a political submission to an administrative power still encumbered with the ideology, the functionaries, and the economic groups whose victims France has been since June, 1940." All Frenchmen could affirm their confidence in Roosevelt's will to safeguard for the duration of the war the rights of the French people. But "with regard to questions relating to France and the political life of her people," they also had a duty "to express clearly and simply their own convictions."

Elsewhere in the French community the same issues were being raised, with perhaps more passion and less eloquence. They lay, for example, at the heart of the feud between the French-language journals, *Pour la victoire* and *France-Amérique*, each of which was, in a different sense, adjusting to the turn of events in North Africa. *Pour la victoire* had been, prior to the North African landings, staunchly Gaullist, although never endorsing the entire doctrine of the London-based *La Marseillaise*, which it was obliged to carry as a supplement.[107] It was therefore somewhat relieved, with the emergence of Giraud, to shed its inconvenient cargo, and henceforth, while ostensibly advocating the union of all French factions, it was unambiguously Giraudist. This campaign was marked by a number of vigorous contributions from the excitable pen of Henri de Kérillis, an early Gaullist recruit now increasingly alarmed at what he saw as the dictatorial and xenophobic tendencies within de Gaulle's entourage: ". . . in becoming a political movement rather than waging war to the death, 'Gaullism' more or less unconsciously appeals to all the secret forces of French nationalism," imperiling Anglo-Saxon friendship toward France.[108] *Pour la victoire*'s enemies ascribed its shift to a subvention from Giraud's associate, Lemaigre-Dubreuil, a charge that de Kérillis angrily rebutted in an "Open Letter to General de Gaulle" in May: "Our paper is poor, but it is pure."[109] Nevertheless it was true that after the editorial policy had been fixed the paper did receive, via the coordinator for inter-American affairs, some financial aid, requested by the State Department, in the form of the purchase of nine thousand copies a week for Latin American distribution.[110]

On the other side the change was not of policy but of vehicle. *France-Amérique* appeared in May as the leading American organ of militant Gaullism after a complex series of maneuvers following *Pour la victoire*'s absorption in March of *La Voix de France*, whose disgruntled editors, Henri Torrès and Emile Buré, thereupon took over an old French weekly, *Amérique*, now re-christened *France-Amérique*. They were encouraged, morally and financially, by the Gaullist delegation under Adrien Tixier; and accordingly the journal embarked on both a fervent defense of the entire Gaullist enterprise and a counterattack upon Giraudist backsliders, for which it made full use of the fierce polemical talents of Torrès. Of his arch-rival, de Kérillis, he wrote: " 'Lunatic,' 'débauche,' 'parvenu' of treason . . .? Let us not exaggerate: poor fellow!"[111] However, when rumors of the impending publication of the journal were first heard, so outraged was the State Department by this fresh onslaught that it sharply protested to the British (via Harry Hopkins who contrived to keep the president uninvolved). And although the journal continued to appear in New York, Tixier himself did not. It had proved his last provocative act in the United States and, never overwhelmingly popular even among his subordi-nates, he was recalled for consultation in London before taking up a new, and more rewarding, post as commissioner for labor and social welfare in the enlarged FCNL in Algiers.[112]

Tixier's passage illustrates nicely the fate of French émigré politics in the United States. For despite all the American involvement and intrusion, and despite the conditions already set by war and diplomacy, these were and remained essentially intra-French conflicts: between the officers and crew of the *Richelieu*, Maritain and Saint-Exupéry, Torrès and de Kérillis. And revolv-ing as they did around the future course of French politics they were soon to be conducted upon more appropriate and hospitable French soil, within the FCNL and the Consultative Assembly at Algiers and thereafter in a liberated France. On this, at least, *Pour la victoire* and *France-Amérique* could make common cause, welcoming both the union of the generals, however precar-ious, and the Allied recognition of the FCNL, however grudging, as markers toward the moment of French self-determination.[113] Any further French influ-ence on American policy would come from a secure and recognized French platform, resting upon the force of arms as well as the force of arguments.

Thus, as a sign of the times, a novel departure occurred in émigré circles in the United States. At the end of March a group of French intellectuals—scholars, scientists, artists, and lawyers, of republican and democratic convic-tions, but without any prior political attachments—gathered under the initia-tive of Boris Mirkine-Guetzévitch, vice-president of the law faculty at the Ecole Libre des Hautes Etudes, to form the Comité Républicain Français, whose declared objective was to promote "a sincere and unequivocal return to the Republican tradition." They plainly saw that tradition as threatened more by Giraud's questionable rule in North Africa than by any supposed Gaullist ambitions.[114] But they set their faces against all factional disputes, and the roster of the committee said almost as much by its omissions as by its inclusions. This was to prove the first occasion that the French journalist André Géraud ("Pertinax") felt able to belong to a French organization in the United States; a former writer for *Pour la victoire*, Philippe Barrès, and an editor of *France-Amérique*, Emile Buré, were united in its ranks; and yet, to steer the discussion away from the personal and the partisan, no politician belonged. No place was found for the ex-deputy Torrès, the ex-deputy de Kérillis, or the ex-minister Pierre Cot. One logical candidate for membership, Jacques Maritain, did not in fact join, following his lifelong practice of taking sides only on the purest questions of principle.[115] But, as was evident from his riposte to Saint-Exupéry, he wished the committee well, and he did contribute a chapter from a forthcoming book, *Principes d'une politique humaniste*, to the first issue of the new journal, *La République française*—named after Léon Gambetta's journal founded in 1871 and, like its predecessor, intended as an open forum for the discussion, and defense, of democratic and republican ideals.[116] And it was likewise a member of this committee, Professor Francis Perrin, who became the representative of Frenchmen in the United States to the French Consultative Assembly, leaving for Algiers early in 1944.[117]

What seemed to so many Frenchmen a new beginning was to most Americans a welcome relief, the end of an uncomfortable episode. The FCNL was installed in Algiers; French troops had contributed to the Tunisian campaign and were about to join in the Italian one. Now most Americans thankfully turned their attention to other matters, the Pacific theater of war or the design of the postwar world, sharing perhaps the lofty view of the *Los Angeles Times* that "the ease with which the two principal French figures appear to have sunk their differences indicates that they could not have been very apart at any time."[118] No public opinion polls were taken on the subject of American policy toward France, possibly because it was no longer regarded as a contentious issue. The only poll taken on French affairs in February revealed simply that among those with some awareness of the French situation sentiment was almost equally divided between supporters of de Gaulle (35 percent) and of Giraud (36 percent).[119]

The issues were now less clear-cut than in the days of the Vichy regime: both Giraud and de Gaulle were actively opposing Germany. And so the familiar deference to government over wartime foreign policy surfaced anew. An opinion poll in July showed that while only 49 percent of the sample approved of Roosevelt's handling of domestic affairs, 73 percent approved of his foreign policy.[120] An anti-Roosevelt paper like the *Miami Herald* and a pro-Roosevelt paper like the *Louisville Courier-Journal* equally applauded the achievement of French unity in June.[121] This acceptance was also due in part to the prevailing view, strengthened by memories of Pearl Harbor and a lurking isolationism, that Japan was America's main foe, and that therefore the European war should be terminated by the most speedy and efficient means. A poll in February revealed that 53 percent of the sample saw Japan as the chief enemy, while only 34 percent saw Germany as such; even in the South, traditionally the most European-oriented section, the poll was Japan 47 percent, Germany 39 percent.[122]

The critics of American policy were not silent, however. Walter Lippmann, unrepentant after his dispute with Hull over the Darlan deal, reiterated in a column published on 19 January his view that the North African muddle was "due to bad judgment based on incorrect information": "Mr. Robert Murphy . . . has been attacked as being Fascist-minded. Having known Mr. Murphy, I do not believe that. But . . . it has seemed to me astonishing that so much reliance has been placed on his judgment. For he is a most agreeable and ingratiating man whose warm heart causes him to form passionate personal and partisan attachments rather than cool and detached judgments."[123] Another column, on 26 June, reminded readers that "when we talk about the difficulty of dealing with [de Gaulle] in Algiers . . . we have done things to him so tactless that they would have tried the patience of a saint" (for example the retention in high office of Peyrouton who had signed de Gaulle's death warrant at Vichy); and Lippmann warned that in view of the evident support for de Gaulle among the French people inside and outside metropolitan France, such cavalier treatment of him by the United States constituted a "disregard of the deepest and most elementary right of self-determination."[124] This was the column that commended itself to the France Forever convention in New York, where a motion was passed praising Lippmann and proposing to send him a telegram of congratulations.[125]

Samuel Grafton took an even more unfavorable view of the administration's motives. Conscious of the campaign afoot to discredit de Gaulle, he wondered, rather unfairly, whether those in the State Department who saw de Gaulle as a fascist were the same as those who had seen Darlan as democratic: "This seems to me a clear case for emergency eye examination. . . . Once they argued against de Gaulle on the grounds that the French population does not want him. Now they find an argument against de Gaulle on the grounds that the French population does want him. They found hope for France in Pétain. They found hope for France in Darlan. Now when France stirs at last and, through de Gaulle, produces a movement of her own, they shake their heads in alarm at this sign of life. . . . Our State Department . . . finds these popular manifestations to be sinister."[126] And Edgar Ansel Mowrer, in a column that appeared regularly from April onward, frequently commented on American policy toward France and urged the recognition of the FCNL. Perhaps wiser after his prematurely ended spell of government service, he directed his charges at the president himself. In an open letter to Roosevelt on 26 June, he observed: ". . . it is no secret that our French policy is being formulated and directed personally by you. It is not the State Department's policy, or Bob Murphy's policy—it is Franklin D. Roosevelt's policy. The State Department's responsibility, if any, is limited to supplying you with false information."[127] Not that the wholesale onslaught on the State Department was quite yet a thing of the past: a "Bill of Indictment" drawn up by the *St. Louis Post-Dispatch* in September used the entire range of recent diplomacy, from Vichy to Japan, to make the familiar point that the department was "tackling a job of twentieth-century diplomacy with nineteenth-century equipment and outlook."[128]

Yet the particular issue of France was now more than ever submerged in a variety of other current debates. Even Lippmann, one of de Gaulle's most prominent defenders, was actually at this time concerned to persuade the American public, and the administration, of the wisdom contained in his latest book on foreign policy. There the argument was not about the course of European politics or the fashionable globalism of Wallace or Willkie; it concerned the seemingly more hardheaded proposition that the United States should recognize the virtues of the unspoken alliance that had long existed with Great Britain, and build thereon a firm "nuclear alliance" among the Great Powers.[129] Elsewhere, among those who had always been chiefly interested in European affairs, France was in 1943 only one country—although it had been the first and a paradigm for the others—to raise acute issues of political warfare. The fall of Mussolini and his replacement by Marshal Badoglio and the king, Victor Emmanuel III, made Italy the next. Further afield, in Austria, Hungary, Greece, as the postwar succession was contested among rival movements and parties, the American administration soon appeared open to charges of favoring the most reactionary and least democratic national elements, charges that the State Department official most involved with the governments-in-exile, Adolf Berle, attempted to refute in toto in a letter to the American Council on Public Affairs in August.[130] That, however, only raised the further issue of the entire management of foreign policy. As Lippmann observed in September, the administration's vulnerability to such criticism was owed to "half a dozen lines of action improvised here, there, and everywhere."[131] So there now took place a most far-reaching public discussion on the whole conduct of American foreign relations—the personnel, the machinery, the relations between the State Department and Congress or other executive agencies, the public information policy—in the course of which the calls for radical reform came no longer just from concerned special-interest groups, but also from sympathetic, if frank, observers.[132] In fact the reorganization of the department rapidly became the special province of Welles's successor as under secretary of state, Edward Stettinius, Jr.[133]

For all these reasons, the specific, and more limited, complaints about

American policy toward France had no more effect on the administration than they ever had. Perhaps they had even less, since the outcry over St. Pierre and Miquelon or the Darlan deal had at least forced in one case a strategic withdrawal, in the other a tactical defense. But usually the only response evoked was a hardening of lines, a more vigorous defense by policymakers of a position already adopted, and even, as we have seen, a counterattack. For these reasons any change in American policy in 1944 would be at once harder to bring about, because the administration's line was so firm, and yet easier to implement, because it could be made without heavy public objection. Thus when American recognition of the FCNL did come about, it was not by the steady accumulation of Gaullist sentiment in the country at large, but, as will be examined in the next chapter, only by a series of extremely delicate maneuvers within the very heart of the Roosevelt administration.

CHAPTER 10
LIBERATION AND RECOGNITION

A t the beginning of 1944, and all through the preparations for the Allied landings in France, the American policy toward the French Committee of National Liberation appeared settled. It was to consist of a military association, uncomplicated by any present or future political commitments.

Such at least was the optimistic view conveyed in a letter, drafted in the State Department, that Roosevelt was to send to the new American representative to the FCNL, Edwin C. Wilson. This was the direct successor to the letter from Roosevelt to Admiral Leahy in December 1940, outlining, and inaugurating, America's Vichy policy, also drafted in the State Department, but equally reflective of Roosevelt's particular approach.[1] The difference between the two letters was the difference between American neutrality and American belligerency, but also between Roosevelt's perceptions of Pétain and of de Gaulle. The twin precepts governing American relations with France were now, in 1944, "that military considerations in the prosecution of the war against Germany are and must remain paramount," and "that sovereignty resides in the people and that as long as over 90 percent of the French people are not free to exercise their political rights, no individual or group will be recognized by the United States as the Government of France or of the French Empire." Furthermore, Roosevelt's administration would not "consciously take any step which may have the ultimate effect of impairing the opportunity of the French people of freely exercising their political rights after their country is liberated from its oppressors."[2] Less formally, Roosevelt explained at a press conference why he had not recognized the FCNL: "What is self-determination? And how do we know what the people of France feel? I don't know. Nobody in this room knows, because I don't think there's anybody in this room that has been in France lately, and even if they had been in France would they have got around to more than just one place?"[3]

The suggested picture of a mute, expectant French populace may have been a convenient one for American planners, and was certainly an attractive one to display before an American public shortly to be cast in the role of liberators. But long before events at the liberation of France rudely corrected that picture, those Americans who were close to the unfolding developments had become fully alive to some awkward discrepancies in it. For while the FCNL possessed none of the attributes of a sovereign state, it was steadily acquiring those of the provisional government which, three weeks prior to D Day, the Consultative Assembly at Algiers declared it to be.[4] All the jockeying for position at the higher levels of the FCNL, which had irritated American officials and left General Giraud without political influence by the end of 1943, could not conceal that the Consultative Assembly, and to a certain extent the FCNL, were increasingly representative of the many political groupings and administrative bodies that had, in name if not always in function, survived the years of defeat. Not only the National Council of the Resistance (which included Communists) but also the Senate, the Chamber of Deputies, and the *Conseils Généraux*, all had representatives in Algiers.[5] And in Brazzaville in January and February 1944, lengthy discussions were held on the future of the French empire, at a conference that stands, in the words of a recent historian, as "one of the seminal events in the resurgence of French colonial trusteeship."[6] Naturally its outcome, which included a reaffirmation of France's overseas mission, may not have entirely suited all American observers, any more than had de Gaulle's recent reassertion of French sovereignty in Lebanon. But, taken together with the proceedings at Algiers, it provided irrefutable evidence of the vitality and resilience of a French political culture that was far from being entirely dependent on foreign arms for its survival. Moreover, it was clear that the renewal of these debates, in both metropolitan France and the Gaullist colonies, had been under way at least since 1941.[7]

Similarly, the various issues that continued to divide de Gaulle from Roosevelt rarely interrupted the real and effective cooperation between their officials handling more tangible matters. Military supplies and Lend-Lease aid continued to pour into North Africa as the material result of Monnet's mission there, and any difficulties that arose were bureaucratic and administrative rather than personal and political.[8] Rather more significantly, in terms of the war effort, Eisenhower was now finding the FCNL most helpful in military planning. Many of the earlier differences had been resolved by the end of 1943, due largely, he wrote to de Gaulle, "to your very understanding attitude toward these matters."[9] Eisenhower now looked forward to close military collaboration not only with the French army of liberation, but also with the domestic resistance, which he rated very highly.[10] All he lacked, and now worked anxiously to secure, was a clear directive from Roosevelt authorizing him to negotiate with the FCNL on the separate but no less important issue of civil affairs in metropolitan France after the landings.[11] But that of course raised the question of the FCNL's political status.

Not until late October 1944 did the American administration grant, or rather concede, formal recognition of the FCNL as the provisional government of France. Until then there continued to be, as Monnet recalled, a disparity between "de facto recognition, at all levels of the administration, and the refusal to establish a legal relationship at the top. . . . [T]he supreme rites had not been observed, and these were the only ones that counted in the liturgy of international affairs."[12] As might be expected, the process whereby Roosevelt was eventually won round was arduous and uneven, punctuated by setbacks and detours: a provocative speech or action by de Gaulle here, a dispute within British circles there, rival and sometimes conflicting pressures within the American administration itself, all occurring at the most perilous military turning-point of the war. Nevertheless, it is possible to discern three distinct steps along the road to recognition, the first of which was the draft directive of 15 March authorizing Eisenhower to consult on his arrival in France with the FCNL at his own discretion, and to make whatever arrangements for civil administration he deemed best, provided that they did not "constitute a recognition of said committee . . . as the government of France even on a provisional basis."[13]

That was, and remained, a draft directive. It did not determine policy, it lay unsigned in London on the day of the invasion of France, and, even if effected, would not really have begun to solve Eisenhower's difficulties. As he himself remarked, it merely proposed "that the whole matter be thrown back on my lap," civil affairs on top of military decisions.[14] For his part, Eisenhower sought neither exclusive reliance upon the FCNL, as he understood the British to be advocating,[15] nor, as the directive offered, a vague mandate that would confer upon him personal responsibility for any unpopular or unfortunate political choice he might, in extremity, be forced to make. All in fact that the directive accomplished was a demonstrable shift in Roosevelt's thinking.

That was never easy to achieve, least of all now, when Roosevelt, absorbed in grander issues, listened attentively only to his most intimate advisers. These did not include British Foreign Office officials who were appalled to learn, early in February, that Admiral Leahy was informing the president that the most reliable person to rally the French population after the Allied landings was Marshal Pétain.[16] The British could not, by themselves, neutralize such advice, although the ambassador, Halifax, was prepared to make an effort. But he was overruled by Churchill, who was content for the moment to employ the ultimate prospect of recognition as a "lever" by which to ensure continued good behavior from the Gaullists. Churchill was thus reluctant to "over-persuade" the president.[17] For he knew, what was increasingly evident, that the more pressure was put on Roosevelt from outside, the more he tended to retreat into a reclusive dependence on his own judgment. "I have been handed pages and pages with detailed instructions and appendices," he had written to Churchill; "I regard them as prophecies by prophets who cannot be infallible."[18] Moreover, to set Roosevelt on an even harder anti-Gaullist course only required a comparatively minor incident, such as occurred on 12 February during the formal transfer to the French navy of a new, American-built destroyer, the *Sénégalais*. Roosevelt chose to present the vessel to Admiral

Fenard, of the French naval mission, in the course of a speech that made no allusion to the FCNL, to which that officer, and that mission, were responsible. Just as Roosevelt was leaving the ceremony, he was accosted by Henri Hoppenot who declared that he, the FCNL's representative in the United States, was the legal recipient of the destroyer. That, according to one observer, Brigadier General Julius Holmes of Eisenhower's staff, "infuriated the President past imagination."[19]

Roosevelt's eventual agreement to the draft directive of 15 March thus represented a marked submission, however vaguely worded. This was owed largely to the prompting of the secretary and the assistant secretary of war, Henry Stimson and John J. McCloy, who were in turn responding to Eisenhower's natural reluctance to gamble on de Gaulle's prolonged goodwill. With the utmost caution they had both begun to present arguments to Roosevelt for a change of policy toward the FCNL, but always on the most rigorously practical of grounds. "There is," Roosevelt was told, "no other representative at hand to help us with the French people when we land, or to help us after the landing in organizing the occupied countries so as to protect our line of communication."[20] In mid-January Cordell Hull lent the advocates his modest support, not, it may be supposed, out of any real affection for de Gaulle, but because he was anxious to avoid a reenactment of the Darlan deal for which his department might once again be abused.[21] No more than Eisenhower did he wish to be a target for partisan charges, and so his draft proposal stressed that the Allies would "have no dealings or relations with the Vichy regime except for the purpose of abolishing it."[22]

Hull and Stimson were agreed upon a narrow definition of recognition, as distinct from a broader proposal offered by McCloy, who was an ardent supporter of de Gaulle, that the FCNL be recognized as the de facto government of France once a portion of the country had been liberated. The two secretaries would have been content to limit recognition to full cooperation within spheres of military operation and those immediately adjacent. But Roosevelt still needed to be convinced. One practical consideration that Stimson took to him was that "in the meantime the British and Churchill are having conferences with de Gaulle abroad and they may work out a formula which we haven't yet done. McCloy is worried about it and thinks we are losing a good deal of position."[23] Casting around for other arguments to present to Roosevelt, Stimson reached into his extensive historical memory and eventually emerged, on 29 February, with a persuasive, if curious, analogy:

> . . . it seemed to me to present a situation much like what would be the case, in the event in the early frontier days one of the western states had gotten into the hands of disorderly elements of such strength that it had been necessary to call in the U.S. Army to restore order. In such a case it might well be the useful source of procedure to have the troops, after

their pacification had been accomplished, turn to some sort of vigilance committee and ask them as men who are acquainted with the local situation and the character of the local inhabitants to help the commander select proper interim sheriffs, county commissioners, etc. to serve until there could be an election. The function of such vigilance committee would be very much like that which we are contemplating in regard to the French Comité, and dealing with such a vigilance committee would of course not be recognizing them as the government of the state.[24]

By such arguments was Roosevelt won round, and the directive—a revision by Stimson of an earlier draft by Roosevelt—was duly signed in Washington.[25]

It remained in such a form—an American draft not an Allied directive—as the result, according to Roosevelt, of an impasse between Churchill and the Foreign Office.[26] But the situation was rather more complex than that. Certainly the draft had served to expose still further the long-standing differences within British circles, with Churchill happy to go along with Roosevelt's settled view, Eden fearful of the confusion that would be sown among the French once Eisenhower started dealing with non-Gaullist officials, and Duff Cooper, the British representative in Algiers, calling the draft "a deliberate insult." Certainly also these differences were weighty enough to be brought before the British cabinet on 19 April.[27] But by that time equivalent differences had been publicly, if inadvertently, aired on the American side. For on 9 April Cordell Hull delivered a major policy address, going much further than would the president himself. "We are disposed," Hull announced, "to see the French Committee of National Liberation exercise leadership to establish law and order under the supervision of the Allied Commander in Chief."[28] Hull was by now not only protective of his department's reputation, but alive also to the dangers posed by a reawakened, hostile France, and by a public rift between Britain and America should Roosevelt refuse recognition. In January Edwin Wilson had warned him that ". . . every effort on our part to thwart [de Gaulle], to diminish his prestige or seem to weaken the position of France, will have only the opposite effect and serve to strengthen his position in the eyes of the French people as the defender of French rights and sovereignty against foreign interference."[29] In June Selden Chapin, Wilson's successor, would also argue for recognition, on the grounds that "the analyses that would have been valid a year ago are valid no longer. De Gaulle's position must not be considered on the basis of outdated diagnoses but by a fresh appraisal of his position at this moment when the liberation of France is in progress."[30]

Hull's speech, not intra-British disputes, thus kept Allied policy in limbo. The British cabinet in fact agreed on welcoming Hull's initiative, and wanted simply "to have the directive brought up into line with it." The only qualification came from Churchill who reserved his "right to agree with the President unless a better arrangement can be made."[31] That, however, was a potential—

not a real—cause for delay. What further confused matters was the remarkable American insistence that Hull's speech and the draft directive "meant the same thing." That view, conveyed by McCloy, de Gaulle's champion, prompted Churchill to remark that "it would be difficult to prove this if any regard were paid to the meaning of words."[32] Amidst all this array of signals, from Roosevelt, Hull, and McCloy, from Churchill, Eden, and Cooper, the best course was no doubt the most prudent: Eden's proposal on 25 April to hold the directive in suspense and to promote more straightforward, and thus more fruitful, negotiations at the military level, between Eisenhower and General Pierre Koenig, de Gaulle's military delegate in London.[33]

Not only the planning but also the execution of the Normandy landings thus took place in a diplomatic vacuum. Roosevelt rejected all suggestions, from whatever quarter and however tactfully phrased, that he should move closer to the FCNL. To Elmer Davis, who recommended in March the start of operational planning with leaders of the French resistance, Roosevelt wrote, "the coming invasion is to be carried out and carried through as a military matter. We shall then find what we shall find."[34] At a cabinet meeting in May he declared that if anyone could give him a certificate proving that de Gaulle was a representative of the French people he would deal with him, but that otherwise he had no intention of changing his position.[35] At the end of May he cabled Churchill repeating "the simple fact that I cannot send anyone to represent me at the de Gaulle conversations with you."[36] Again, at the beginning of June, when Davis sought permission to refer in OWI propaganda broadcasts to the FCNL as a "provisional government" (as the FCNL itself was doing), Roosevelt sternly refused, calling that issue "the meat in the coconut": "No person outside France or in France knows whether the people of France consider it [the FCNL] the provisional government of France."[37] And finally, almost on the eve of the invasion, when, for a fleeting moment it had seemed, to Churchill among others, that Roosevelt was about to invite de Gaulle over to America for talks, he hastily corrected such optimism: if de Gaulle asked to come over, they would certainly meet. But, Roosevelt added, "the whole point of it is that I decline absolutely as head of the State to invite him to come over here."[38]

All this time Eisenhower was laboring under a distinct handicap. Any military operation, but particularly one conducted on foreign soil, aiming at the liberation of occupied territory, demands clear, but also flexible planning. Unable to predict an exact timetable of events after an invasion, military commanders rely perforce on the sort of guidance that can determine a long-range strategy while also permitting short-term changes of course, adjustable to momentary and hazardous shifts in the campaign. Nor are these purely military considerations. Questions of economic supply, of civic administration, of billetting, currency, and labor will, in such a fluid situation, move constantly back and forth across those boundaries between civilian and political and military affairs which Roosevelt, more than anyone else, was striving to lay down. Knowing this, Eisenhower was becoming increasingly restless under Roosevelt's instructions, at once vague where Eisenhower needed precision, and rigorous where he needed flexibility.

Again and again, in the weeks leading up to D day, Eisenhower asked for a formal, but plainly worded, joint directive. He was requesting that he be allowed to commence open and full negotiations with the FCNL, unhampered by code restrictions or security restraints, in order to discuss the initial approach to be made to the French people and the organized resistance groups. He was asking, that is, to have American policy brought into line with the very latest intelligence arriving out of France, from undercover agents and escaped prisoners of war, that there were "in France today only two major groups, of which one is the Vichy gang, and the other characterized by unreasoning admiration for De Gaulle."[39] But he made no headway, even with Churchill eventually supporting the idea of a meeting between Roosevelt and de Gaulle,[40] and that exposed a further source of embarrassment. For Eisenhower was not an American theater commander. He was the Supreme Allied Commander, with responsibilities toward two governments, as his chief of staff in London, General Walter Bedell Smith, had to remind General Marshall: "The Prime Minister always says . . . that he stands with the President on all questions dealing with the French. This statement, of course, can be taken for what it is worth but it must always be remembered that the one ministry which the Prime Minister does not control is the Foreign Office."[41] Eisenhower did nonetheless retain a soldierly optimism. "I believe," he noted in his diary on 22 May, ". . . that once the operation is started I can secure from the French the cooperation that I need."[42] After D day, as after the North African landings, he would at last be left to his own devices.

Some damage had, however, already been done. These two separate strands, in effect two distinct policies—military collusion and diplomatic boycott—were bound at some point to intersect; and so they did, on D day, 6 June, with altogether foreseeable results, as the greatest amphibious landings since ancient times seemed for a while endangered, not by bad weather or enemy action, but by unresolved political disagreements. Viewed in straightforward military terms, the landings did proceed very much according to plan. Three airborne divisions, comprising American, British, and Canadian troops, disembarked on various Normandy beaches in overwhelming numbers, possessing, moreover, the extraordinary advantage of surprise. The swift action of the first days was then succeeded by the arduously slow, but still appreciable, progress inland, the struggle for Caen and for Cherbourg, the advance on Rouen, the long sweep across Brittany, and thence on to the liberation of Paris, by which time General Patton's Third Army was using to the full the French division under General Leclerc attached to it, and liberating French soil already cultivated, and French communities already revived, by the "secret army" of the resistance.[43] De Gaulle meanwhile had struck. As the invasion commenced, he declined to broadcast his support of it to the French people; he refused to permit French liaison officers to accompany the troops; and he would not endorse the occupation currency, the supplemental francs with which the troops were to be supplied.[44]

The refusal to cooperate with Roosevelt and Churchill was perhaps de Gaulle's greatest wartime gamble. For he risked alienating even those whom he most needed to sway Allied councils. In Stimson's opinion, de Gaulle's action over the currency was "a dangerous blow at our advancing troops just as much as if he had deprived them of their arms or their ammunition,"[45] and Eden now agreed with Churchill that there was no point in having any further discussion, on civil or military affairs, with de Gaulle, who might just as well return to Algiers.[46] Yet these provocations, for all the outrage they occasioned, did not quite amount to open revolt, as de Gaulle knew perfectly well. They belonged rather to that recurrent pattern—of irritation and then reconciliation—which had characterized his relations with the Allies from the time of the Syrian campaign, the Brazzaville interview, and the St. Pierre-and-Miquelon affair. This situation too would eventually be eased, the issues having been carefully selected for their public and diplomatic repercussions and not for any military damage they might inflict. De Gaulle, it soon turned out, would broadcast a message to the French people, albeit not, as originally proposed, in too obvious a subordinate role in the enterprise.[47] French liaison officers would accompany the troops, though they would be civilian not military officials.[48] Finally, de Gaulle would not expressly repudiate the occupation currency (only complain, at a press conference, about Allied arrangements).[49]

But there was one critical difference between these and earlier disputes. De Gaulle was now, as of 26 May, speaking and acting on behalf of a provisional government, whether or not recognized as such by the Allies. And there are certain basic functions that a government must perform, if its claims to sovereignty are to carry any conviction. One is to control the nation's currency. Another is to control its foreign relations—to negotiate, for example, an entente with the Soviet Union. (Thus, in a speech on 7 May, de Gaulle predicted a reorientation of French foreign policy toward a traditional ally, "dear and powerful Russia,"[50] and he did indeed effect such a change the following autumn.) Sovereignty was, in essence, what the invasion crisis was all about.

Moreover, de Gaulle did get out of the crisis some part of what he wanted: the start of negotiations on various practical matters—local jurisdiction, currency, property, and publicity—which, while leaving open the troubled question of recognition, could at least serve as a basis for future agreements.[51] It was as true in London as it had been in Algiers that the most fruitful negotiations were those conducted at a relatively junior level; and by 4 July American

Treasury officials and French army officers had at least resolved the currency issue.[52] Nor was that all. De Gaulle also made that long-deferred visit to the United States. "I will do my best," Roosevelt told Churchill, "to attract his interest to the Allied war effort."[53] In fact there was not that much for the two men to discuss once the specific question of recognition had been ruled out, and Roosevelt went to great pains to exclude it from the agenda at his press conference on 7 July: they would be talking about "anything that's of interest," but not, emphatically, about recognition.[54] De Gaulle's eventual visit to the United States, from 6 to 11 July, needed, for that very reason, to be almost as rigorously planned as the Normandy landings.[55] It became more ceremonial and festive than diplomatic or contractual. He was fêted at dinner parties;[56] he was garlanded by his admirers in the American press;[57] he met his supporters in New York; he visited General Pershing in hospital;[58] and he secured an audience with President Roosevelt.

But the conversation, by common consent, turned away from pressing political differences toward grander, and more distant, geopolitical explorations. There, in their very different ways, both men felt more at home. De Gaulle instructed Roosevelt on the crucial postwar role of a renewed French state; Roosevelt educated de Gaulle on the need to extend American power across the world.[59] And later de Gaulle, the old mischief-maker, did not let slip the opportunity to pass on to Duff Cooper the news that their discussions had also concerned that well-known anomaly, British imperialism, the military ally but ideological foe of American idealism, the current partner but historical rival of French nationalism. According to de Gaulle, Roosevelt had held himself responsible for the future security of the whole American continent and had spoken of the "authority" that the United States would have to exercise in such places as Dakar, the Dutch East Indies, Singapore, and India. Churchill was furious when he heard of this, and, knowing that Roosevelt had never dared to speak so frankly to him, wanted to let the president know that this sort of indiscretion was how de Gaulle treated friendliness: "I have now had four years' experience of him and it is always the same."[60] Even without such vexations it is unlikely that either man adjusted his view of the other on the basis of a few such conversations. To de Gaulle it seemed that Roosevelt's "will to power cloaked itself in idealism."[61] To Roosevelt de Gaulle seemed "very touchy about the honor of France . . . but essentially selfish."[62]

So it cannot properly be said that either of these developments—the military campaign in France, which had initially created friction, or the visit to Washington, which overlooked it—hastened Roosevelt much further along the path toward recognition. Yet the fact is that on 11 July, the day de Gaulle left for Canada, Roosevelt did take the second major step in that direction. He announced at his press conference that he, the president, would accept the FCNL as "the de facto authority for the civil administration of France," although he stressed that that was not to be construed as recognition. Such powers as the

FCNL possessed would be temporary, pending the opportunity shortly to be given to all the French people to choose their own form of government; and Eisenhower would meanwhile retain considerable powers—to exercise, if need be, a military veto over civilian appointments and to determine what were in fact the areas to be thus placed under civilian control. For, Roosevelt emphasized, at the time he was speaking only about o.1 percent of French metropolitan territory had been liberated by the Allies.[63] (He had made the same points in a telegram to Churchill the previous day.)[64]

No doubt, as Walter Lippmann observed, it was necessary to conclude de Gaulle's visit on a note of progress;[65] brushing aside the more detailed and speculative questions that his statement had provoked, Roosevelt went straight into a coincidental announcement of his candidacy for an unprecedented fourth term as president.[66] But the new policy was not simply an electoral ploy. There was no critical Gaullist or even French vote in the United States, although one member of the cabinet, Harold Ickes, did believe that the French issue, if it continued to be conspicuously mishandled, could lose Roosevelt the 1944 election.[67] The change was due, rather, to private, semiofficial, and painstakingly discreet overtures from sources close to Roosevelt himself.

In the first weeks after D day it had begun to seem as if the whole of Washington officialdom had stalled on the question of recognition. Eisenhower, however, was granting a measure of de facto recognition to the French forces under his command, elevating on 23 June their senior officer, General Koenig, to a status equal to other Allied commanders, with the identical right to refer decisions to his own national authority.[68] Throughout the liberated areas, in Rennes, Bayeux, Vercors, local committees were appearing—whether spontaneously, out of the netherworld of Resistance activity, or else ably coordinated by de Gaulle's delegates in the wake of the army's advance—all acknowledging as a matter of course de Gaulle's authority.[69] And an Anglo-French draft agreement, based on those earlier negotiations, lay waiting in London.[70] What that agreement lacked was Roosevelt's approval; but this, as the summer wore on, seemed almost impossible to obtain.

For Roosevelt was now, in turning down appeals for recognition, emphasizing a novel and, to him, more compelling argument. This went beyond the familiar, neo-Wilsonian reasons for postponing the establishment of a provisional government in France, and pointed instead to the presumed fact, which Roosevelt learned from Leahy, that the precipitate recognition of de Gaulle's forces would only provoke a civil war and revolution in France.[71] Leahy in turn owed that line of reasoning to Ralph Heinzen, a journalist whom he had known well in Vichy and who, although interned by the Germans after 1942, had never been known for any pronounced hostility toward the figure of Marshal Pétain.[72] All that was necessary was for the Allies to bide their time and de Gaulle would "crumple"; "the British supporters of de Gaulle will be confounded by the progress of events." Moreover, there were "other parties" far more deserving of American backing; they were waiting in the wings and would emerge as the liberation advanced. Roosevelt owed that piece of intelligence to Colonel Donovan.[73]

Stimson was astounded by all this, as much by the quality of the information as by its provenance, an inner circle of personal advisers that effectively excluded the responsible cabinet and military officials. "Leahy," he commented later, "is not a very acute person and, although he has had the advantage of being stationed in Vichy for several years, I don't think his advice is good."[74] So he battled resourcefully to overturn such advice. "The President's position," he concluded, "is theoretically and logically correct but . . . it is not realistic." Once again Stimson delved into his memory to recall instances that would confound what he saw as the prevailing complacent Wilsonianism. After all, he noted, "very few countries outside the English-speaking countries know what a fair election is." A border dispute between Chile and Peru during his term as governor of the Philippines had been won by Chile simply by virtue of her current occupation of the land and consequent conduct of the plebiscite; a later election in Nicaragua, when Stimson was Hoover's secretary of state, had only been fairly conducted once Stimson had insisted that it be supervised by a neutral constabulary trained by American officers who remained in command until after the election. However, he observed, "America cannot supervise the elections of a great country like France." All she could do was "insist upon a pledge of free elections from De Gaulle and his party, who apparently are the only available representatives of the French people at the present time . . . and we should devote the rest of our time to winning the war instead of quarreling with De Gaulle's efforts to gradually inch himself forward into a position where he and his Committee will be the Provisional Government of France pending such an election." In short, it was better "not to run the risk of bickerings now which will serve not only to divide us from de Gaulle but will divide us from the British who more and more are supporting de Gaulle."[75]

Yet however eloquently he argued his case Stimson lacked strategic allies. His position was, if anything, weaker than it had been in the spring. Cordell Hull, feeling perhaps that he had overreached himself with that speech on 9 April, was at best a lukewarm supporter of de Gaulle's case. Moreover, he had been attending to Adolf Berle's dark predictions of the course a Gaullist administration would take—exploiting all the powers that would accrue to it under an *état de siège*, stringently controlling the flow of information and press freedom in general, and moving toward an uncomfortably anti-Western entente with Russia.[76] Hull wanted above all else to avoid risking his department's reputation in a public controversy from which it would be unlikely to emerge unscathed; and in the troubled state of affairs immediately after the invasion that aim could be more reliably assured by adopting a neutral stance. If Roosevelt insisted on making policy, then let him be identified with it. So while Hull wished Stimson well he was not yet to be counted a powerful ally.[77] The third member of the cabinet formerly most involved in these discussions, the elderly secretary of navy, Stimson's fellow Republican, Frank Knox, had died in April, and was succeeded by James Forrestal, an ardent and excitable foe of de Gaulle, closer in sympathy to Leahy than to Stimson; he relished the opportunity that his new post afforded him to stimulate anti-Gaullist propaganda.[78]

Help, when it arrived, came from a different quarter, the secretary of the treasury, Henry Morgenthau; and the deadlock was resolved the only way it could be, semantically. Anxious to end those damaging arguments over the French currency, Morgenthau, together with McCloy and, more hesitantly, Hull, presented Roosevelt on 7 July with a memorandum proposing what they disingenuously called "a fresh approach to the French situation." This supposedly new approach was to deal with the FCNL by some such designation as the "Civil Authority" or the "Administrative Authority," or the "De Facto Authority" or the "French Authority"—in any case, as an "Authority." The term "government" was nowhere mentioned in the memorandum. As Morgenthau said privately to McCloy, "we're going to forget there ever was such a word." That was in fact, as Morgenthau also noted, the principle inherent in Hull's speech of 9 April. It is noteworthy that both McCloy and Morgenthau spoke of the president as someone who needed to be coddled, nudged along, before he would accept such a proposal. Morgenthau considered it vital to stress to Roosevelt that this approach was a complete novelty, unlike anything he had considered before: "I think this thing should be done—that this is something fresh, that this is something new and in a way that he can say 'Well, now'— maybe that he thought of it or dreamt of this." McCloy similarly thought that the memorandum should contain a few sweeteners to make it palatable to Roosevelt, such as mention of the need for democratic elections in France at the earliest opportunity: "I mean those things are the things that he clutches at, and if you put them in there, he's awfully apt to say 'Yes—that's right,' and take an awful lot of other stuff along with it."[79] Both spoke of "selling" the president a proposal, the basic principle of which he was known already to have rejected. In any event the technique worked. Roosevelt did accept the memorandum, which thus became the basis of his statement at the press conference on 11 July.

There was now a pause, and not until late August were the papers signed and delivered to the Combined Chiefs of Staff.[80] This delay was due not to any further prejudice on Roosevelt's part (as de Gaulle supposed),[81] but rather, his associates believed, to his distractions, not least the impending elections.[82] He appears to have regarded his own statement of 11 July as a satisfactory basis on which to proceed, and was not thereafter unduly perturbed by the periodic disagreements that the Allied military authorities continued to have with French officials over the next few months. On the other hand, he was passionately concerned to prevent any further elevation of the FCNL's status. An incident such as the attempt on Giraud's life in late August—which may or may not have been committed by some overexcited Gaullists—only confirmed Roosevelt's view, which according to Stimson had developed into an obsession, that to recognize the FCNL as a provisional government would cause a revolution in France.[83] In vain did Stimson protest that such a revolution could only occur after the war was over, with American troops no longer in France, and the United States possessing independent lines of communication to a defeated Germany.[84] Thus it was not until almost the last week in October, after two more months had passed, that recognition was finally granted. And by then it appeared that the Americans—unlike the Russians and the British— were in effect capitulating before the press of events rather than engaging in a generous and open act that might, as Stimson and others had long urged, have greatly increased the overall stock of goodwill.

For what had taken place in the intervening months? On 15 August, in one of the most resonant episodes of modern French history, the inhabitants of Paris arose with the decisiveness born of impatience. Spontaneous and un-coordinated though it was, their insurrection nonetheless paralyzed the German administration of the city. Within a matter of days Resistance forces were in control of police stations, town halls, government offices, and newspaper buildings and had forced an armistice out of the German commander, General Dietrich von Choltitz. He had not been one of Hitler's more lenient gauleiters, but he now chose prudently to act contrary to Hitler's express wish to see Paris burned to the ground and ravaged, without water supplies, by cholera and typhus.[85] It was a moment that nicely reversed the events of May and June 1940 when, with the German armies advancing, Paris had been declared an open city by the last government of the Third Republic. But, quite aside from its symbolic and romantic importance, the event required an immediate response from Eisenhower. Instead of bypassing Paris along the route to the German frontier, as his original strategy had proposed, he now had sound military reasons, with the armistice expiring on 24 August, to send Allied, and of course French, troops in to occupy the city.[86] It was a French general, Philippe Leclerc, who received the formal surrender of von Choltitz on 24 August and who did so, moreover, in the name of the provisional government of France; and thereafter, in accordance with the terms of the most recent Allied-French agreement, the capital city, no longer a battle zone, passed under French control.[87]

Henceforth Paris, not Algiers, would be the source of the FCNL's bid for recognition, and it was a Paris that increasingly resembled a government center. Governmental authority seemed, to Eisenhower at least, to follow logically from administrative control; and more than ever the FCNL seemed, in both military and political affairs, not to be an instrument of de Gaulle's personal rule but rather an arena for the resolution of competing tendencies and traditions. So Eisenhower listened with respect to French requests for aid in upholding order in the liberated areas, in absorbing disparate resistance units within the French regular army, and in easing the flow of food and coal to the liberated areas.[88] De Gaulle for his part began to broaden still further the scope of the Consultative Assembly to include a full range of political parties, trade unions, and resistance groupings.[89] By the second half of September Eisenhower and de Gaulle both knew that the time had come to set up a Zone of the Interior, the largest feasible area of French liberated territory over which the French could themselves have control.[90] A harsh winter was looming and Eisenhower understandably preferred that a provisional French government, and not the Allied liberators, be blamed for the ensuing hard times. These, and related considerations, were now being pressed on the State Department by its two successive representatives to the FCNL, Selden Chapin and Jefferson Caffery.[91]

Hull and his colleagues were firmly persuaded. In an uncharacteristic burst of activity he sent a series of memoranda to Roosevelt outlining in the strongest possible terms the case for recognition: de Gaulle had, by all accounts, been acclaimed as the national leader in liberated France; the likelihood of his establishing a personal dictatorship was getting more and more remote, as he was working all the time with popular, democratic, and republican elements; and the withholding of recognition by the United States would at once jeopardize American prestige in France, now very high, and weaken the FCNL's in its task of maintaining the internal stability necessary for the successful prosecution of the war.[92] But, once again, and for the last time, Roosevelt hesitated: "It is best to let things go along as they are for the moment." Recognition would be "premature."[93]

That was on 21 September. A few days later H. Freeman Matthews, head of the State Department's European desk and until recently a stout opponent of Gaullist claims, confessed to Harry Hopkins that there was little further point in pressuring Roosevelt to concede. Such pressure threatened, in Roosevelt's current mood, to be counterproductive: "We would not wish him to feel that we were trying to deluge him with material in support of our suggestion."[94] The citadel would not fall until the ramparts had been taken. So on 25 September Matthews went to see his old chief at the Vichy embassy, Leahy, to ask him to tell the president that "it would be definitely to the advantage of the United States" to confer recognition on the FCNL as the provisional government of France.[95]

At some point in the next few weeks Roosevelt evidently yielded. It was a logical, almost inescapable step, yet one that, characteristically, he was reluctant to take. He waited until all his arguments had been proved wrong, his fears—of civil war, revolution, dictatorship—shown to be groundless, his hopes for rival French leaders to emerge dashed. He waited until every responsible official in his administration was impressing on him the urgent need for full recognition of the FCNL. Even Churchill, up to then his loyal lieutenant, had by 14 October been won round by equivalent persuasion from his foreign office, as well as manifest French realities.[96] All Churchill clung to was a distinction between what he intended, to recognize the FCNL as the provisional government of France, and, as it might otherwise appear, to recognize the French provisional government that had been proclaimed on 30 August.[97] Perhaps toward the end Roosevelt was unimpressed by his own arguments. For at his press conference on 13 October he now called the distinction between "authority" and "government"—a distinction he had been laboring at least since 11 July and which was still firmly upheld in OWI broadcasts[98]—"really legalistic": "I am not splitting hairs—you can call it either way—authority or government."[99] Yet a week later he referred to the diplomatic status of the FCNL as an "iffy" question.[100]

Now, as if by way of light relief, the whole system went into reverse. Once the decision was made in principle it had to be correctly implemented. OWI officials had long agreed that should recognition be granted it must be presented as an acknowledgment of the national effort of the French and not credited to the work of a single man; and they would add that the course had been recommended to the president by the Department of State the moment justification for it was seen.[101] That much was clear. What now ensued was a contest between the Foreign Office and the State Department to ensure that neither recognized the FCNL first, and thus be able to blame the delay on the other. The contest reached its peak outside the office of the French foreign minister, Georges Bidault, where, according to Caffery, Duff Cooper made an attempt to exclude Caffery from the formal joint delivery of the message, alongside the Russian and Canadian ministers.[102] But the attempt was thwarted, and on 23 October the announcement of full recognition of the FCNL was made, the American statement coming, with singular appropriateness, from the State Department.[103] For in seeking to win that contest with the Foreign Office, the State Department moved rather more swiftly than Roosevelt had intended. On 22 October Roosevelt had only told Churchill that he would communicate with him again about recognition "within the next few days," thus startling Churchill, who knew very well that the State Department and the Foreign Office were going ahead with it;[104] and on 24 October, with recognition completed, Roosevelt wired again to express his regret that his absence from Washington had "resulted in more precipitate action by the State Department than was contemplated."[105]

America's wartime French policy thus ended, in formal terms, as it had begun, with a decision by Roosevelt. But more than the passage of time distinguishes the manner in which the two decisions were reached: the first, to enter into full diplomatic relations with the Vichy regime, had seemed a bold and imaginative enterprise, however much it may have been in harmony with the basically conservative policy the United States adopted toward Europe before Pearl Harbor; the second, to enter into full diplomatic relations with the FCNL, made by a president wheedled and cajoled, and in the end circumvented by his advisers, was virtually a capitulation. It cannot even be said that Roosevelt surrendered to the logic of events, which was much more compelling than the logic of his policy. It was to his trusted servants that he ultimately bowed—Stimson and Hull in March, McCloy and Morgenthau in July, Matthews and Leahy in October. He followed to the end the practice of court diplomacy.

For what was the logic of American policy? At the close of this review of the tortuous and prolonged sequence of events by which the United States did come round to according diplomatic recognition to the FCNL, it may well seem as if the issue scarcely merited the attention it received. There was a war to be won, a country to be liberated, and yet both the conduct of the war and the affairs of that country seemed to be forever caught up in a mere diplomatic technicality. However, the question of recognition or nonrecognition is in fact rather more than a technicality, as the international situation of Israel and both Chinas since then, and, previously, of the Soviet Union, amply demonstrates, although there is the ever-present paradox that at least as much attention is paid to governments and states that are not recognized as to those that are. What matters is that such a policy be seen to be grounded upon principles that are explicit, cogent, and well established. Roosevelt's declared objectives—self-determination, collective security, anticolonialism—were in outline perfectly clear, but hardly adequate as principles to justify a policy toward France that, especially in its final stages, obscured even when it did not flatly contradict them. Yet, ironically, Roosevelt had been offered a rationale for his policy, a proper, legal justification for withholding recognition from the FCNL, but he and his advisers, for reasons that are themselves of some interest, chose not to employ it.

This was contained in the Tréveneuc Law of 15 February 1872, first drawn to Roosevelt's notice by the exiled diplomat, Alexis Leger, in a long, closely reasoned letter in January 1944.[106] According to Leger this was a fundamental law of the Third Republic, predating the constitution of 1875 and providing, as that later document did not, for the reestablishment of republican legality after the expulsion of an occupying power. In an argument that harmonized well with American objectives, Leger insisted that this law offered the only correct procedure to restore the Third Republic and evade Gaullist, or any other intrusions, by reconstituting republican authority from below, from venerable democratic sources, the *Conseils Généraux* (the locally elected regional councils).[107] That was not the view which then prevailed in Algiers or, in due course, Paris, and it was open to objection on a variety of grounds. Constitutionally, it could be held that the 1875 constitution had implicitly abrogated the Tréveneuc Law; it had not confirmed the considerable, albeit provisional, powers conferred on the *Conseils Généraux* by the Tréveneuc Law, which referred in any case to the original system of a single assembly, not the bicameral legislature of 1875.[108] It was also noted that some *Conseils* had been purged by Vichy and that others might be hostile to de Gaulle. Furthermore, how long would it take, in the thick of battle, to reanimate the required one-half of the *Conseils Généraux*, which only then could elect an Assembly, itself to be the only validly constituted provisional authority? It was clear that the Tréveneuc Law specifically prescribed the reconstitution of the Third Republic, rather than a republic per se, and that was an objective somewhat at variance with the reforming impetus generated, in different ways, by both the domestic Resistance and de Gaulle.[109]

But more fundamental still was the question of the nation's recovery. To the Gaullists the Tréveneuc Law, with its crucial stress on local, regional initiatives, smacked too much of that fracturing of the national identity which had been threatened by the German occupation, division, exploitation, and general enfeebling of metropolitan France, as well as by four years of American policy—always dealing with distinct, local, often detachable authorities, Pétain in Vichy, a Gaullist high commissioner in Brazzaville or Guyana, Darlan in North Africa. The Tréveneuc Law likewise inverted Gaullist priorities, since to de Gaulle the first order of business was always to "re-establish the State."[110] Nevertheless, these were French, not American, debates, and Roosevelt could, with perfect consistency, have based his case for denying recognition to the FCNL on the sturdily republican grounds of the Tréveneuc Law. That he missed his opportunity and instead took the advice of Stettinius that "it would seem wise to avoid taking a position on a matter which primarily concerns the French people"[111] suggests that American imperatives, not French traditions, determined his policy, and also that the doctrine of self-determination, so simple in conception, could yield paradoxical and, for its expounders, disconcerting results. One French constitutional scholar, wrestling with American policy toward the FCNL, was reminded of the man who jumped into the water to avoid getting wet in the rain.[112]

The inspiration for the entire policy remains therefore Roosevelt himself. But before taking a retrospective look at the president, it is worth noting briefly the outcome of his policy. Recognition, he and Churchill had long agreed, was but a word, signifying nothing in itself but at least auguring a change in the pattern of relations. Yet what happened? At every point of intersection between the two countries, France and the United States, there reappeared all the old disputes and debates, dampening somewhat the ardor that should properly have accompanied the aftermath of liberation and recognition as the war drew to a close. Jefferson Caffery sent a series of memoranda to the State Department outlining "French grievances against the United States," which ranged from resentment at recent American diplomacy to more current objections to the behavior of the American liberators, whose conduct included, according to well-publicized rumors, leniency toward German prisoners, a patronizing attitude toward the French civilian population, and a lavish requisitioning of French property.[113] On the other hand, Walter Lippmann was moved to complain that American representatives abroad, whether in Paris or Algiers, were not themselves well suited to ease the strain between the two countries.[114] And distinguished French visitors to the United States, like Jean-Paul Sartre, found themselves, like their émigré forbears, regarded with suspicion both in governmental quarters and in certain sections of the press.[115]

At the higher reaches, Franco-American relations continued on their bumpy course. Roosevelt and de Gaulle did not prolong even that limited cordiality which had been achieved during de Gaulle's July visit to Washington. The French were not admitted to the Yalta conference in February 1945 (although they were there granted an occupation zone in Germany), and de Gaulle declined to meet Roosevelt in Algiers afterwards.[116] Militarily, the conclusion to the war in Europe was punctuated by tactical disagreements and near crises, such as in January the threatened exposure of newly liberated Strasbourg to German attack and in April the threatened eviction of the French occupying forces from Stuttgart.[117] Meanwhile, in the Far East the issue of Indochina began to loom ominously. By the time of Roosevelt's death in April, his initially firm refusal to countenance the reestablishment of any French rule there had considerably softened, and the insistent French requests for aid in repelling the Japanese were being more sympathetically treated.[118] But Roosevelt thereby bequeathed to his successors an unsettled policy and, as later events would show, an artificial dilemma: either an "anticolonial" policy that would, perhaps, serve American interests in Asia, or a "pro-French" policy that would strengthen them in Europe.[119] With the liberation of France, however, spokesmen for the two peoples resumed their characteristic modes of regarding one another. Elmer Davis could now perceive a new "vigor and resolution in the French people which offers good hope."[120] From Sartre's point of view "the conflict that divided the Americans on the French question" over the previous five years had "showed by its very virility the strength of their friendship toward us."[121]

CHAPTER 11
FRANKLIN ROOSEVELT:
A RETROSPECT

The closing weeks of Roosevelt's administration, that is to say, of his life, were at least as crowded as the first. The conclusion to the Yalta conference and the planning for the San Francisco conference, the battles of Iwo Jima and Okinawa, the advance on Berlin and the horrific reports about German concentration camps that now appeared, the visits from the Canadian prime minister and the Philippine president, the drafting of a major address to a Democratic rally on Jefferson Day, the long hours of posing for a commissioned watercolor portrait—all these pressed upon the attention of a tired, ailing president.[1] He found time, nonetheless, to attend to one other item that, though smaller than the rest, would matter at least as much to posterity as the watercolor by Mme Shoumatoff.

A Harvard historian, William Langer, serving during the war as head of the Research and Analysis branch of the OSS, had been asked by Cordell Hull to write an account of American relations with Vichy France. In the expectation that it was not for immediate publication but for the use of government officials, he was given access to the records of various departments and agencies. He needed also to consult White House files, and Hull first sought permission for him in September 1943.[2] Direct access to the files was not granted, but by March 1945 a digest of the records, prepared at Roosevelt's direction, was complete; and on 6 April Roosevelt reviewed the material before it was sent to Langer.[3] Within a week the president was dead of a massive cerebral hemorrhage. He had not read Langer's original draft, only at that point seen by members of the Department of State,[4] and he was not to see the later, revised version, published in 1947 as *Our Vichy Gamble*. But he had, in a typically oblique fashion, determined much of the interpretation it would offer.

For what is the thesis of Langer's book? It is the same in both versions, before and after the White House digest, and it can be quite easily summarized. It is that the American policy toward Vichy France was the correct one, and a credit to the State Department, and that those who criticized it were misguided and wrong. As Langer concluded, "From the standpoint of American interests, the policy was always a substantially sound one even though it may have been an unattractive one."[5] Such a bald outline cannot of course convey the painstaking research, the richness of detail, and the vivid and lucid

225

style that are all evident throughout the book. So, in strict justice, before considering a somewhat different conclusion—one that arises from a closer scrutiny of Roosevelt's behavior than Langer was in a position to have—we should reflect on the nature of that book.

The American government did not, like the British, commission volumes of official histories on the civilian side of the war effort. Neither American diplomacy, nor the economic programs, nor the new agencies were commemorated in volumes as counterparts to the British Official History of the Second World War or the diplomatic studies of Sir Llewellyn Woodward.[6] The closest we have, what might be termed semiofficial histories, are the works of Langer and S. E. Gleason on prewar diplomacy, sponsored by the Council on Foreign Relations, and of Herbert Feis, the former adviser on international economic affairs in the State Department, on such areas as the background to the attack on Pearl Harbor, the inter-Allied cooperation during the latter part of the war, and the decision to drop the atom bomb on Japan.[7] While these are not official histories, their authors' privileged access to source material only much later made available to other historians, as well as their personal association with the inner circles of government, undeniably lends their work at least the flavor of officialdom; it is to this twilight zone that Langer's *Our Vichy Gamble* belongs.

Langer recalled in the preface of the book, and later in his autobiography, how he was asked by Hull to write the study. The invitation came in mid-1943, a period, it may be recalled, when, with events in North Africa slipping out of American control, State Department officials were especially concerned about their declining prestige, inside and outside the administration.[8] Langer nevertheless insisted that he could not undertake the assignment merely to compile a case for the defense; and Hull replied that he did not want that either, only a detailed, independent, objective account of the policy, assembling all the facts so that a balanced judgment could be formed. Moreover, he added, "if . . . the government's policy had been wrong, it was important to know how and why."[9] It was on this understanding that Langer commenced his labors and gained not only access to much classified source material, but also the cooperation of many of the informed participants: Bullitt, Hull, Leahy, Murphy, Matthews, with Stimson making available the correspondence between Murphy, Eisenhower, and the War Department, which even Hull had not seen.[10] Langer thus emerged from his experience much more knowledgeable about the policy than any single individual actually connected with it; and both the conditions on which he agreed to the task, and the resources open to him, suggest the considerable value of the resulting book. But the question necessarily arises as to whether there was any tension between the two. Did Langer's immersion in governmental sources narrow his own perspective? Did his reliance upon the memories of governmental officials induce him to accept their biases?

At the outset it can be allowed that not all American officials subscribed to Langer's version. Sumner Welles (whose retirement was not disturbed by any intrusive inquiries from Langer) denied that any thought was ever given, as Langer alleged, to allowing relations with Vichy to lapse in 1940. According to Welles, the only question was whether to have "an effective ambassador" to strengthen Vichy's resistance to German demands (as between January 1941 and April 1942), or to rely simply on the embassy staff as an expression of disapproval (as between April and November 1942).[11] Neither course could properly be termed a gamble. Murphy registered a similar doubt in his memoirs, that the title of Langer's book implied a choice between alternatives of which Murphy, chargé d'affaires in the American embassy in 1940, had not been aware. More interestingly, he added that Langer's limited access to White House material had led him to discount the advantages of the policy that flowed through channels outside the State Department. For example, as Murphy well knew, Roosevelt's own deep interest in North Africa led him to bypass both the State Department and the military establishment, and rely instead on a personal and clandestine diplomacy operated through such emissaries as Murphy himself: the " 'Vichy policy,' " he writes, ". . . in fact was Roosevelt's personal policy . . . which the President often shaped without consulting his Secretary of State."[12] Similarly, Matthews, Murphy's successor as chargé d'affaires, wrote a long memorandum to Langer when the first draft was complete, offering a number of amendments. Some of them (for example, that the maintenance of relations did actually inhibit Vichy's collaboration with Germany) Langer did incorporate into the published version. Others (for example, that American action had kept the fleet and North Africa out of German hands), he did not.[13]

Clearly then, Langer's claim to have made an independent assessment of the policy is at least partially valid. On the other hand, these remain points of detail, not interpretation. Langer remained in broad agreement with the State Department on the fundamental matters, that the policy was "sensible [and] purely opportunist"[14] and that it yielded distinct benefits. Indeed Murphy's complaint that Langer underestimated the role of the White House is actually a fair illustration of the degree to which he accepted the interpretation of the State Department. And there were other examples. He might have been expected to criticize what many State Department officials regarded as British obstructionism, the intervention of a rival power. But he also sided with the department in the bureaucratic squabbles within the American administration, especially marked before and after the North African excursion. Despite plain talk from Leahy on the strategic importance of the program for economic aid to North Africa, the Board of Economic Warfare (BEW), it seems, remained "unenlightened and unregenerate."[15] As for the War Department, it "was slow in taking advantage of the opportunities that had been prepared."[16] There was much in this to gladden State Department hearts: when the book's publication was being considered, Matthews noted that "some of the sections dealing with the stupidity of the British on our North African program may be toned down a bit (though I am quite agreeable to leaving in the strictures on the B.E.W.)."[17] Leahy too, from a slightly different standpoint, observed, when Langer gave him the first draft to read, that it had apparently been prepared "with the purpose of justifying the attitude and performance of the State Department," although he added that it was "interesting, well written and generally correct."[18]

It was, of course, the sources that he used, rather than the auspices under which he wrote, that influenced Langer's final judgment. But that this judgment coincided with that of the State Department emerges with startling clarity if one turns from the policy itself to the domestic criticism it encountered. This was after all the public context in which the book came to be written and published. It was that bitter, unrelenting criticism directed at Hull, over this policy more than any other, which had compelled him to seek Langer's services;[19] and, as we have seen, it is striking that nearly all this criticism fastened on the State Department, not the War Department, or the Chiefs of Staff, or the White House. Hull's own views of his critics were perfectly straightforward; they thought, he believed, "largely of ideologies, less of American interests." In his memoirs, published in 1948, he concluded that it was "unfortunate that that policy aroused so many emotions in the United States."[20] This explanation of the criticism, in terms of ideology and emotion, occurred equally in Langer's book, published the previous year, where he commented that "the only real arguments against [the policy] were . . . of a sentimental or ideological character. . . . [But] the Department of State could hardly have been expected to deal in terms of sentiment." They were, in short, "liberals and radicals"[21] who attacked Hull, his department, and his policy. This may seem a curious way to account for a movement of opinion that included, at various times, Henry Luce, Walter Lippmann, and Wendell Willkie.[22] But, as we have also seen, it was a commonplace around the State Department in the war years to ascribe all criticism to ideologies and emotions.[23]

What, in any case, does "ideology" mean in this context? If it means "the integrated assertions, theories and aims that constitute a sociopolitical program" (*Webster's Ninth New Collegiate Dictionary*), then the Atlantic Charter propounded an ideology, as had, before it, Roosevelt's "Four Freedoms" speech. In that case the force of the distinction between the administration and its critics is greatly weakened, unless, as was attempted in preceding chapters, an examination is made of ideological *differences*. But of course the term also has a more pejorative meaning: the first definition offered in the dictionary, "visionary theorizing." In this case the distinction would appear to be one between the practical approach of the State Department and the abstract approach of its critics. Yet a debate over practicality can never be historically resolved. It cannot be known, for example, what would have been the effect of more wholehearted American support of de Gaulle in 1941, though it is worth noting that even Langer admits that "the man himself might have become less rambunctious and his following might have become more comprehensive and united."[24] Herein lies the difficulty in disentangling the polemical and factual threads in the memoirs of the time, and even in subsequent histories, although Langer made a much more conscientious effort to keep the two apart than did, for example, Basil Rauch in his much cruder assault on the writings of Robert Bendiner and Waverley Root.[25]

It is equally hard, even at this distance, to detach the policy from the debate it engendered, a debate even Langer's book did not wholly still. When the reviews started to appear in 1947 they were as mixed as the contemporary commentary on the policy had been, although no historian questioned the integrity of Langer's scholarship. On the contrary, those who differed with him argued that his views could actually be refuted on the basis of his own material.[26] The present study has not therefore sought to prolong or reanimate that wartime controversy, but rather to include it as part of the historical record, and, by so doing, to explore two closely related matters—the nature of Roosevelt's management of foreign policy and the public discussion of such policy—which are largely absent from Langer's work.

The relationship between governmental actions and public opinion may not be an orderly one, but it is, particularly in wartime, intimate; and it is a subject that has engaged at some time the attention of most commentators on American society. Tocqueville devoted a famous chapter of *Democracy in America* to showing how foreign policy was exempt from the general rule of the benign effect on political life of democratic forms. There, he argued, the aristocratic principle had proved more wholesome, and had indeed been acted upon by George Washington: "Foreign policy," Tocqueville wrote, "does not require the use of any of the good qualities peculiar to democracy, but does demand the cultivation of almost all those which it lacks."[27] It is in fact public opinion, and not "democracy" narrowly conceived, which is the main subject of the whole work, and the source of that Tyranny of the Majority which the author so feared. But it was Lord Bryce, half a century later, who embarked on a more sustained analysis of public opinion (a term unused by Tocqueville), making it literally the center of his examination of *The American Commonwealth*. To Bryce, writing near the end of the nineteenth century, public opinion had emerged as a significant component of the political culture of both Britain and the United States, and he accordingly anatomized its virtues and defects. Of particular interest here is his attribution to public opinion of the quality of "fatalism," a word not easy to define but which to Bryce clearly partook of both deference and solidarity (what later came to be called "consensus").[28] Walter Lippmann's understanding of public opinion as "primarily a moralized and codified version of the facts" has already been cited.[29] We should also consider what D. W. Brogan discerned as the combination of curiosity and credulity in the American public:

> The American man-in-the-street expects to get the low-down on all secret conferences, to have international decisions supplied to him before the participants have had time to put their smiles on and pose for the group photograph. If this demand is not forthcoming from official sources, it is provided from unofficial sources. Commentators of varying degrees of knowledge, candor, truthfulness, ingenuity, intelligence, explain and announce. Wildly conflicting guesses are made with equal confidence, and the reader and listener are given a wide range of confidential misinformation—as is their right. The outsider may wonder at the willing suspension of disbelief on which the commentators can count.[30]

Some of the evidence presented in this study does bear out the warnings and judgment of those commentators. At least with regard to Vichy, Roosevelt did engage in a kind of court diplomacy that was "aristocratic" rather than "democratic" in flavor. It is evident also that public opinion, as distinct from active pressure groups, did display a measure of deference and fatalism. In the second half of 1940 a rising expectation that America would go to war was combined with a dwindling desire to do so; in July 1943 Roosevelt's foreign policy was supported by nearly half as many again as his domestic policy; in April 1944 he was the presidential choice of 55 percent of one sample if the war was still on, 42 percent if it was over.[31] Finally it is also clear that public opinion was, throughout this period, both ill-informed and misinformed. In July 1942 a third of the 51 percent who could correctly identify de Gaulle believed that it was with the Free French that the United States had formal relations; as late as June 1944 exactly one half of one sample had neither read nor heard about de Gaulle's Committee.[32] In some cases, too, public opinion might be deliberately misled by propaganda or censorship: for example, the handling by Vichy of news about the Dakar expedition, or the attempts by American administration spokesmen to make the Darlan deal appear more Eisenhower's decision than it in fact was—both of which seem to have had the desired effect on public opinion. And there were other, subtler means. Roosevelt's kittenish behavior at press conferences is justly famous; and the favored journalists (Arthur Krock, Forrest Davis, Anne O'Hare McCormick)[33] and the planted story (the dissemination in 1943 and 1944 of black propaganda about de Gaulle's headquarters in London) also proved useful tools. There are, in short, a variety of ways by which information, once selected, can be distributed.

But the evidence on which such conclusions are based, public opinion polls, is significantly different from that which nineteenth-century writers employed. The activities in which Tocqueville and Bryce engaged have suffered from a division of labor. Today there are those who design questionnaires, those who ask questions, those who analyze responses; and before accepting any general conclusions from the polls' findings one would do well to note two important reservations about their reliability. The period under consideration falls midway between two historic opinion poll fiascos, that of the *Literary Digest* in 1936 and that of virtually every pollster in 1948, and it would be rash to assume that the scientific study of public opinion was other than in its infancy. Techniques of sampling and of framing questions were still at the experimental stage. Gallup used a nationwide survey of 3,000; *Fortune* polled 5,000 businessmen.[34] Apart from their limited predictive success (which is more of a problem for the political scientist than the historian), polls cannot adequately register the expression of ideas. It is significant that the findings of public opinion polls, and indeed the nature of the whole exercise, are rarely satisfactory to people of pronounced political convictions.[35] The wording of the question, and the manner, even the tone of voice, in which it is asked, immediately introduce an element of subjectivity. Thus it is possible, for example, to imagine a question such as "What do you think we should do with Germany, as a country, after the war?" being asked in a variety of ways, each suggesting a different response. Nor is it clear that the questions themselves were entirely free from oversimplification or complexity or ambiguity. A question such as "Do you think Russia can be trusted to cooperate with us when the war is over?" presupposes general agreement on American postwar aims. Another question, "As soon as Germany is defeated do you think she will start making plans for another world war?" seems to be putting ideas into respondents' heads. Still another, "If peace could be obtained today on the basis of Germany holding the countries it has conquered so far, and with Britain keeping the British Empire as it now stands, would you be in favor of such a peace?" yokes together two distinct controversies.

Public opinion polls have then proved of greater worth to the political scientist—who can, when informed by a sense of historical discipline, employ them to great effect[36]—than to the historian, who may appropriately reserve them for two rather limited purposes: to supplement conclusions arrived at from other sources (for example, the widespread support given to the American administration's French policy) and to establish simple matters of fact (for example, the proportion of the American public that had actually heard of Pétain or de Gaulle). They do, however, illuminate one further area that, given Roosevelt's intense interest in public opinion generally, is of some consequence for the present study. This is the broad question of "isolationism." To view it through the lens of wartime public opinion is to see it not as a doctrine, or a policy, or a social movement, or even as a uniquely American cast of mind, but, at its simplest, as an attachment to a particular kind of strategy —independent, expedient, and short-term. Its starting-point is an intense patriotism, which—translated into diplomatic and strategic terms—becomes

unilateralism. It thus blends well with a lack of interest (bordering on ignorance) in the affairs of countries outside the American hemisphere. Hence,
once engaged in a common war with those countries, the American public will
extend the widest tolerance to a diplomacy of opportunism or a strategy of *pis
aller*, if they promise to win the war in the shortest possible time.

The implications with regard to wartime France are clear. Public opinion
was not greatly exercised over America's French policy simply because the
policy fulfilled this most urgent requirement. It was not greatly aroused against
Pétain because he did not actively obstruct American policy (at least not with
that degree of visibility which was needed to cause complaints). Nor was it
greatly enthused by the figure of de Gaulle who, as after Dakar, had a military
record that could be easily disparaged and who, defiantly and publicly, did
inconvenience American policymakers, over St. Pierre and Miquelon, in
North Africa, and before and after the Normandy landings. He also had the
added liability, from this point of view, of the backing of a narrow, exclusive,
intellectual, and journalistic clique, widely, though mistakenly, identified with
the radical left.

These conclusions are not substantially affected by the fact that the Second
World War was clearly a transitional period, in the course of which internationalist goals were expounded by the most diverse spokesmen inside and outside
the administration, and at the end of which the United Nations was founded,
on American soil, with moral and material support from the United States. For
there is little evidence that the internationalist rhetoric of Roosevelt, or even
Henry Luce, struck a particularly vibrant chord in the American public at
large. When, a few months after Pearl Harbor, Roosevelt invited all Americans to think up a good name to call the present war, pollsters found that the
vast majority were content with "World War II," or sometimes "The Second
World War."[37] A year after Pearl Harbor, when 68 percent of one sample
declared that they had a clear idea of what the war was all about, the results were unimpressive; and the gloomy reflections of the pollster are worth
preserving:

> Among those who say they do have a clear idea of why we are fighting,
> there is some evidence of a failure to understand the underlying issues.
> Many of those people, when asked to state what they thought the war
> was about, indulged in catch phrases such as "We're fighting for free-
> dom and liberty," or "We're fighting to lick the Nazis," or "We're fight-
> ing to keep Democracy." Only a negligible number of those questioned
> mentioned the Atlantic Charter or the "Four Freedoms" as our purpose
> in the war. And even fewer of those who brought up the Four Freedoms
> could name them.[38]

The same is true of the United Nations. Its acceptance by the American
public hardly reflected a new adoption of broadly internationalist goals. As the

answers to the polls, and the questions themselves, make abundantly clear, the increasing majorities in favor of a successor to the League of Nations were attracted to the idea of an "international police force," "a world organization to maintain the future peace of the world."[39] That is a rather different objective from the internationalization of such American virtues as justice, freedom, and democracy; and the popular acceptance of that, the internationalist goal, awaited a different war, the Cold War, and a different set of principles, anti-Communism. In the meantime, insofar as one is able to judge from the polls, the American public was prepared to endorse its government's various dealings with Pétain in 1940, Darlan in 1942, Giraud in 1943, and finally de Gaulle in 1944 all on the same principle, that they were called for by American strategic requirements.

This was not, however, the public that most exercised Roosevelt. It was, for him, placid and deferential, content with his revision of Wilsonian internationalism so as to embrace the notion of great powers policing their areas of influence, albeit without the trappings of European colonialism. Thus did "isolationism" bury itself within "interventionism." But just as abroad Roosevelt tended to think in terms of great powers, so too at home, always the aristocrat, he thought in terms of powerful, organized blocs of opinion—Congress, lobbies, the press—and worked hard to manage or undermine them.[40] "I want," he told an aide in February 1943, after reading one unfavorable editorial, "all the releases in *PM* in the last three weeks about de Gaulle, Giraud, Peyrouton, etc. I want to see Max Lerner or whoever the editor of *PM* is."[41] It was in such circles as these that the American policy toward France proved controversial, among those, the attentive or informed public, who, while lacking political office, still sought to communicate their views on public affairs: journalists, publicists, lobbyists. They did so in various ways, by airing their views in public or by confiding them to government officials; and the relative emphasis varied from writer to writer. Samuel Grafton, loudly and belligerently, tried through his newspaper columns to arouse popular fury against the administration's policy. Alfred Bergman, more surreptitiously, sent his news and advice to key administration officials, flaunting his supposed contacts and building up a veritable network of Anglo-American correspondence. Walter Lippmann, with a somewhat more dispassionate air, attempted to engage both the readers of his column and the administration in an educated dialogue about American policy.

Yet overall the results were meager. If public opinion was sluggish, the administration was inflexible. The State Department was particularly obdurate: the chief effect of the opposition to its stand on St. Pierre and Miquelon was to stiffen its resistance (prior to a quiet, belated tactical retreat); and the similar, though weaker agitation over North Africa in 1943 only brought down a vigorous counterattack. Even those, like Elmer Davis, Archibald MacLeish, and Edgar Ansel Mowrer, who actually entered government service, did not exercise any very profound influence on policy; for Mowrer indeed it was a deeply saddening experience. Perhaps the enduring symbol of all this is the headmasterly figure of Henry Stimson, in the wake of the Darlan deal, calling on MacLeish, Felix Frankfurter, Henry Morgenthau, and Wendell Willkie, to stifle their criticism and show loyalty to the school.

Instead, then, of a well-organized group guiding public opinion while advising officials on public policy, there was only an anarchic, impotent array of competing voices. Of course this does not mean that organizations such as the Union for Democratic Action, the Free World Association, and Freedom House did not serve as valuable forums for public discussion; or that France Forever did not engage in useful charitable works; or that some French émigrés did not help to keep alive Franco-American cultural links; or that a great number of journalists, of all political persuasions, did not, by interpreting events in the light of their readers' presumed allegiances, perform a valid task. But as against these achievements, the failures were considerable. The internationalist organizations, with their interlocking directorates and a frequently demogogic style of argument, gained neither mass support nor political respectability, and soon had all the traits of a self-conscious, self-enclosed élite. France Forever, barred from political activity, suffered from both bureaucratic malaise and financial starvation. The French émigrés, while separately they may have been talented, energetic persons, rapidly acquired a not altogether undeserved reputation for intrigue, dissension, and petulance. The Gaullists among them had, to be sure, an extraordinarily difficult task. But their very failure to build up a coherent bloc, or lobby, of opinion—a failure imposed as much by circumstance as by personalities—naturally robbed them of all interest for Roosevelt. As for American journalists, with one or two exceptions (Lippmann being the most conspicuous), they interpreted French developments within such a narrow, domestic frame of reference as to strip their arguments of any real utility. They allowed them to be judged by ideological criteria. Thus, to take two contrasting examples, the *Chicago Tribune* did not succeed in having starving French civilians fed, and the *Nation* and the *New Republic* did not secure an American break in relations with Vichy.

The point here is not just that French affairs were analyzed, discussed, and debated in an American idiom. To some extent this may be inevitable in any attempt to understand the affairs of another society; the effort at comprehension may require a domestication of the issues. But what occurred in the American discussion of France went much further than that. Even allowing for the varied preoccupations of the writers concerned, it is remarkable that the correlations they found were always exact, between French and American democracy, the Popular Front and the New Deal, Vichy reaction and State Department conservatism, the Free French and American liberalism; and the intention, in portraying French affairs in this paradigmatic fashion, was nakedly polemical. For the habit was most apparent in those quarters with distinctive domestic grievances: the isolationists, finding themselves in an undesired war, conducted by a hated administration; the interventionists, finding the war fought with an alarming disregard for their ideals; each in addition fearing (and exaggerating) the influence of the other in Washington. Moralism and insularity were here paradoxically combined: while American standards were being prescribed for France, such European notions as "appeasement," "totalitarianism," and "fascism" were, in crossing the Atlantic, being stripped of their limited, precise meanings and harnessed to peculiar, American controversies.

The most peculiar, and the most recurring, of all these controversies was over the State Department, which was vulnerable to domestic criticism while powerless to direct policy. Time and again critics who objected to America's foreign policy directed their complaints at the State Department, and betrayed a fundamental misunderstanding of Roosevelt's whole approach to wartime government, for he sought to make satellites of his executive departments rather than confide in them. Such a widely held and rarely challenged misapprehension requires some explanation; and although part of the explanation certainly lies in Roosevelt's astute manipulation of people and agencies, he was only exploiting the unusual situation in which, by the Second World War, the department found itself.

The department over which Cordell Hull presided for twelve years had greatly changed from that created by the Founding Fathers, whose modest though implacable diplomatic objectives had enabled them to confer on it not only the management of foreign policy but also responsibility for patents and copyrights, the national census, the preparation of executive pardons, and the supervision of territorial affairs.[42] Then too the office of secretary of state, combining broad administrative experience with statesmanlike duties, was seen as the natural route to the presidency. But in time America's more widespread international rights and obligations, and a more disorderly world, brought about a huge expansion in the department, the greatest period of which was under Hull and during the Second World War. Between 1939 and 1945 the number of employees in the department rose from 974 to 3,767 and the budget reached fifty million dollars. The department also temporarily acquired a Board of Economic Operations, an Office of Foreign Territories (later merged into the Office of Foreign Economic Coordination), a Caribbean Office, an Office of Foreign Relief and Rehabilitation, an Advisory Committee on Postwar Foreign Policy, and an Office of Public Information.[43] Yet this piecemeal and haphazard growth was not balanced by any reorganization of the department (until 1944) or by any clearer definition of its duties.

To anyone outside Washington it might well have seemed as if the department had had a new access of power and influence. But the reverse is true. As, in Roosevelt's words, Dr. New Deal became Dr. Win-the-war, so too the secretary of state was transformed from a statesman into a spokesman. "The President told me," Henry Wallace noted in his diary in 1942, "that the one thing which he had determined to do back in 1932 was to clean up the State Department. . . . There is no question but that the President has it in for the State Department and at the right time will move in on them."[44] But having delayed for ten years, Roosevelt was unlikely now to seek a direct collision with the department or its chief; nor was there any need for one with so many alternative channels through which to direct policy, particularly during a war when Roosevelt's powers as commander in chief were truly formidable.

His French policy alone provides abundant illustrations of his techniques. The department's diplomatic activities were supplemented by those of Roosevelt's personal emissaries, Bullitt, Leahy, and Murphy. Its usefulness as a source of information and advice was progressively diluted by the intelligence services of the army, the navy, and Colonel Donovan, not to mention that eloquent supplicant, Winston Churchill. Perhaps most tellingly of all, foreign policy itself was depreciated by Roosevelt's declared resolve to postpone all political decisions until the end of the war, and his practice of permitting the armed forces to make the interim decisions. Nor, finally, while the president was outlining grand strategy and global ideals, could the secretary be the leading expounder of American foreign policy, only someone who filled in the details (admittedly a somewhat exacting task).

What then, aside from remaining part of the machinery for more formal diplomatic intercourse and having occasional dealings with Congress, was the function of the wartime State Department? The new bureaus were essentially concerned with two areas. One was the theoretical, hypothetical work of postwar planning, an activity rendered even more abstract by the department's virtual exclusion from major policy decisions.[45] Only in the detailed exploration of other people's ideas—for example the United Nations Charter—did the department do valuable service. The second area was economic warfare, where there soon arose the most bitter jurisdictional feuds. For in addition to the State Department there were at various times a host of other agencies working on related matters, the Board of Economic Warfare, the Petroleum Coordinator, the Office of Lend-Lease Administration, and of course the Treasury. The resulting conflicts lined Hull up against such figures as Wallace and Morgenthau, who were significantly located on the left of the New Deal. Nor did Hull invariably win all his battles. Roosevelt might concede to him formal administrative hegemony while dispersing effective power elsewhere.[46] And on general conflicts of policy it may be said that the department lost whenever it stood alone, and won only when it had strategic allies outside (as when Stimson helped to defeat Morgenthau's plan for the pastoralization of the German economy).[47] In short, the position had been exactly reversed since the early days of the New Deal when, confronting the administration's economic isolationism, Hull won acceptance of his pet scheme, a reciprocal trade program.

The ensuing demoralization had far-reaching effects. Those internal factional disputes which so weakened the department's effectiveness were directly related to its dwindling autonomy: the conflict between Hull and Welles to Welles's greater familiarity with the president, that between Berle and Acheson to Acheson's known loyalty to the meddlesome Felix Frankfurter.[48] The newly diminished role of the department also explains why it reacted to domestic criticism with such harsh fury. If the critics were animated by a sense of their own powerlessness, how much more so was this true of their target. The siege mentality of the department, surrounded by New Dealers and their agencies, prompted it to turn with unaccustomed bitterness on its most accessible, public adversaries, thereby provoking even more criticism. But in thus entering the fray the department only further exposed itself; and if now most of the critics came from a largely powerless left wing, they would later be drawn from a newly dangerous right, rather more adept at deploying the language of patriotism and the charge of disloyalty. In the meantime the department and its critics, each seeing only a portion of the truth, became locked in a relentless contest from which the only conceivable beneficiary could be Roosevelt.

The nature of Roosevelt's policy management was much debated at the time by his colleagues. Breckinridge Long, listening to Hull's mournful complaints about Roosevelt's treatment of him, thought that it was still "child's play" compared to Woodrow Wilson's eclipse of his secretaries of state.[49] By contrast Stimson, who suffered no less than Hull from Roosevelt's disdain for his executive departments, considered that while there were parallels this was still a particularly alarming and dangerous practice. On one occasion Stimson actually asked Roosevelt "what a Cabinet is for and what Departments were for," but then confessed in his diary: "I have small hopes of reforming him. The fault is Rooseveltian and deeply ingrained. Theodore Roosevelt had it to a certain extent but never anywhere nearly as much as this one. . . . I told him frankly that, if the process of whittling down the powers of the Secretary of War should continue, I would be in a very embarrassing position, for I had no desire, in the words of Churchill, to go down in history as the person who consented to the liquidation of the great historical powers of my office."[50]

Clearly any major war will cause a certain amount of centralization, or at least some departure from conventional administrative procedures. What appears to have happened in Roosevelt's case is that those wartime requirements—for immediate and immediately effective decisions—tempted him toward a more extreme self-reliance because he was a man temperamentally averse to the detailed work of administration, supremely confident in his ability to dispense with it, and above all more interested in the broad goals of

strategy, diplomacy, and the postwar world than in adopting the bureaucrati-
cally correct means of securing them.

In Roosevelt's defense, it must be recalled that the American Constitution
makes no mention of a cabinet. That most exacting task of a newly elected
president—the nomination of executive department heads—occupies him far
more than the Founding Fathers ordained it should. Cabinet members may like
to think of themselves as colleagues within a corporate body, but the reality is
closer to a model of competitive individualism, with each member reproduc-
ing, at cabinet level, the same patterns and habits that he confronts presiding
over his own department. Roosevelt understood this well, as did, possibly, the
increasingly dejected Hull. The "imperial presidency" did not require any self-
aggrandizement on the part of the incumbent to sustain its growth; it was, at
least with regard to the cabinet, always there. If a cabinet, in the British sense,
had ever existed—as, presumably, Stimson desired—then there would have
been cabinet minutes for a future historian to inspect.

Roosevelt does then belong at the center of a study of American behavior
toward France, and this not merely because he authored the policy that others
upheld. He appears also to have addressed the concerns of a public wider than
his immediate circle of officials. His French policy is thus instructive about
more than just his diplomatic technique, but also his overall vision, and to a
large extent that of his fellow citizens. It is of course hazardous to generalize
about the behavior of a statesman on the basis of his dealings with just one
country, as was discovered by Roosevelt's conservative critics who found
themselves asserting that Roosevelt had been cunning and deceitful in his
relations with prewar Japan shortly before he became naive and gullible in
handling wartime Russia. A more rounded picture is probably drawn by those
scholars who, examining Roosevelt's attitudes and policies toward the outside
world as a whole, presented their conclusions in the form of either an analysis
of the changing pattern of his views ("Roosevelt the Isolationist," "Roosevelt
the Realist")[51] or a discussion of the general areas he surveyed ("The Abolition
of Imperialism," "A Global New Deal")[52] or a richly detailed narrative of his
performance.[53]

Nevertheless, there is an advantage to be gained from concentrating on one
country, in this case France, where the internal conflicts, and the ensuing
debates within America, served to expose an entire range of domestic issues
and to make relations between the two countries a test case of American
principles. Seen in this light the American policy toward France might appear
to have revealed a classic dilemma of ends and means: the ends, for the
French, were the expulsion of the Nazi invader and the choice of their own
future government; the means, for the Americans, were a series of compromis-
ing and expedient arrangements with some of the uglier forces in French
society, newly risen to prominence in the wake of the German occupation.

Whatever else may be said about the motives of de Gaulle's American supporters, it is hardly surprising that for them the adoption of such means far outweighed even the considerable material aid that, beginning in November 1941, was being extended to the forces they backed.

Yet Roosevelt did not see it like this, as an awkward moral dilemma, and the French policy is also important for revealing a president harder and colder than the gay, convivial, genial Roosevelt of folklore. At the time of the Darlan deal he might be quoting, on every conceivable occasion, "an old Bulgarian proverb of the Orthodox Church: 'My children, you are permitted in time of great danger to walk with the Devil until you have crossed the bridge.' "[54] But that was consciously invoked to appease critics. It was an afterthought to a measure about which Roosevelt never himself had any doubts. Similarly he did from time to time display a sympathy for the liberal, democratic politicians undergoing various ordeals in Vichy. He wanted to read a transcript of the Riom trials;[55] he gratefully acknowledged a copy of Léon Blum's collected speeches and writings, as well as a gift of the original draft of Blum's prison reflections.[56] But all this was on a par with his equally sincere concern for the welfare of Darlan's son, Alain, stricken, as Roosevelt had been, with infantile paralysis, and who was thus welcomed for treatment at Warm Springs;[57] or his charmingly disingenuous remarks to the visiting French journalists in March 1945 that he had loved France ever since he had toured it on bicycle as a boy and that they were not to think that he and de Gaulle were currently on bad terms.[58]

For Roosevelt never allowed personal or, more important, idealistic considerations to intrude upon his conduct of the intermediate affairs of coalition warfare. An exception to this—the insistence, in January 1943, on an Allied requirement for unconditional surrender by the Axis powers—only serves to prove the rule. By threatening to harden German resistance this may have seemed to prolong the war in the interest of a just and lasting peace.[59] Yet what had caused it? The occasion on which it was announced, after months of discussion in American official circles, clearly exposes other Rooseveltian objectives. By revealing to the world, just after the Darlan deal, that the ability of Germany and Japan to wage another war would be utterly destroyed, Roosevelt simultaneously affirmed to Russia that the United States would not be neglecting the European front, and reassured an uneasy press, in Britain and the United States, that Darlan's counterparts in Germany would receive no similar favors.[60] He was thus trying to cement the anti-Axis alliance, an immediate, not a long-term goal and one required of him by the outcome of his own Vichy policy.

There was then for Roosevelt no inconsistency in his actions. The political ideals were reserved for the postwar world, with details to be worked out then. Meanwhile, military strategy would remain the prime determinant of policy. It is here that Roosevelt, for all his personal and highly individual control over policy-making, proved more attuned to public opinion as a whole than to his own liberal supporters or certain members of his administration. He was no doubt an intensely private man, as was detected by an admiring French observer, the diplomat Alexis Leger. "The man I have heard," he wrote after one of Roosevelt's campaign speeches in 1940, "is not 'cheap.'" To Leger, Roosevelt's "supreme accomplishment" was his ability never to sacrifice "his private needs, his secret wants, for essential political success." He seemed to retain a certain loneliness "in the midst of the crowd": "the condition of every leader having a mission to fulfill in this world."[61]

Such a man could be private without being introspective, possessing nothing of the brooding melancholy of earlier war presidents like Lincoln or Wilson. His death left behind no scraps of autobiography, no memoirs, no personal diaries, only a busy public record of memoranda and official correspondence. At once self-reliant and exuberant, he was well suited to be the first president continuously exposed, in various media, to a mass public. This is perhaps why his personal popularity and his afterlife in the American folk memory[62] bear little relation to the wisdom or effectiveness of his policies.

For his appeal was not, in the end, a practical one. As the United States shifted from a broadly isolationist to a broadly interventionist posture toward the outside world—a shift imposed as much as willed—there was this transitional period when many of the older patterns of thought were retained: the desire for a wholly independent foreign policy, a confidence in the superiority of American institutions, a moralistic suspicion of European power politics as a generator of war and imperialism. Some of those sentiments have of course persisted much longer, creating still further difficulties. But even during the war they hardly provided a comfortable setting for a supposedly common struggle.

Roosevelt understood or intuited this, and attempted, in that vague but idealistic rhetoric, to ease the adjustment of his bewildered countrymen. His attitudes and policies toward France epitomize his, and their, changing mood: the contempt for a nation proven incompetent at social and economic reform, unable to defend itself against its neighbor even while claiming a preemptive right to rule underprivileged peoples; the relentlessly independent line he pursued with regard to both Vichy and de Gaulle; the constant stress on short-term efficacy in his military dealings with Darlan, Giraud, and de Gaulle; and, towering over it all, the breezy, Rooseveltian assurance that the compromises, the expedient measures, and even the insults would all serve the cause of peace, justice, and self-determination. That last claim may perhaps be left as an open question, although the responsibility for raising it is not.

ABBREVIATIONS
AND ACRONYMS

AIPO	American Institute of Public Opinion
BLI	British Library of Information
BPS	British Press Service
CHDGM	Comité d'histoire de la deuxième guerre mondiale
Cong. Rec.	*Congressional Record*, followed by volume, Congress, session, part, and page numbers
FCNL	French Committee of National Liberation
FDR	Franklin Delano Roosevelt
FDRL	Franklin D. Roosevelt Library, Hyde Park, New York. For these documents the following abbreviations are also used:

OF   Official File
PPF President's Personal File
PSF President's Secretary's File

FDR Press Conferences	*The Complete Presidential Press Conferences of Franklin D. Roosevelt* (New York, 1972)
FO	British Foreign Office records, followed by division, box, and file numbers
FRUS	*Foreign Relations of the United States* (Washington, D.C., 1957–65)
LCMD	Library of Congress, Manuscript Division
PREM	Prime Minister's Files
ONI	Office of Naval Intelligence
OSS	Office of Strategic Services
OWI	Office of War Information
R and A	Research and Analysis division of the Office of Strategic Services
SD	State Department records, followed by the number of the decimal file and of the document within the file
WSC	Winston Spencer Churchill

NOTES

CHAPTER I

1. See, for example, Chatfield, "Alternative Antiwar Strategies of the Thirties"; Ferrell, "The Peace Movement"; Divine, *Illusion of Neutrality*; Bolt, *Ballots before Bullets*.
2. Hull, *Memoirs*, 1:518–30; Allen, "Cordell Hull and the Defense of the Trade Agreements Program, 1934–1940."
3. See, for example, Loewenheim, "An Illusion That Shaped History."
4. For the importance, and sometimes self-importance, of American ambassadors abroad in this period, see, for example, Davies, *Mission to Moscow*; Dodd and Dodd, *Ambassador Dodd's Diary*; Bowers, *My Mission to Spain*; Phillips, *Ventures in Diplomacy*; Dallek, *Democrat and Diplomat*; Kaufmann, "Two American Ambassadors, Bullitt and Kennedy"; Wright, "Ambassador Bullitt and the Fall of France."
5. Bullitt and Freud, *Thomas Woodrow Wilson, Twenty-eighth President of the United States*.
6. Bullitt to FDR, 29 Jan. 1943, in O. H. Bullitt, ed., *For the President*, 575–90; complete text in President's Secretary's File (PSF) 34, William C. Bullitt, 1941–43, Franklin D. Roosevelt Library, Hyde Park, New York (FDRL).
7. See, for example, W. C. Bullitt, "How We Won the War and Lost the Peace," *Life*, 6 Sept. 1948, and idem, *The Great Globe Itself*.
8. Bullitt, *For the President*, 512–17; see also Berle and Jacobs, *Navigating the Rapids*, 445, 828–29; Acheson, *Present at the Creation* 77; Harold L. Ickes Diary, Library of Congress, Manuscript Division (LCMD), 8 June, 28 June, 27 July, 30 Nov., 7 Dec. 1941, 14 Feb., 25 Apr., 9 May, 15 Aug., 29 Aug. 1943.
9. Barnet, *Intervention and Revolution*, 189.
10. On the disillusioned intelligentsia, see Mayer, *Politics and Diplomacy of Peacemaking*, 875–93; Rochester, *American Liberal Disillusionment*.
11. Freidel, *Franklin D. Roosevelt: The Ordeal*, 17–18, 122–37.
12. Steel, *Walter Lippmann and the American Century*, 165.
13. Farnsworth, *William C. Bullitt and the Soviet Union*, 72–74.
14. Bullitt to Sinclair, 8 Apr. 1920, Upton Sinclair Papers, Lilly Library, Indiana University, Bloomington.
15. Bullitt to Sinclair, 22 Jan. 1920, ibid.
16. Bullitt to FDR, 18 May 1934, Bullitt, *For the President*, 88.
17. Bullitt to Hull, 20 Apr. 1936, ibid., 156.
18. Farnsworth, *William C. Bullitt*, 143–49.
19. Bullitt to Hull, 20 Apr. 1936, Bullitt, *For the President*, 154.

20. Bullitt to FDR, 7 Dec. 1937, ibid., 242.

21. Bullitt to FDR, 20 May 1938, ibid., 262.

22. Haight, *American Aid to France*, 13, 33–35, 70–71, 91–92.

23. Ickes Diary, 22 Mar. 1939.

24. M. E. Lehand to Bullitt, 20 March, FDR to Bullitt, 27 July 1940 ("Will you let me have your slant on the enclosed?"), FDRL PSF, 43, France, William C. Bullitt, 1940.

25. Bullitt, *For the President*, 376–96; see also R. Walton Moore (counselor of State Department) to Rep. Sol Bloom of the House Committee on Foreign Affairs, 23 Jan. 1941, enclosing full text of Bullitt's letter to Moore, 29 Nov. 1936 (edited version in Bullitt, *For the President*, 191–93) outlining Bullitt's advice to the French, R. Walton Moore Papers, Box 3, Bullitt, W.C., 1940–41, FDRL.

26. Memo of Anthony Eden, 13 Mar. 1940, Prime Minister's Office Papers, Public Record Office, London (PREM) 4, 25/2; see also memo by Sir Robert Vansittart quoted in Bullitt, *For the President*, 404–5.

27. See the views of Alexis Leger, permanent secretary general of the French Foreign Office, as reported by Welles, *Foreign Relations of the United States (FRUS)* (1940), 1:66; and the notes passed to the British Foreign Office by the French ambassador, Charles Corbin, 9 Mar., 10 Mar. 1940, PREM 4, 25/2.

28. Wiskemann, *Rome-Berlin Axis*, 241–43.

29. Offner, "Appeasement Revisited," esp. 384–93.

30. Bullitt to FDR, 18 Apr. 1940, Bullitt, *For the President*, 410.

31. Ickes Diary, 19 May 1940.

32. Bullitt, *For the President*, 415–20, 425–36, 439–46.

33. Ibid., 415.

34. Ibid., 426.

35. Ibid., 436.

36. Hoare to Foreign Office (F.O.), 31 July 1940, FO 371 24384, C 7825 5 18.

37. Bullitt, *For the President*, 427–28.

38. Ibid., 432, 424, 441, 458, 465–66, 473–78.

39. Bullitt to Ickes, 29 Oct. 1939, Ickes Papers, Box 371, War, 2.

40. Bullitt to Hull, 31 July 1940, Bullitt, *For the President*, 478–80.

41. Ickes Diary, 27 June 1940.

42. Adolf Berle Diary (FDRL), Box 212, 13 June 1940.

43. Bullitt to FDR and Hull, 1 July 1940, *FRUS* (1940), 2:462–69, esp. 462, 464, 467, 469.

44. Ibid., 468; an edited version of this dispatch, omitting one of the quoted passages, is in Bullitt, *For the President*, 481–87.

45. Baudouin, *Neuf mois au gouvernement*, 219; and see in general Warner, *Pierre Laval and the Eclipse of France*.

46. Pétain to FDR, 4 July 1940, *FRUS* (1940), 2:469.

47. Bullitt to FDR and Hull, 1 July 1940, ibid., 466.

48. Ibid., 464, 467.

49. Bullitt to Hull, 5 July 1940, ibid., 471.

50. Ibid., 470.

51. Bullitt to FDR and Hull, 12 July 1940, ibid., 472.

52. Bullitt to FDR and Hull, 1 July 1940, ibid., 464–65; cf. Murphy to Hull, 29 July 1940, ibid., 378.
53. *New York Times*, 21 July 1940.
54. Henry L. Stimson Diary (Sterling Library, Yale University), 1 Aug. 1940; Ickes Diary, 4 Aug. 1940.
55. Bullitt, *Report to the American People*.
56. Bullitt memo, 9 Nov. 1940, Bullitt, *For the President*, 505–6.
57. Review of these various attempts, May 1944, in Henry L. Stimson Papers, Box 145.
58. Bullitt, *For the President*, 529–45; Ickes Diary, 13 Dec. 1942.
59. Bullitt to FDR, 13 June 1942, Bullitt, *For the President*, 555.
60. Ickes Diary, 2 July 1944.
61. Bullitt, *Address*.
62. See above, note 25; John C. Wiley Papers (FDRL), Box 6, Bullitt, Wiley to Bullitt, 28 Jan. 1941; cf. Bullitt's response to personal attacks, Stimson Papers, Box 142, Bullitt to Stimson, 16 June, Stimson to Bullitt, 17 June, 18 June 1943.
63. Ickes Diary, 10 Oct. 1943.
64. Bullitt, *For the President*, 604–5.
65. *Life*, 14 Aug. 1944.
66. Haight, *American Aid to France*, 189–231.
67. Porter, *Seventy-sixth Congress*, 172–73.
68. Text for FDR speech, 3 Sept. 1940, U.S. Department of State, *Peace and War*, 565.
69. Ibid., 545–49; Bullitt to FDR and Hull, 31 May 1940, Bullitt, *For the President*, 445.
70. FDR to Reynaud, 14 June 1940, *FRUS* (1940), 1:248.
71. Hull's telegram to Chiefs of Diplomatic Missions in the American Republics, 17 June 1940, *FRUS* (1940), 5:180–81.
72. *FRUS* (1940), 2:513–16.
73. See also Bullitt's conversation with Stimson, 1 Aug. 1940, Stimson Diary.
74. Biddle to FDR, 1 July 1940, FDRL, PSF 39, France, 1940.
75. Murphy, *Diplomat among Warriors*, chapter 3.
76. The terms of the armistice were made available for American readers in *New York Times*, 26 June 1940.
77. Views as reported in telegrams from Lothian to F.O., 24 June 1940, FO 371 24258, A 3465 3465 45; 5 July 1940, FO 371 24321, C 7483 839 17; 12 July 1940, FO 371 24323, C 7795 1101 17; 27 June 1940, FO 371 24333, C 7418 7328 17.
78. Matthews to Hull, 14 Oct. 1940, *FRUS* 1940, 2:393.
79. Pétain, *Quatres années*, 62; on Montoire, see Paxton, *Vichy France*, 74–76.
80. FDR to Pétain, 24 Oct. 1940, *FRUS* (1940), 2:475.
81. Pétain to FDR, 2 Nov. 1940, ibid., 481–82.
82. Matthews to Hull, 27 Oct. 1940, ibid., 398.
83. Matthews to Hull, 4 Nov. 1940, ibid., 407.
84. Barnes to Hull, 15 Nov. 1940, ibid., 411.
85. Murphy to Hull, 9 Dec. 1940, ibid., 417.

86. Matthews to Hull, 16 Nov. 1940, ibid., 412–14.

87. Murphy to Hull, 14 Dec., 16 Dec. 1940, ibid., 422, 423; cf., concerning Laval's unpopularity, Matthews to Hull, 19 Nov. 1940, SD 740.0011 European War/6794.

88. Matthews to Hull, 18 Dec. 1940, ibid., 424.

89. Lothian to F.O., 21 Dec. 1940, FO 371 24263, A 5226 5226 45.

90. FDR to Leahy, 20 Dec. 1940, *FRUS* (1940), 2:425.

91. *Department of State Bulletin* 3, no. 61 (24 Aug. 1940): 138–39; for French misgivings before and after the Havana Conference, see *FRUS* (1940), 2:499–500, and 5:215, 230–31.

92. Churchill to Gen. Ismay, 16 May 1941, PREM 3, 178/1.

93. *FRUS* (1940), 2:505–36.

94. Welles memos, 20 July, 24 July 1940, ibid., 509–11.

95. Berle memos, 20 Apr., 9 Sept. 1940, ibid., 361, 516.

96. Ministry of Defence (Joint Intelligence Subcommittee) to Churchill, 17 May 1941, PREM 3, 178/1.

97. F.O. to Lothian, 18 Oct. 1940, FO 371 24333, C 10670 7327 17.

98. Hull memo, 30 Sept. 1940, *FRUS* (1940), 2:523.

99. *FRUS* (1940), 4:145, and for earlier agreements, 30–31.

100. Blum, ed., *Morgenthau Diaries: Years of Urgency*, 353, and chap. 10.

101. *FRUS* (1940), 4:40, 65.

102. Ibid., 29, 63–65, 80–81, 86–87, 100–101, and esp. 132–34.

103. Ibid., 65.

104. Quoted in French memo presented to U.S. chargé d'affaires, 19 Sept. 1940, ibid., 133; see also Baudouin, *Neuf mois*, 297.

105. Quoted in French memo cited above in note 104; see Charles-Roux, *Cinq mois tragiques*, 255.

106. State Department press release, 23 Sept. 1940, *Peace and War*, 573; cf. Lothian to Foreign Office, 13 Sept. 1940, FO 371 24353, C 10022 7407 17.

107. Hull: "Acquiescence may be a matter of necessity. Giving assent, however, is quite another matter," quoted in Langer and Gleason, *Challenge to Isolation*, 601; cf. Welles, refusing a French request to urge the Japanese to make their occupation only temporary: that "would be accepting the principle of it [the occupation]. But this would be a violation of the *status quo*, the maintenance of which we shall continue to insist upon," quoted in Langer and Gleason, *Undeclared War, 1940–1941*, 12.

108. See *FRUS* (1940), 4:100–101, 104–5.

109. Matthews to Hull, 19 Dec. 1940, *FRUS* (1940), 2:535.

110. See, e.g., Langer and Gleason, *Challenge to Isolation*, 573; Welles memo, 24 Sept. 1940, *FRUS* (1940), 2:590–91.

111. Felix Cole in Algiers to Hull, 18 Nov. 1940, *FRUS* (1940), 2:619.

112. Hull to Mallon, 7 Sept., 18 Nov. 1940, ibid., 641, 644.

113. For the reactions of colonial officials to the armistice, see the reports by American consuls in ibid., 570–79, and the discussion in Paxton, *Parades and Politics*, 68–71.

114. For Baudouin's comments, see State Department (SD) Decimal File (Record

Group 59, National Archives, Washington, D.C.) 740.0011 European War 1939/7070; for Pétain's and Boisson's comments, see *FRUS* (1940), 2:418–19, 519.

115. Ibid., 579–87.
116. Murphy to Hull, 12 Dec. 1940, ibid., 419.
117. Matthews to Hull, 8 Nov. 1940, ibid., 614–15.
118. Cole to Hull, 18 Oct. 1940, ibid., 597–99.
119. Goold to Hull, 31 Oct. 1940, ibid., 609.
120. Matthews to Hull, 8 Nov. 1940, ibid., 614–15.
121. Hull to Cole, 26 Oct. 1940, ibid., 604; Welles memo, 31 Oct. 1940, ibid., 608–9.
122. H. S. Villard memo (Division of Near Eastern Affairs), quoting Paul Guerin, assistant director of Moroccan Railways, 9 Dec. 1940, ibid., 627.
123. Hull to Murphy, 13 Dec. 1940, ibid., 420.
124. Hull to Joseph P. Kennedy, 5 Sept. 1940, ibid., 503; Lothian to F.O., 24 Aug. 1940, FO 371 24341, C 9148 7328 17.
125. From a French memo presented to Welles, 7 Oct. 1940, *FRUS* (1940), 2:386.
126. *FDR Press Conferences*, 15:489.
127. See note 80 above.
128. FDR to Leahy, 20 Dec. 1940, *FRUS* (1940), 2:428.
129. In a speech to American journalists, see *New York Times*, 21 Aug. 1940.
130. Murphy to Hull, 19 July 1940, *FRUS* (1940), 2:380.
131. For example, FDR's remarks at Philadelphia, 23 Oct. 1940, "It is for peace that I have worked and for peace that I shall work every day of my life," were headlined in Vichy newspapers, see ibid., 394 and n.
132. Matthews to Hull, 1 Nov. 1940, ibid., 399.
133. E.g., MacMurray (Ankara) to Hull and Welles, 12 Nov. 1940, SD 851.01/175; cf. Matthews to Hull, 25 Oct. 1940, *FRUS* (1940), 2:395.
134. Matthews to Hull, 14 Nov., 14 Oct. 1940, ibid., 405, 392.
135. For Bullitt's approval, see FDRL, Official File (OF), France 1940, Welles to FDR, 25 July 1940, and Ickes Diary, 22 Sept. 1940; for Murphy's, see *New York Herald Tribune*, 6 Sept. 1940; on Henry-Haye's early career, Henry-Haye, *La grande éclipse*, 13–156.
136. Henry-Haye, *La grande éclipse*, 85–86, 92–98, 101–3. For the spying rumors, see Berle, *Navigating the Rapids*, 345; de Roussy de Sales, *Making of Yesterday*, 162–3; Office of Strategic Services (OSS) report 25665C (Record Group 226, National Archives, Washington, D.C.) from a member of the French Embassy; *New York Times*, 11 Sept., 12 Sept., 12 Oct., and *PM* (New York), 28 Oct., 30 Oct., 1 Nov. 1940; and below, chapter 5.
137. For Henry-Haye's first meeting with FDR, see the marginally different accounts in Ickes, *Secret Diary*, 3:332, and de Roussy de Sales, *Making of Yesterday*, 162; for the meetings with Hull and Welles, *FRUS* (1940), 2:517, 521.
138. Welles memo, 31 Oct. 1940, 609.
139. Hull memo, 4 Nov. 1940, ibid., 400; cf. Harrison (Berne) to Hull, 11 Nov. 1940, SD 851.9111/65, for the use of the Swiss press to understand Vichy's policy.

140. Welles memo, 11 Dec. 1940, ibid., 532.
141. Matthews to Hull, 15 Nov., 19 Dec. 1940, ibid., 533; for Chauvel's views, Matthews to Hull, 15 Nov. 1940, SD 740.0011 European War 1939/6706.
142. Matthews to Hull, 26 Oct. 1940, ibid., 477.
143. Minute by A. Speaight, 21 Oct. 1940, FO 371 24361, C 12050 12050 17; Halifax to Churchill, 14 Oct. 1940, FO 371 24306, C 10760 45 17.
144. On British policy in 1940, see Bell, *A Certain Eventuality*; Thomas, *Britain and Vichy*, 5–87; Johnson, "Britain and France in 1940." On the proposal for Anglo-French Union, see Thomson, *Proposal for Anglo-French Union*; and Beloff, "The Anglo-French Union Project."
145. Lothian to F.O., 25 June, 27 June 1940, FO 371 24338, C 7418 7328 17, and FO 371 24352, C 7430 7407 17.
146. FO 371 24333, C 10646 7327 17.
147. Matthews to Hull, 11 Nov. 1940, *FRUS* (1940), 2:451.
148. Kennedy to Hull, 21 Oct., Johnson (London) to Hull, 10 Nov. 1940, ibid., 474, 484–85.
149. FO 371 20306, C 12601 45 17.
150. Memo by Wallace Murray (Division of Near Eastern Affairs), 27 Nov. 1940, *FRUS* (1940), 2:620.
151. Villard memo, 18 Dec. 1940, ibid., 634.
152. FO 371 24336, C 12384 7327 17.
153. Lothian to F.O., 28 Nov. 1940, ibid.
154. Chautemps, *Cahiers secrets*, 285–94, and, for Welles's testimony at his trial, 323–24; for Henry-Haye's hostility, see Henry-Haye, *La grande éclipse*, 381–84.
155. Langer and Gleason, *Challenge to Isolation*, 734–35 and n., and C. L. de Chambrun, *Shadows Lengthen*, 381–94. For FDR's comments, FDR to Welles, 16 March 1943, FDRL, PSF 94, Sumner Welles, State 1943, 4.
156. Monnet's memo to FDR, in Freedman, ed., *Roosevelt and Frankfurter: Their Correspondence*, 566–68, and Stimson Diary, 2 Dec. 1940.
157. Roosevelt, ed., *Roosevelt Letters*, 3:339–40.
158. Full biographical material is in FDRL, General Correspondence, 1940, Drawer 2, 16 Nov. 1940; see also below, chapter 3.
159. William D. Leahy Papers (LCMD), Diary, 22 Dec. 1940; War Notes 1, 3.
160. SD 123 Leahy William D./16¼, 30½; final instructions, FDR to Leahy, 20 Dec. 1940, *FRUS* (1940), 2:425–29.
161. Minute by Scott, 12 Aug. 1940, FO 371 24323, C 8601 1101 17.

CHAPTER 2

1. See, in particular, Gallup, *Gallup Poll*, vol. 1 (1935–48) (henceforth *Gallup*, followed by date of survey); Cantril and Strunk, *Public Opinion* (henceforth AIPO, standing for American Institute of Public Opinion, followed by date of survey); Cantril, "America Faces the War" (ms.); "Movements of Opinion in the United States in the First Year of the War, September 1939 to September 1940," compiled by Survey Department, British Press Service, New York, Oct. 1940,

in FO 371 24243, A 4696 131 45; Jacob, "Influences of World Events"; *Twohey Weekly Analysis of Newspaper Opinion* (1940).
2. *New York Herald Tribune: Tenth Annual Forum*, 3, 31, 107.
3. Rosenberg, "The Fall of Paris."
4. AIPO Poll, 22 Sept. 1940; see in general Cantril, "America Faces the War."
5. Rosenman, ed., *Public Papers and Addresses of Franklin D. Roosevelt*, 8:646.
6. Strout, *American Image*, 204; Adler, *The Isolationist Impulse*, chaps. 11, 12; Cantril, "America Faces the War," 404–5.
7. U.S. Department of State, *Peace and War*, 326–28.
8. Cited in Ekirch, *Ideologies and Utopias*, 208.
9. Divine, *Illusion of Neutrality*, 193–99.
10. Chatfield, *For Peace and Justice*, 112–17, 278–81; Doenecke, "The Non-Interventionism of the Left"; for a contemporary appraisal, see Masland, "The 'Peace' Groups Join Battle."
11. For example, Bausmann, *Let France Explain*.
12. Quoted in Jonas, *Isolationism in America*, 228.
13. Taylor, *Awakening from History*, 227.
14. Text of speech, 9 Feb. 1940, in the collection of transcripts of meetings of the Chicago Council on Foreign Relations, in the library of the University of Illinois at Chicago Circle.
15. Ibid., 12 Apr. 1940.
16. *New Republic*, 1 Apr. 1940, 423.
17. In the absence of available French sources this discussion draws heavily upon the study commissioned by the Institute for Propaganda Analysis at Yale University, published in Lavine and Wechsler, *War Propaganda*; see also Amaury, *Les deux premières expériences*; Richard de Rochemont, "France and Propaganda," *Life*, 25 Mar. 1940.
18. Lavine and Wechsler, *War Propaganda*, 234.
19. AIPO Polls, 28 Mar., 29 May 1940.
20. De Roussy de Sales, *Making of Yesterday*, 89.
21. Lavine and Wechsler, *War Propaganda*, 98–109.
22. Ibid. For an account of one such function, see "A Tribute to France," *New York Herald Tribune*, 20 Feb. 1940.
23. *Louisville Courier-Journal*, 14 Nov. 1939.
24. See, e.g., *New York Times, Wall Street Journal, Washington Post*, 20 Nov. 1939.
25. Bliven writing in *Boston Transcript*, 28 Nov. 1939.
26. See, e.g., dispatch of John Elliot to *New York Herald Tribune*, 21 Oct., and P. J. Philip to *New York Times*, 10 Nov. 1939.
27. 13 Nov. 1939.
28. 5 Nov. 1939.
29. *New York Herald Tribune*, 2 Nov., 23 Nov., 29 Nov. 1939.
30. De Roussy de Sales, *Making of Yesterday*, 147–48.
31. *Nation*, 18 May 1940, 618–23; see subsequent issues for discussion of what MacLeish had to say.
32. *New Republic*, 6 May 1940, 603–8.
33. 10 Nov. 1939.

34. 1 June 1940.
35. *New Republic*, 102, 17 June 1940, 808.
36. See above, chapter 1.
37. *New York Times*, 28 May 1940.
38. *Peace and War*, 549–53; see also British Library of Information (BLI) report no. 293, "Reynaud's Appeals for American Aid," 21 June 1940, in FO 371 24240, A 3427 131 45.
39. 16 June 1940.
40. In a review of Brogan, *France Under the Republic*, in *Nation*, 12 Oct. 1940, 338.
41. *Scribner's Commentator*, Jan. 1941, 13–19.
42. *Cong. Rec.*, 86, 76th Cong., 3d session, appendix, pt. 17, 5173–75.
43. 8 July 1940.
44. E.g., *New York Times*, 1 Sept., 20 Dec. 1940.
45. *PM* (New York), 13 Nov. 1940.
46. Melvin M. Fagen, "Liberalism and the French Defeat," *New Republic*, 2 Sept. 1940, 341.
47. Ehrman, "The Blum Experiment."
48. *New Republic*, 20 Jan. 1941, 86; see also the *Nation*, 2 Nov. 1940, 417.
49. Guérard's articles in *Nation*, 21 Sept., 19 Oct. 1940, 247–48, 367–68. For a hostile survey of how American liberals, in particular the *Nation*, criticized Anglo-French policies in the 1930s, see Martin, *American Liberalism and World Politics*, esp. 2:998.
50. Heinz Pol, "The Suicide of the Left," *Nation*, 13 July 1940.
51. *PM*, 21 Aug. 1940.
52. Taylor, "Democracy Demoralized."
53. *New York Herald Tribune*, 7 June 1940; see also D. Thompson, "The Maginot Line: A Fort in Action," *Current History*, June 1940, 51–52.
54. 9 July 1940; cf. *New York Herald Tribune*, 12 Aug., *Chicago News*, 3 June 1940.
55. 4 July 1940.
56. E.g., *Des Moines Register*, 20 Oct. 1940; for more about censorship, see BLI report no. 326, "Authoritarian France," 13 July 1940, in FO 371 24241, A 3628 131 45.
57. 2 Aug. 1940.
58. *New York Times*, 3 July, 12 July 1940.
59. Ibid., 5 Aug. 1940.
60. Ibid., 22 Nov. 1940.
61. BLI report no. 399, "Vichy Attempts to Court U.S. Opinion," 8 Sept. 1940, in FO 371 24242, A 4365 131 45.
62. 10 July 1940.
63. 7 July 1940.
64. 9 July 1940.
65. 18 Aug. 1940. On the Dakar incident in general, see BLI report no. 432, "Dakar," 3 Oct. 1940, in FO 371 24242, A 4364 131 45.
66. 17 Sept. 1940.
67. *Twohey Weekly Analysis of Newspaper Opinion*, week of 28 Sept. 1940.

68. *Nation*, 5 Oct. 1940, 285.
69. 26 Sept. 1940.
70. 30 Sept. 1940; and see above, note 61.
71. *New York Times*, 25 July 1940.
72. Quoted in Brown, "American Isolation," 30.
73. See Bruce Bliven, "The Road to Hysteria: 1940," *Virginia Quarterly Review* 16 (Spring, 1940): 190–201.
74. See above, note 17.
75. E.g., Frank C. Hanighen, "What England and France Think About Us," *Harper's Magazine*, Sept. 1939, esp. 383–85.
76. Raoul de Roussy de Sales, "America Looks at the War," *Atlantic Monthly*, Feb. 1940, 152.
77. See, in general, Fritsch-Estrangin, *New-York*, esp. 27–28; see also below, chapter 5.
78. *New York Times*, 16 July, 13 Aug., 4 Sept. 1940; see also below, chapter 5.
79. *Christian Science Monitor*, 31 July, *Washington Star*, 21 Aug. 1940; Murphy in *New York Times*, 6 Sept. 1940.
80. Henry-Haye, *La grande éclipse*, 156–62.
81. See above, chapter 1, note 136.
82. 12 Oct. 1940.
83. Quoted in British Press Service (BPS) report no. 18, 29 Oct. 1940, FO 371 24243, A 4694 131 45.
84. See above, chapter 1, note 155.
85. De Chambrun, *I Saw France Fall*, 114, 117, 122, 126.
86. *Chicago Tribune*, 19 Oct. 1940; Stanton B. Leeds, "De Chambrun—Soldier of France," *Scribner's Commentator*, Jan. 1941.
87. Stimson Diary, 17 Oct. 1940.
88. 17 Oct. 1940.
89. Telegram, Lippmann to Cordell Hull, 18 July 1940, Walter Lippmann Papers (Sterling Library, Yale University), Box 75, Folder 88.
90. *New York Times*, 26 June 1940.
91. See White, *Seeds of Discord*, 114–21; *New York Times*, 29 Sept. 1940; and see below, chapter 5.
92. De Gaulle–de Sieyès correspondence in FO 371 24342, C 10276 7328 17.
93. See letter from Strathallan in New York to Oliver Harvey at the Ministry of Information, 30 Sept. 1940, "The French in America and the propaganda possibilities," FO 371 24343, C 10521 7328 17.
94. London, 1940.
95. L. H. Leach (in New York Consulate) to British Embassy, Washington, 24 Aug. 1940, FO 371 24342, C 10276 7328 17.
96. *New York Times*, 23 Aug. 1940.
97. Séguin to S. T. Early (White House), 19 Oct. 1940, in FDRL, OF 203 A, 1940.
98. See letter from Assistant Attorney General Wendell Berge to Hull, 20 April 1941, SD 851.202011/25.
99. Séguin to Hull, 10 April 1941, SD 851.202011/21.
100. Strathallan to Harvey, 16 Aug. 1940, FO 371 24341, C 8994 7328 17.
101. Strathallan to Harvey, 7 Aug. 1940, FO 371 24341, C 8528 7328 17.

102. Minute by Frank Darvall (Deputy Director, American Division, Ministry of Information), 2 July 1940, FO 371 24230, A 3508 26 45.
103. Geneviève Tabouis, "Credo of a Frenchwoman," *Current History*, Sept. 1940, 19–20; see also BPS report no. 78 on her lecture tour, 3 Dec. 1940, FO 371 24244, A 4995 131 45.
104. 23 July 1940.
105. *Greensboro* (N.C.) *Record*, 6 Aug.; *New York Daily Worker*, 23 July 1940. See also *New York Evening Post*, 23 July; *Miami Herald*, 13 Aug.; *Birmingham* (Ala.) *Herald*, 27 July; *Chicago Journal of Commerce*, 3 Aug. 1940.
106. *Nation*, 24 Aug. 1940; see also Martin, *American Liberalism and World Politics*, 2:1010–11.
107. *New York Times*, 17 June 1940.
108. *New York Herald Tribune, New York Sun, New York Post, Boston Globe, Philadelphia Enquirer, Baltimore Sun, Washington Post*, 5 July 1940.
109. *Washington Post*, 26 July; *Christian Science Monitor*, 12 Aug.; *Philadelphia Enquirer*, 9 Sept. 1940.
110. 9 Aug. 1940.
111. 27 Oct. 1940.
112. De Roussy de Sales, *Making of Yesterday*, 149.
113. *Time*, 30 Dec. 1940, 17–18.
114. All quotations, 16 Dec. 1940.
115. *PM*, 15 Jan. 1941.
116. Lippmann, *Public Opinion*, 125.
117. See Cantril, Rugg, and Williams, "America Faces the War," 655.
118. *Gallup*, 2 June, 15 Sept. 1940.
119. Ibid., 30 June, 5 Sept. 1940.
120. Ibid., 8 Dec. 1940.
121. Ibid., 19 May, 2 Dec., 7 July, 30 Dec. 1940.
122. Cantril, "America Faces the War," esp. 405–7; see also Leigh, *Mobilising Consent*, 16, 21.
123. Cantril, "America Faces the War," 390.
124. Ibid., 406.
125. Friedlander, *Prelude to Downfall*, 138–39.
126. See Cantril, Rugg, and Williams, "America Faces the War," 651–56.
127. See Divine, *Foreign Policy and U.S. Presidential Elections, 1940–48*, 24–25.
128. Jonas, *Isolationism in America*, chapter 5.
129. Johnson, *Battle against Isolation*, chapters 3, 4; Chadwin, *Hawks of World War II*, chapters 2, 4.
130. Cole, *America First*, 131–54.
131. *New York Times*, 11 Aug. 1940.
132. 21 Dec. 1940.
133. Fight for Freedom Papers (Princeton University Library), Miscellaneous Publications, release of 27 Oct. 1940; the White committee had made such a scheme one of its earliest proposals, see Tuttle, "Aid-to-the-Allies Short-of-War versus American Intervention, 1940," esp. 844.
134. *Chicago Daily News*, 11 June 1940, reproduced in Johnson, *Battle against Isolation*, 86.

135. Taylor, *Awakening from History*, 228. See also Taylor, "Democracy Demoralized"; Taylor, Snow, and Janeway, *Smash Hitler's International*; Taylor, *Strategy of Terror*.

136. Taylor, *Awakening from History*, 228.

137. Taylor, *Strategy of Terror* (2d ed.), v, vi, 239–40, 273.

138. "Indiscretions of a Democratic Well-Poisoner" is the title of chapter 17 of *Awakening from History*. See, in general, "A French Officer," "Bolstering National Morale"; Allport, "Liabilities and Assets in Civilian Morale."

139. Robinson, *Roosevelt Leadership*, 253–55; Burns, *Roosevelt: The Soldier of Freedom*, 36–40. See also Burke, "The Election of 1940," esp. 383–84; Divine, *Foreign Policy and U.S. Presidential Elections*, 84–89.

140. *New York Times*, 23 Oct. 1940.

141. Hoover, *Addresses upon the American Road, 1940–41*, 251–52; Hoover, "It Needn't Happen Here," *American Mercury*, July 1940, 263–70.

142. Both cited in Parmet and Hecht, *Never Again*, 214, 222.

143. Quoted in Divine, *Foreign Policy and U.S. Presidential Elections*, 49–50; *New York Times*, 20 Aug., 30 Aug., 15 Sept. 1940.

144. *New York Herald Tribune*, 18 Sept.; see also Arthur Krock in *New York Times*, 17 Sept. 1940.

145. *PM*, 25 June 1940.

146. Quoted in Divine, *Foreign Policy and U.S. Presidential Elections*, 63, 81; *New York Times*, 8 Oct., 24 Oct. 1940.

147. Barnard, *Wendell Willkie*, 269–320, 347–48, 411–15, 480–84.

148. William Henry Chamberlain, "France in the Shadows," *Current History*, Sept. 1940, 21–24.

149. *Harper's Magazine*, Oct. 1940, 49–60.

150. *Christian Century*, 30 Apr. 1941, 558–90.

151. New York, 1940, v.

152. André Maurois, "The Case for France," *Life*, 6 Jan. 1941, 62–64.

153. *Newsweek*, 19 Aug. 1940.

154. *Saturday Evening Post*, 23 Mar. 1940, quoted in Strout, *American Image of the Old World*, 207.

155. *Cong. Rec.*, 86, 76th Cong., 3d session, pt. 8, 8640–41, 8 June 1940.

156. Special Report to Congress, "Investigation of Un-American Propaganda Activities in the U.S.," 20–21, cited in Ogden, *The Dies Committee*, 230; *Cong. Rec.*, 87, 77th Cong., 1st session, pt. 1, 898, 11 Feb. 1941.

157. John T. Flynn, "Plain Economics," *Washington News*, 12 July 1940.

158. *Cong. Rec.*, 87, 77th Cong., 1st session, pt. 3, 2684, 27 March 1941.

159. Rosenman, *Public Papers and Addresses of FDR*, 1940, 284–85 (press conference), 672 (Four Freedoms).

160. Lippmann to Mrs. Robert Lovett, American Friends of France, Inc., 13 May 1940, Lippmann Papers, Box 51, Folder 55.

161. Fight for Freedom Papers, Box 5, questionnaire by Henry Sloane Coffin, Nov. 1940.

162. Armstrong to Frankfurter, 27 Nov., 4 Dec. 1940, Felix Frankfurter Papers, LCMD, Box 21.

CHAPTER 3

1. William D. Leahy Diary, LCMD, 29 May 1943.
2. In the absence of a biography of Leahy, information comes from *Who Was Who in America*, vol. 3; the biographical sketch in FDRL, General Correspondence, 1940, Drawer 2, 16 Nov. 1940; and various contemporary articles, e.g., *Life*, 28 Sept. 1942; *Time*, 28 May 1945; and, more critically, *Nation*, 1 Aug. 1942; and *New Republic*, 9 Nov. 1942.
3. E.g., FDR to Leahy, 26 June 1941, reprinted in Leahy, *I Was There*, 533–34.
4. Welles, *Seven Major Decisions*, 56.
5. Ickes Diary, 9 Mar. 1940, 4 June 1939, 1 Dec. 1940.
6. Ibid., 27 Jan. 1940.
7. Ibid., 12 June 1940.
8. Ibid., 9 Mar., 12 June 1940.
9. Ibid., 1 Aug. 1942.
10. Leahy Diary, 22 Dec. 1940.
11. FDR to Leahy, 20 Dec. 1940, *FRUS* (1940), 2:425–29.
12. FDR to Leahy, 16 Nov. 1940, FDRL, PSF, France 1940, Box 5.
13. FDR to Pétain, 19 Dec. 1940, ibid.
14. H. F. Matthews to Hull, SD 123 Leahy, William D/2.
15. H. F. Matthews memo, Oct. 1941, in Leahy Diary, 1942 volume.
16. Welles to Leahy, 6 Feb. 1941, ibid.
17. Welles to Leahy, 15 Aug. 1941, ibid.
18. Leahy to FDR, 25 Jan. 1941, reprinted in Leahy, *I Was There*, 520–22; Leahy to Hull, 11 Jan., *FRUS* (1941), 2:93–96; Leahy to Hull, 6 Feb., ibid., 110–12.
19. Leahy Diary, 23 Jan. 1941.
20. Leahy to FDR, 25 Jan. 1941; see above, note 18.
21. Ibid.
22. Leahy Diary, 3 Mar. 1941.
23. Leahy to Hull, 18 Mar. 1941, *FRUS* (1941), 2:129.
24. Leahy to Hull, 18 Apr. 1941, ibid., 151.
25. Leahy to Hull, 4 May 1941, ibid., 160.
26. Leahy to Hull, 13 May 1941, ibid., 167.
27. Leahy to FDR, 21 April 1941, in Leahy, *I Was There*, 529–30.
28. Hull to FDR, 13 May 1941, *FRUS* (1941), 2:166; the file copy, SD 711.51/165a, indicates that the memo was drafted by J. C. Dunn, the State Department's adviser on political relations.
29. A full account, with press cuttings, of Leahy's visit to Marseilles is in William Peck (American Consul, Marseilles) to Hull, 23 April 1941, SD 123 Leahy, William D./50; see also Leahy, *I Was There*, 37–39, 47–49.
30. Hull to FDR, 13 May 1941, SD 123 Leahy/William D./60.
31. Leahy Diary, 13 May 1941.
32. Leahy to FDR, 26 May 1941, in Leahy, *I Was There*, 531.
33. Leahy Diary, 16 July 1941.
34. Leahy to Hull, 15 May 1941, *FRUS* (1941), 2:180–81.
35. Leahy Diary, 22 May 1941.

36. The terms have since been published in Langer, *Our Vichy Gamble*, 402–12.
37. Leahy to Hull, 13 May 1941, *FRUS* (1941), 2:167–70.
38. Memo by J. C. Dunn, 16 May 1941, ibid., 172.
39. *Department of State Bulletin*, no. 99 (17 May 1941): 584.
40. Hull memo, 19 May 1941, *FRUS* (1941), 2:174; see also Hull, *Memoirs*, 2:959.
41. Hull memo, 20 May 1941, *FRUS* (1941), 2:177–80.
42. Text of Chautemps's letter in Leahy Papers, Correspondence File, Welles to Leahy, 24 May 1941.
43. Hull, *Memoirs*, 2:959.
44. Ibid., 963.
45. On the French cabinet discussions, see Langer, *Our Vichy Gamble*, 157–59; Hytier, *Two Years of French Foreign Policy*, 264–65, and Paxton, *Vichy France*, 118–22; nowhere does American aid to North Africa emerge as a telling consideration.
46. Leahy to Welles, 11 June 1941, Leahy Diary, 1942 volume.
47. Leahy Diary, 21 July 1941.
48. Ibid., 9 Oct. 1941.
49. Ibid., 27 Oct. 1941.
50. Ibid., 21 Nov. 1941.
51. Ibid., 12 Dec. 1941.
52. Ibid., 27 Jan. 1942.
53. Leahy to Hull, 19 Nov. 1941, *FRUS* (1941), 2:464–66.
54. Hull to Leahy, 20 Nov.; Leahy to Hull, 22 Nov. 1941, ibid., 469–70, 474.
55. Leahy, *I Was There*, 37–40.
56. Leahy to Hull, 18 Apr. 1941, *FRUS* (1941), 2:295; Leahy, *I Was There*, 40.
57. Leahy Diary, 12 Aug. 1941.
58. Leahy to Welles, 29 Sept. 1941, Leahy Diary, 1942 volume.
59. Leahy Diary, 21 Feb. 1942.
60. Churchill to FDR, 3 Jan. 1941, *FRUS* (1941), 2:89; see also telegrams of 12 Mar., 29 Mar., ibid., 119–20, 134.
61. Leahy Diary, 18 Mar. 1941; Leahy to FDR, 19 Mar. 1941, in Leahy, *I Was There*, 527; Leahy to Hull, 18 Mar. 1941, *FRUS* (1941), 2:130.
62. Rosenman, *Public Papers and Addresses of FDR*, 9:640.
63. Leahy Diary, 21 Mar. 1941.
64. Leahy to Hull, 12 Sept. 1941, *FRUS* (1941), 2:431.
65. Leahy to FDR, 28 July 1941, in Leahy, *I Was There*, 534–36.
66. For a summary of American information about the Riom trials, see "The French 'War-Guilt' Trial at Riom," OSS records, Research and Analysis Branch report no. 279.
67. Leahy to Hull, 4 June 1941, SD 711.51/157.
68. Ibid.
69. Welles memo, 27 Dec. 1941, *FRUS* (1941), 2:205.
70. Matthews to Atherton, 26 June 1941, SD 711.51/174.
71. Leahy to Hull, 6 Nov. 1941, SD 711.51/174.
72. Leahy to Welles, 30 Mar. 1942, Leahy Diary, 1942 volume.
73. Matthews memo to embassy staff, 26 June 1941, SD 124.516/376.

74. Steele, *The First Offensive*, 72.
75. Matthews letter, 17 Jan. 1945 (lent by the writer); a brief extract is in *FRUS: Washington and Casablanca*, 68.
76. *FRUS: Washington and Casablanca*, 234–35.
77. Ibid., 244.
78. Ibid., 235–36; Weygand, *Recalled to Service*, 391–92.
79. Leahy to FDR, 25 Jan. 1942, in Leahy, *I Was There*, 548–49; Leahy to Hull, 22 Jan. 1942, SD 123 AT 4/425; Leahy Diary, 22 Jan., 25 Jan. 1942.
80. Weygand, *Recalled to Service*, 392; Bankwitz, *Maxime Weygand*, 352.
81. Leahy Diary, 27 Jan. 1942; Leahy to Hull, 27 Jan. 1942, *FRUS* (1942), 2:124–25.
82. Leahy to Welles, 30 June, Welles to Leahy, 21 July 1941, Leahy Diary, 1942 volume.
83. E.g., *FRUS* (1941), 2:466–68, 470–72, 479–81.
84. Leahy to Welles, 10 Dec. 1941, ibid.
85. Leahy to Hull, 12 Dec. 1941, SD 124.51/231.
86. Hull to Leahy, 13 Dec. 1941, SD 124.51/232a.
87. Leahy to FDR, 20 Feb. 1942, in Leahy, *I Was There*, 550–52.
88. *FRUS* (1942), 2:131–34; Leahy Diary, 11 Feb. 1942.
89. FDR to Leahy, n.d., in Leahy, *I Was There*, 552–53.
90. Leahy to Welles, 4 Mar., 11 Mar. 1942, ibid., 140–46, 150–51.
91. Welles to Leahy, 27 Mar. 1942, *FRUS* (1942), 2:160–61.
92. Memo of Atherton-Leahy telephone conversation, 15 Apr. 1942, SD 124.51/236a.
93. Welles to Leahy, 15 Apr. 1942, *FRUS* (1942), 2:170.
94. Leahy to Hull, 27 Apr. 1942, SD Leahy/William D./102.
95. Leahy Diary, 27 Apr. 1942.
96. Ibid., 28 Apr. 1942.
97. Ibid., 22 Dec. 1943.
98. Ibid., 20 Nov. 1942.
99. Ibid., 22 Aug. 1945.
100. Ickes Diary, 28 July 1945.
101. Leahy Diary, 31 Mar. 1943.

CHAPTER 4

1. E.g. Henry-Haye, *La grande éclipse*, 173–79.
2. Fritsch-Estrangin, *New-York*, 42–48.
3. *PM*, 27 Oct., 28 Oct., 30 Oct., 1 Nov. 1940; *New York Herald Tribune*, 21 Aug.–4 Sept. 1941.
4. Henry-Haye, *La grande éclipse*, 165–72, 284–90.
5. OSS report no. 25565C from an unidentified member of the embassy; letter of resignation of Hervé Alphand, financial attaché, July 1941, SD 701.511/806.
6. FDRL, PSF, Box 162, Binder 4 to Box 164, Binder 13.
7. Donovan to FDR, 27 Apr. 1942, FDRL, PSF, Box 163, Binder 9.

8. John Wiley (of OSS) to Morgenthau, 31 July 1941, Henry M. Morgenthau Diaries, FDRL.

9. Henry-Haye, *La grande éclipse*, 172.

10. Welles memo, 11 Mar. 1942, SD 701.4111/1334.

11. Henry-Haye, *La grande éclipse*; de Gaulle, *War Memoirs*; Muselier, *De Gaulle contre le gaullisme*; Soustelle, *Envers et contre tout*; Bouthillier, *Le drame de Vichy*; Peyrouton, *Souvenirs*; Pucheu, *Ma vie*.

12. Giraud, *Un seul but*.

13. Henry-Haye, *La grande éclipse*, 275.

14. Ibid., 366–67.

15. Ibid., 173–79, 229, 223.

16. Welles memo, 11 Dec. 1940, SD 851.01/202.

17. Henry-Haye, *La grande éclipse*, 187–88.

18. Ibid., 78–79.

19. Ibid., 347–53; cf. Murphy, *Diplomat among Warriors*, 264–65.

20. Henry-Haye, *La grande éclipse*, 153. For Bullitt's recommendation, see also Welles to FDR, 25 July 1940, FDRL, OF, Box 203, France, 1940, and the note on Henry-Haye, FDRL, PSF, Box 5, France, 1940.

21. Henry-Haye, *La grande éclipse*, 246, 248, 162, 234 (in order of citation).

22. De Gaulle, *War Memoirs*, 1:207.

23. For Saint-Quentin's popularity, see *Washington Post*, 31 July 1940.

24. Henry-Haye, *La grande éclipse*, 381–84. See Fritsch-Estrangin, *New-York*, 122–25, for an important, hitherto unpublished interview with Chautemps in 1944.

25. *Annuaire diplomatique et consulaire*, 1941, passim.

26. A "Liste du personnel des affaires étrangères en fonctions aux Etats-Unis au moment de la rupture diplomatique," kindly supplied to the author by Martial de la Fournière, Directeur des Archives et de la Documentation, Ministère des Affaires Etrangères.

27. See, in general, the resignations and statements of intent in *New York Times*, 4 Sept. 1940, 15 June 1941, 23 Apr. 1942.

28. Henry-Haye, *La grande éclipse*, 92–98; Griffiths, *Pétain*, 200–203.

29. Henry-Haye, *La grande éclipse*, 42–47.

30. Ibid., 80–90, 101–3; Hytier in *Two Years of French Foreign Policy*, 193, has noted Henry-Haye's articles in *Cahiers Franco-Allemands* (Paris, 1937): "Zwei Wege und die Ziel: der Friede" (45–49), and "Unser Glaube an eine Deutsch-Französiche Verständigung" (172–80).

31. *New York Times*, 2 Mar. 1942.

32. De Chambrun and de Chambrun, eds., *France during the German Occupation*, 1330–35.

33. *Washington Star*, 21 Aug. 1940.

34. Henry-Haye, *La grande éclipse*, 17ff.

35. Ibid., 54–59.

36. Leahy to Hull, 27 April 1942, *FRUS* (1942), 2:181; see also Tuck (chargé d'affaires in Vichy) to Hull, 5 May, 13 June 1942, ibid., 700, 188.

37. Henry-Haye, *La grande éclipse*, 280–82; Welles memo, 11 Aug. 1942, *FRUS* (1942), 2:193–94; and, for an analysis of the speech itself, Warner, *Pierre Laval*, 301–3.

38. Hull, *Memoirs*, 1:847.
39. Bullitt to Hull, 1 July 1940, *FRUS* (1940), 2:468.
40. Vansittart minute, 16 Oct. 1940, FO 371 24354, C 11132/7407/17.
41. De Gaulle, *Discours aux français*, 217, press conference of 27 May 1942.
42. WSC minute (n.d., in response to Vansittart minute; see above, note 40), PREM 3, 184/1.
43. Chautemps, *Cahiers secrets*, 285–94; Fritsch-Estrangin, *New-York*, 115–26. See also above, note 8.
44. E.g., Welles to Ray Atherton (acting chief of the Division of European Affairs), 29 Mar. 1941, SD 711.51/146½; Hull to Leahy, 18 May 1941, SD 740.0011 European War 1939/11115b.
45. See, in general, the file on Chautemps in FDRL, PSF, Box 5042, especially Welles to FDR, 15 Oct. 1941.
46. See above, note 24.
47. E.g., Chautemps to Welles, 13 Oct. 1941, SD 851.00/2404¼; Chautemps to Welles, 15 Oct. 1942, SD 851.01/721; Chautemps to Welles, 2 Feb. 1943, SD 740.0011 European War 1939/27852.
48. Matthews (chargé d'affaires in Vichy) to Hull, 15 Nov. 1940, *FRUS* (1940), 2:409; cf. ibid., 403.
49. According to the reports cited above, notes 5, 8.
50. Welles memo, 30 Apr. 1941, Breckinridge Long Papers, LCMD, Box 211, Folder Undersecretary, Mr. Welles, 1940–42.
51. Welles memo, 19 Feb. 1941, SD 741.51/465.
52. Hull memo, 2 May 1941, SD 740.0011 European War/10664.
53. Murphy to Welles, 12 Aug. 1941, SD 701.5111/811; for Esteva's conversion, Childs (chargé d'affaires in Tangier) to Hull, 14 June 1941, *FRUS* (1941), 2:381; for Monick's dismissal, Leahy to Hull, 26 July, Childs to Hull, 29 Aug. 1941, ibid., 402–4, 423–24.
54. Welles to Murphy, 18 Aug. 1941, SD 701.5111/811; for Leahy's espousal of Requin, see Leahy, *I Was There*, 115.
55. Murphy to Welles, 24 Aug. 1941, SD 701.5111/815.
56. Leahy to Hull, 26 Sept. 1941, SD 701.5111/839.
57. Ibid.
58. Leahy to Hull, 13 Oct., 30 Oct. 1941, SD 701.5111/846, 848.
59. *New York Times*, 6 Nov. 1941.
60. See above, note 6.
61. Adolf A. Berle Diary, FDRL, 24 Jan. 1942.
62. Berle to Hoover, 13 Jan. 1943, SD 851.20211 Leger, Alexis/7. Despite the strange phrasing, Berle's meaning is clear.
63. Breckinridge Long memo, 8 July 1941, Long Papers, Box 195, Folder on France.
64. War Dept. to Berle, 31 July 1941, SD 851.20211/36.
65. Justice Dept. to Berle, 16 Sept. 1941, SD 701.5111/841.
66. ONI report, "French colony and consulate in Los Angeles," 16 April 1942, SD 851.20211/93.
67. Hoover to Berle, 24 Nov. 1942, SD 702.5111/1046½.

68. E.g., Fritsch-Estrangin, *New-York*, 42–43, 71, and see the press speculation cited above, note 3.
69. Hoover to Berle, 5 Oct., 15 Oct. 1940, SD 701.5111/723, 1025; also 26 Oct. 1940, 800.20211/16; 5 May, 12 Aug. 1942, 800.20211/851, 924; and ONI report, 23 Oct. 1941, 851.20211/50.
70. OSS report no. 173186C, 9 Jan. 1942.
71. See Paxton, *Vichy France*, 340–41.
72. See above, note 69, and Fritsch-Estrangin, *New-York*, 89.
73. See above, note 27; Alphand's letter of resignation was passed to the State Dept. on 2 July 1941, SD 701.5111/806.
74. Welles memo, 8 April 1942, *FRUS* (1942), 2:558–59.
75. Hull memo, 11 May 1942, ibid., 627–29.
76. Welles memo, 11 Aug. 1942, ibid., 193–94.
77. Welles memo, 29 Oct. 1942, ibid., 408.
78. Henry-Haye, *La grande éclipse*, 315.
79. Ibid., 316–21, 327–28.
80. Long memos, 9 Nov., 15 Nov., 27 Nov. 1942, Long Papers, Box 210, Folder on representation of French interests in the U.S.
81. E.g., Long memo, 18 Mar. 1943, ibid.
82. Long memo, 22 June 1943, ibid.
83. Copy in S. Reber to J. C. Dunn, 29 Dec. 1944, SD 740.0011 EW 1939/12-2944.
84. *New York Times*, 11 Jan. 1941.
85. *New York Herald Tribune*, 6 Dec. 1940.
86. *New York Times*, 6 Dec. 1940.
87. 12 Dec. 1940.
88. 6 Mar. 1941.
89. *New York Times*, 6 Mar. 1941.
90. See above, chapter 2, note 81.
91. E.g., *Scribner's Commentator*, 9 Jan. 1941, 13–19.
92. E.g., *Louisville Courier-Journal*, 15 Oct. 1940.
93. E.g., *New York City News*, 4 Oct. 1940.
94. (London) *Daily Herald*, 26 Feb. 1941.
95. 6 Mar. 1941.
96. 7 Mar. 1941.
97. Original text in Fight for Freedom Papers (Princeton University Library), Miscellaneous Publications.
98. De Roussy de Sales, *Making of Yesterday*, 184.
99. See in particular Henry-Haye's press conference reported in *New York Times*, 16 Oct., the articles in *PM*, 27 Oct. and 1 Nov., and Henry-Haye's letter to the editor, 30 Oct. 1940.
100. Hyde, *The Quiet Canadian*, 95–103.
101. Replies of Henry-Haye and Musa in *New York Herald Tribune*, 3 Sept., 4 Sept. 1941.
102. *New Republic*, 18 Aug. 1941.
103. *Des Moines Register*, 14 Sept. 1941.

104. *New York Herald Tribune*, 10 Sept. 1941.
105. Ibid., 1 Oct. 1941.
106. Ibid., 4 Sept. 1941.
107. Quoted in OSS report no. 173186C, 9 Jan. 1942.

CHAPTER 5

1. See the analysis by W. Henry Cooke, "Writers' Inquest on France," *Current History*, Feb. 1942, 560–62.
2. Raoul Aglion, "Rapport sur la régression de l'enseignement du français aux Etats-Unis," 20 Jan. 1943, Comité d'histoire de la deuxième guerre mondiale, Paris (CHDGM).
3. "The French Press in the United States," memo by Foreign Nationalities Branch of OSS, 31 Oct. 1944, OSS records (Record Group 165, National Archives, Suitland, Maryland), Box 1959.
4. "Considérations sur la colonie française aux Etats-Unis," n.d., CHDGM.
5. Fritsch-Estrangin, *New-York*, passim.
6. *New York Times*, 14 Dec. 1941.
7. Leger to Archibald MacLeish, 4 Dec. 1940, Perse, *Oeuvres complètes*, 936–37.
8. Berle to Hull, 3 Sept. 1941, Adolf Berle Papers (FDRL), Box 58, Folder Hull, memoranda, July–Dec. 1941.
9. Foreign Office review of relations with de Gaulle, 1940–43, PREM 3, 121/5.
10. Churchill interview with de Gaulle, 12 Sept. 1941, PREM 3, 120/2.
11. *Chicago Daily News*, 27 Aug. 1941; Desmond Morton to Churchill, 28 Aug. 1941, PREM 3, 120/1.
12. Churchill to Eden, 27 Aug. 1941, PREM 3, 120/5.
13. See above, note 11.
14. Churchill to de Gaulle, 2 Sept. 1941, PREM 3, 120/5.
15. Churchill to Morton, 1 Sept. 1941, PREM 3, 120/10A.
16. See above, note 10.
17. Churchill interview with de Gaulle, 1 Oct. 1941, PREM 3, 120/3.
18. Full correspondence in PREM 3, 120/4.
19. *New York Herald Tribune*, 14 Nov. 1940.
20. *New York Times*, 7 Dec. 1940.
21. *Christian Science Monitor*, 8 Nov. 1940.
22. E.g., ibid., 18 Dec.; *Atlanta Constitution*, 19 Nov.; *New York Times*, 5 Dec. 1940.
23. De Gaulle to de Sieyès and Garreau-Dombasle, 9 Jan. 1941, FO 371 28328, Z 228 56 17.
24. De Roussy de Sales, *Making of Yesterday*, 183.
25. De Kérillis, *De Gaulle dictateur*; see also *Pour la victoire* (New York), 1 May 1943.
26. De Kérillis to de Gaulle, 17 Feb. 1941, FO 371 28319, Z 1998 56 17.
27. De Gaulle to de Roussy de Sales, 12 Aug. 1940, CHDGM ("la décomposition voulue de la patrie").
28. Garreau-Dombasle to de Gaulle, 19 May 1941, FO 371 28320, Z 4082 56 17.

29. De Sieyès to de Gaulle, 19 May 1941, FO 371 28320, Z 4173 56 17.
30. Témoignage de Raoul Aglion, 6 Dec. 1948, CHDGM.
31. See above, chapter 4.
32. Hankey minute, 21 May 1941, to telegram cited above in note 28.
33. R. D. Barclay to Michael Huxley (Inter-allied Information Centre, New York), 10 July 1941, FO 371 28322, Z 5706 56 17.
34. Huxley to Barclay, 4 July 1941, ibid.
35. Témoignage de Mme Pleven, 12 Dec. 1948, CHDGM.
36. "France Libre Unie," report, 18 Feb. 1942, CHDGM; *New York Times*, 25 Apr. 1941.
37. Témoignage de Raoul Aglion, 6 Dec. 1948, CHDGM.
38. De Gaulle to Garreau-Dombasle, 17 Feb. 1941, FO 371 28328, Z 1128 56 17.
39. E.g., *New York Herald Tribune*, 17 May, 24 May 1941.
40. De Gaulle to de Sieyès, 21 May 1941, FO 371 28319, Z 1674 56 17.
41. De Gaulle to Garreau-Dombasle, 27 May 1941, FO 371 28320, Z 4082 56 17.
42. De Gaulle to Garreau-Dombasle, 8 June, and to de Sieyès, 13 June 1941, FO 371 28321, 2 5285, Z 4812 56 17.
43. See above, chapter 3.
44. Morton to Mack, 9 May 1941, FO 371 28436, Z 3735 368 17.
45. Somerville-Smith to Morton, 16 May 1941, FO 371 28320, Z 3945 56 17.
46. Halifax to F.O., 22 May 1941, FO 371 28320, Z 4286 56 17; cf. Hull memo, 21 May, *FRUS* (1941), 2:180.
47. Christopher Bramwell minute, 6 June 1941, FO 371 28321, Z 4681 56 17.
48. Markham, *America Next*.
49. Bergman to Eden, 30 June 1941, FO 371 28322, Z 6652 56 17.
50. Bergman to Churchill, 3 July 1941, FO 371 28323, Z 6802 56 17.
51. FDRL, PPF 5237: especially Bergman to Eleanor Roosevelt, 17 Apr. 1941; Bergman to Col. M. McIntyre, 31 Aug. 1940; Ickes to FDR, 30 Apr. 1941; Bergman to Ickes, 16 Apr. 1941; Bergman to McIntyre, 13 Feb. 1941. See also PSF 115, Bergman to Ickes, 4 Feb. 1941; Ickes Papers, Boxes 377–79, War, Bergman files.
52. Pleven to de Gaulle, 19 July, de Gaulle to Pleven, 3 Aug., Pleven to de Gaulle, 6 Aug. 1941, FO 371 28322, Z 6342, Z 7174 56 17.
53. Bergman to de Saint-André, 7 May 1941, Ickes Papers, Box 378, War, Bergman, Folder 9.
54. Témoignage de Raoul Aglion, 6 Dec. 1948, CHDGM.
55. Bergman to Ickes, 19 June 1941, Ickes Papers, Box 378, War, Bergman, Folder 10.
56. Ickes to Bergman, 24 June 1941, ibid.
57. Bergman to Eden, 1 Aug. 1941, FO 371 29322, Z 7174 56 17, which includes the text of the exchange between Bergman and de Saint-André.
58. FDRL, PPF 5237, Bergman to FDR, 14 Dec. 1941.
59. Biographies of the members of the delegation were wired by Pleven to de Gaulle, 19 Sept. 1941, FO 371 28324, Z 8043 56 17.
60. Témoignage de Mme Aglion, 21 Dec. 1948, CHDGM.
61. De Roussy de Sales, *Making of Yesterday*, 226.
62. Ibid., 223.

63. Pleven to de Gaulle, 19 Sept. 1941, FO 371 28324, Z 8042 56 17.
64. De Gaulle to Pleven, 2 July 1941, FO 371 28322, Z 5631 56 17.
65. Morton to Speaight, 14 Aug. 1941, FO 371 28323, Z 6998 56 17.
66. Hankey minute, 30 Aug. 1941, FO 371 28323, Z 7355 56 17.
67. See Pleven to de Gaulle, 19 Sept. 1941, FO 371 28324, Z 8042 56 17.
68. Butler to F.O., 30 July 1941, FO 371 28323, Z 6682 56 17.
69. Ibid., and Speaight minute, 10 Aug. 1941.
70. Somerville-Smith (on liaison with Free French h.q. in London) to Mack, 27 Aug. 1941, FO 371 28323, Z 7355 56 17.
71. Morton to Speaight, 19 Aug. 1941, FO 371 28323, Z 6998 56 17.
72. Somerville-Smith (quoting Pleven) to Mack, 7 June 1941, FO 371 28321, Z 4804 56 17.
73. Butler to F.O., 30 July 1941, FO 371 28323, Z 6682 56 17.
74. Campbell to F.O., 23 Sept. 1941, FO 371 28329, Z 8186 56 17.
75. Mack minute, 29 Sept. 1941, ibid.
76. Barclay to F.O., 10 Oct. 1941, FO 371 28325, Z 9338 56 17.
77. Makins minute, 28 Nov. 1941, FO 371 28326, Z 10028 56 17.
78. See letter from Campbell to F.O., 1 Dec. 1941, enclosing minute by military attaché, R. C. Benton, 27 Nov., FO 371 28326, Z 10064 56 17.
79. Biddle to FDR, 12 May, 17 May, 9 June 1941, FDRL, PSF, A. J. D. Biddle, 1937–41.
80. Stimson Diary, 23 July 1941.
81. Frankfurter-Morgenthau telephone conversation transcript, 8 July 1941, Morgenthau Diaries.
82. Hopkins-Morgenthau telephone conversation transcript, 8 July 1941, ibid.
83. Morgenthau to FDR, 8 July 1941, ibid.
84. Pleven to de Gaulle, 13 July, 23 July 1941, in de Gaulle, *War Memoirs*, Documents, 1:218–19.
85. Lippmann to Pleven, 1 July 1941, Walter Lippmann Papers (Sterling Library, Yale University), Box 96, Folder 1719.
86. FDR to Morgenthau, 9 July 1941, Morgenthau Diaries.
87. Hopkins-Morgenthau telephone conversation transcript, 8 July 1941, ibid.
88. Pleven to de Gaulle, 4 Oct. 1941, FO 371 28325 56 17; see below, note 93.
89. Morgenthau-Frankfurter telephone conversation transcript, 8 July 1941, Morgenthau Diaries.
90. Butler to Mack, 29 July 1941, FO 371 28323, Z 6698 56 17.
91. Butler to F.O., 26 June 1941, FO 371 28322, Z 5645 56 17.
92. Welles memo, 8 July 1941, *FRUS* (1941), 2:573–74; Pleven's memo, ibid., 574–78.
93. Pleven to de Gaulle, 4 Oct. 1941, FO 371 28325, Z 8477 56 17; that text includes passages omitted from the published version (de Gaulle, *War Memoirs*, Documents, 1:229) which show Welles in a slightly more favorable light, e.g., with regard to a proposed call on Hull, ". . . he would be pleased to facilitate my audience."
94. Pleven to de Gaulle, 7 Oct. 1941, FO 371 28325, Z 8530 56 17.
95. *FRUS* (1941), 2:478n.; Makins minute, 28 Nov. 1941, FO 371 28326, Z 10028

56 17; Campbell to F.O., 1 Dec., and Hankey minute, 19 Dec. 1941, FO 371 28326, Z 10664 56 17; *New York Times*, 25 Nov., 26 Nov. 1941.

96. FDR to E. R. Stettinius, Jr., 11 Nov. 1941, quoted in *FRUS* (1942), 2:435.

97. Boegner to de Gaulle, 28 Nov. 1941, FO 371 28326, Z 10146 56 17; again, de Gaulle (*War Memoirs*, Documents, 1:232–33) published only a severely edited version of this dispatch.

98. New York Consul General (Haggard) to F.O. 19 Dec. 1941, FO 371 28326, Z 10731 56 17.

99. Gallup poll, 26 Aug. 1941.

100. *Cong. Rec.*, 87, 77th Cong., 1st session, pt. 8, 9040.

101. See below, chapter 7.

102. *New York Times*, 28 Aug. 1941.

103. *FRUS* (1941), 2:570–72.

104. *New York Post*, 17 Oct. 1941.

105. *FRUS* (1941), 2:578–86.

106. *New York Times*, 25 Nov. 1941.

107. Halifax to F.O., 27 Dec. 1941, FO 371 28326, Z 10945 56 17.

108. See below, chapter 7.

109. "Tendencies in the French Language Press of New England," 17 Feb. 1942, OSS files, R and A branch report, no. 244.

110. See the regional reports on France Forever compiled by the Free French delegation in the spring of 1942, CHDGM.

111. Fritsch-Estrangin, *New-York*, 154–55, and see following note.

112. Raoul de Roussy de Sales to Ulric Bell, 20 July 1941, Fight for Freedom Papers, Box 32, enclosing letter (dated 13 July, copy in Box 61) from a friend in Hollywood; also, reports by Robert G. Spivack, 17 June 1941, on the "Vipers from Vichy."

113. FBI report from Los Angeles, 6 Dec. 1941, SD 851.20211 GABIN JEAN/2; Bernstein had informed the FBI on 20 Aug. that he suspected Gabin of pro-Nazism.

114. The manuscript for 1941 is in the Dorothy Thompson Papers (George Arendts Research Library, Syracuse University, New York); henceforth, de Roussy de Sales ms. The edited, published account of these events is in de Roussy de Sales, *Making of Yesterday*.

115. De Roussy de Sales, "Love in America."

116. De Roussy de Sales ms., 19 Jan. 1941.

117. Ibid., 26 June 1941.

118. Ibid., 4 Jan. 1941.

119. Ibid., 4 Jan., 14 Jan., 30 Mar. 1941.

120. Maurois, *Memoirs*, 284–85. See above, note 112; see also *New York Times*, 20 July 1941, for a letter by Bernstein about Pétain.

121. Fritsch-Estrangin, *New-York*, 155–56.

122. De Roussy de Sales ms., 30 Mar. 1941.

123. Ibid., 26 Jan. 1941.

124. Ibid., 15 May 1941.

125. Ibid., 27 Sept. 1941.

126. Ibid., 24 Aug. 1941.

127. Ibid., 23 Feb. 1941.
128. Ibid., 7 Feb. 1941.
129. Ibid., 14 June 1941.
130. Ibid., 16 Mar. 1941.
131. Ibid., 7 Feb. 1941.
132. Ibid., 2 Apr. 1941.
133. Ibid., 23 Mar. 1941.
134. De Roussy de Sales, Curie, and Barrès, eds., *They Speak for a Nation.*
135. De Roussy de Sales ms., 20 Apr. 1941.
136. Ibid., 23 Feb., 12 Jan. 1941.
137. Ibid., 19 Jan. 1941.
138. Ibid., 3 Oct. 1941.
139. Ibid., 9 Sept. 1941.
140. Ibid., 11 July 1941.
141. See the letter about Pobers from Lucien Vogel to Geneviève Tabouis, 7 Jan. 1942, in Edgar Ansel Mowrer Papers, LCMD, Box 28, Folder TA.
142. De Roussy de Sales ms., 27 Sept. 1941.
143. See above, notes 61, 62.
144. De Roussy de Sales to Ulric Bell, 18 June 1941, Fight for Freedom Papers, Box 5; de Roussy de Sales ms., 1 Aug. 1941; *New York Times*, 5 Aug. 1941.
145. De Roussy de Sales ms., 23 Aug. 1941.
146. Ibid., 25 Oct. 1941.
147. Ibid., 12 Oct. 1941.

CHAPTER 6

1. Walter Lippmann, *Washington Post*, 6 Jan. 1942; Dorothy Thompson, *New York Herald Tribune*, 30 Dec. 1941.
2. *New York Herald Tribune*, 26 Dec.; *PM*, 28 Dec. 1941. FDR is also said to have used the same term; see Sherwood, *Roosevelt and Hopkins*, 488.
3. Sherwood, *Roosevelt and Hopkins*, 489.
4. *FRUS* (1941), 2:499–500.
5. Ibid., 546, 549–50; Eden to Halifax, 25 Dec. 1941, PREM 3 377.
6. Muselier, *De Gaulle contre le gaullisme*, 327.
7. 26 Dec. 1941, and following issues.
8. Christian, *Divided Island*, especially 162–72.
9. Anglin, *St. Pierre and Miquelon*, 147–48.
10. *FRUS* (1941), 2:551.
11. 5 Jan. 1942.
12. 14 Jan. 1942.
13. 17 Jan. 1942.
14. Acheson, *Present at the Creation*, 63. For the resignation note, see below, note 66.
15. J. Pierrepont Moffat to Hull, 25 Dec. 1941, *FRUS* (1941), 2:552; cf. State Dept. memo, 26 Dec. 1941, *FRUS: Washington and Casablanca*, 383–86.
16. Memo, 6 Jan. 1942, Long Papers, Box 195, France folder.

17. *Department of State Bulletin* 5, no. 129 (13 Dec. 1941): 519–20. See in general reports of the Foreign Nationalities Branch, OSS.
18. Hull, *Memoirs*, 2:1125–26.
19. Israel, ed., *War Diary of Breckinridge Long*, 241–42.
20. Ibid., 243.
21. Berle and Jacobs, *Navigating the Rapids*, 393.
22. Ibid., 395.
23. Ibid., 399.
24. *New York Times*, 14 Feb. 1942.
25. Israel, *War Diary of Breckinridge Long*, 240–41; see also the memo by the State Department's legal adviser, G. H. Hackworth, 9 Jan. 1942, *FRUS: Washington and Casablanca*, 396–98.
26. Campbell to Atherton, 17 Feb. 1942, FO 115 3475.
27. Undated British memo, *FRUS: Washington and Casablanca*, 381.
28. Leahy to Hull, 12 Dec. 1941, *FRUS* (1941), 2:200–201.
29. Ibid., 499.
30. Memo by J. D. Hickerson, Division of European Affairs, 17 Dec. 1941, ibid., 549; de Gaulle, *War Memoirs*, 1:217.
31. De Gaulle, *War Memoirs*, Documents 1:238–39.
32. Ibid. (text), 1:216.
33. Ibid., 217, Documents, 1:238–39.
34. Muselier, *De Gaulle contre le gaullisme*, 263–64; de Gaulle, *War Memoirs*, 1:217.
35. Berle and Jacobs, *Navigating the Rapids*, 390–91.
36. Minute of 8 Oct., to letter from Pleven, 4 Oct. 1941, FO 371 28325, Z 8477 56 17 (italics in original).
37. Minute of 28 Nov., to letter from Campbell, 5 Nov. 1941, FO 371 28326, Z 9885 56 17.
38. *Twohey Weekly Analysis of Newspaper Opinion*, week ending 29 Dec. 1941.
39. 26 Dec. 1941.
40. 27 Dec. 1941.
41. 26 Dec. 1941.
42. 26 Dec. 1941.
43. 30 Dec. 1941.
44. 31 Dec. 1941.
45. 27 Dec. 1941.
46. *New York Post*, 2 Jan. 1942.
47. *New York Herald Tribune*, 30 Dec. 1941, italics in original.
48. *Nation*, 3 Jan. 1942.
49. *New Republic*, 12 Jan. 1942.
50. *New York Times*, 27 Dec. 1941.
51. Hull memo, 26 Dec., *FRUS* (1941), 2:558–59.
52. 28 Dec. 1941.
53. 26 Dec. 1941.
54. 26 Dec. 1941.
55. 27 Dec. 1941.
56. *New Republic*, 5 Jan. 1942.

57. 30 Dec. 1941.

58. *PM*, 31 Dec. 1941.

59. 29 Dec. 1941.

60. 26 Dec. 1941.

61. 14 Feb. 1942.

62. *Washington Post*, 2 Jan. 1942.

63. "Campaign to Undermine the State Department," undated ms. (67 pp.), in Hull Papers, Box 95, Folder 403. The ms. was evidently written early in 1942: it contains no reference to events after January, although in April, with Laval's return, a more determined campaign against the department was mounted.

64. *Nation*, 17 Jan. 1942.

65. 28 Dec. 1941.

66. Pencilled draft, 16 Jan. 1942, Hull Papers, Box 50, Folder 148.

67. *Nation*, 3 Jan. 1942.

68. Text in *New York Times*, 31 Dec. 1941.

69. Pickersgill, *Mackenzie King Record*, 1:322.

70. 31 Dec. 1941.

71. Hull, *Memoirs*, 2:1134.

72. Hull to FDR, 31 Dec. 1941, *FRUS: Washington and Casablanca*, 382.

73. Hull draft statement, FDR memo, 1 Jan. 1942, ibid., 386–87.

74. E.g., Hull's personal "memo for the files," 15 May 1941, Hull Papers, Box 49.

75. Hull to FDR, 31 Dec. 1941, *FRUS: Washington and Casablanca*, 382.

76. Halifax to Churchill, 24 Dec., Morton to Churchill, 26 Dec. 1941, PREM 3, 377.

77. Memo, 4 Feb. 1942, J. Pierrepont Moffat Papers (Houghton Library, Harvard University), Box 47.

78. Pickersgill, *Mackenzie King Record*, 1:345–46.

79. Malcolm MacDonald (British High Commissioner, Canada) to Halifax and Dominions Office, London, 26 Dec. 1941, PREM 3, 377.

80. Halifax (recording Campbell's report) to Eden, 10 Jan. 1942, PREM 3, 377.

81. Donovan to FDR, 23 Dec. 1941, *FRUS: Washington and Casablanca*, 404.

82. Halifax to Churchill, 26 Dec. 1941, PREM 3, 377.

83. Eden to Churchill, 20 Jan. 1942, PREM 3, 377.

84. De Gaulle to Churchill, 27 Dec. 1941, PREM 3, 377.

85. Morton minute, 6 Jan. 1942, PREM 3, 120/10A.

86. Churchill to Eden, 10 Jan. 1942, PREM 3, 377.

87. FDR to Churchill, 14 Jan. 1942, PREM 3, 377.

88. Pickersgill, *Mackenzie King Record*, 1:320–22.

89. Leahy to Hull, 30 Dec. 1941, *FRUS* (1941), 2:502–3.

90. They may be followed in Anglin, *St. Pierre and Miquelon*, 112–26; *FRUS* (1942), 2:654–71; *FRUS: Washington and Casablanca*, 106–7, 111–12, 131, 140–41, 156–58, 376–405.

91. Hull to FDR, 2 Feb. 1942, *FRUS* (1942), 2:669–70.

92. Hull to FDR, 2 Feb. 1942, FDRL, PSF, Box 39, France 1942.

CHAPTER 7

1. See above, chapter 2, note 31.
2. AIPO poll, 25 Nov. 1941.
3. AIPO polls, 29 July, 19 Aug. 1941, 1 July 1942. That total, one-third, would be very slightly increased if allowance were made for a slip in polling technique; on the earlier question, 56 percent claimed to know who the Free French were, but only 51 percent were correct. Nevertheless, the second question, on American policy, was asked of all 56 percent.
4. AIPO poll, 29 July 1941; Gallup poll, 16 Aug., 5 Sept. 1941; AIPO poll, 25 Nov. 1941, 1 July 1942. Some of the above figures are based on the author's own calculations, as follows: the poll of 16 Aug. 1941 showed 58 percent regarding Vichy as helping Germany, and 25 percent not having any opinion; that yields 77 percent as the proportion of those informed about France who thought Vichy was helping Germany. Similarly the AIPO poll of 25 Nov. 1941 showed 47 percent informed about France. Therefore, if 17 percent favored American recognition of the Free French, that amounts to 36 percent of those so informed, and if 9 percent took a favorable view of Vichy, then the total proportion of those so informed who were against it was 81 percent.
5. See above, chapter 2.
6. Quoted in Mott, *American Journalism*, 765.
7. Broughton, "Government Agencies and Civilian Morale," 171; on Taylor, *Strategy of Terror*, see above, chapter 2.
8. Winkler, *Politics of Propaganda*, 40–42.
9. MacLeish to Ickes, 9 April 1942, Felix Frankfurter Papers, LCMD, Box 82, MacLeish.
10. Elmer Davis, "Report to the President: Office of War Information, 13 June 1942, 1 Sept., 15 Sept. 1945," OWI records (National Archives, Suitland, Maryland, Record Group 208), Box 64, Entry 6.
11. See above, chapter 2.
12. Quoted in Mott, *American Journalism*, 766.
13. *FDR Press Conferences*, 22 Dec. 1944, 24:276–78.
14. Mowrer to MacLeish, 11 April 1942, Archibald MacLeish Papers, LCMD, Box 14, Mowrer file.
15. Steele, *The First Offensive*, 64–65, 89.
16. Creel to Davis, 4 Aug. 1942, Elmer Davis Papers, LCMD, Box 1.
17. *New York Times*, 2 Aug. 1941.
18. Ibid., 29 Dec. 1940.
19. Ibid., 5 Jan. 1941.
20. Ibid., 7 Jan., 8 Jan. 1941.
21. *New York Herald Tribune*, 9 Jan. 1941.
22. *New York Times*, 21 Jan. 1941.
23. See above, chapter 3.
24. See above, chapter 2.
25. A useful survey of American interpretations of the trial is in "The French 'War-Guilt' Trial at Riom," R and A report no. 279, OSS files.

26. Leahy to Hull, 14 Mar., Welles to FDR, 15 Mar., FDR note, 16 Mar. 1942, FDRL, OF 203, France, 1942.
27. *New York Times*, 20 Feb., 21 Feb. 1942.
28. E.g., *Baltimore Sun*, 21 Feb. 1942.
29. 23 Feb. 1940.
30. *Nation*, 7 Mar. 1942.
31. 27 Oct. 1941.
32. 16 Apr. 1942.
33. 20 Mar. 1941.
34. Thompson to Feis, n.d., Herbert Feis Papers, LCMD, Box 20, Thompson file; Thompson to Luce, 12 Mar. 1941, Dorothy Thompson Papers, Series 2, Box 1, Jan.–Apr. 1941.
35. E.g., *New York Times* editorials, 16 May, 24 May, 28 May, 16 June, 12 June, 17 June, 4 Aug., 21 Nov., 25 Nov., 26 Dec. 1941, 3 Mar., 15 Apr., 16 Apr., 17 Apr., 24 Sept. 1942; for dissent from "Pertinax," ibid., 6 June, 6 Aug., 13 Aug., 24 Aug., 26 Sept., 7 Dec., 17 Dec., 26 Dec. 1941, 25 Mar., 15 Apr. 1942.
36. *Wall Street Journal*, 22 Apr. 1942; see also, ibid. for Woodlock, 20 May, 27 May, and Morley, 23 May 1942.
37. E.g., *Washington Post*, 6 Jan., 21 Mar., 16 Apr., 18 Apr., 16 July, 29 Oct., 12 Nov. 1942.
38. *Commonweal*, 7 Mar. 1941, 487–89 (my italics).
39. Ibid., 4 Apr. 1941, 590–92.
40. Henry Luce, "The American Century," *Life*, 17 Feb. 1941; Wallace, *Price of Free World Victory*; Welles, *World of the Four Freedoms*, including speeches from 1941 and 1942; Wendell Willkie, speech in New York, reported in *New York Times*, 7 Nov. 1942 (including views later developed in his *One World*); Hoover and Gibson, *Problems of Lasting Peace*; Streit, *Union Now*, reprinted fourteen times in the next two years (see Divine, *Second Chance*, 38); Spykman, *America's Strategy in World Politics*.
41. Morton to Churchill, 19 April 1941, PREM 4, 26/6.
42. De Roussy de Sales, *Making of Yesterday*, 239.
43. Lippmann, *U.S. War Aims*, recapitulating many of the themes evident in the columns cited above, note 37.
44. *Wall Street Journal*, 20 May 1942.
45. E.g., the articles by C. G. Paulding, *Commonweal*, 5 Dec., 12 Dec., 19 Dec. 1941, 16 Jan., 15 May 1942, and see above, note 38.
46. *Chicago Tribune*, 14 Apr., 11 Nov. 1942.
47. FDR to Wallace, 9 Sept. 1942, FDRL, PPF 5107.
48. *Chicago Tribune*, 14 Apr. 1942.
49. *New Republic*, 2 July 1942, 57.
50. *Nation*, 12 July 1941.
51. E.g., SD 711.51/255, 257, 263, 279, 280, 281, 283, 284.
52. Mrs. Brewster to André Leloup, 18 July 1942, statement of accounts after the fête, 13 Aug. 1942, France Forever Papers, Chicago Historical Society, Chicago, Illinois.
53. Témoignage de Pierre André Weil, 26 Nov. 1948, CHDGM.

54. De Roussy de Sales, *Making of Yesterday*, 268.
55. Berle Diary, 3 Apr. 1942.
56. Berle Diary, 1 Oct. 1942.
57. Berle Diary, 30 Apr. 1942.
58. E.g., Berle Diary, 16 Feb., 2 May, 5 May, 7 May, 12 May, 15 May, 26 May, 11 June, 17 June, 20 June, 21 Oct., 28 Oct., 31 Oct.
59. OSS Files 184195, 21781C, 22716C; memos from Carter in SD 851.01/378.
60. SD 851.01/558.
61. Carter memo, 8 Oct. 1942, FDRL, PSF, Box 121, J. F. Carter, Aug.–Dec. 1942.
62. *Pour la victoire*, 30 Aug., 2 Oct., 3 Oct., 24 Oct., 31 Oct. 1942.
63. Tabouis to John Wiley, 5 April 1942, FDRL, John Wiley Papers, Box 9, Gen. Corr., Tabouis, Geneviève.
64. For various perspectives on this feud, see de Kérillis, *De Gaulle, dictateur*, 87–114; de Kérillis, open letter to de Gaulle, *Pour la victoire*, 1 May 1943; Témoignage de Pierre André Weil, cited above, note 53; Fritsch-Estrangin, *New-York*, 126–32.
65. *New York Times*, 6 May 1942.
66. Ibid., 13 Apr., 16 Apr., 18 Apr.; *New York Herald Tribune*, 14 Apr., 15 Apr., 16 Apr., 17 Apr.; *New York Sun, Chicago Sun, Atlanta Constitution, Baltimore Sun*, 15 Apr. 1942.
67. *New Republic*, 27 Apr. 1942.
68. *Nation*, 25 Apr. 1942.
69. *New York Herald Tribune*, 23 June 1942.
70. *New York Post*, 22 June 1942.
71. *Chicago Sun*, 21 June 1942.
72. *New York Times*, 15 July 1942.
73. *Cong. Rec.*, 87, 77th Cong., 1st session, appendix, pt. 10, 267, pt. 11, 1621, pt. 13, 3404–5, 4039.
74. Ibid., pt. 8, 9040.
75. Ibid., pt. 12, 2872–73.
76. Ibid., 88, 77th Cong., 2d session, pt. 3, 3471.
77. Ibid., 3485.
78. Ibid., 3687.
79. *New York Times*, 18 June 1942; Israel, *War Diary of Breckinridge Long*, 273.
80. *New York Times*, 13 Aug. 1941.
81. *Cong. Rec.*, 88, 77th Cong., 2d session, pt. 6, 7665–72.
82. *New York Times*, 27 July, 2 Aug., 4 Aug., 12 Aug., 24 Aug., 12 Oct., 7 Sept., 27 Dec. 1941.
83. Memo by Dewitt C. Poole, 16 Apr. 1943, OSS, Foreign Nationalities Branch.
84. *New York Times*, 5 Aug. 1941.
85. This information has been extracted from a number of sources, including the notepaper of the UDA, three memoranda in the Cordell Hull Papers, Box 95, Folder 403, and a report of the OSS Foreign Nationalities Branch on Freedom House, 17 Feb. 1943; Kingdon's article, *Free World*, 3 Mar. 1942; the first of Alvarez del Vayo's "Political War" supplements, *Nation*, 26 Sept. 1942.
86. Niebuhr to Eleanor Roosevelt, FDRL, OF 203A, France 1941.
87. *Free World*, Oct. 1941, Oct. 1942.

88. Memos of 9 Sept. 1943, 1 June 1944, FDRL, OF 5422, FWA.

89. William Agar to Eleanor Roosevelt, 22 Apr., FDR to Eleanor Roosevelt, 5 May, FDR memo, 21 May 1942, FDRL, OF 203A, France, Jan.–Aug. 1942.

90. *Daily Worker*, 30 April 1941, "Campaign Against the Department of State," n.p., n.d., Hull Papers, Box 95, Folder 403.

91. *New York Times*, 5 July, 9 July, 15 July 1942.

92. Wallace to FDR, 4 May 1942, FDRL, OF 5422, FWA, enclosing a copy of the speech.

93. *New York Times*, 28 June 1942.

94. See above, chapter 2, note 147.

95. Survey of "Statements on People's War," OWI, Master File, Bureau of Publications and Graphics, 4 Jan. 1943.

96. FDRL, OF 5422, FWA.

97. See above, chapter 2.

98. *Nation*, 4 Jan., 28 Apr., 24 May 1941, 12 July, 19 July, 26 July, 2 Aug. 1941, and almost every issue thereafter.

99. *New Republic*, 16 June 1941, 7 July, 18 Aug., 8 Sept., 15 Sept. 1941, 12 Jan., 9 Feb., 16 Feb., 23 Feb., 16 Mar., 30 Mar., 27 Apr., 4 May, 18 May 1942, and almost every issue thereafter.

100. See above, chapter 6, notes 46, 47.

101. *PM*, 3 Feb., 4 Feb., 5 Feb., 6 Feb., 11 Feb., 12 Feb., 24 Feb., 25 Feb., 26 Feb., 4 Mar. 1941.

102. *Nation*, 25 July, 1 Aug., 8 Aug., 15 Aug. 1942.

103. New York, 1942.

104. New York, 1945–46.

105. "The Department of State," *Fortune*, Dec. 1939.

106. Feis to Felix Frankfurter, 26 Feb. 1941, Feis Papers, Box 16, Frankfurter file.

107. Berle Diary, 5 Feb. 1942.

108. Berle Diary, 24 Oct., 27 Oct. 1942.

109. Ingersoll to Frankfurter, 28 Feb. 1941, Feis Papers, Box 34, 1941 file.

110. Berle to Welles, 5 Oct. 1942, Berle Papers, Box 73, Welles, Sumner (1938–42).

111. Acheson, *Present at the Creation*, 38–39.

112. Murphy, *Diplomat among Warriors*, 544.

113. E.g., Blum, ed., *The Price of Vision*, 26–27, 67–68, 734.

114. E.g., Blum, *Years of War*, 332–37.

115. Berle Diary, 26 Dec. 1941.

116. Transcript of telephone conversation, Morgenthau-Frankfurter, 8 July 1941, Morgenthau Diaries, FDRL.

117. Transcript of telephone conversation, Morgenthau-Frankfurter, 14 Jan. 1941, ibid.

118. E.g., Ickes Diary, 2 July, 23 Sept. 1939, 17 Nov. 1940, 30 May, 14 Dec. 1941.

119. Ibid., 12 July, 18 Oct. 1942.

120. Ibid., 10 May 1941, 1 Feb., 29 Mar. 1942.

121. Ickes to Lippmann, 15 May 1943, Lippmann Papers, Box 79, Folder 1116.

122. Ickes Diary, 19 Apr. 1942.

123. Ickes Diary, 10 May, 15 May 1941; *New York Times*, 28 May 1941; Welles memo to Hull, 28 May 1941, SD 711.51/170.

124. *FDR Press Conferences*, 15:598; 17:120; 18:154, 314, 380; 19:136, 279.
125. Bendiner, *Riddle of the State Department*, 6–7.

CHAPTER 8

1. See Paxton, *Vichy France*, 317–26.
2. See the OSS memo on Darlan prepared by Morgenthau, 16 Nov. 1942, Morgenthau Diary, 584:280–82.
3. Bullitt to Hull, 1 July 1940, *FRUS* (1940), 2:466.
4. Melka, "Darlan between Britain and Germany," 64.
5. E.g., *FRUS* (1941), 2:502–3, and *FRUS* (1942), 2:127–29.
6. Melka, "Darlan between Britain and Germany," 71.
7. E.g., *FRUS* (1941), 2:189, 440–41, 457–58, and *FRUS* (1942), 2:248–49, 283–84.
8. Donovan to FDR, 21 April 1942, FDRL, PSF, Box 163.
9. Steele, *First Offensive*, 54, 167–79.
10. Murphy, *Diplomat among Warriors*, 127–29.
11. Memo enclosed with Murphy's letter to Welles, 12 Jan. 1942, *FRUS* (1942), 2:229–36.
12. Giraud, *Un seul but*, 13–14.
13. De Gaulle, *Discours aux français*, 218.
14. *FDR Press Conferences*, 20:244–47, 17 Nov. 1942.
15. See Funk, "Negotiating the 'Deal with Darlan,' " which together with the same author's *Politics of Torch*, provides the definitive account of the affair.
16. Stimson Diary, 18 Nov. 1942.
17. Ibid., 16 Nov. 1942.
18. Eisenhower to Marshall, 17 Oct. 1942, Chandler, ed., *Eisenhower Papers*, 1:625–26.
19. Leahy to Murphy, 17 Oct. 1942, *FRUS* (1942), 2:396–97.
20. *New York Times*, 9 Nov. 1942.
21. *FRUS* (1942), 2:340–42, 367–70; Dougherty, *Politics of Wartime Aid*, 43–46.
22. Dr. Graham H. Stuart, "The Role of the Department of State in the North African Economic and Political Program from its Inception to the Invasion" (ms., 1944), Hull Papers, Box 65, Folder 287, condensed as chapter 29 of Stuart, *The Department of State*.
23. *FRUS* (1942), 2:392n.
24. Stimson Diary, 8 Nov. 1942.
25. Ibid., 16 Nov., 17 Nov. 1942.
26. Stimson memo, 10 Nov. 1942, Stimson Papers, Box 171, Folder 18.
27. J. P. Moffat memo, reporting Welles's views, "Notes on Trip to Washington," 13–17 Nov. 1942, Moffat Papers, vol. 24.
28. Stimson Diary, 3 Nov. 1942.
29. Morgenthau Diary, 16 Nov. 1942.
30. FDR to Churchill, 2 Sept. 1942, in Loewenheim et al., *Roosevelt and Churchill*, 247–48 (henceforth *Roosevelt-Churchill Correspondence*).
31. Woodward, *British Foreign Policy in the Second World War* (1962), 206–7; cited

in Funk, "Negotiating the 'Deal with Darlan,'" 96n.
32. Churchill to Roosevelt, 12 Mar. 1941, *Roosevelt-Churchill Correspondence*, 134.
33. Memo by Hoyar-Millar, 12 Nov. 1942, FO 115 3529.
34. CAB 65/28, WM 153(42)2, 16 Nov. 1942.
35. Minute, 11 Jan. 1943, FO 371 36007, Z 47 47 17.
36. Winant to FDR, 3 Dec. 1942, Harry Hopkins Papers, FDRL, Box 330, Book 7, Casablanca.
37. CAB 65/28, WM 156(42), 21 Nov. 1942.
38. *FRUS* (1942), 2:437, 442–43.
39. Halifax to Eden, 14 Nov. 1942, PREM 3, 442/9.
40. Churchill to FDR, 22 Nov. 1942, PREM 3, 120/8.
41. Eade, ed., *War Speeches*, 2:377.
42. Churchill to FDR, 17 Nov. 1942, *FRUS* (1942), 2:445–46; see above, note 14.
43. Eisenhower to Marshall, 1 Nov. 1942, Chandler, *Eisenhower Papers*, 1:651.
44. Eisenhower to Gen. Smith, 9 Nov. 1942, ibid., 2:677.
45. Eisenhower to Marshall, 9 Nov. 1942, ibid., 2:680.
46. Eisenhower to Combined Chiefs of Staff, 14 Nov. 1942, ibid., 2:707–11; Langer, *Our Vichy Gamble*, 357, 360; Sherwood, *Roosevelt and Hopkins*, 651–53.
47. Cantril, "Evaluating the Probable Reactions to the Landing in North Africa in 1942."
48. Smith, *OSS*, 60.
49. *FRUS* (1941), 2:466–68, 470–72, 479–81.
50. Murphy to Hull, 26 Sept. 1942, Hull Papers, Box 65, Folder 287.
51. Quoted in Stuart study, 56–57, see above, note 22.
52. Murphy, *Diplomat among Warriors*, 158–63.
53. FDR to Murphy, 22 Sept. 1942, *FRUS* (1942), 2:379n-381; Murphy, *Diplomat among Warriors*, 96, 134.
54. E.g., *FRUS* (1942), 2:227, 265, 278, 332. Cited in Funk, "Negotiating the 'Deal with Darlan,'" 92n.
55. *FRUS* (1942), 2:379.
56. See above, note 19.
57. Eisenhower to Combined Chiefs of Staff, 8 Nov. 1942, Chandler, *Eisenhower Papers*, 2:670.
58. Funk, "Negotiating the 'Deal with Darlan,'" 110–11, 114–15; Thomas, *Britain and Vichy*, 153–54.
59. E.g., Langer, *Our Vichy Gamble*, 337–64; Murphy, *Diplomat among Warriors*, 159–76; Pendar, *Adventure in Diplomacy*, 102–18.
60. Winner to Sherwood, 1 Jan. 1943, OWI records, Box 57, Entry 6.
61. Ibid., and Paxton, *Parades and Politics*, 344–90.
62. Matthews to Leahy, 10 Dec. 1942, Leahy Diary, 1942 volume.
63. Leahy Diary, 20 Nov., 1 Dec., 5 Dec., 7 Dec. 1942.
64. Ibid., 25 Dec. 1942.
65. *FRUS* (1942), 2:546–47 (the original of this memo by Welles, which was cut for publication, could not be traced in the National Archives); de Gaulle, *War*

Memoirs, Documents, 2:94; Témoignage de M. André Philip, 13 June 1947, CHDGM.
66. Hull memo, 14 Nov. 1942, Hull Papers, Box 58, Folder 209.
67. Berle memo, 7 Dec. 1942, Berle Papers, Box 214, Diary, Nov.–Dec. 1942.
68. Moffat memo of conversation with Berle, 23 Dec. 1942, Moffat Papers, vol. 24.
69. Berle memo, 21 Dec. 1942, Berle Papers, Box 214, Diary, Nov.–Dec. 1942.
70. Chandler, *Eisenhower Papers*, 2:700 n. 3.
71. Steele, *First Offensive*, 149–58, 178.
72. FDR to Eve Curie, 10 Nov. 1942, FDRL, PSF, 39, France, 1942.
73. Ickes Diary, 22 Nov. 1942.
74. Stimson Diary, 20 Nov. 1942.
75. Eisenhower to Gen. Smith, 18 Nov. 1942, Chandler, *Eisenhower Papers*, 2:732–35.
76. Elmer Davis to FDR, 16 Nov. 1942, FDRL, PSF, 170, OWI; see above, notes 14, 42.
77. FDR to Hull, 17 Nov. 1942, Hull Papers, Box 50, Folder 152.
78. Murphy, *Diplomat among Warriors*, 157.
79. Quoted in Elson, *World of Time, Inc.*, 59.
80. *Time*, 14 Dec. 1942.
81. Quoted in Root, *Secret History of the War*, 2:512–13.
82. *Cong. Rec.*, 77th Cong., 2d session, pt. 7, 9546–48, 15 Dec. 1942.
83. Memos of 10 Nov. 1942, 12 Jan. 1943, Master File, OWI records; cf. weekly OWI reports sent to Foreign Office, FO 371 34167, A 156/156/45.
84. *American Foreign Service Journal*, 12 Dec. 1942; *New York Sun*, 11 Nov.; *New York World-Telegram*, 10 Nov.; *Baton Rouge State-Times*, 16 Nov. 1942.
85. *New York Times*, 9 Nov. 1942.
86. Reported in ibid., 18 Nov. 1942.
87. Ibid., 24 Nov. 1942.
88. *Chicago Tribune*, references in order, 12 Nov., 11 Nov. (invasion), 28 Nov., 30 Nov., 2 Dec. 1942 (Toulon).
89. Ibid., 23 Nov. (MacArthur and Rickenbacker), 17 Dec. (critics), 16 Nov. (FDR), 21 Nov. (Darlan and Fighting French), 25 Nov. 1942 (Four Freedoms).
90. *Christian Century*, 25 Nov. 1942.
91. De Gaulle, *Discours aux français*, 266–7.
92. Eisenhower, *The President is Calling*, 141.
93. See above, chapter 7.
94. *New York Herald Tribune*, 13 Nov. 1942.
95. Quoted in *Nation*, 21 Nov. 1942.
96. *New York Times*, 15 Nov. 1942.
97. *Nation*, 21 Nov. 1942.
98. *New Republic*, 30 Nov. 1942.
99. See the British cabinet discussions, CAB 65/28, WM 166(42)3, 9 Dec. 1942.
100. *New York Post*, 9 Dec. 1942.
101. *Christian Science Monitor*, 8 Dec. 1942.
102. *New Republic*, 14 Dec. 1942.

103. *Nation*, 12 Dec. 1942.
104. Stimson Diary, 16 Nov. 1942.
105. Quoted in Jay Hayden, "Willkie Speech Censored," *Atlanta Constitution*, 22 Nov.; TRB's column in *New Republic*, 30 Nov. 1942; Barnard, *Wendell Willkie*, 393.
106. See above, notes 14, 76.
107. Willkie to MacLeish, 24 Nov., MacLeish to Willkie, 30 Nov., Willkie to MacLeish, 2 Dec. 1942, MacLeish Papers, Box 20.
108. *Washington Post*, 12 Nov. 1942.
109. Lippmann to Stimson, 19 Nov. 1942, Stimson Papers, Box 141.
110. A copy of this memo, dated 17 Nov. 1942, is in Hull Papers, Box 50, Folder 152; a handwritten draft in Lippmann Papers, Box 106, Folder 2112.
111. The entire correspondence is in Hull Papers, Box 50, Folder 152, including a memo to Hull, 19 Nov., from Wallace Murray, a State Dept. adviser on political relations, about a conversation with General J. E. Hull of the War Dept.; Lippmann's columns in order: *Washington Post*, 19 Nov. 1941, 6 Jan., 21 Mar. 1942.
112. See above, chapter 7, note 16.
113. See the unsigned memo "Willkie Influence on O.W.I.," 21 July, and Robert Sherwood's rebuttal, 9 Aug. 1943, in FDRL, PSF, Box 10, OWI; cf. Smith, *OSS*, 63–66.
114. Stimson Diary, 22 Jan., 23 Jan., 27 Jan., 28 Jan., 2 Feb. 1943.
115. Demaree Bess, "The Backstage Story of Our African Adventure," *Saturday Evening Post*, 3 July, 10 July, 17 July 1943.
116. *Washington Post*, 10 July 1943.
117. FDRL, OF 144.
118. J. C. Dunn (adviser on political relations), "An Analysis of the Reaction to the North African Situation from after the 'Cease Fire' Order Was Given to the Present," 17 Feb. 1943, Hull Papers, Box 65, Folder 287.
119. Material in Hull Papers, Box 51, Folder 153; *PM*, 29 Jan. 1943.
120. "Specimen Day in Washington," 5 Jan. 1943, Davis Papers, Box 10, OWI file.

CHAPTER 9

1. Funk, *Politics of Torch*, 275–77, Thomas, *Britain and Vichy*, 152–53, 168–70.
2. Stimson Diary, 26 Dec. 1942.
3. Harley Notter Files, SD, Box 43.
4. The view of Kolko, *Politics of War*, 67.
5. Crusoé, *Vicissitudes*, 152–54.
6. Monnet, *Memoirs*, 198.
7. *Roosevelt-Churchill Correspondence*, 335.
8. FDR to Hull, 18 Jan. 1943, Hull Papers, Box 51, Folder 153.
9. Ickes Diary, 9 Jan. 1943.
10. Murphy to Hull and FDR, 30 May 1943, FDRL, Map Room Papers, Box 30, Folder 001, North Africa, French National Committee (1), Section 1; cf. *Roosevelt-Churchill Correspondence*, 335, 338, 347.

11. *Roosevelt-Churchill Correspondence*, 338.
12. Macmillan, *Blast of War*, 237–38.
13. Macmillan, "The Road to Recognition," 27 Aug. 1943, PREM 3, 181/4.
14. Macmillan to Eden, 4 Oct. 1943, PREM 3, 177/6.
15. CAB 65/38, WM 53(43)2, 13 Apr. 1943.
16. De Gaulle, *War Memoirs*, 2:106–7; Funk, *Charles de Gaulle*, 114–15.
17. CAB 65/38, WM 75(43)1, 23 May 1943.
18. Churchill to FDR, 21 July 1943, PREM 3, 181/2.
19. FDR to Churchill, 22 July 1943, ibid.
20. *FRUS* (1943), 2:185.
21. PREM 3 181/6.
22. Churchill to FDR, 15 Aug. 1943, PREM 3, 181/3.
23. Churchill minute, 24 July 1943, PREM 3, 181/2.
24. Separate memos of Churchill and Eden, 1943, PREM 3, 181/8.
25. Stimson Diary, 5 Jan. 1943.
26. Stimson and Bundy, *On Active Service*, xx, xxi, 110–52.
27. Stimson Diary, 1 Feb. 1943.
28. Ibid., 10 Aug. 1943.
29. Macmillan to Churchill, 22 June 1943, PREM 3, 181/7.
30. Churchill to Macmillan, 23 June 1943, ibid.
31. FDR to Churchill, 8 July 1943, PREM 3, 181/2.
32. Chandler, *Eisenhower Papers*, 2:1273.
33. Acheson, *Present at the Creation*, 131.
34. Boston, 1943.
35. Long to Hornbeck, 28 Aug. 1943, and various memos, all in Long Papers, Box 194, Foreign Policy: Walter Lippmann book.
36. Notter, *Postwar Foreign Policy Preparation* is a useful account of these discussions.
37. Louis, *Imperialism at Bay*, 27–47, 159–74.
38. E.g., Hull, *Memoirs*, 2:1313–14.
39. Stimson Diary, 2 Feb., 16 Feb., 7 Sept. 1943; Ickes Diary, 2 Jan., 6 March 1943; CAB 65/38, WM 53(43)2, 13 Apr. 1943.
40. As reported in *New York Times*, 16 Jan. 1944.
41. Lippmann to Stettinius, 17 Jan., Stettinius to Lippmann, 22 Jan., Lippmann to Stettinius, 25 Jan. 1944, Lippmann Papers, Box 103, Stettinius.
42. See above, chapter 6, note 63.
43. Matthews to Hull, 23 Aug. 1943, H. Freeman Matthews Papers (State Department Records, National Archives), Box 1, Memoranda for the Secretary, 1943–45.
44. H. D. Gideonse, "In Defense of the State Department," transcript of address to Chicago Council on Foreign Relations, 13 Aug. 1943, Manuscript Division, University of Illinois at Chicago Circle.
45. *New Leader*, 21 Aug. 1943.
46. The case may be followed, on the British side, in CAB 65/42, WM 71(44)5, 1 June 1944; CAB 66/50, WP (44)286, 31 May 1944; CAB 66/51, WP (44)325, 15 June 1944. See also, Funk, *Charles de Gaulle*, 221; Pendar, *Adventures in Diplomacy*, appendix; and Mengin, *No Laurels for De Gaulle*, 273–74.

47. Matthews to Hull, 9 Sept., Matthews to Berle, 17 Sept. 1943, Matthews Papers, Box 1, Memoranda for the Secretary, 1943–45.
48. K. Smith, "Spotlight on the State Department," *Reader's Digest*, May 1944, 1–7, esp. 5; see also the critique of this article in Michael Clark, "The Maquis's Plan for France," *Nation*, 1 July 1944, 16–17; cf. K. Smith, "Our Government's Case for Appeasement," "Our Foreign Policy Goes Realist," "Unrevealed Facts about Robert Murphy," *American Mercury*, Feb. 1943, 135–42, Dec. 1943, 165–70, and Nov. 1944, 528–36.
49. Matthews to Murphy (Washington), 15 May 1943, FDRL, Map Room Papers, Box 166, Naval Aide's File—France and the French Empire, Part II.
50. Winant to FDR, 14 June 1943, FDRL, Map Room Papers, Box 30, Folder 001, N. Africa (1) Section 1.
51. *Washington Post*, 12 July, and *Newsweek*, 19 July 1943; cf. the criticism of them in *Nation*, 31 July 1943, 115–16.
52. See PREM 3, 121/1.
53. British embassy in Washington to London, press survey, 11 July 1943, FO 371 36308, Z 7766 6659 69.
54. CAB 65/35, WM 99(43)1, 14 July 1943; cf. Halifax to F.O., 13 July 1943, PREM 3, 181/11.
55. Winant to FDR, 16 July 1943, FDRL, Map Room Papers, Box 30, Folder 001, N. Africa, French National Committee, section 2; cf. Winant to FDR, 9 July 1943, ibid.
56. Matthews to Atherton, 25 June 1943, Leahy Diary, July 1942 volume.
57. Welles to FDR, 16 Aug. 1943, FDRL, PSF, Box 96, Sumner Welles, 1943 and 1944.
58. E.g., Ickes Diary, 8 June, 28 June, 27 July, 7 Dec. 1941, 28 Apr., 9 May 1943; Bullitt, *For the President*, 512–17; Berle, *Navigating the Rapids*, 445; Acheson, *Present at the Creation*, 77.
59. Hull, *Memoirs*, 2:1230–31.
60. Lippmann to Hull, 2 Nov., Hull to Lippmann, 20 Nov. 1943, Lippmann Papers, Box 79, Folder 1104.
61. Halifax to F.O., 5 Nov. 1943, FO 371 35994, Z 11341 2 47.
62. Halifax to F.O., 5 Dec. 1943, FO 371 35994, Z 12262 2 17.
63. PREM 3, 181/11.
64. FDR to S. T. Early, 8 June 1943 (comment on R. E. Sherwood of OWI to FDR, 6 June), FDRL, PSF, Box 40, France, 1943.
65. FDR to Eisenhower, 17 June 1943, FDRL, Map Room Papers, Box 30, Folder 001, N. Africa, French National Committee (1).
66. FDR to Eisenhower, 17 June 1943, Hopkins Papers, Box 330, Sherwood Collection, Book 7, Post-Casablanca, N. Africa.
67. FDR to Eisenhower, 22 Dec. 1943, *FRUS* (1943), 2:195.
68. See FDR to Leahy, 23 Dec., Marshall to FDR, 25 Dec. 1943, FDRL, Map Room Papers, Box 30, Folder 0011, French National Committee, Section 3; cf. Matthews memo, 22 Dec. 1943, *FRUS* (1943), 2:195–96.
69. FDR to Eisenhower, 26 Dec. 1943, *FRUS* (1943), 2:197.
70. Kaspi, *La mission de Jean Monnet*; Monnet, *Memoirs*, 178–211.

71. Monnet memo, 24 Dec. 1942, Hopkins Papers, Box 330, Sherwood Collection, Book 7, Casablanca.
72. Sherwood, *Roosevelt and Hopkins*, 678–79.
73. FDR to Hull, 5 Feb. 1943, FDRL, OF, 203, France, 1943; FDR to Eisenhower and Murphy, 22 Feb. 1943, FDRL, Map Room Papers, Box 12, Folder 2B.
74. Monnet, *Memoirs*, 187–90; Giraud, *Un seul but*, 120–22.
75. Monnet to Hopkins, 11 March 1943, Hopkins Papers, Box 330, Sherwood Collection, Book 7, Post-Casablanca, North Africa.
76. E.g., J. Maritain, in *New York Times*, 25 April 1943.
77. Monnet, *Memoirs*, 190.
78. Lash, ed., *Diaries of Frankfurter*, 222–24.
79. Monnet to Hopkins, 6 May 1943, Hopkins Papers, Box 330, Sherwood Collection, Book 7, Post-Casablanca, North Africa.
80. Monnet to Hopkins, 22 July 1943, ibid.
81. See Lash, *Diaries of Frankfurter*, 260, for Hull's view of Monnet.
82. Monnet, *Memoirs*, 211.
83. Halifax to F.O., 5 Dec. 1943, PREM 3, 177/6.
84. *Roosevelt-Churchill Correspondence*, 344–45.
85. E.g., Lash, *Diaries of Frankfurter*, 193.
86. Quoted in Funk, *Charles de Gaulle*, 158.
87. Roosevelt, *As He Saw It*, 74, 114–6, 256.
88. E.g., Hull, *Memoirs*, 2:1597.
89. Churchill to Eden, 21 Dec. 1943, PREM 3, 178/2; cf. State Department memo listing official pronouncements on the future of French territory after the war, 15 Dec. 1942, Hull Papers, Box 50, Folder 152.
90. E.g., Varian Fry, "Giraud and the Jews," *New Republic*, 10 May 1943, 626–29; Representative Emanuel Celler's petition to the FCNL, 27 Sept. 1943, *Cong. Rec.*, 89, 78th Cong., 1st session, appendix, pt. 11, 4000–4001.
91. Kaspi, *La Mission de Jean Monnet*, 82–87; Raoul Aglion, "Enquête sur le ralliement des marins à la France Combattante," 1 April 1943, CHDGM; *FRUS* (1943), 2:202–19.
92. Matthews to Jacob Beam at the American embassy in London, 23 Aug. 1943, Matthews Papers, Box 1, Correspondence, File 13.
93. See above, notes 43–56.
94. Halifax to F.O., 5 Nov. 1943, FO 371 35994, Z 11341 2 47.
95. De Roussy de Sales, *Making of Yesterday*, 303.
96. E.g., Perse, *Oeuvres complètes*, 615–16.
97. E.g. above, chapter 3, note 10.
98. FO 371 32079, passim; see also Perse, *Oeuvres complètes*, 614–15, 617, and *Honneur à Saint-John Perse*, 727–29.
99. Quoted in J. P. Moffat, "Notes on Trip to Washington, November 13–17," Moffat Papers, vol. 24; see also, Halifax to F.O., 11 Dec. 1942, FO 371 31954, Z 10064 90 17; Campbell in Washington to F.O., 31 Dec. 1942, FO 371 35993, Z 694 2 17.
100. Leger to Welles, 29 Dec. 1942, SD 851R.01/281.
101. E.g., Matthews memo, 23 Aug. 1943, SD 851.01/2819.

102. See above, chapter 5.
103. See Berle memo, 7 July 1943, Berle Papers, Box 215.
104. *New York Times*, 29 Nov. 1942.
105. See above, chapter 5, note 119.
106. *Atlantic Monthly*, April 1943, 43–48; both letters had appeared in French in *Pour la victoire*, 19 Dec. 1942.
107. See above, chapter 7, note 64.
108. *Pour la victoire*, 24 July 1943; cf. ibid., 26 Dec. 1942, 3 July, 17 July, 4 Sept. 1943.
109. Ibid., 1 May 1943.
110. Unsigned memo for the President, 18 Dec. 1943, Matthews Papers, Box 1, Memos for the President.
111. *France-Amérique*, 12 Sept. 1943; cf. ibid., 23 May.
112. The whole episode can be followed in Hopkins Papers, Box 330, Sherwood Collection, Book 7, Post-Casablanca, North Africa: Welles to FDR, 12 Apr., Hopkins to FDR, 14 Apr., Halifax to Hopkins, 15 Apr., 17 Apr.; PREM 3 120/10A: Halifax to Eden and Churchill, 14 April, Eden to Halifax, 15 April; and Michael Wright of the Washington embassy to Mack at the F.O., 1 May 1943, FO 371 35994, Z 558 2 17. On Tixier's unpopularity with his colleagues, see Témoignage de Mme Aglion, 21 Dec. 1948, CHDGM.
113. *Pour la victoire*, 4 Sept.; *France-Amérique*, 5 Sept. 1943.
114. *New York Times*, 2 Apr.; *New York Herald Tribune*, 2 Apr., 11 May 1943.
115. "Rapport de M. R. Aglion sur le Comité Républicain Français," 12 April 1943, CHDGM.
116. *La République Française*, Dec. 1943.
117. *New York Times*, 22 Dec. 1943; see also d'Ornano, *L'action gaulliste*, 129–33.
118. *Los Angeles Times*, 1 June 1943.
119. AIPO poll, 3 Feb. 1943.
120. Gallup poll, 11 July 1943.
121. *Miami Herald*, 7 June; *Louisville Courier-Journal*, 1 June 1943.
122. Gallup poll, 24 Feb. 1943.
123. *New York Herald Tribune*, 19 Jan. 1943.
124. Ibid., 26 June 1943.
125. Ibid., 27 June 1943; telegram from France Forever to Lippmann, 26 June 1943, Lippmann Papers, Box 72, Folder 810.
126. *Philadelphia Record*, 10 July; cf. ibid., 5 May, 13 May, 2 June, 3 June, 10 June 1943.
127. *New York Post*, 26 June.
128. *St. Louis Post-Dispatch*, 20 Sept. 1943.
129. Lippmann, *U.S. Foreign Policy*, 119–29, 161–68; cf. his columns in *New York Herald Tribune*, 3 June, 14 June, 23 June 1943.
130. *New York Times*, 30 Aug. 1943.
131. *New York Herald Tribune*, 30 Sept. 1943.
132. E.g., the articles by Joseph M. Jones in *Fortune*, Aug. and Sept. 1943.
133. Campbell and Herring, *Diaries of Stettinius*, xxiv–xxv, 9, 15–16, 20.

CHAPTER 10

1. See above, chapter 1, note 160.
2. FDR to Wilson, 5 Jan. 1944, SD 711.51/341A.
3. *FDR Press Conferences*, 23:134, 28 March 1944.
4. Chapin (U.S. representative to FCNL) to Hull, 16 May 1944, *FRUS* (1944), 3:685.
5. Listed in de Gaulle, *War Memoirs*, 2:231–33.
6. Louis, *Imperialism at Bay*, 43.
7. See the articles by Lapie, "The New Colonial Policy of France," and Rueff, "The Future of French Indo-China."
8. Dougherty, *Politics of Wartime Aid*, 53–122.
9. Eisenhower to de Gaulle, 29 Dec. 1943, Chandler, *Eisenhower Papers*, 3:1637.
10. E.g., Eisenhower to Gen. François d'Astier de la Vigerie, 17 March 1944, ibid., 1771–72.
11. E.g., Eisenhower to Marshall, 19 Jan. 1944, ibid., 1667–68.
12. Monnet, *Memoirs*, 218–19.
13. *FRUS* (1944), 3:675–77.
14. Eisenhower memo, 22 Mar. 1944, Chandler, *Eisenhower Papers*, 3:1784.
15. See, e.g., Campbell and Herring, *Diaries of Stettinius*, 64.
16. Halifax to F.O., 3 Feb. 1944, FO 371 41922, Z 1146 275 17.
17. Churchill to Eden, 26 Feb.; Churchill minute, 2 Mar.; Churchill to Halifax, 13 Mar., PREM 3 177/3.
18. FDR to Churchill, 29 Feb. 1944, ibid.
19. As reported in minute by Charles Peake, 23 Feb. 1944, FO 371 41957, Z 1555 1555 17.
20. Stimson Diary, 13 Jan. 1944.
21. Ibid., 14 Jan. 1944.
22. Hull to FDR, 5 Jan. 1944, SD 851.01/3369B.
23. Stimson Diary, 18 Jan. 1944; see also Stimson and Bundy, *On Active Service*, 546–48.
24. Stimson Diary, 29 Feb. 1944.
25. Ibid., 1 Mar., 3 Mar., 15 Mar. 1944.
26. Ibid., 17 May, 14 June, 20 June, 27 June 1944.
27. Minutes by Churchill, 20 Mar., and Eden, 22 Mar.; telegram from Cooper, 24 Mar. 1944, PREM 3, 177/2.
28. Hull, *Memoirs*, 2:1429–30.
29. Wilson to Hull, 21 Jan. 1944, Hull Papers, Box 53, Folder 169.
30. Chapin to Hull, 24 June 1944, ibid.
31. Cabinet conclusions, 19 Apr. 1944, PREM 3, 177/3; cf. Campbell and Herring, *Diaries of Stettinius*, 62, 68–69.
32. Churchill to Cooper, 23 Apr. 1944, PREM 3, 177/3.
33. Eden to Churchill, 25 Apr. 1944, ibid.
34. Davis to Grace Tully, 22 Mar., FDR to Davis, 22 Mar. 1944, FDRL, PSF, Box 10, OWI.
35. As reported in E. Stettinius to J. C. Dunn and H. F. Matthews, 24 May 1944, SD 851.01/3589; cf. Hull, *Memoirs*, 2:143.

36. FDR to Churchill, 31 May 1944, *FRUS* (1944), 3:694.

37. FDR to Davis, 1 June 1944, FDRL, PSF, 170, OWI.

38. FDR to Churchill, 4 June 1944, FDRL, Map Room Papers, Box 31, Folder 011, France, Civil Affairs, for 8 Apr.–22 Sept. 1944.

39. Eisenhower to Marshall, 16 May 1944, Chandler, *Eisenhower Papers*, 3:1867; cf. ibid., 1852–53, 1857–58, 1904.

40. Churchill to FDR, 12 May, 27 May 1944, FDRL, Map Room Papers, Box 31, Folder 011, France, Civil Affairs for 8 Apr.–22 Sept. 1944; and see above, note 38.

41. Smith to Marshall, 15 May 1944, FDRL, Map Room Papers, Box 31, Folder 001, France, Civil Affairs, 8 Apr.–22 Sept. 1944.

42. Memo for Diary, 22 May 1944, Chandler, *Eisenhower Papers*, 3:1881.

43. Military events can be followed in ibid., 3:1913–2037, 2041–97; cf. the narrative in Aron, *France Reborn*.

44. See de Gaulle's account of these affairs, in *War Memoirs*, 2:256–58.

45. Stimson Diary, 8 June 1944.

46. CAB 65/46, WM (44)72, 5 June 1944.

47. De Gaulle, *War Memoirs*, 2:256.

48. Cooper to Eden, 6 June 1944, PREM 3, 177/4.

49. De Gaulle, *War Memoirs*, Documents, 2:341.

50. Quoted in Funk, *Charles de Gaulle*, 247.

51. Eden to Churchill, 30 June 1944, PREM 3, 177/4.

52. Chandler, *Eisenhower Papers*, 3:1922 n. 3; cf. McCloy memo to FDR, 10 June 1944, FDRL, PSF, Box 42, France, De Gaulle, 1944–45.

53. FDR to Churchill, 9 June 1944, PREM 3, 177/4.

54. *FDR Press Conferences*, 24:9–10, 7 July 1944.

55. See Stimson Diary, 27 June 1944, for how carefully the visit needed to be planned; see also FDRL, OF, 203 A, Visit of General de Gaulle.

56. Ickes Diary, 9 July; Leahy Diary, 6 July, 7 July 1944; Hull, *Memoirs*, 2:1433.

57. E.g., *Time*, 17 July; *Christian Century*, 19 July; *Cleveland Plain Dealer*, 7 July 1944.

58. De Gaulle, *War Memoirs*, 2:268, 272–73; Témoignage de Pierre André Weil, 26 Nov. 1948, CHDGM.

59. De Gaulle, *War Memoirs*, 2:269–71.

60. Cooper to F.O., 17 July, Churchill minute to Eden, 19 July 1944, FO 371 41958, Z 4942 1555 17.

61. De Gaulle, *War Memoirs*, 2:269.

62. FDR to Representative Joseph Clark Baldwin, 19 July 1944, FDRL, OF, 203, 1944. The letter's contents were subsequently leaked to de Gaulle; see de Gaulle, *War Memoirs*, 2:272.

63. *FDR Press Conferences*, 24:12–20, 11 July 1944.

64. FDR to Churchill, 10 July 1944, *FRUS* (1944), 2:723–24.

65. See Campbell in Washington to F.O., 6 July 1944, FO 371 41957, Z 4326 1555 17.

66. *FDR Press Conferences*, 24:13–25, 11 July 1944.

67. Ickes Diary, 24 June 1944.

68. Pogue, *Supreme Command*, 237.

69. Foulon, *Le pouvoir en province*, 61–131; cf. Novick, *Resistance versus Vichy*, 60–66.
70. See above, note 51.
71. Stimson Diary, 8 June, 25 Aug., 9 Sept. 1944.
72. Leahy Diary, 30 Mar. 1944.
73. Stimson Papers, Box 172, Folder 5, Record of the Day, 14 June 1944.
74. Stimson Diary, 14 Sept. 1944.
75. See above, note 73.
76. E.g., Berle to Hull, 6 July 1944, Berle Papers, Box 59, Hull, Cordell, memos, 1944; cf. Berle memo, 9 May, Berle to Hull, 22 July, Berle Diary, Box 216, May–Aug. 1944.
77. Stimson Papers, Box 172, Folder 5, Notes after talk with Hull, 20 June 1944.
78. Ibid.; Campbell and Herring, *Diaries of Stettinius*, 90–91; cf. S. T. Early to W. Hallett, 19 June 1944, FDRL, PSF, Box 40, de Gaulle, 1944–45, enclosing a copy of David Lawrence's article in *Washington Star*, 19 June 1944.
79. Morgenthau Diaries, 750, 137–40 (Morgenthau-McCloy telephone conversation, 5 July 1944, 12:30 P.M.), 328 (memo to FDR, dated 1 July 1944); see also Blum, *Years of War*, 175–76.
80. Pogue, *Supreme Command*, 319.
81. De Gaulle, *War Memoirs*, 2:333.
82. Morgenthau Diaries, 23 Aug. 1944.
83. Stimson Diary, 9 Sept. 1944; FDR to de Gaulle, 2 Sept. 1944, FDRL, PSF, Box 42, France, de Gaulle, 1944–45.
84. Stimson Diary, 25 Aug. 1944.
85. Aron, *France Reborn*, 236–69.
86. Eisenhower to Smith, 22 Aug. 1944, Chandler, *Eisenhower Papers*, 4:2089–90.
87. Ibid., and Pogue, *Supreme Command*, 240–43.
88. Eisenhower to de Gaulle, 28 Aug. 1944, Chandler, *Eisenhower Papers*, 4:2097–98; cf. ibid., 2138–39, 2181–82.
89. De Gaulle, *War Memoirs*, 3:46.
90. Eisenhower to General Juin, 25 Sept. 1944, Chandler, *Eisenhower Papers*, 4:2189.
91. Chapin to Hull, 15 Sept., 21 Sept., Caffery to Hull, 20 Oct. 1944, *FRUS* (1944), 3:733–35, 736–37, 742–43.
92. Hull to FDR, 17 Sept., 21 Sept., 3 Oct. 1944, ibid., 735–39.
93. FDR to Hull, 19 Sept., 21 Sept. 1944, FDRL, PSF, Box 40, France, 1944–45.
94. Matthews to Hopkins, n.d., Hopkins Papers, Sherwood Collection, Box 334, Civil Affairs in France.
95. Leahy Diary, 25 Sept. 1944.
96. Churchill to FDR, 14 Oct. 1944, *Roosevelt-Churchill Correspondence*, 585–86.
97. Churchill to Eden, 18 Oct. 1944, PREM 3, 182/4.
98. "Special Guidance on F.C.N.L.," 31 Aug. 1944, OWI records, Office of Policy Coordination, Box 107, FCNL, Policy.
99. *FDR Press Conferences*, 24:165, 13 Oct. 1944.
100. Ibid., 191, 20 Oct. 1944.
101. London office to OWI, 25 Sept. 1944, OWI records, Office of Policy Coordination, Box 107, FCNL, Policy.

102. Matthews to Hopkins, 26 Oct. 1944, Hopkins Papers, Sherwood Collection, Box 334, Civil Affairs in France.
103. *Department of State Bulletin* 11, no. 279 (29 Oct. 1944): 491.
104. FDR to Churchill, 22 Oct., Churchill to FDR, 23 Oct. 1944 (2 telegrams), *Roosevelt-Churchill Correspondence*, 592–94.
105. FDR to Churchill, 24 Oct. 1944, ibid., 594.
106. Leger to FDR, 31 Jan. 1944, SD 851.01/3445; original in Perse, *Oeuvres complètes*, 619–27.
107. See the commentary on Leger's letter in Etienne, "Saint-John Perse et le politique," which draws heavily upon Flory, *Le statut international*, 233–45.
108. Esmein, *Eléments de droit constitutionnel*, 416–18.
109. Novick, *Resistance versus Vichy*, 197.
110. Speech of 25 July 1944, de Gaulle, *War Memoirs*, Documents, 2:278.
111. Stettinius to FDR, 14 Feb. 1944, SD 851.01/3445.
112. Flory, *Le statut international*, 240.
113. E.g., Caffery to Stettinius, 3 Jan. 1945, SD 711.51/1–345.
114. Lippmann to Stettinius, 25 Dec. 1944, Lippmann Papers, Box 103, Folder 2001.
115. MacLeish memo, 26 Jan., Hickerson to Dunn, 26 Jan., MacLeish to Dunn, 2 Feb. 1945, MacLeish Papers, Box 6, James C. Dunn folder; Sartre letter to *New York Times*, 1 Feb. 1945.
116. See PREM 3, 185/3.
117. Pogue, *Supreme Command*, 398–402, 459–61.
118. Thorne, "Indochina and Anglo-American Relations."
119. Herring, "The Truman Administration and the Restoration of French Sovereignty in Indochina."
120. Speech, 24 Oct. 1944, in Richmond, Virginia, Elmer Davis Papers, Box 10.
121. Letter to *New York Times*, 1 Feb. 1945.

CHAPTER 11

1. Bishop, *FDR's Last Year*, 471–578; Hassett, *Off the Record with FDR*, 319–35.
2. Hull to FDR, 25 Sept. 1943, FDRL, OF, 203, France, 1943.
3. Wilson Brown (naval aide) to Dorothy Brady (secretary), 26 March 1945, FDRL, PSF, 82, Navy, Wilson Brown.
4. It is now declassified and may be examined in the State Department records in the National Archives.
5. Langer, *Our Vichy Gamble*, 398.
6. Woodward, *British Foreign Policy in the Second World War*.
7. See the books by Feis: *Road to Pearl Harbor*; *Churchill, Roosevelt, Stalin*; *Japan Subdued*.
8. See above, chapter 9, note 40.
9. Langer, *In and Out of the Ivory Tower*, 195.
10. Stimson memo, 6 July 1943, Stimson Papers, Box 171, memoranda; the date incidentally suggests that Hull's invitation to Langer had come in the summer of

1943, not, as Langer recalled, the autumn (Langer, *In and Out of the Ivory Tower*, 194).

11. Welles, *Seven Major Decisions*, 54; Langer, *Our Vichy Gamble*, 76.
12. Murphy, *Diplomat among Warriors*, 90, 157.
13. Matthews memo to Langer, and his accompanying letter of 17 Jan. 1945, loaned by the writer after an interview in Washington, D.C., July 1972.
14. Langer, *Our Vichy Gamble*, 389.
15. Ibid., 269.
16. Ibid., 396.
17. Matthews to Woodruff Wallner, 29 July 1946, Matthews Papers, Box 1, Folder W.
18. Leahy Diary, 18 Aug., 29 Aug. 1944.
19. Langer, *Our Vichy Gamble*, preface; Langer, *In and Out of the Ivory Tower*, 194.
20. Hull, *Memoirs*, 2:1192, 1194.
21. Langer, *Our Vichy Gamble*, 257, 300, 382, 394, 398.
22. See above, chapter 8, notes 79, 105, and 111.
23. See above, chapter 8, note 118.
24. Langer, *Our Vichy Gamble*, 395.
25. Rauch, *Roosevelt from Munich to Pearl Harbor*, chapter 10.
26. E.g., Gottschalk, "Our Vichy Fumble."
27. Tocqueville, *Democracy in America*, 1:282.
28. Bryce, *American Commonwealth*, 2:341–50.
29. Lippmann, *Public Opinion*, 125.
30. Brogan, *American Character*, 160.
31. Gallup polls of 10 May, 2 July, 23 Oct., 6 Dec. 1940, 11 July 1943, 24 Apr. 1944.
32. AIPO poll, 1 July 1942, Gallup poll, 28 June 1944.
33. For McCormick, FDRL, PPF, 675; for Davis, OF, 4278 (*Saturday Evening Post*).
34. See introduction to Cantril and Strunk, *Public Opinion*, viii–ix.
35. See, e.g., Sheldon Wolin's review of Wattenberg, *The Real America, New York Review of Books*, 6 Feb. 1975, 15–20; James L. Payne, "Will Mr. Harris Ever Learn?" *National Review*, 21 June 1974, 701–2.
36. E.g., Leigh, *Mobilising Consent*.
37. Gallup poll, 29 Apr. 1942.
38. Gallup poll, 16 Dec. 1942.
39. E.g., Gallup polls, 28 Dec. 1942, 24 Mar., 3 May, 5 June, 26 Sept. 1943, 2 July 1944.
40. Sussmann, "FDR and the White House Mail"; Dorothy Borg, "Notes on Roosevelt's 'Quarantine' Speech"; Steele, "The Pulse of the People"; see FDRL, PPF, 200, Public Reaction letters, for samples of mail received at the White House.
41. Roosevelt to Early, 5 Feb. 1943, FDRL, PPF, 6646.
42. Hunt, *Department of State*, 117–57.
43. Stuart, *Department of State*, 350–415.

44. Blum, *Price of Vision*, 91.
45. See above, chapter 9, note 33.
46. E.g. on the Board of Economic Warfare, Blum, *Price of Vision*, 78–81.
47. E.g. Blum, *Years of War*, 359–83, 390–91; Stimson and Bundy, *On Active Service*, 568–83.
48. E.g. Berle and Jacobs, *Navigating the Rapids*, 377, 405–6, 408.
49. Israel, *War Diary of Breckinridge Long*, 176.
50. Stimson diary, 1 Feb. 1942.
51. Divine, *Roosevelt and World War II*.
52. Range, *Franklin D. Roosevelt's World Order*.
53. Dallek, *Franklin D. Roosevelt and American Foreign Policy*.
54. E.g., *FDR Press Conferences*, 20:247, 17 Nov. 1942; Blum, *Years of War*, 151; Stimson and Bundy, *On Active Service*, 545; *Roosevelt-Churchill Correspondence*, 282.
55. Welles to FDR, 15 Mar. 1942, FDRL, OF, 203, France, 1942.
56. Bullitt to FDR, 3 Aug., enclosing book edited by Suzanne Blum, FDR memo, 27 Sept. 1943, FDRL, PPF, 8529; see also, PSF, Box 40, Léon Blum.
57. FDR to Leahy, 26 Nov. 1942, FDRL, PPF, 8405; A. Darlan in Warm Springs to FDR, 21 Dec., FDR to Darlan, 29 Dec. 1943, PSF Box 40, France, 1943.
58. Substance of remarks at private meeting, 9 Mar. 1945, FDRL, OF, 36.
59. For this view of FDR's motives, see Burns, *Roosevelt: Soldier of Freedom*, 548–49.
60. See, e.g., the discussion in Gaddis, *The United States and the Origins of the Cold War*, 8–10.
61. Leger to Mrs. Francis Biddle, 13 Sept., 6 Nov. 1940, Perse, *Oeuvres complètes*, 898–900.
62. Leuchtenburg, *In the Shadow of FDR*.

BIBLIOGRAPHY

A. MANUSCRIPT SOURCES

Official documents

GREAT BRITAIN
London
  Public Record Office
    Cabinet conclusions, CAB 65
    Cabinet memoranda, CAB 66
    Consular records, FO 117
    Foreign Office records, FO 371
    Prime Minister's Office files, PREM 3, 4

UNITED STATES
Hyde Park, New York
  Franklin D. Roosevelt Library
    Franklin D. Roosevelt Papers, Map Room Papers, Official File, President's Personal File, President's Secretary's File
Washington, D.C.
  National Archives
    State Department: Decimal Files; Matthews, Hickerson Files; Harley Notter Files, Record Group 59
    Office of Strategic Services Files, Record Group 226
    Office of War Information Files, Record Group 208

Private Collections

FRANCE
Paris
  Comité d'histoire de la deuxième guerre mondiale
    Various reports, interviews, correspondence, and memoirs, including those of Raoul Aglion, André Philip, and P. A. Weil

UNITED STATES
Bloomington, Indiana
  Lilly Library, Indiana University
    Upton Sinclair Papers
Cambridge, Massachusetts
  Houghton Library, Harvard University
    J. Pierrepont Moffat Papers

Chicago, Illinois
  Chicago Historical Society
    France Forever Papers
  University of Illinois at Chicago Circle
    Chicago Council on Foreign Relations records
Hyde Park, New York
  Franklin D. Roosevelt Library
    Adolf Berle Diary and Papers
    Harry Hopkins Papers
    R. Walton Moore Papers
    Henry Morgenthau, Jr., Diaries and Papers
    John C. Wiley Papers
New Haven, Connecticut
  Sterling Library, Yale University
    Walter Lippmann Papers
    Henry L. Stimson Diary and Papers
Princeton, New Jersey
  Princeton University Library
    Cantril, Hadley, *America Faces the War: A Study in Public Opinion* (MS., 1940)
    Fight for Freedom Papers
Syracuse, New York
  George Arendts Research Library, Syracuse University
    Dorothy Thompson Papers
Washington, D.C.
  Library of Congress, Manuscript Division
    Elmer Davis Papers
    Herbert Feis Papers
    Felix Frankfurter Papers
    Cordell Hull Papers
    Harold Ickes Diary and Papers
    William D. Leahy Diary and Papers
    Breckinridge Long Papers
    Archibald MacLeish Papers
    Edgar Ansel Mowrer Papers

B. PUBLISHED OFFICIAL DOCUMENTS

Annuaire diplomatique et consulaire de l'Etat français pour 1941. Vichy, 1941.
Congressional Record, vols. 86–90, 76th Congress, 3d session, to 78th Congress, 1st session. Washington, D.C., 1940–45.
U.S. Department of State, *Department of State Bulletin*. Washington, D.C., 1940–45.
———. *Foreign Relations of the United States*. 1940, vols. 1–4. 1941, vol. 2. 1942, vol. 2. 1943, vol. 2, 1944, vol. 3. *The Conferences at Washington, 1941–1942, and Casablanca, 1943*. Washington, D.C., 1955–68.

_____. *Peace and War: United States Foreign Policy, 1931–1941*. Washington, D.C., 1943.

C. JOURNALS AND NEWSPAPERS

Journals consulted: an asterisk denotes systematic study; other references obtained from the *Reader's Guide to Periodical Literature*.

American Foreign Service Journal	*Harper's Magazine*
American Mercury	*Life**
Annals of the American Academy of Political and Social Science	*Nation**
	*Newsweek**
Atlantic Monthly	*New Republic**
Chicago Journal of Commerce	*Pour la victoire**
*Christian Century**	*Public Opinion Quarterly**
*Commonweal**	*Reader's Digest*
Current History	*Saturday Evening Post*
*Department of State Bulletin**	*Scribner's Commentator*
*Foreign Affairs**	*Time**
*France-Amerique**	*Virginia Quarterly Review*
*Free World**	

Newspapers consulted: an asterisk denotes systematic study; other references obtained from the Press Library, Royal Institute of International Affairs, Chatham House, London, or the files of press cuttings in the Office of War Information records, National Archives, Washington, D.C.

*Atlanta Constitution**	*Miami Herald*
Baltimore Evening Sun	*New Orleans Times-Picayune*
Baton Rouge State-Times	*New York Daily Mirror*
Birmingham Herald	*New York Daily News*
Boston Globe	*New York Daily Worker*
Boston Transcript	*New York Herald Tribune**
Bridgeport (Conn.) *Post*	*New York Journal-American*
Charleston News and Courier	*New York Post**
Chicago Daily News	*New York Sun*
Chicago Sun	*New York Times**
Chicago Sunday Times	*New York World-Telegram*
*Chicago Tribune**	*Omaha World Herald*
*Christian Science Monitor**	*Philadelphia Enquirer*
Cleveland Plain Dealer	*Philadelphia Record*
Daily Herald (London)	*PM**
Des Moines Register	*Providence* (R.I.) *Evening Bulletin*
Greensboro (N.C.) *Record*	*St. Louis Post-Dispatch*
Greenville (S.C.) *News*	*Wall Street Journal**
Lancaster (Pa.) *Intelligencer Journal*	*Washington News*
*Los Angeles Times**	*Washington Post**
Louisville Courier-Journal	*Washington Star*

D. BOOKS

Acheson, Dean. *Present at the Creation*. New York, 1969.
Adler, Selig. *The Isolationist Impulse*. New York, 1957.
Amaury, Philippe. *Les deux premières expériences d'un "ministere de l'information"
en France*. Paris, 1969.
Anglin, Douglas George. *The St. Pierre and Miquelon Affair of 1941: A Study in
Diplomacy in the North Atlantic Quadrangle*. Toronto, 1966.
Aron, Robert. *France Reborn*. New York, 1964.
Bankwitz, P. C. F. *Maxime Weygand and Civil-Military Relations in Modern France*.
Cambridge, Mass., 1967.
Barnard, Ellsworth. *Wendell Willkie: Fighter for Freedom*. Marquette, Mich., 1968.
Barnet, Richard J. *Intervention and Revolution*. London, 1972.
Baudouin, Paul. *Neuf mois au gouvernement*. Paris, 1948.
Bell, P. M. H. *A Certain Eventuality*. London, 1974.
Bendiner, Robert. *The Riddle of the State Department*. New York, 1942.
Berle, B. B., and Jacobs, T. B., eds. *Navigating the Rapids, 1918–1971: From the
Papers of Adolf A. Berle*. New York, 1973.
Bishop, Jim. *FDR's Last Year*. New York, 1974.
Blum, J. M., ed. *From the Morgenthau Diaries: Years of Urgency, 1938–1941*. Bos-
ton, 1965.
———. *From the Morgenthau Diaries: Years of War, 1941–1945*. Boston, 1967.
———. *The Price of Vision: The Diary of Henry Wallace, 1942–46*. Boston, 1973.
Bolt, Ernest C., Jr. *Ballots before Bullets: The War Referendum Approach to Peace in
America, 1914–1941*. Charlottesville, Va., 1977.
Bouthillier, Yves. *Le drame de Vichy*. 2 vols. Paris, 1950–51.
Bowers, Claude G. *My Mission to Spain: Watching the Rehearsal for World War II*.
New York, 1954.
Brogan, D. W. *The American Character*. New York, 1956.
———. *France under the Republic*. New York, 1940.
Bryce, James. *The American Commonwealth*. 2 vols. Edited by Louis Hacker. New
York, 1959.
Bullitt, Orville H., ed. *For the President: Personal and Secret Correspondence be-
tween Franklin D. Roosevelt and William C. Bullitt*. London, 1973.
Bullitt, William C. *Address*. N.p., 1943 (Library of Congress D761.B8).
———. *The Great Globe Itself*. London, 1947.
———. *Report to the American People*. Philadelphia, 1940.
Bullitt, William C., and Freud, Sigmund. *Thomas Woodrow Wilson, Twenty-eighth
President of the United States: A Psychological Study*. London, 1967.
Burns, J. M. *Roosevelt, The Soldier of Freedom*. London, 1971.
Campbell, Thomas M., and Herring, George C., eds. *The Diaries of Edward R. Stet-
tinius, Jr., 1943–1946*. New York, 1975.
Cantril, Hadley, and Strunk, Mildred, eds. *Public Opinion, 1935–46*. Princeton,
N.J., 1951.
Chadwin, Mark Lincoln. *The Hawks of World War II*. Chapel Hill, N.C., 1968.
Chandler, Alfred D., ed. *The Papers of Dwight David Eisenhower: The War Years*.
Vols. 1–4. Baltimore, Md., 1970.

Charles-Roux, François. *Cinq mois tragiques aux affaires étrangères.* Paris, 1949.
Chatfield, Charles. *For Peace and Justice: Pacifism in America, 1914–1941.* Knoxville, Tenn., 1971.
Chautemps, Camille. *Cahiers secrets de l'armistice.* Paris, 1963.
Christian, William A. *Divided Island: Faction and Unity on St. Pierre.* Cambridge, Mass., 1969.
Cole, Wayne S. *America First: The Battle Against Intervention, 1940–41.* Madison, Wis., 1953.
Complete Presidential Press Conferences of Franklin D. Roosevelt. New York, 1972.
Crusoé (pseud.). *Vicissitudes d'une victoire.* Paris, 1946.
Dallek, Robert. *Democrat and Diplomat: The Life of William E. Dodd.* New York, 1968.
———. *Franklin D. Roosevelt and American Foreign Policy, 1932–1945.* New York, 1979.
Davies, Joseph E. *Mission to Moscow.* New York, 1941.
de Chambrun, Clara Longworth. *Shadows Lengthen—The Story of My Life.* New York, 1949.
de Chambrun, René. *I Saw France Fall—Will She Rise Again?* London, 1941.
de Chambrun, René, and de Chambrun, José, eds. *France during the German Occupation.* Vol. 3. Stanford, Calif., 1958.
de Gaulle, Charles. *Discours aux français.* N.p., n.d.
———. *War Memoirs.* 3 vols., with 3 vols. of *Documents.* Translated by Jonathan Griffin and Richard Howard. London, 1955–61.
de Kérillis, Henri. *De Gaulle dictateur.* Montreal, 1945.
de Roussy de Sales, Raoul. *The Making of Yesterday.* New York, 1947.
de Roussy de Sales, Raoul; Curie, Eve; and Barrès, Philippe, eds. *They Speak for a Nation.* New York, 1941.
Divine, Robert A. *Foreign Policy and U.S. Presidential Elections, 1940–48.* New York, 1974.
———. *The Illusion of Neutrality.* Chicago, 1962.
———. *Roosevelt and World War II.* Baltimore, Md., 1969.
———. *Second Chance.* New York, 1967.
Dodd, William E., Jr., and Dodd, Martha, eds. *Ambassador Dodd's Diary, 1933–1938.* New York, 1941.
Dougherty, James J. *The Politics of Wartime Aid.* Westport, Conn., 1978.
Eade, Charles, ed. *War Speeches of the Right Honourable Winston S. Churchill.* Vol. 2. London, 1965.
Eisenhower, Milton S. *The President is Calling.* New York, 1974.
Ekirch, A. A., Jr. *Ideologies and Utopias.* Chicago, 1964.
Elson, Robert R. *The World of Time, Inc..* New York, 1973.
Esmein, Adhemar. *Eléments de droit constitutionnel français et comparé.* Vol. 2. Paris, 1928.
Farnsworth, Beatrice. *William C. Bullitt and the Soviet Union.* Bloomington, Ind., 1967.
Feis, Herbert. *Churchill, Roosevelt, Stalin: The War They Waged and the Peace They Sought.* Princeton, N.J., 1957.
———. *Japan Subdued: The Atomic Bomb and the End of the War in the Pacific.*

Princeton, N.J., 1961.

───. *The Road to Pearl Harbor*. Princeton, N.J., 1950.

Flory, Maurice. *Le statut international des gouvernements refugiés et le cas de la France Libre, 1939–1945*. Paris, 1952.

Foulon, Charles-Louis. *Le pouvoir en province à la libération*. Paris, 1975.

Freedman, Max, ed. *Roosevelt and Frankfurter: Their Correspondence, 1928–1945*. Boston, 1967.

Freidel, Frank. *Franklin D. Roosevelt: The Ordeal*. Boston, 1954.

Friedlander, Saul. *Prelude to Downfall: Hitler and the United States*. London, 1967.

Fritsch-Estrangin, Guy. *New-York entre de Gaulle et Pétain*. Paris, 1967.

Funk, A. L. *Charles de Gaulle: The Crucial Years, 1943–1944*. Norman, Okla., 1959.

───. *The Politics of Torch*. Lawrence, Kan., 1974.

Gaddis, J. L. *The United States and the Origins of the Cold War*. New York, 1972.

Gallup, George H. *The Gallup Poll: Public Opinion, 1935–1971*. Vol. 1. New York, 1971.

Giraud, Henri. *Un seul but, la victoire*. Paris, 1949.

Griffiths, Richard. *Pétain*. London, 1970.

Haight, John McVickar, Jr. *American Aid to France, 1938–1940*. New York, 1970.

Hassett, William D. *Off the Record with FDR*. London, 1960.

Henry-Haye, Gaston. *La grande éclipse franco-américaine*. Paris, 1972.

Honneur à Saint-John Perse. Preface by Jean Paulhan. Paris, 1965.

Hoover, Herbert. *Addresses upon the American Road, 1940–41*. New York, 1941.

Hoover, Herbert, and Gibson, Hugh. *The Problems of Lasting Peace*. New York, 1942.

Hull, Cordell. *Memoirs of Cordell Hull*. 2 vols. New York, 1948.

Hunt, Gaillard. *The Department of State of the United States*. New Haven, Conn., 1914.

Hyde, H. Montgomery. *The Quiet Canadian: The Secret Service Story of Sir William Stephenson*. London, 1962.

Hytier, A. D. *Two Years of French Foreign Policy*. Paris, 1958.

Ickes, Harold. *The Secret Diary of Harold Ickes*. Vol. 3. New York, 1955.

Israel, Fred L., ed. *The War Diary of Breckinridge Long*. Lincoln, Neb., 1966.

Johnson, Walter. *The Battle against Isolation*. 1944. Reprint. New York, 1973.

Jonas, Manfred. *Isolationism in America, 1935–41*. Ithaca, N.Y., 1966.

Kaspi, André. *La mission de Jean Monnet à Alger, mars–octobre 1943*. Paris, 1971.

Kolko, Gabriel. *The Politics of War*. New York, 1968.

Langer, William L. *In and Out of the Ivory Tower: The Autobiography of William L. Langer*. New York, 1977.

───. *Our Vichy Gamble*. New York, 1947.

Langer, William L., and Gleason, S. Everett. *The Challenge to Isolation, 1937–1940*. New York, 1952.

Langer, William L., and Gleason, S. Everett. *The Undeclared War, 1940–1941*. New York, 1953.

Lash, Joseph P., ed. *From the Diaries of Felix Frankfurter*. New York, 1975.

Lavine, Harold, and Wechsler, James. *War Propaganda and the United States*. New Haven, Conn., 1940.

Leahy, William D. *I Was There*. London, 1950.
Leigh, Michael. *Mobilising Consent: Public Opinion and American Foreign Policy, 1937–47*. London, 1976.
Leuchtenburg, W. E. *In the Shadow of FDR: From Harry Truman to Ronald Reagan*. Ithaca, N.Y., 1983.
Lippmann, Walter. *Public Opinion*. New York, 1929.
————. *U.S. Foreign Policy: Shield of the Republic*. Boston, 1943.
————. *U.S. War Aims*. Boston, 1944.
Loewenheim, Francis L.; Langley, Harold D.; and Jonas, Manfred, eds. *Roosevelt and Churchill: Their Secret Wartime Correspondence*. London, 1975.
Louis, William R. *Imperialism at Bay, 1941–1945: The United States and the Decolonisation of the British Empire*. Oxford, 1977.
Macmillan, Harold. *The Blast of War*. London, 1967.
Markham, Peter. *America Next*. New York, 1940.
Marlow, James. *De Gaulle and the Coming Invasion of Germany*. London, 1940.
Martin, James J. *American Liberalism and World Politics*. 2 vols. New York, 1964.
Maurois, André. *Memoirs*. Translated by Denver Lindley. London, 1970.
Mayer, Arno J. *Politics and Diplomacy of Peacemaking: Containment and Counter-revolution at Versailles, 1918–1919*. London, 1968.
Mengin, Robert. *No Laurels for de Gaulle*. London, 1966.
Monnet, Jean. *Memoirs*. Translated by Richard Mayne. London, 1978.
Mott, F. L. *American Journalism*. Rev. ed. New York, 1956.
Murphy, Robert D. *Diplomat among Warriors*. London, 1964.
Muselier, Emile Henri. *De Gaulle contre le gaullisme*. Paris, 1946.
New York Herald Tribune: Tenth Annual Forum on Current Problems, 1940. New York, 1941.
Notter, Harley. *Postwar Foreign Policy Preparation*. Washington, D.C., 1949.
Novick, Peter. *The Resistance versus Vichy*. London, 1968.
Ogden, A. R. *The Dies Committee*. Washington, D.C., 1945.
d'Ornano, H. F. *L'action gaulliste aux Etats-Unis, 1940–1945*. Paris, 1948.
Parmet, Herbert S., and Hecht, Marie B. *Never Again: A President Runs for a Third Term*. New York, 1968.
Paxton, Robert O. *Parades and Politics at Vichy*. Princeton, N.J., 1956.
————. *Vichy France: Old Guard and New Order, 1940–1944*. London, 1972.
Pendar, Kenneth. *Adventure in Diplomacy*. New York, 1945.
Perse, Saint-John [Alexis Saint-Leger Leger]. *Oeuvres complètes*. Paris, 1972.
Pétain, Philippe. *Quatres années au pouvoir*. Paris, 1944.
Peyrouton, Marcel. *Souvenirs*. Paris, 1950.
Phillips, William. *Ventures in Diplomacy*. Boston, 1953.
Pickersgill, J. W. *The Mackenzie King Record*. Vol. 1 (1939–44). Toronto, 1960.
Pogue, Forrest C. *The Supreme Command. The United States Army in World War II. The European Theater of Operations*. No. 4. Washington, D.C., 1954.
Pol, Heinz. *Suicide of a Democracy*. New York, 1941.
Porter, David L. *The Seventy-Sixth Congress and World War II*. Columbia, Mo., 1979.
Pucheu, Pierre. *Ma vie*. Paris, 1948.
Range, Willard. *Franklin D. Roosevelt's World Order*. Athens, Ga., 1959.

Rauch, Basil. *Roosevelt from Munich to Pearl Harbor*. New York, 1950.
Robinson, E. E. *The Roosevelt Leadership, 1933–45*. Philadelphia, 1955.
Rochester, Stuart I. *American Liberal Disillusionment in the Wake of World War I*. University Park, Pa., 1977.
Roosevelt, Elliott. *As He Saw It*. New York, 1946.
———. *The Roosevelt Letters*. Vol. 3 (1928–45). London, 1952.
Root, Waverley. *The Secret History of the War*. 3 vols. New York, 1945–46.
Rosenman, S., ed. *Public Papers and Addresses of Franklin D. Roosevelt*. Vols. 8–13. London, 1941–50.
Sherwood, Robert. *Roosevelt and Hopkins*. New York, 1948.
Smith, R. Harris. *OSS: The Secret History of America's First Intelligence Agency*. New York, 1972.
Soustelle, Jacques. *Envers et contre tout*. 2 vols. Paris, 1947–50.
Spykman, Nicholas. *America's Strategy in World Politics*. New York, 1942.
Steel, Ronald. *Walter Lippmann and the American Century*. Boston, 1980.
Steele, Richard W. *The First Offensive, 1942: Roosevelt, Marshall, and the Making of American Strategy*. Bloomington, Ind., 1973.
Stimson, Henry Louis, and Bundy, McGeorge. *On Active Service in Peace and War*. New York, 1948.
Streit, Clarence. *Union Now*. New York, 1939.
Strout, Cushing. *The American Image of the Old World*. New York, 1963.
Stuart, G. H. *The Department of State: A History of its Organization, Procedures, and Personnel*. New York, 1949.
Taylor, Edmond. *Awakening from History*. London, 1971.
———. *The Strategy of Terror*. Boston, 1940 (1st ed.); 1941 (2d ed.).
Taylor, Edmond; Snow, Edgar; and Janeway, Eliot. *Smash Hitler's International: The Strategy of a Political Offensive against the Axis*. New York, 1941.
Thomas, R. T. *Britain and Vichy: The Dilemma of Anglo-French Relations, 1940–42*. London, 1979.
Thomson, David. *The Proposal for Anglo-French Union in 1940*. Oxford, 1966.
Tocqueville, Alexis de. *Democracy in France*. 2 vols. Edited by J. P. Mayer and Max Lerner. London, 1963.
Twohey Weekly Analysis of Newspaper Opinion. Compiled by James S. Twohey Associates. Washington, D.C., 1940–43.
Wallace, Henry. *The Price of Free World Victory*. New York, 1942.
Warner, Geoffrey. *Pierre Laval and the Eclipse of France*. London, 1968.
Wattenberg, Ben J. *The Real America*. New York, 1975.
Welles, Sumner. *Seven Major Decisions*. London, 1951.
———. *The World of the Four Freedoms*. New York, 1943.
Weygand, Maxime. *Recalled to Service*. Translated by E. W. Dickes. London, 1952.
White, Dorothy Shipley. *Seeds of Discord: de Gaulle, Free France, and the Allies*. Syracuse, N.Y., 1964.
Who Was Who in America. Vol. 3. Chicago, 1966.
Willkie, Wendell. *One World*. New York, 1943.
Winkler, Allan M. *The Politics of Propaganda: The Office of War Information, 1942–45*. New Haven, Conn., 1978.
Wiskemann, Elizabeth. *The Rome-Berlin Axis*. London, 1966.

Woodward, Llewellyn. *British Foreign Policy in the Second World War*. London, 1962.

————. *British Foreign Policy in the Second World War*. 5 vols. London, 1970–76.

E. ARTICLES

"A French Officer." "Bolstering National Morale in Wartime France." *Public Opinion Quarterly* 4, no. 1 (Mar. 1940): 66–74.

Allen, William R. "Cordell Hull and the Defense of the Trade Agreements Program, 1934–1940." In *Some Pathways in Twentieth-Century History*, ed. D. R. Beaver, 177–220. Detroit, Mich., 1969.

Allport, Gordon W. "Liabilities and Assets in Civilian Morale." *Annals of the American Academy of Political and Social Science* 216 (1941):88–94.

Beloff, Max. "The Anglo-French Union Project of June, 1940." In Beloff, *The Intellectual in Politics, and Other Essays*, 172–99. London, 1970.

Borg, Dorothy. "Notes on Roosevelt's 'Quarantine' Speech." *Political Science Quarterly* 72, no. 3 (Sept. 1957): 405–33.

Broughton, Philip S. "Government Agencies and Civilian Morale." *Annals of the American Academy of Political and Social Science* 220 (1942):168–77.

Brown, John Crosby. "American Isolation: Propaganda Pro and Con." *Foreign Affairs* 18, no. 1 (Oct. 1939): 29–44.

Burke, Robert. "The Election of 1940." In *The Coming to Power: Critical Presidential Elections in American History*, ed. A. M. Schlesinger, Jr., and F. L. Israel, 355–84. London, 1973.

Cantril, Hadley. "America Faces the War: A Study in Public Opinion." *Public Opinion Quarterly* 4, no. 3 (Sept. 1940): 387–407.

————. "Evaluating the Probable Reactions to the Landing in North Africa in 1942: A Case Study." *Public Opinion Quarterly* 29, no. 3 (Fall 1965): 400–10.

Cantril, Hadley; Rugg, Donald; and Williams, Frederick. "America Faces the War: Shifts in Opinion." *Public Opinion Quarterly* 4, no. 4 (Dec. 1940): 651–66.

Chatfield, Charles. "Alternative Antiwar Strategies of the Thirties." *American Studies* 13, no. 1 (Spring 1971): 81–93.

de Roussy de Sales, Raoul. "Love in America." In *America in Perspective*, ed. Henry Steele Commager, 280–90. New York, 1947.

Doenecke, Justus D. "The Non-Interventionism of the Left: The Keep America Out of War Congress." *Journal of Contemporary History* 12, no. 2 (Apr. 1977): 221–36.

Ehrmann, Henry W. "The Blum Experiment and the Fall of France." *Foreign Affairs* 20, no. 2 (Oct. 1941): 152–64.

Etienne, Bruno. "Saint-John Perse et le politique, ou, à propos de la lettre d'Alexis Leger au President Roosevelt, 31 janvier 1944." In *Espaces de Saint-John Perse*, 3 (Aix-en-Provence, 1981): 157–88.

Ferrell, Robert H. "The Peace Movement." In *Isolation and Security*, ed. Alexander de Conde, 82–106. Durham, N.C., 1957.

Funk, A. L. "Negotiating the 'Deal with Darlan.'" *Journal of Contemporary History* 8, no. 2 (Apr. 1973): 81–117.

Gottschalk, Louis, "Our Vichy Fumble." *Journal of Modern History* 20, no. 1 (Mar. 1948): 47–56.

Herring, George C. "The Truman Administration and the Restoration of French Sovereignty in Indochina." *Diplomatic History* 1, no. 2 (Spring 1977): 97–117.

Jacob, Philip E. "Influences of World Events on U.S. 'Neutrality' Opinion." *Public Opinion Quarterly* 4, no. 1 (Mar. 1940): 48–65.

Johnson, D. W. J. "Britain and France in 1940." *Transactions of the Royal Historical Society*, 5th ser., 22 (1972):141–57.

Kauffmann, W. W. "Two American Ambassadors, Bullitt and Kennedy." In *The Diplomats, 1919–1939*, ed. Gordon A. Craig and Felix Gilbert, 2:649–81. Princeton, N.J., 1953.

Lapie, P. O. "The New Colonial Policy of France." *Foreign Affairs* 23, no. 1 (Oct. 1944): 104–11.

Masland, John W. "The 'Peace' Groups Join Battle." *Public Opinion Quarterly* 4, no. 4 (Dec. 1940): 664–73.

Melka, Robert L. "Darlan between Britain and Germany, 1940–41." *Journal of Contemporary History* 8, no. 2 (Apr. 1973): 57–80.

Offner, Arnold A. "Appeasement Revisited: The United States, Great Britain, and Germany, 1933–1940." *Journal of American History* 64, no. 2 (Sept. 1977): 373–93.

Payne, James L. "Will Mr. Harris Ever Learn?" *National Review* 26 (21 June 1974): 701–2.

Rosenberg, Harold. "The Fall of Paris." In Rosenberg, *The Tradition of the New*, 209–20. New York, 1965.

Rueff, Gaston. "The Future of French Indo-China." *Foreign Affairs* 23, no. 1 (Oct. 1944): 143–49.

Steele, Richard W. "The Pulse of the People: Franklin D. Roosevelt and the Gauging of American Public Opinion." *Journal of Contemporary History* 9, no. 4 (Oct. 1974): 195–216.

Sussmann, Leila A. "FDR and the White House Mail." *Public Opinion Quarterly* 20, no. 1 (Spring 1956): 5–16.

Taylor, Edmond. "Democracy Demoralized: The French Collapse." *Public Opinion Quarterly* 4, no. 4 (Dec. 1940): 630–49.

Thorne, Christopher. "Indochina and Anglo-American Relations, 1942–1945." *Pacific Historical Review* 45, no. 1 (Feb. 1976): 73–96.

Tuttle, William M., Jr. "Aid-to-the-Allies Short-of-War versus American Intervention, 1940: A Reappraisal of William Allen White's Leadership." *Journal of American History* 56, no. 4 (Mar. 1940): 840–58.

Wright, Gordon. "Ambassador Bullitt and the Fall of France." *World Politics* 10 (Oct. 1957): 63–90.

INDEX

Acheson, Dean, 108, 158, 191, 237
Act of Havana (1940), 18; applicability
  to St. Pierre and Miquelon, 123, 124,
  126, 129
Agar, Herbert, 37, 146, 154
Agar, William, 132, 134, 154
Aglion, Raoul, 109
Algeria, 22, 162, 169, 176, 185, 202
Algiers, 22–23, 164, 170, 186, 194,
  197, 208, 211, 212, 219, 224
Alphand, Hervé, 92, 109
America First, 59
American Council of Churches, 89
American Council on Public Affairs, 205
American Foreign Service Journal, 174
American Friends of France, 36, 66
American Political Science Association,
  131
American Union for Nationalist Spain,
  36
Anderson, Maxwell, 95, 132
André Simon (pseudonym), 99
Anglin, Douglas, 121
Anglo-French Purchasing Commission,
  34, 37, 112
Anglophobia, French, 9–10, 101, 162
Anti-Communism, 4, 58, 140, 148
Anti-Semitism: Vichy's, 53, 71, 103,
  178, 185, 196, 199; Henry Ford's, 59
Appeasement: Allied, 3, 6, 40, 56, 131,
  134, 153; American, 7, 25, 59–60,
  61, 62–63, 64, 153, 154, 193, 235;
  alleged over St. Pierre and Miquelon,
  131; alleged over Darlan deal, 168,
  177–78
Archambault, G. H., 45
Armistice, Franco-German (1940), 9,
  13, 51, 58, 65; terms of, 14, 87;
  American views of, 14–15, 39

Armstrong, Hamilton Fish, 39, 40, 66,
  192
Atherton, Ray, 68, 81, 112
Atlanta Constitution, 39–40, 128
Atlantic Charter (1941), 129, 142, 143,
  155, 176, 177, 228, 232
Atlantic Monthly, 116
Attlee, Clement, 8, 37, 189
Auboyneau, Captain Philippe, 110

Badoglio, Marshal, 205
Baeyens, Baron James, 91
Baltimore Evening Sun, 128
Barclay, Hartley W., 41
Barclay, R. E., 111
Barnes, Maynard, 16–17
Barrès, Philippe, 118, 151, 154, 203
Barton, Bruce, 63
Baton Rouge State-Times, 174–75
Battle of Britain (1940), 56
Baudouin, Paul, 9, 10, 17, 21, 22, 144
Beard, Charles, 58
Belgium, 8, 39
Bell, Ulric, 50
Bendiner, Robert, 154, 157, 158, 160,
  229
Benét, Stephen Vincent, 132
Bergman, Alfred, 107–8, 109, 233
Berle, Adolf A., Jr., 8, 28, 151, 154–
  55, 156, 157, 158, 171, 192, 237; on
  Martinique, 19; and foreign nation-
  ality groups, 91, 101, 123, 205; justi-
  fies stance over St. Pierre and Mique-
  lon, 126; predicts course of a Gaullist
  regime, 217
Bernstein, Henri, 41, 100, 115, 117,
  119, 154, 155
Bess, Demaree, 182
Bidault, Georges, 221

Yale University, 4
Yalta Conference (1945), 224, 225
Yugoslavia, 71

Zola, Emile, 32